**Tradition and
Modernization
in China and Japan**

◆

New Horizons in Comparative Politics

edited by Howard J. Wiarda

V HORIZONS IN
ARATIVE POLITICS

Tradition and Modernization in China and Japan

Peter R. Moody, Jr.
University of Notre Dame

Wadsworth Publishing Company
Belmont, California
A Division of Wadsworth, Inc.

Political Science Editor: Brian Gore
Editorial Assistant: Jennifer Dunning
Production Editor: Michelle Filippini
Print Buyer: Diana Spence
Permissions Editor: Jeanne Bosschart
Designer: Andrew Ogus
Copy Editor: Rebecca McDearmon
Cover Designer: Andrew Ogus
Cover Photograph: Keren Su/Allstock
Signing Representative: Jay Honeck
Compositor: Steven Bolinger, Wadsworth Digital Productions
Printer: Malloy Lithographing, Inc.

 This book is printed on acid-free recycled paper.

International Thomson Publishing
The trademark ITP is used under license.

Printed in the United States of America
1 2 3 4 5 6 7 8 9 10—99 98 97 96 95

Library of Congress Cataloging-in-Publication Data
Moody, Peter R.
    Tradition and modernization in China and Japan / Peter R. Moody, Jr.
      p. cm.
    Includes bibliographical references and index.
    ISBN 0-534-24546-3 (alk. paper)
    1. China—Politics and government—20th century. 2. Japan—Politics
and government—20th century. 3. Taiwan—Politics and government—1945–
I. Title.
    DS774.M62 1994
320.951—dc20
                                                         94-16413

Contents

✦

CHAPTER 7
....
China's Political and Social Structure   171

CHAPTER 8
....
Politics and Policy in Contemporary China   222

CHAPTER 11
················
Politics and Policy in Contemporary Japan   315

CHAPTER 12
················
Tradition and Modernization   337

Index   346

Foreword

✦

The Wadsworth series New Horizons in Comparative Politics seeks to present timely, readable, up-to-date books in that exciting and booming political science field. Convinced that other Comparative Politics series are outdated or no longer suitable for classroom use, Wadsworth launched this series to remedy the situation. The time is ripe for fresh perspectives in view of changing world events and new disciplinary approaches.

Books in the series may take one of several forms: country studies, regional studies, or studies of topical issues such as "Democracy in Comparative Perspective," "The New Europe," or "Corporatism in Comparative Perspective." The books in the series will be brief (in the neighborhood of 200 pages), readable, and designed for introductory and upper division courses in comparative politics. But it is hoped that more senior students and scholars will find their data and interpretations of interest as well. The goal of the series is to provide political science students with texts that are accessible, yet enhance their understanding of the vital themes, approaches, and analyses in comparative politics. So far as is feasible and to facilitate comparative analysis, parallel chapter outlines will be used for the country and area books in the series. Books for series have already been published on such topics as Great Britain (Jorgen Rasmussen), France (Ronald Tiersky), and Eastern Europe (Ivan Volgyes). Other books that are of related interest are *An Introduction to Comparative Politics* by Howard J. Wiarda, *Comparative Politics in Transition* by John McCormick, as well as recently commissioned books on Mexico and the Middle East.

In launching this new series we have sought to get balanced scholars and lively, readable authors. We also made a conscious decision to move to a new generation of scholars who see things from a fresh perspective. Our goal is to provide short, versatile volumes that can be used in a myriad of comparative politics courses or area studies. We hope some of the excitement and enthusiasm that our authors feel for their subject areas is contagious.

We are pleased to include in our series this study of "Tradition and Modernization in China and Japan" by Peter R. Moody, Jr. Dr. Moody is Professor of Government and International Studies at the University of Notre Dame.

As East Asia continues to develop at impressive rates, and as United States foreign policy increasingly turns its attention to trade with Asia, it is important that we understand thoroughly the countries and societies with which we are dealing. East Asia has probably been more successful in adapting to modernization than any other non-Western society. The primary example is Japan. But the "four tigers" (Hong Kong, Singapore, South Korea, Taiwan) have also demonstrated remarkable growth rates. China is now making its great leap into the modern world, and countries like Indonesia, Malaysia, and Thailand are all doing quite well.

What accounts for this remarkable resurgence and growth in Asia? There are, clearly, multiple causes. Professor Moody analyzes these causes but his main focus is on the changing political culture of the region. He traces the origins and evolution of Confucian concepts in China and throughout East Asia. In the past, Confucianism was often thought a barrier to modernization, but now we know this traditional concept is both adaptable to, and encouraging of, development. Hence the title of Professor Moody's book: the interweaving of traditional and modern in East Asia to achieve phenomenal growth.

The focus of the book in its early chapters is on the development and modernization of Confucian thought and societal norms in China. But it is clear that when Professor Moody writes of China, he means "greater China," including Hong Kong, Singapore, and Taiwan, as well as the dynamic Chinese communities resident in other countries of Asia. Moreover, his analysis further broadens to include Korea and, especially, Japan, and to demonstrate how Confucian values helped stimulate rapid modernization in those societies, too.

The result is a book that could be used as a text in a course in China, a course comparing China and Japan, or a course encompassing all of East Asia. The book is rich not just in facts but also in interpretation and insight. As with others in our series, it is not just a text but and eminently enjoyable, well-written, provocative, and highly readable book as well.

HOWARD J. WIARDA
Amherst, Cambridge, and Washington, D.C.

Preface

✦

Cultural diversity became a topic of controversy on American college campuses during the 1990s; it was not always clear what was meant by the term. Some critics thought it denoted a hostility to the western cultural heritage, whether traditional or modern, and adherence to a political agenda justifying that hostility. Part of this agenda, the critics asserted, was the affirmation of different cultural traditions, as long as everyone thought the same things. More constructive interpretations of cultural diversity urge respect for the heritage of people of varying backgrounds and a critical appreciation of perspectives and visions of the world different from those current in one's own circles. In this sense, cultural diversity would simply be a normal part of a proper liberal education.

I am not sure whether my own interest in the politics and cultures of Asia (nurtured now for more than a quarter of a century) counts as an application of the principle of cultural diversity. I think, however, that a study of even moderate depth of this great civilization is a step toward realizing such an objective. My own motivation for study was curiosity about the profound humanistic tradition of Confucianism and a fascination with the tumult then characteristic of the Confucian area, especially China. At that time there was still some serious effort to identify general empirical theories of politics, and I was also interested in discovering to what extent such generalizations applied in vastly different cultural contexts. In those days, a westerner's interest in East Asian culture was probably something very different from an East Asian's interest in western culture. In spite of occasional explicit warnings to the contrary, it was still too easy to identify the western with the modern, and to take contemporary western culture as normative for the entire world. This is no longer possible, given Asia's dramatic emergence as a political and economic center. The power of the Asian states and economies enhances the incentive to take their cultures seriously. But beyond all the pragmatic considerations, the study of culture and its relation to politics is important for what it reveals about human experience and the human potential. Becoming aware of the differences among cultures and societies and becoming aware for the rationale for those differences enhances our understanding of our common humanity.

This book grew from a course I have been teaching for many years, entitled, as it so happens, Tradition and Modernization in China and Japan. The writing provided an opportunity to draw together some of the things I have learned while teaching the course, although I can't claim that it represents anything like the sum of knowledge about the subject, and would prefer not to think that it reveals even the extent of my own understanding. I have assumed that these two countries (or societies) are best understood in a comparative perspective. Taken together, they share a common general cultural heritage distinct from other cultures; taken separately, differences within the Confucian culture they both share become apparent.

The East Asian region has not yet been accommodated in a completely comfortable way within the general discipline of political science, China perhaps less comfortably than Japan. This may represent a perennial tendency of those who study China, whether natives of China or not, to treat that country as something unique and special—a propensity shared with those who study the United States. But it may also represent a shortcoming of mainstream political science, which has not tried hard enough to come to terms with the East Asian experience.

This book takes a cultural perspective on the politics of the region. The concept of political culture passed somewhat out of style around 1970, but is enjoying something of a revival as events of the post-Cold War era make its general relevance once again obvious. It did not pass out of style among students of East Asia, perhaps partly because they were somewhat isolated from the "mainstream," but also because the politics of the region simply could not be understood apart from the culture.

I believe that the current situations in China and Japan must be understood as both stemming from, and reacting against, their earlier traditions. Since traditions are not stagnant, and to a certain extent may even be reconstructed by each generation, the political culture of each country must also be studied as it shows itself in the historical process. It is not, of course, always necessary to go back to the Warring States or the Fujiwara Regency to explain everything about contemporary Chinese or Japanese politics (and, in fact, overly intrusive attempts to explain the present in terms of the past can be pretentiously irritating). But discussions of contemporary affairs completely divorced from an awareness of the traditions and their transformations risk shallowness. It is not merely that certain patterns may recur (for, of course, others may not) or that by failing to try to understand how others think we too easily and erroneously assume they think just the same as us. In East Asia, a concern for tradition and for modernization as a historical and social process shapes the discourse of active politicians and of thinkers who attempt to interpret their own societies.

In this book I have tried to present a synthesis of the various interpretations and approaches I take to be current in the field, and so owe unpayable debts to those who have undertaken detailed studies and offered original theses. I have tried to present both the scholarly and the political controversies in a fair manner. On some of these issues I have my own opinions, and have sometimes even offered them. But I hope to have done so in a way that makes it clear why others might not agree. Furthermore, readers have access to material that allows them to develop their own interpretations.

A synthesis such as this is bound to reflect the limitations of the author. This book should certainly not be taken as the last word on tradition and modernization in China and Japan, but as the first word, an introduction. It will succeed to the extent that it furthers an understanding of China and Japan as societies in comparison with others, and to the extent that it serves as a foundation for practical engagement with, or further scholarly study of, the region.

Job in the Bible remarks: "Would that my enemy had written a book." In science and scholarship, of course, the work is everything, and the fallible ego of the one offering the work is nothing; as Confucius might point out, even a flawed work is valuable, showing us what is not the case, and the kind of thing we should not do. Nonetheless, in making a work public one cannot but be aware of one's manifold deficiencies; the nagging sense that however much attempt was made to overcome lapses in knowledge, judgement, or energy, there will still be such lapses. I am in debt to students and colleagues, and to the reviewers who commented on this manuscript: Joel Glassman, University of Missouri-St. Louis; Richard K. Franklin, University of Akron; Stephen K. Ma, California State University, Los Angeles; Donald C. Hellman, University of Washington. My gratitude also goes to Howard Wiarda, the general editor of this series, and to the staff at Wadsworth, particularly Brian Gore, Jennifer Dunning, and Michelle Filippini. Finally, I'd like to thank my family.

An Essay on Chinese and Japanese Pronunciation

✦

Chinese is not written with a phonetic alphabet, but in "characters" or "ideograms," which do not systematically link shape and the sound. Japanese is intrinsically more suited to phonetic writing than is Chinese, and, in fact, it has two different systems for indicating pronunciation (showing syllables rather than what we would call individual letters). Japan first received its writing system from China, and these phonetic elements are used in conjunction with Chinese characters. In western works it is necessary to use letters to represent Chinese and Japanese sounds, especially, of course, for proper names. This process is called romanization (because English and other western European languages use the Roman or Latin alphabet).

Chinese Pronunciation

There are two internationally used systems for romanizing Chinese—the traditional Wade-Giles system (devised by Western sinologists) and the newer *pinyin* (that is, "phonetic spelling") system, endorsed by the government of the People's Republic. During the 1980s pinyin was widely adopted in writing about China, although some traditionalists, and writers on traditional subjects, continue to prefer Wade-Giles. Those used to Wade-Giles often think that system has an elegance not found in pinyin, although pinyin may, once its sometimes not obvious principles are mastered, be more efficient in giving a sense of the sound. This book uses mainly pinyin, although the chapter on Taiwan uses Wade-Giles for personal names. Wade-Giles continues to be the officially approved system on that island, and people from Taiwan tend to use it when romanizing their own names. Both systems, as will immediately become obvious, have their eccentricities.

Pinyin

We might begin with the vowels in pinyin. Remember that the given correspondences are only approximate.

a   as in f*a*ther
e   as in s*u*ch (except when followed by i or y: see below)
i   normally, as in s*ee*k. However, i's pronunciation changes, in not always intuitively obvious ways, according to the consonants it is used with.
o   roughly, as in *aw*, shucks. There is often a slight u or w sound before the o sound. With some consonants this is made explicit: thus, *luo*, to fall, rather than lo; but *bo*, to peel, rather than buo. You don't need to worry too much about this, but try not to pronounce bo like bow and arrow.
u   normally, as in m*oo*n. Following j, q, x, and y, u in pinyin is pronounced in the French fashion or the German ü, a sound that does not occur in English. Try to pronounce *oo* while forming your mouth to say *ee* and you should have it.

Another refinement: l and n may be followed by either u sound; with these letters, the "French" pronunciation is indicated by two dots (an umlaut) over the u: ü. For example, *nu* (noo), slave, but *nü*, woman; *lu*, road, but *lü*, green.

Y, when used as a vowel, is pronounced as i (as in seek) when it begins a syllable. Yi, however, is itself a single syllable, pronounced ee (not yee). Y before u, again, is the ü sound, and the y is not pronounced.

Chinese has several vowel combinations, or diphthongs:

ai   as in *ai*sle
ao   as in c*ow* (but don't close your mouth at the end of the word)
ei   l*ay*
ia   y*a*rd (as a word by itself, *ya*)
iao   *yow* (when this is a word by itself, it is written *yao*)
ie   *yeah* (but don't slur the pronunciation; when by itself, *ye*)
iu   *yo*yo (but the yo sound as a word by itself is written *you*)
ou   l*ow* (but with the final consonant left open; it is about the same as the iu sound, but without the initial i)
ua   *wah*, like a baby's cry (when a word by itself, it is written *wa*)
ui   *way* (this occurs only after certain consonants; when it is a word by itself, the sound is rendered *wei*)
uo   *waw* (approximately; as a word by itself, *wo*)

Mandarin Chinese has only two final consonants:[1] -n and -ng. Neither really presents any problems, but the following may be of technical interest.

an is not pronounced like the English article, but more like *aun*t in British English, or, in American English, the version of that word that does not sound like "ant."

ang also keeps the broad *a* sound. *Sang*, mulberry tree, is pronounced less like English *sang* (a song), and more like French *sang*, blood— except the Chinese, like the English, clearly sounds the *ng*.

en *un*done

eng h*ung*

-ian, or, when used alone, yan
as in *yen*ta. Wade-Giles uses -ien for this sound, and that is probably a more appropriate rendition for speakers of English.

in as in p*in*

ing as in p*ing*-pong

ong has no equivalent in most English dialects. Think of "oong." *Long*, dragon, is not pronounced like a "long time," unless, perhaps, one were speaking with a Yorkshire accent. The Wade-Giles version of this sound is -ung, and, here again, is probably more conducive to correct pronunciation.

un somewhere between the *en* sound, above, and m*oon*; the sound begins with a hint of a w.

-uan, or -uang
the u here functions as a w would in English, and when these sounds are words unto themselves, they are spelled *wan* and *wang*.

-üan and -üang (or uan and uang following j, q, or x)
are probably difficult for English speakers. In principle, all you need to do is sound out the letters in their regular pronunciations, but pack the whole thing into a single syllable. The ü sound has the effect of changing the connected *a* sound toward *Anne*, pronounced with an American accent.

The pinyin consonants present fewer problems of pronunciation than do the vowels. Unless otherwise noted, they are sounded as you would expect. From an English speaker's point of view, the more peculiar renditions include:

c pronounced *ts* (as in Polish spelling; pinyin was devised during the period of Soviet influence in China, and the scholars responsible for developing it were probably influenced by the Slavic languages).

g is always hard, as in *g*arden, not as in *g*ender.

---

1. This does not count the final -r sound for many nouns in the colloquial speech of Peking and other northern regions.

h   pronounced with a more vigorous expulsion of breath than in English, with the breath coming from the back of the mouth.

r   is, as it happens, pronounced much as it is in English, but that is a rare variety of r. It is not vibrated in either the front or the rear of the mouth, as it is in many other languages. The tongue is curled behind that upper ridge toward the front of the mouth.

x   as in *sh*eep. The tongue is flat, the tip toward the top front of the mouth. Contrast this with the pinyin sh, pronounced as in *sh*ould, the tongue curled behind the ridge on the top of the mouth.

z   might be more usefully spelled *dz*—a sort of buzzing sound.

Another group of letters requires more extended explanation. Pinyin, in what might be an excess of sophistication, distinguishes between two pronunciations of what in English are usually spelled *j* or *ch*.[2] Compare these pairs of words:

1. *ch*eap *j*eep
2. *ch*arred *j*unk

In (1) the tongue is flat on top of the mouth, the tip near the top front teeth. In (2) the tongue is curled behind the ridge in the top of the mouth. The relationship here is the same as that discussed above between *x* and *sh*. In (1) the ch is rendered by q, while j is still j. In (2) ch is rendered by ch, while j becomes zh.[3] Pinyin distinguishes all these different sounds.

J and q (and x as well) must always be followed by an i or ü (or their variants, -ian and the like). This is the reason pinyin does not use the umlaut with these letters. If you see *qu*, to go, you know the u is pronounced ü; if you see *chu*, out, you know the u is long, as in prune. An exercise: say *chu qu*, to go out.

A consequence of the above rules is that the i takes on different sounds in different contexts. Thus, there is no shi syllable in Chinese in which the i is sounded as ee (rather, if it is, the sh- becomes an x instead). After sh, ch, and zh, the i takes a certain r sound, as in *sir*. Thus, *shi*, that's so, is pronounced *shir*, as in *shir*t. By the same logic, *chi* is pronounced *chir* (as in *chir*p); the *chee* sound (as in *chee*se) is rendered, of course, as *qi*. Analogously, *zhi* is pronounced *jir* (if there is such a sound in English; it should rhyme with the -ir in chirp), while *gee* is rendered *ji*.

Si, however, is pronounced neither *see* nor *sir* (neither sound exists in northern-accented Mandarin). The i here, and also in ci, ri, and zi, indicates that the consonant sound is drawn out, with only a hint of an undefined vowel at the end. The Wade-Giles equivalent of si, *ssu* or *szu*, probably gives a better approximation of the sound to English speakers.

---

2. Note that these sounds are produced in the same way in the mouth: ch- is j- with an expulsion of breath. This aspect is developed in the discussion of the Wade-Giles system.

3. Note that all these sounds are hard, as in English, not soft, as in French. Beijing is pronounced like *jing*le bells.

Wade-Giles

The Wade-Giles system is generally more flexible, and so less precise, than pinyin. Except as noted below, the vowels in Wade-Giles are much the same as in pinyin. The main exceptions, I think, include:

the pinyin -ian or yan become -ien or yen in Wade-Giles.

the pinyin -ong becomes -ung in Wade-Giles.

the -ir sound, for which pinyin uses the letter i, becomes, maddeningly, -ih in Wade-Giles.

the pinyin *shi*, that's so, becomes *shih* in Wade-Giles.

the pinyin *yu* (with the "French" u) is *yü* in Wade-Giles. The Wade-Giles *yu* is equivalent to *you* in pinyin. Generally, the "French" u sound is indicated by an umlaut in Wade-Giles, although it may be omitted in those places where u must always be pronounced in the French manner. Thus, pinyin *xu* may be either *hsu* or *hsü* in Wade-Giles.

the pinyin *yi* may be either *i* or *yi* in Wade-Giles—at the writer's choice.

the pinyin e, in some cases, can be either e or o in Wade-Giles. For example, the province Henan, in pinyin, may be either Henan or Honan in Wade-Giles.

The Wade-Giles system of consonants has some peculiarities. First, let's get some easy things out of the way:

as already noted, the pinyin si sound is rendered ssu or ssz (your choice) in Wade-Giles.

pinyin x becomes hs in Wade-Giles.

pinyin r becomes, of all things, j in the Wade-Giles system.

In pinyin, the *People's Daily*, the official newspaper of the Communist party, is *Renmin Ribao*; in Wade-Giles, it is written *Jen-min Jih-pao*. Notice that the pinyin b has become a Wade-Giles p. This brings up the problem of "aspirated" and unaspirated consonants.

Note the following pairings, in English:

b and p
d and t
g and k
j and ch

The sounds in each pair are formed by the same positions and movements of the lips and tongue; the second sound in each pair, however, also requires an expulsion of breath, an "aspiration." The Wade-Giles system, in its own exercise in oversophistication, takes this similarity into account. Apparently, if we are really technical about it, Chinese does not have the "d" sound, at least as that figures in English. Rather, Chinese has an "unaspirated t," which to almost all English speakers sounds just like a d.

Yet English does have examples of an unaspirated t. Loosely hold a piece of paper next to your mouth and say the following words:

top
stop

The paper moves at the t sound in top: you are blowing air on it. On the t sound in stop, however, it is relatively still (and in both cases the paper moves on the p sound). The t in stop is unaspirated. Pinyin treats the unaspirated sounds as the English letters they most nearly sound like.

The pinyin Deng Xiaoping, for example, becomes Teng Hsiao-p'ing in Wade-Giles. The t is not aspirated. The p is, and this fact is indicated by the aspiration mark, ', which in modern texts is almost always indicated by an apostrophe (older texts used a reversed apostrophe).

The equivalents in both systems are as follows:

pinyin	Wade-Giles
b	p
c	ts'
ch	ch'
ci	tz'u
d	t
j	ch
k	k'
p	p'
q	ch'
t	t'
z	ts
zh	ch
zi	tzu

Note that Wade-Giles does not make pinyin's distinction between the frontal and back ch- and j- sounds.

One more convention might be noted. In pinyin, a term consisting of more than one character is spelled as a single word. In Wade-Giles the character sounds, or syllables, are separated by a hyphen (except in geographic terms that are commonly used in English, such as the names of provinces or major cities). Thus, China ("Central Country"), in pinyin, is *Zhongguo*; in Wade-Giles it is *Chung-kuo*.[4] Where there is an ambiguity, pinyin separates syllables by an apostrophe. Thus, the Communist wartime capital should properly be romanized Yan'an, to avoid its being mispronounced as Ya'nan.

Chinese is a tonal language, and the tone of each syllable is as much a part of its pronunciation as the vowels and consonants. This text, however, ignores the tones.

---

4. Although a geographic term, it is hyphenated because English uses the word *China* instead.

Japanese Pronunciation

The most-used system for romanizing Japanese is the Hepburn system. It is probably less complicated for English speakers than the various Chinese romanizations. Japanese has fewer syllable sounds than Chinese, but most Japanese words have more than one syllable.

The vowels include:

a   as in f*a*ther
e   as in b*e*nd
i   as in s*ee*k
o   as in *o*ld
u   as in m*oo*n (sometimes, however, it is barely sounded; for example, one greeting is *arigato desuka*, which sounds almost like *arigato des'ka*)

Japanese has only two vowel combinations, or diphthongs:

ai   as in *ai*sle
ei   as in Y*a*le

Otherwise, when two vowels appear together, they are sounded as separate syllables. Sometimes the ai combination indicates two different syllables. In that case, there is an umlaut over the i, as in Aïnu.

Japanese consonants are pronounced much as the English equivalents, but h is more strongly exhaled, r is trilled in the front of the mouth, and g is always hard.

Proper Japanese pronunciation requires distinction between long and short vowels. Like the tones in Chinese, but perhaps with less justification, these are ignored in the text.

About the Author

✦

Peter R. Moody, Jr., teaches in the Department of Government and International Studies at the University of Notre Dame. He was educated at Vanderbilt and at Yale, and has conducted research in China, Taiwan, Japan, Korea, and Vietnam. He is the editor of *China Documents Annual*, and has written on Chinese politics, comparative politics, international relations, and Chinese political thought. His books include *Opposition and Dissent in Contemporary China* (Hoover Institution, 1977); *Political Opposition in Post-Confucian Society* (New York, 1988); and *Political Change on Taiwan* (New York, 1992).

1
—
◆
Introduction

It is common to hear that we are approaching the "Asian Century." The speculation takes its inspiration from the economic dynamism of East Asia, especially of those societies in the region that have been influenced by Confucian culture. Japan, despite its dearth of natural resources, boasts the world's second largest economy. China has not done as well, but its potential remains enormous. As China and Japan become major world economic and cultural centers, they will be resuming what for centuries had been their normal place in the world's scheme of things. The Confucian societies (Korea and Vietnam along with China and Japan) have lengthy, complex, sophisticated cultural traditions. This Confucian culture region was also the most isolated and self-contained of the world's great cultures. The process some call modernization—the changes resulting directly or indirectly from the industrial, technological, and scientific revolutions that began in Europe a few centuries ago—did not occur spontaneously in East Asia. The confrontation of an aggressive, modernized West with traditional Confucian civilization disrupted the old order, bringing the collapse and revolutionary transformation of the official Chinese order and a no-less-radical transformation of Japanese life, society, and politics. But while the process of modernization began as an imposition from the outside, the East Asian societies have perhaps been more successful on the whole than any other non-Western societies in adapting to modernization. The prime example is, of course, Japan, but further evidence for this hypothesis is the "four dragons"—the Chinese societies of Taiwan, Hong Kong, and Singapore, as well as South Korea. There is also reason to wonder whether in the long run the East Asian societies may not adapt to modern life more successfully than the Western societies that first gave it birth.

This book hopes to make sense of the contemporary political systems of China and Japan and of the relationship between politics and the broader economies and societies. It begins with several assumptions. One is that understanding is furthered by the comparative method. China and Japan and the changes they have undergone can be analyzed, on the one hand, in comparison with other areas of the world, especially the West (meaning western Europe and North America) and, from within, in comparison with each other. China and Japan began with a somewhat similar background and faced very similar external pressures. The difference in their reactions should allow insight into how politics works in each country (and also, perhaps, into how politics works more generally).

Another assumption is that politics and political change are usefully understood in terms of their cultural context. This similar culture forms the basis for the comparison of the two societies.[1] The modern state everywhere is modeled upon the systems of western Europe and North America, but the institutions do not work everywhere exactly as they do in the West. Students of China and Japan have never really been able to ignore the cultural context. Modernization is itself in part a question of cultural change (although this does not mean that the change is always toward greater similarity with the West; we should be careful to maintain a distinction between modernization and westernization), and the fate of the traditional culture in the modern world and the compatibility of that culture with modernization have been major political themes in both China and Japan for more than a hundred years.

Modernization is itself a major political issue in both countries.[2] In both cases, a complex and sophisticated traditional culture was challenged by a new world order imposing itself from outside, and examining the adaptation (or failure to adapt) to the modern world order becomes a way of organizing

---

1. It would not necessarily be the only way to approach a comparative study of either country. Thus, comparisons, say, of China and Russia can be informative as can, perhaps, comparisons of Japan and Great Britain.
2. The term went somewhat out of fashion among political scientists in the West around 1970 or so. One reason I am using it as if there were no problem with it is that it continues to be a viable concept in the Chinese and Japanese political discourse.

information about and making sense of political institutions and processes in both countries.

We hope to understand China and Japan for the intrinsic interest of their societies and cultures and for their importance in world affairs. Most of this book deals directly and explicitly with the countries themselves. This introductory chapter, however, treats matters of theory, to clarify the ways in which terms such as *culture*, *tradition*, and *modernization* are being used.

Political Culture and the Cultural Approach

Students of politics have always had to take into account cultural differences among different peoples, but self-conscious attention to political culture is associated with political scientists of the generation following the Second World War.[3] There was a concern at that time with making political science truly scientific, and many scholars maintained (on the whole somewhat unfairly) that their predecessors had been content to give accounts of the laws and formal institutions of different countries without worrying about how those laws and institutions actually worked. At the same time, the number of independent countries in the world was increasing. These new states were for the most part non-Western former colonies of Western empires.[4] Their formal institutions resembled those of their former imperial masters, but the content of politics often seemed to have little to do with the formal institutions. In hoping to understand the stuff of politics, it was natural to try to systematically take cultural differences into account.

The concept of political culture was introduced to help explain why similar formal institutions did not work the same way in different places and circumstances, and it also pointed to aspects of politics not evident from formal descriptions of institutions. While originally invented to help explain the politics of societies that people in the United States might find a little exotic, the concept applies to comparative politics generally. It should be as helpful to study the political culture of the United States or Great Britain as of China, Japan, or Mozambique. A classic exploration of the concept, for

---

3. For a survey of the ways in which the concept has been used, see Michael Brint, *A Genealogy of Political Culture* (Boulder, 1991).

4. China and Japan had not, of course, been colonies, although China had lost effective control over much of what went on within the country. Japan was anything but a passive recipient of outside forces. But neither China nor Japan had been incorporated into the body of the discipline of political science. In fact, even today political science as a whole fails to take sufficient account of the East Asian nations—a condition partly attributable, I think, to the cultural differences.

example, attempts to discover whether culture helps explain differences in democratic stability among Western countries.[5]

Culture so far has not been defined, and it may not be usefully amenable to an overly rigid definition: we discover what the term means from the ways it is used. Most generally, culture refers to all the nonbiological aspects of human life.[6] That we eat is a biological necessity. What we eat, when we eat, what we consider edible, what we consider palatable, the significance we attribute to different kinds of foods are all (within certain still-undiscovered limits[7]) matters of culture. An uncontroversial assumption is that different groups of humans have different sorts of acquired traits, which may change over time, and that within any given group each trait is somehow systematically related to other traits.

Culture includes language, art, diet, family structure, politics, religion, clothing styles, humor, and much else characteristic of any group of people. Since politics is a part of culture, *political culture* would seem to be nothing else than the politics characteristic of a particular human group. This definition may be too broad to be useful, however; it may be better to allow the concept some content of its own, making it refer, say, to the place of politics within a particular culture, to the relations of other aspects of culture to politics, and to the political expression of the group's culture.

Political scientists tend in practice to use the term even more narrowly— probably too narrowly. In one influential formulation, "political culture is the set of attitudes, beliefs, and feelings about politics current in a nation at a given time."[8] There is a tendency to formulate statements about the attitudes and the like in psychological terms, with the culture defined in terms of the personalities of the various individuals found within the group held to have that culture. This is in effect a newer version of the older theories of national

---

5. Gabriel Almond and Sidney Verba, *The Civic Culture: Political Attitudes and Democracy in Five Nations* (Princeton University Press, 1963). For criticisms, reappraisals, and reassertions, see *The Civic Culture Revisited*, edited by Gabriel Almond and Sidney Verba (Boston, 1980).

6. In English, Chinese, and Japanese usage a cultured person is one who has acquired those attributes most highly valued in the particular society. This usage is probably still the most common meaning of the term in all three languages; it is different from, but related to, the more general anthropological usage.

7. There may be no reason dogmatically to make an overly rigid and absolute distinction between the biological and the cultural. There may be cultural universals somehow innate in human nature—perhaps the capacity to form language, perhaps, as the Chinese philosopher Mencius asserts, a capacity for empathy with other human beings. These propensities, however, take different forms and are realized in different ways among different groups of humans.

8. Gabriel Almond and G. Bingham Powell, *Comparative Politics: System, Process, and Policy*, second edition (Boston: 1978), p. 25.

character, which speculate that people of different types sort themselves out by country: Americans are loud and pragmatic, Germans are efficient and ruthless, the French are sophisticated and amorous, the English are cold and snooty, the Chinese are sociable and inscrutable, the Japanese are hardworking and clever, and so on. The more scientifically ambitious essays in this vein try to identify culture by comparing answers to questionnaires asking people in different countries similar things about politics.[9]

Political culture is used in this book a little more broadly than it often is in political science. It may not be useful to think of culture as something specific in itself, which directly explains things about a society. Rather, culture is the *context* in which political action takes place. It is not cause or effect ("independent variable" or "dependent variable") so much as the general structure of conditions influencing the ways in which causes produce effects.

The original political science approaches, perhaps reflecting the liberal individualism of the American culture in which they were formed, reduced cultural patterns to statements about numbers of separate individuals. Culture, however, is a characteristic of societies as a whole, not simply of collections of individuals. At least in principle, culture should be kept distinct from the psychological characteristics of the particular people in a culture (there may, of course, be empirical or factual connections, but this is a matter to be discovered through research, not assumed beforehand). The structure or pattern we identify as culture would then shape behavior independently of the personalities of those who participate in it. Someone with an aggressive personality may possibly be a better football player than a gentler person who is equally strong, fast, and coordinated; and a good football player will certainly be aggressive on the practice and playing fields. But no one is particularly surprised to find football players who are not at all aggressive off the field. Traffic habits in Taipei, the capital of Taiwan, are abominable, whereas in the United States, all things considered, the rules of the road are followed. But after coming to the United States those who learned to drive in Taipei are soon driving like Americans, and Americans in Taipei soon drive like everyone else there. It is not that Americans are careful drivers while Chinese are not; rather, in order to drive effectively in any given environment, one must follow the prevailing pattern.

There is also, we have seen, a tendency to identify culture with "attitudes" and "values." These must be a part of culture. Values, here, however, should not indicate merely arbitrary preferences people happen to have. A cultural focus points as well to the *rationale* for those preferences. Once we get into questions having any degree of complexity (questions of right and wrong, or good and evil, for example), people prefer certain things because they believe

---

9. Almond and Verba, *The Civic Culture*.

they have reasons for those preferences, and these reasons are likely to be connected to or derived from a general mentality or vision of how the world works. Part of the job of cultural analysis is to reconstruct (or, if you are a postmodernist, to deconstruct) the logic behind these mentalities or views of the world.

Nor, I think, should cultural analysis be confined to the mental level. It should also attempt to discover how ways of thinking about the world are linked to the way people behave or act, and to the political, social, economic, and other institutions through which action takes place. Since culture is intrinsically such an all-embracing concept, to say something is caused by culture is close to saying nothing at all. Culture may be a general explanation for certain outcomes if we are comparing across different cultures. More normally, however, culture is not itself an explanation but a setting or a context for explanation, a way of making sense of what is done. Culture is a way of looking at things, not itself a thing. That is why it would rarely be sufficient to explain a phenomenon simply by pointing to culture: we would want to know what it is, specifically, that produces that phenomenon. Political factionalism may be an element of Japanese culture, but it is unhelpful to say that culture causes factionalism. Rather, we should investigate specific relationships—say those between the electoral system and the party system. The cultural focus, however, leads us to inquire further, to see if there is a systematic relationship among, for example, factionalism, the electoral system, and other specific Japanese institutions, practices, and values (for the electoral system does not exist in isolation from the rest of Japanese life, and it itself has its causes).[10]

The political culture approach is an alternative to formalistic descriptions of political institutions (a way of studying politics no one from ancient times on has probably ever deemed completely satisfactory). Political culture does not mean that institutions are ignored but should help explain how institutions actually work in different contexts. Some Marxian critics object that the approach, by focusing on values, is both morally and intellectually deficient. They may assert that the cultural approach looks at the problem of "underdevelopment" by "blaming the victim"—attributing poverty, say, to a "culture of poverty," neglecting the specific institutions and practices that contribute to keeping people poor. Some in this same school consider the approach nonhistorical, saying it forgets that attitudes and values are themselves contingent, that they arise, change, and perish for particular reasons at

---

10. For a work that, despite its age (and, to my mind, an overly psychological orientation), remains insightful, see Ruth Benedict, *Patterns of Culture* (New York, 1934), especially Ch. IV. Ruth Benedict also wrote, using her particular mode of analysis, an influential study of Japanese culture that remains worth reading: *The Chrysanthemum and the Sword* (New York, 1947).

particular times. The emphasis on values gives the impression that everyone in a society sees things the same way, whereas sometimes the official set of values in a society might be a rationalization for the powerful and privileged, an instrument to make people think that things as they are, are just as they should be.[11]

Obviously, there are errors here to avoid. Particular studies may or may not have such shortcomings, but they are probably not inherent in the approach. Someone offering a cultural explanation, however, might in turn wonder whether all this class struggle is not itself a cultural artifact, present sometimes in some societies but not in others. The charge that a cultural focus leads to a static analysis is not entirely fair either. To identify a society as having a certain culture probably does imply that some things about it do not change, or do not change very rapidly, over time. If we could think of a society as having a new culture every day, the concept would not help us very much in understanding that society.[12] On the other hand, many of the more significant changes in the world today, whether for good or for bad, are cultural changes, and these, by definition, can hardly be understood without reference to culture. The political culture approach has in fact been invaluable in giving insights into changes in the world.[13] Analysis of culture gives clues both to the possibilities for change inherent in any particular society, and to the ways in which that society might react to changes forcing themselves in from the outside.

Another popular approach sometimes taken as an alternative to political culture, "rational choice," focuses on individuals rather than on classes or groups, and assumes individuals are all pretty much alike. Here the critic will assert that the student of culture explains people's actions in terms of in themselves inexplicable cultural peculiarities and idiosyncrasies, whereas in fact most of what we do can be understood as a rational action geared toward the logic of the situation, what anybody would do in the circumstances. Some of the political culture literature may make too much of a distinction between what is culturally contingent and what is rational. A possible fallacy of the rational choice approach, however, is to fail to consider that there may be no such thing as rationality in the abstract. An action or statement is rational in a certain context, based on certain assumptions, or moving toward a certain

---

11. For a strong statement of these last points, see Barrington Moore, *Social Origins of Dictatorship and Democracy* (Boston, 1968).

12. Harry Eckstein, "A Culturalist Theory of Political Change," *American Political Science Review*, 83, 2 (September 1988), pp. 789–804.

13. For example, Ronald Inglehart, *Cultural Shift in Advanced Industrial Society* (Princeton University Press, 1990); Samuel P. Huntington, *The Third Wave: Democratization in the Late Twentieth Century;* also *New Directions in Comparative Politics*, edited by Howard J. Wiarda (Boulder, 1991).

end. Rational choice theorists usually point in practice to the so-called rationality of means—that is, is an action an efficient way to achieve one's desires (values). This approach neither can nor does say anything about the rationality of the ends, about whether what we might want is itself reasonable or not. This must depend in part on the cultural context. Beyond that, different groups of people not only value different things, but differ in how they think about what they value. Part of the job of cultural analysis is to show that what to the outsider may seem strange or irrational is understandable in human terms. Culture provides the context for rational choice.[14]

Political culture is a theoretical concept. A theory's purpose (or function) is to explain the world. It must be measured against facts and cannot be a substitute for facts. The analysis in this book assumes a general comparability between Chinese and Japanese culture, but in any specific instance we have to look at the facts to see just what the similarities and differences might be. On some specific points the culture of either country may be closer to that of some Western society than it is to that of the other. Thus, baseball, which came to Japan from America, not China, is as much a part of Japanese culture as Confucianism or Buddhism (which came from China and India). The Japanese lifetime employment system seems to work quite well in Japan, but probably would not work out so well in the United States. Chinese reformers believe a similar system used in their country to be responsible for perpetuating China's backwardness. Thus, in some ways Chinese and American culture may share traits neither shares with Japan.

Tradition and Modernization

The self-conscious analysis of political culture was part of a movement in comparative politics sometimes called political development or modernization theory.[15] This, too, fell out of favor for a while, with critics finding the approach too ethnocentric, too inclined to hold up the contemporary capitalist West as the standard for everyone else, too negligent of the possible lack of autonomy of weak states from an external transnational economic system, and too optimistic about the relationship between social and economic

---

14. This understanding need not imply approval for the choices made or actions taken; nor does it imply that all ways of looking at the world are equally rational in some abstract sense.

15. Almond and Powell, *Comparative Politics*, is a good epitome of the most influential trend in this approach.

modernization and political democracy. More recently it has made something of a comeback, with scholars coming to feel its defects had been exaggerated.

For more than a century a major theme in East Asian politics has been whether the traditional cultures can modernize and yet retain their shape and identity, or whether modernization, a need imposed by the modern world system, requires abandoning the traditional culture in its entirety. East Asian rulers and citizens have, like the modernization theorists, seen connections among ideas, values, social forms, and technology and, like modernization theorists, have not always known quite what to make of these connections. All seem to agree that economic and technological changes influence, and are influenced by, other elements in the society and culture.

Beyond this somewhat uncontroversial observation, things are less clear. Sometimes (although this may be an old-fashioned view) modern society is contrasted with traditional society. Modern society is secular, complex, differentiated, while traditional society is dominated by religion, has a relatively simple distribution of labor and relatively simple structures of status relationships. This view of traditional society, however, does not adequately describe that of China or Japan or, if it comes to that, of Europe before modern times. Nor is it certain that modern society always has the characteristics ascribed to it. It may not be useful to make too absolute a distinction between modern and traditional. Religion is certainly traditional, and in some modern societies it has lost its force—but it has not lost its force in all modern societies, including those of the United States and Japan. In China in the 1980s, when the country was "modernizing" at perhaps a more rapid rate than it ever had been, there was also a revival of religion, both of Christianity and of the traditional religions. Some traditional elements may actually help advance modernization. For example, the modern Japanese office may reproduce social relations similar to those of the traditional village work teams; the strong family system in China and Japan may help ameliorate the psychologically disruptive aspects of modernization (although in some of its aspects modernization undermines that family system).

But even if we avoid too absolute a distinction between tradition and modernization, we should still probably keep the two separate terms. Modern society is said to be secular, and there is a sense in which this remains valid even if we still recognize the continuing influence of religion. To say that traditional society is religious or "sacred" would fit Chinese (and maybe Japanese) society only uneasily, but there may be a legitimate way of expanding on the meaning of these terms. In traditional societies there is a sense of a universal, objectively valid moral order, which is reflected in relations among individuals. Not everyone necessarily shares this same moral sense (and certainly not everyone adheres to it), but dissenting opinions are typically structured in specific contrast to the dominant orthodoxy (Daoism to some extent defining itself against Confucianism, for example). In modernizing society, the formerly accepted moral order loses much of its former rational credibility. This does not mean that it has been refuted; it may simply be that the social conditions that supported the old moral sense and were supported by it have changed, making the assumptions underlying the old rationality more difficult to accept. Modernization in this sense need not be restricted to what we usually consider modern times. The so-called Warring States period in ancient China (roughly 500 to 200 B.C.), the formative period of Chinese civilization, was an age of both social and technological change and of intellectual ferment—with the ferment motivated by a desire to rediscover a lost order, or to understand why order had been lost. In modern society there is no officially sanctioned order (unless it is secular rationalism itself, a way of thinking that denies objective status to "values"); in our ethical and social relations, knowledge has been replaced by opinion.[16]

In common usage—the usage for the most part employed in this book—modernization refers to the consequences of the industrial and scientific revolutions that began in Europe in the 1700s and 1800s. Prior to that time Europe and East Asia were technologically comparable (in some respects Europe was more advanced, in others Asia was more advanced). With the industrial revolution Europe became more powerful than any culture had ever been, able to project itself on a global scale. One consequence of the industrial revolution is what is sometimes called the European conquest of the world. It is impossible to know whether the East Asian societies would have undergone a similar process on their own (scholars will argue the question either way), but the fact is they did not. They were brought into a new world order for which their traditional institutions did not prepare them as a result of European (and American) imperialism and had to adapt, with greater or lesser success, to this unfamiliar international environment.

An assumption or hypothesis of some of the older modernization theory was that economic and social development would lead to democracy. The scientific revolution and the cultural revolution that went along produced a cast of mind in which we believe that nature has been brought under human control (although environmental degradation and the like can also cause us to wonder whether nature doesn't get its own licks in). By extension this can cause us to consider that the social order is not some natural given, but, rather, can be shaped to our heart's desires. The idea that the way things are

---

16. Some argue that totalitarian societies based on an ideology—and these are modern societies—do in fact enforce an absolute moral standard. I don't think, however, that this standard is really a moral one. In totalitarian ideologies morality is always reducible to something else—the progress of the revolution, the interests of the proletariat, the master race, or the like.

is subject to control is perhaps a necessary condition for democratic government, and democratic governments are on the whole found in the more successfully modern societies. But sometimes rapid technological change simply undermines the existing structure of authority without substituting anything for it, and this may encourage authoritarian or totalitarian political reactions[17] (with modern technology sometimes making oppressive rule more effective than it would otherwise be and moral skepticism and relativism removing previous restraints on human cruelty). It is safe to say that there is no single political consequence of modernization and also that it may not be easy to predict what in a particular case the consequence will be.

The more general cultural consequences of modernization are also ambiguous. On one level modernization implies increasing human freedom. Yet control over nature, given by technology, may often be no more than a synonym for the increased ability of some people to control others. Another consequence of modernization is the increased scope of state power, and increased power for the state within that scope. Modernization may mean liberation from certain kinds of bonds—women and grown children become free from undesired subservience to husbands and parents—but increased dependence on impersonal forces—the marketplace, the organization, remote political bureaucracies. Modernization opens up new ranges of personal choices, but chances are our values are formed by our environment, so modernization also conditions the choices we make. Modernization may breed alienation—a freedom, to be sure, from personal obligations, but one that deprives us of automatic personal support from others. We may feel shaped and guided by impersonal, unpredictable forces that are products of human action but not under human control.

East Asian society may represent a different version of modernization. Modernization historically began in the West, but modernization is not necessarily the same thing as westernization. However modern they get, China and Japan remain China and Japan. A tentative hypothesis might be that the overall political and economic structures of the traditional societies could not be easily adapted to modernization, and the intrusion of the new world order brought about the collapse or radical transformation of those structures and an erosion of the credibility of the ideologies supporting them. But at the "bottom" level, the personal bonds holding society together remained strong, and human interactions continued to have a personalized basis, modeled on that of the family. Once obstacles to modernization (including those derived from the traditional order) have been overcome, it can come about

---

17. Samuel P. Huntington, *Political Order in Changing Societies* (Yale University Press, 1968); Guillermo O'Donnell, *Modernization and Bureaucratic Authoritarianism* (University of California, Institute of International Studies, 1973).

without much of the demoralization and alienation that has characterized it in the West.

China and Japan

This book compares China and Japan because both were Confucian societies (and so have sufficient similarity to each other to make comparison interesting and meaningful). Both countries have faced similar challenges revolving around the concept of modernization. The main focus of this study is on *politics*, the formation of public choices. The interest in politics extends both to its smaller aspects—power struggles, personal and factional rivalries—and to its larger significances—determining the directions that the societies as a whole will take. Culture is an indication of what is important in politics in a particular society. It gives insights into the concerns of those who participate in or are victims of politics and points to the constraints they operate under, including, perhaps, some of those they might not consciously be aware of.

In China and Japan, culture is itself perhaps, in modern times, the major perennial political issue. At least since their exposure to the power of the industrialized West, thinkers, political elites, and ordinary people in China and Japan have wondered and argued about whether the traditional way of life is compatible with the demands of modernization; if there is any incompatibility, whether that way should be sacrificed for the sake of modernization; whether modernizing change is possible if people are to keep some sense of cultural integrity. The contemporary politics of both countries can be analyzed partly in terms of this debate, one that is not fully resolved even as the twentieth century lurches to its end.

This chapter has been rather abstract. The others concentrate much more closely on two countries. The second chapter discusses the general East Asian environment—the people, the languages, the geography. The third chapter deals with the intellectual background—Confucianism and the other philosophies and ways of thinking that helped shape the two societies. In these chapters there is rather more attention given to China than to Japan. China is larger and more diverse than Japan, and so requires more space in exposition. Also, while the original folk cultures of China and Japan were quite different from each other, Japan's literate culture derives almost entirely from China, so (perhaps influenced by a kind of Middle Kingdom mentality) I take China as the standard. Confucianism and the other systems of ideas must be understood first in their Chinese context, and most of what is said about their content in China applies equally to Japan. The section on Japan, then, focuses mainly on ways of thinking unique to Japan (such as, probably, the Shinto religion) and to those aspects of Confucianism in which Japanese practice differs from that of China.

The fourth chapter gives a schematic comparative overview of traditional society in China and Japan, showing how the manners of thinking discussed in Chapter 3 were expressed in political, social, and economic life. The culture of any country is never static, but changes through time, and so cultural generalizations need to be put into historical context. This is especially true when a powerful foreign culture intrudes itself. The fifth chapter compares the way in which the modern industrial order made itself felt in China and Japan, and the sixth chapter compares the ways in which the two societies tried to adapt to their new international environment. The remainder of the book also has a comparative purpose, but devotes separate chapters to discussions of the contemporary political structures and processes in each country. There is also a discussion of the government and politics of Taiwan, whose ruling regime was a remnant of that defeated by the Communists on the mainland in 1949. Whether Taiwan should someday reunify with the mainland, or whether it should someday become explicitly independent, or whether it remains in limbo, it shows some potentials in contemporary Chinese political culture different from those made kinetic in the People's Republic.

2

✦

The East Asian Environment

The culture of any society is in part an adaptation to its physical environment, although there are a multitude of ways of making this adaptation. To understand the politics of society we no doubt need to have some feel for the daily life and preoccupations of the people who live in it. This chapter sketches the geographic and human setting of China and Japan.

East Asia was the most isolated of the great civilizations and perhaps for this reason the most distinct. The particular cultural configuration is centered in China and extends to Japan, Korea, and Vietnam, and nowhere else. Obviously the region was not completely cut off from outside influences. Confucianism is, in effect, confined to this East Asian region, but so are other cultural practices perhaps less obviously connected with a particular view of life—eating with chopsticks, for example. The region was obviously not impervious to outside influences— Buddhism, which originated in India, is pervasive and gives the culture much of its substance and flavor. But Buddhism became radically transformed in the process of adapting itself to the larger Confucian environment, and East Asian Buddhism is different from Buddhism elsewhere. Practices and artifacts did not spread easily beyond the region. It has become commonplace in development studies to assert that the technology of one culture (such as the modern West) cannot be imported piecemeal to other cultures without much wider cultural and social ramifications. Yet Chinese technology in early times (paper, gunpowder, the compass, efficient types of rudders, the stirrup, pasta, perhaps the burning of coal) was transferred to the rest of the world without causing the foreign societies and cultures to become any more like those of China (although certainly there were great social consequences). The spread of the Chinese pattern has little to do with direct political influence; states that had been under some form of subordination to China for centuries (Siam—today's Thailand—and even Tibet) do not share the Chinese culture, whereas Japan was never subordinate to China. There may be a negative political association, however. In the 1200s the Mongols conquered a huge portion of East Asia, from the Pacific Ocean virtually to the Danube, but this empire broke up within a single generation. The economic and cultural core of that empire was China: the Mongols could rule China only in a Chinese fashion, and rule in a Chinese fashion was not suited for rule anywhere else.

China

China is the world's largest country, with a 1990 population of about 1.1 billion, roughly a fifth of the human race. In area it is the third largest country, behind Russia and Canada. China is also the world's oldest continuous civilization: Babylon, Egypt, and some others are more ancient, but they are also gone. Chinese civilization, including the written (and, presumably, the spoken) language, can be traced in a straight line from the present day back to ancient times.

China has always been an agrarian civilization. The Great Wall has been thought to divide the regions suited to farming from the areas to the north more suited to herding and grazing. As recently as 1980, about 80 percent of the people earned their living by agriculture, a ratio that may have been constant for several centuries. By the mid-1980s those earning their living exclusively from farming had decreased (apparently) to a little over 60 percent, a result of increased agricultural productivity and the opening up of new economic opportunities in rural areas.[1] While China's food problem has perhaps been basically (a word that in Communist jargon means "not quite") solved (the last major famine was in 1960–61, a result of bad policy rather than natural conditions by themselves), the area of arable land is small and has in recent decades been decreasing, a result of environmental degradation

---

1. John Gittings, *China Changes Face: The Road from Revolution, 1949–1989* (Oxford University Press, 1989), p. 4.

and the diversion of farmland to other uses. Most of the good farmland, and, hence, most of the people, are in the eastern part of the country, concentrated within the great river basins.

Chinese civilization originated in the region drained by the Yellow River, which flows through the arid northern plains. The river picks up dirt as it flows and, with the relatively flat terrain, this means it tends to spread out beyond its earlier banks. Since ancient times, the water has been held in by a system of dikes. Silt continues to accumulate, so that if the riverbed is not periodically dredged, that bed may be higher in elevation than the surrounding countryside, making for disaster should the dikes not be properly maintained. The mouth of the Yellow River has changed several times in history, most recently in the 1850s, when it shifted from the southern to the northern side of the Shandong Peninsula. The dry climate of northern China means that agriculture cannot depend upon rainfall but also requires irrigation. Although wheat is the main crop of the Yellow River region today, rice, which is grown in the other regions of China, requires an elaborate irrigation system even in areas of plentiful rainfall. This need for water control has been a mark of Chinese civilization and for some students even a determining element shaping that civilization.

Language

The civilization of the Yellow River area spread southward in ancient times, assimilating the local populations into itself. At the time there was presumably a fair amount of ethnic diversity, but by 400 B.C. the larger part of what is now China proper shared a common culture, including a common written language. This written language dates to the beginnings of a distinctly Chinese civilization and may even have given it its identity.

Farmers sometimes found old bones with strange markings on them. They would sell them to pharmacies as dragon bones, to be ground up for medicine. Around the turn of the twentieth century, Chinese and foreign scholars determined that the markings were in fact an early version of Chinese writing. The bones, called by the scholars oracle bones, had been used for divination during the Shang period (roughly 1700 to 1100 B.C.). The collarbone of an ox or the shell of a tortoise would be dried and a question would be scratched on it ("Is tomorrow a good day for hunting?" for example). The bones would then be heated on the fire, and the answer to the question would be deduced from how the bone cracked. The oracle bones corroborate in some detail aspects of ancient history skeptics had considered legendary (they confirm, for example, the names and dates traditionally ascribed to the rulers of the Shang dynasty), and also show that 3,000 years ago people were using the same general writing system that is used today.

Of course, only specialists can read the bone writing. The written language has changed, but those who study such things can trace the evolution of the characters (as the individual units of Chinese writing are called) from the bone writing to the present form. The present system took shape about 200 B.C., based on the handwriting of the prime minister who masterminded the unification of the whole country at that time. Beginning in the 1950s, the Peking regime sponsored a simplification of the writing system, but the overall changes (which have not been adopted outside the China mainland) are marginal.

Chinese writing is unusual—it is not alphabetic or phonetic; rather, each character represents a general meaning.[2] Chinese is itself a family of languages. Pronunciations vary in different parts of the country, but the written language is standard. An analogy, perhaps, is the number 5—pronounced *five* in English, *cinque* in French, *wu* in Chinese, but carrying the same meaning everywhere. Until the first decades of the twentieth century, Chinese was usually written in a "classical" format, perhaps bearing some relationship to the spoken language of 2,000 years ago but existing primarily as a medium for writing and close to unintelligible if spoken. The classical writing may have served to maintain the unity of the culture, as it provided a way of communication that avoided local variations of usage. Since the 1920s most Chinese has been written in the vernacular, based on the vocabulary and grammar of the Peking region.

We sometimes hear about the tens of thousands of Chinese characters. This is not untrue, but most characters are not used very much, and one approaches basic literacy with a knowledge of 700 or so. A college graduate may have a passive recognition of 10,000 characters. It is often assumed that the writing system is difficult to learn. It probably does put a premium on ability to memorize, but as far as one can tell about these things literacy rates in traditional China were no lower than those in traditional Europe, and Chinese children learn to read about as fast as children whose languages use phonetic systems. There is no evidence that the simplified characters introduced recently are any easier to remember than the standard forms, and they may even be more difficult to recognize (they are, however, much easier to write).

While the written language seems daunting to the foreigner, it is well adapted to the spoken language. People sometimes speak of the many Chinese dialects. Actually, about 80 percent of the people speak one form or another of what Westerners call Mandarin and what the Chinese call the common or national language. It is spoken with a great variety of accents (which differ more from each other than do accents of English). The radio-announcer, language-school standard is the Peking pronunciation (sometimes purged of its purely local Peking features). The 20 percent who speak non-Mandarin Chinese languages are found mainly in the south and southeast.

---

2. The Egyptian hieroglyphics were originally picture writing, but the signs soon came to be used for their phonetic value.

Spoken Chinese is tonal—that is, each syllable not only has a certain "sound" but also has a certain pitch or tone. It seems to be difficult for people not raised speaking a tonal language to adapt to one, and while Chinese has a rather simple grammar, most foreigners find it difficult to pronounce. Mandarin has only four tones, but some of the southern languages have twelve.

It may be no coincidence that Chinese is not written phonetically (for the Chinese have long been familiar with the concept of phonetic writing). It is difficult to devise a really satisfactory system. This book uses (for the most part) the "romanization" system (that is, the spelling of Chinese in Roman letters) developed under the auspices of the government of the People's Republic and given official status by that government. It is not a bad system, although somewhat inelegant, and once mastered (and used correctly) gives an unambiguous approximation of the sound of the word. It is not intuitively appealing to English speakers. The ts sound, for example, is rendered by c (a feature perhaps adapted from the Slavic languages—the Soviet Union was China's model at the time the system was devised). Q is used to represent the ch- sound when it appears before the vowels i (when i is pronounced *ee*) or ü (when, that is, u is pronounced in the French fashion), whereas elsewhere the ch- sound is represented by ch-. The two sounds are in fact formed differently, in different parts of the mouth; the difference is relatively obvious to Chinese speakers but English speakers must listen carefully to detect it.[3]

Linguists sometimes argue about whether Chinese is a monosyllabic language. The untutored may consider the issue semantic. Each character has a single-syllable sound, and virtually all sounds (syllables) have some kind of meaning (the exceptions are a few "empty terms" that do not have any meaning in themselves but perform grammatical functions). But there is a paucity of separate sounds in Chinese—not taking the tones into account, there are only about 400 separate syllables in Mandarin. In practice, many, perhaps most, terms in spoken Chinese consist of two syllables. *Lu*, for example, by itself means road, but there are many other words that would be pronounced exactly the same way (land, kill, deer, dew, and many other words are also pronounced *lu*), so that in common speech road is usually rendered *malu*, "horse road." Sometimes the two-syllable combination has only a remote relationship

---

3. The names of historical personages are kept in the form that is most familiar: Chiang Kai-shek, for example, not Jiang Jieshi. Certain cities are also kept in what is probably the more familiar form: for example, Peking, Chunking, and Canton, rather than Beijing, Chongqing, and Guangzhou, respectively. The reasoning here is that the familiar form is in effect an English, not a Chinese word (just as we say Moscow for the capital of Russia, not Moskva, or Vienna rather than Wien). The chapter on Taiwan uses the once-standard Wade-Giles romanization system for personal names, since that is the system still used on the island and so is the form most people will be familiar with.

to the meaning of each syllable. The word for crisis, for example, is *weiji*, and Richard Nixon used to point out that it is made of a combination meaning danger (wei) and opportunity (ji)—thus supposedly giving insight into the general nature of crises and to how Chinese think of crises. It does not in fact seem to be the case that Chinese necessarily think of crises as a conjunction of danger and opportunity. Rather, the term for crisis stands on its own, meaning simply crisis—and the meaning is not easily guessed simply by knowing the meaning of each separate term.[4] The general lack of different sounds means that Chinese will probably always be written with characters, even though the government once had a long-term plan to phase them out. In conversation the meaning, if not clear, can be explained, and in writing the words having the same sound but different meanings are rendered in different characters. But a romanized text is often simply unintelligible.[5]

Regions and Peoples

China rises gradually from the Pacific Ocean to the Himalayas. Naturally, then, all the major rivers flow eastward—so much so that "water flowing east" has become a poetic cliché for the passing nature of earthly pleasures, the vanity of human existence, and the like. The Yellow River drains the northern part of the country. It rises in the western province of Sichuan, flows through the northern plains, around the Taihang Mountains, and into the ocean. It was the cradle of Chinese civilization. Confucius came from what is now Shandong province. The first capital of the unified country was near Sian, now a sleepy provincial town but once a major metropolis along the Silk Road leading out of China through central Asia. Peking (Beijing), the present capital, first held this position under the Mongols, because it was close to their homeland. Subsequent dynasties for the most part kept the capital there, partly to be able to keep an eye on the Mongols. For most Chinese the staple food is rice, and rice is generally considered the best tasting of the grains. The staple in the north, however, is wheat, served mainly in the form of steamed bread, pancakes, or dumplings (baking is not much used in Chinese cooking).

Central China is drained by the Yangtze River (or, the Chinese term for the river as a whole—Yangtze technically refers only to a part of it—the

---

4. *Wei* means danger and *ji* can mean opportunity (or, rather, means opportunity when used in conjunction with a certain other term). Chinese would probably not derive the meaning the way Nixon did, however. Rather, if anything crisis would be interpreted as meaning an occasion for danger.

5. At one point modern communications seemed to require the elimination of characters —they take a long time to write by hand and Chinese typewriters are very cumbersome. The characters can, however, be adapted to computer use, and the computer revolution helped make their obsolescence itself obsolete.

Changjiang, "Long River"). It, too, begins in Sichuan, meeting the ocean near Shanghai. The area north of Shanghai is also drained by the Huai River, and the region between the Huai and the Yangtze is rather poor. South of Shanghai, however—Jiangnan, "south of the river"—is fertile, pleasant in climate, rich. Upstream are Hunan and Hubei provinces, exemplars of central China. Relatively unsettled until a few centuries ago, the region has more recently become known as the home of military leaders and revolutionaries: Mao Zedong and an impressive proportion of the first-generation Communist leadership hailed from Hunan. Hunan is also famous in China and abroad for its pepper-spiced cuisine.

West of Hunan and Hubei, the Yangtze falls through a series of spectacular gorges; above the gorges is Deng Xiaoping's home area, Sichuan—mountainous, rich, and remote. A famous poem has it that the road to Sichuan is as hard as climbing to the blue heavens. Sichuan is China's largest province, with a population of more than 70 million—more than most countries of the world. According to the proverb, Sichuan is the first province to rebel and the last to be pacified. Its cooking is even spicier than that of Hunan: in Hunan cuisine the peppers are chopped large; in the Sichuan style they are finely minced, so that their flavor permeates every bite.

Southwest China is mountainous and in places heavily forested. A generally poor region, it is home to many minority nationalities.

In this description I have used the word *Chinese* where technically I should have said Han. The Chinese are all those who are citizens of China, while Han refers to the dominant ethnic group, language, and culture. The word is taken from the Han dynasty, which ruled the country from 206 B.C. to A.D. 220 (the southernmost regions were not really incorporated into the empire until the Tang dynasty, A.D. 618–907, and southerners sometimes call themselves "Tang people"). In addition to the Han, China has 55 officially recognized minority nationalities, although altogether they constitute less than 7 percent of the population. The largest of these is the Zhuang, who live in the southwest, especially Guangxi, and have on the whole taken on Han culture.

The regions north and west of the Great Wall are the (originally) non-Han regions of the greatest historical importance. In the northeast is the region foreigners usually call Manchuria (although the Chinese themselves rarely use this word, calling the area instead simply the northeastern provinces). The Manchus were a tribe that conquered China in 1644 and ruled it until 1911. They have become almost completely assimilated into the Han. Their old homeland was opened to agricultural settlement in the late 1800s and is now overwhelmingly Han, with a substantial Korean minority as well (and even a small Russian community). The area is rich in forests, minerals, and other natural resources. Because of the large expanses of open land, it is one of the few places in China where mechanized agriculture is practical. During China's period of weakness, various imperial powers contended for control of Manchuria, with the Japanese being the most successful, and the Japanese left behind a substantial industrial base. The major drawback of the northeast may be its harsh continental climate: broiling in summer, freezing in winter. A generation of young Chinese became familiar with the "great northern wastes" when they were sent to state farms and military-run construction camps in the late 1960s and early 1970s, in the aftermath of the Cultural Revolution.

West of Manchuria is Inner Mongolia. In the 1100s and 1200s the Mongols conquered China and, for that matter, much of Eurasia; after Mongol rule had been overthrown in China, Mongolia became subject to the Chinese state. The northern part of that territory—what used to be called Outer Mongolia—became independent (actually a client of the Soviet Union's) in the 1920s, and its sovereignty was grudgingly recognized by Peking in 1949. Inner Mongolia remained under Chinese sovereignty. The Mongols, now a minority in their own homeland, by tradition are herdsmen.

Beyond Mongolia is Xinjiang (the "new frontier"), formerly called Chinese Turkestan. The Uighurs are the major indigenous group; they are Moslem in religion. In the northwestern part of China proper (and throughout the rest of the country, although in lesser numbers) there is also a Moslem population that is Han in ethnicity and language but whose customs are sufficiently distinct from those of their neighbors that they are classified as a separate nationality.

The Moslems, whether Uighur or Han, have sometimes resisted central authority, and Uighurs and Mongols have sometimes cherished desires for autonomy. The most troublesome national minority, however, has been the Tibetans. There has been interaction between Tibet, to the south and west of Xinjiang, and China proper for centuries, some of it friendly and some of it not. The Tibetan rulers recognized, most of the time, a vague overlordship by the Chinese emperor. The Tibetans, however, are different from the Han in language, ethnicity, and customs. They have their own distinctive type of Buddhism and traditionally were ruled by the Buddhist clergy, headed by the Dalai and Panchen Lamas. After the Revolution of 1911 Tibet more or less went its own way, until it was reabsorbed into the Chinese realm in 1951. Although on paper Tibet enjoyed much autonomy, Peking worked to increase central control, undermine the power of the clergy, and enforce socialist reforms. The tensions exploded in a rebellion in 1959, which was brutally suppressed in a military and political campaign in which the Communists tried to eradicate all of traditional Tibetan culture. In the 1980s the government repented of its excesses and matters improved. This, however, only provoked bolder demands for independence.

We have looked at China in terms of geographic regions and in terms of China proper and the border regions. Another culturally important distinction is between the coast and the interior. The eastern coast, from Canton

(Guangzhou) in the south, through Shanghai and Tianjin, and then up to Manchuria, was the part of China most directly under the influences of modern forces after 1840. The coastal area after the Opium War (1839–1842) became increasingly integrated into the larger world capitalist economy and less within the ability of the traditional Chinese state to control it. The interior enjoyed few of the benefits of the new economic system, but felt the consequences of the general weakening of the state. The division split Chinese political culture, with a modernized coast and a nonmodernized (it would probably not be entirely accurate to say traditional) interior.

Geography, Culture, and Politics

The easiest justification for this lengthy excursus on geography is that an appreciation for the shape of the land is necessary for an understanding of politics. We cannot understand American politics and history, for example, without some insight into the regions of the country—the South, New England, the West, the Midwest, California, and so forth—and their traditions and histories, their flavors and textures, their rivalries, the visions they have of themselves and each other. This kind of consideration is probably necessary for the understanding of any large country. Regional rivalries also play a role in Chinese politics as, of course, do rivalries between the Han and the non-Han nationalities.

The coast–interior distinction can even be a framework for overarching interpretations of contemporary politics. Western imperialism (it can be argued) created a new, modernized Chinese society on the coast, economically, culturally, and politically detached from the older Chinese state. The anti-Manchu Nationalist party (Kuomintang or KMT) originated in the coastal regions and had its greatest strength there. The Communist Party of China (CPC) was also originally a part of the new coastal culture, but in its conflicts with the KMT was forced to retreat to the interior and there adapt itself to local interests. The 1949 CPC victory could then be interpreted as (among other things) a vindication of the more backward interior over the more modernized coast and also (in good Marxist form) the basis for a new synthesis of coast and interior. In fact, as a result both of U.S. hostility and its own choices, the new regime for several years after its triumph was cut off from the world influences that had previously dominated the coast, and the Maoist regime (1949–1976) in its more radical phases was actively hostile to the values and foreign influences associated with the coastal culture. At the same time there was little real respect for the premodern cultural tradition. The result was an oppressive politics, puerile culture, and stagnant economy. Some Communist reformers after 1979 proposed a "coastal policy," letting the already more highly advanced areas take the lead in general economic development, with the coast linking up with the other dynamic Pacific Rim economies—Japan, Taiwan, Hong Kong, South Korea, Singapore—and the entire process prompting growth in the interior. More conservative officials feared this would reinforce the coast–interior distinction while exposing the country at large to "spiritual pollution" from foreign countries and that spontaneously generated in the process of this kind of economic growth. It would also challenge, if not national unity, at least the control of the central government over the country.

This interpretation neither is nor should be the only way to understand Chinese politics, but it provides a beginning framework for some of the more important contemporary themes. In its turn it provides a foundation for an even more overarching (and probably less sound) interpretation. The coastal areas of China and the Chinese-style states of the Pacific Rim suggest there is nothing inherently incompatible with modernization in Chinese culture taken as a whole. The question, then, is why China (as a whole) has had so much trouble modernizing. Karl Marx made some offhand comments to the effect that China, along with India, was an "Asiatic society." In this pattern the state overwhelms the social structures, preventing their autonomous development. The "surplus value" in the society (in this case meaning the difference between what is actually produced in the society as a whole and what it takes to keep the population alive and reproducing itself) is expropriated by the state and is used either for luxury consumption by big officials or for public works that serve to keep the society in a stable state. The most elaborate working out of this thesis is associated with the work of Karl Wittfogel, an anticommunist Marxist—a somewhat unusual turn of mind.[6] Wittfogel centers on the need for water control, which, he argues, requires community effort coordinated by an educated elite. This elite comes to monopolize power and privilege and by hindering the development of either the economy or knowledge heads off any possible challenges to itself. The incorporation of China into the world system promised to break this pattern, but this promise was thwarted by the victory of the Communists, who represented the most regressive forces of the interior, and Chinese Communist rule becomes a reversion to the traditional despotism.

Wittfogel's theory has been much criticized. It probably exaggerates the degree to which the traditional state was in fact "despotic," and also ignores the genuine amount of social and technological change that did take place during the term of the Chinese Empire. The Chinese state was certainly capable of great public works, but water works for agricultural purposes were for the most part not under state control. Irrigation and drainage networks seem to have been undertaken mainly by local people with their own private organization. Wittfogel and others of this general persuasion are probably

---

6. Karl Wittfogel, *Oriental Despotism* (Yale University Press, 1957).

right to focus on the relative strength of the Chinese state ruling a weak society, but geographic determinism based on ideas about water control probably does not explain much of this state strength.

Theories about politics should help us understand how politics actually works; often, however, they also point their own political morals. Wittfogel, for example, wishes to emphasize the harsh quality of Communist rule and to deny that the Communists represent anything progressive or liberating (and this also helps explain why the Communist establishment itself is not much taken with his analysis). But when political theories are used to make political points, they themselves become political facts, and in the 1980s ideas such as Wittfogel's found an audience among Chinese intellectuals eager to understand and eliminate what they took to be their country's backwardness.

The theme was popularized in a 1988 television series, "River Elegy," which uses the Yellow River as a symbol of China and the forces governing it. Some early scenes show an attempt by young canoeists to negotiate the river's upper reaches. They are killed by the treacherous waters, and themselves become symbols of the human sacrifice the River has always demanded. The River, then, stands for the inhuman powers that have shaped Chinese civilization. The spirit of the river is the dragon, and the dragon is the symbol of the imperial throne. This (allegedly) shows the propensity of the Chinese people to identify political power as superhuman—which is to say, inhuman—and then to subordinate themselves completely to it. China's stagnant agrarian society is contrasted with the dynamic, open, democratic, commercial society of the West; China must leave the inward-looking, earth-clogged "yellow" civilization of the river and adopt the values represented by the blue skies and blue waters of the ancient Mediterranean West.

This is certainly not a fair picture of Chinese civilization and, indeed, some of its authors, forced into exile after the June 4, 1989, tragedy, came to see the shallowness of their idealization of the West and found unsuspected virtues in parts of their own tradition. The episode is interesting not only for the interpretation it makes of Chinese civilization, but even more for itself, as an indication of the cultural rifts present in Chinese society as a result of social change. These rifts are not a product of geography pure and simple, but of the cultural meaning assigned to certain geographic data.

Japan

Japan lacks China's geographic, cultural, and linguistic diversity. The country is a chain of islands stretching north to south. The main ones are Hokkaido, Honshu, Shikoku, and Kyushu, and in addition there are hundreds of smaller islands. Hokkaido, the northernmost island, was incorporated into Japan relatively late. Much to the south is Okinawa (or the Ryukyu Islands), which at one time had its own king who was technically subordinate to the Chinese emperor, and which remains to some degree culturally distinct from the rest of Japan.

The Japanese islands are volcanic rocks jutting up from the floor of the Pacific Ocean. The terrain is very hilly and only a small part of it is cultivatable—although that part has been cultivated very intensely. The country lacks most kinds of natural resources—except, it would appear, human talent. Japan has been a major world power since at least the 1890s, and by the 1980s was the world's second largest economy.

Japan's "higher" culture is adapted from China, although there is no relationship in language or ethnicity. The Japanese people originally came from several places but mainly, it seems, from central Asia by way of Korea. The original inhabitants of the islands were the Äinu, a "proto-Caucasian" people, now very few in number, living mainly on Hokkaido. The main ethnic group migrated to the islands perhaps from around 200 B.C. to about A.D. 400 (although Japanese mythology traces the imperial line—and the origin of the islands themselves—to about 700 B.C.). At that time the southern part of Korea and the southern Japanese islands probably formed a single cultural area, and how much influence there was on Japan from Korea remains a matter for scholarly and even political polemics. Japan's "little tradition" may be part of a broader "northern Pacific" culture. Original Japanese religion shares shamanistic traits with that of Korea, the Äinu, Eskimos, and northwestern American Indians, whereby the spirit of another person or an animal enters into and communicates through a priest (or, more commonly, a priestess). There are totem poles in Korea that, to the untrained eye anyway, look remarkably like those of the American northwest, and the unadorned wooden pillars of Japanese Shinto shrines are survivals of that original practice (although the architecture of the shrines has absorbed overwhelmingly Chinese forms). If there is such a common pattern it is, of course, the result of cultural diffusion rather than common origin.

The analogy is sometimes made between Japan and Britain in respect to their position relative to their respective continental neighbors. Actually, Japan is much farther out to sea than England is and historically has been less involved in continental affairs. Both have a seafaring tradition involving, in the early days, both trade and piracy, but prior to contemporary times Japan, more isolated from international politics on the continent, which, in any case, were dominated by China, did not develop into a naval power. At some times in the past the English had ambitions to conquer France, and in the 1500s certain Japanese warlords hoped to subdue Korea and, with luck, China itself. After 1600, however, Japan withdrew into self-imposed isolation, a choice geography and history would have made impossible for England.

Around A.D. 500 the Japanese began taking over and adapting the Chinese civilization of that time, including Chinese philosophy and religion and China's political and writing forms. The Japanese language in its origin and structure is no closer to Chinese than it is to English, although it now contains many loan words from Chinese (as well as many loan words from English, although these are much more recent). While Japanese is not closely related to any other language, it is probably part of the Altaic family, a language group spread through northern and central Asia. It would, then, be remotely related to Turkish and Mongolian. Its closest relation is probably Korean, but even that relationship is pretty distant. The two tongues are remarkably similar in structure (with Korean being rather more complex), but not in vocabulary.

Japanese is written with Chinese characters. A character may be used either for its meaning or for its sound, and it is not always obvious which is intended. The characters are, therefore, supplemented by a phonetic system—not strictly an alphabet but a syllabary. A second syllabary is used to transcribe loan words from languages other than Chinese—for example, *besu baru*, baseball. Each Chinese character has at least two pronunciations, one the native Japanese term for what the character represents, the other a Japanese adaptation of the Chinese pronunciation of that character. Thus, the word for mountain is pronounced, according to context, either as *yama* (the original Japanese term), or as *san* (Japanese–Chinese; the contemporary northern Chinese pronunciation is *shan*). Both sounds are rendered by the same character.

In earlier centuries the language of serious business was Chinese, just as medieval Europe used Latin. There remains a sense that the Chinese terms are somehow more dignified than the Japanese, although foreign popular culture is more apt to be familiar with the less-dignified forms. Everyone knows about the *kamikaze*, the "divine wind," the suicide pilots who fought against the Americans in the last days of World War II. In Japan, however, kamikaze has come to have a somewhat comic connotation. It might be used to refer, say, to a reckless Tokyo taxi driver doped up on amphetamines. The young men who voluntarily sacrificed their lives for the honor of their country are more properly called by the Chinese pronunciation of the characters, *shimpu*. Another famous Japanese term is *hara kiri*, "belly cutting," in colloquial American usually pronounced "hairy Kerry." Japanese referring to ritual suicide, however, would usually use the Chinese rendition, *sepuku*. There are a few cultural distinctions in the use of the different terms. Educated people are said to use "square" words, words of Chinese origin that would be written with Chinese characters; ordinary people speak "round" words, the indigenous terms usually written in the syllabary. An English analogy is perhaps the relatively greater use of words with Latin roots by people with more education. Personal names are written with Chinese characters, but are almost always given the Japanese pronunciation.

The Japanese consider themselves to be a culturally and racially homogeneous people—an attitude imprudent conservative politicians are sometimes given to voicing in a bigoted, offensive manner. Strictly speaking this is not true. There are even regional differences in Japan, although hardly as pronounced as in China. The fertile, urbanized eastern part of the country (the "front") has a flavor different from that of the sparsely populated mountainous west (the "back"). For centuries there has been a difference of style between commercially oriented Osaka and the political and cultural center, Tokyo; both are different from the old imperial capital, Kyoto. There are also general urban-rural differences, with the highly valued peasant way of life surviving in this most modern country partly as a luxury. In strict economic terms Japanese agriculture is not worth the investment, but protectionist and pro-rural policies by the government have allowed the rural communities not only to survive but to enjoy a standard of living comparable with that of the cities. In much of the country farming has become a part-time occupation, with various family members working in factories in the vicinity and working the farms in the evening or on days off.

The predominant ethnic strain in Japan is probably north Asian, but there is a mixture of peoples from the south and also the Äinu. An Äinu minority survives, and there is a much larger minority from Korea. As labor costs have gone up Japan has attracted large numbers of mostly illegal guest workers from southeast Asia and elsewhere. There is even a hereditary outcaste minority, the burakumin (or, less politely, the eta) whose ancestors were butchers, tanners, night-soil collectors, circus performers—holders of occupations considered unclean in a society obsessed with physical and ritual cleanliness. The burakumin have enjoyed legal equality since the 1800s and are physically and linguistically identical with all other Japanese. Yet they are discriminated against in employment, and families will employ marriage brokers to make sure their son or daughter does not marry a burakumin.

In Japan, as elsewhere, homogeneity is more a cultural claim than a physical fact. It is an important element in the self-definition of the Japanese. It can mean that those who do not fall under the social definition of homogeneity do not always have a pleasant time. Koreans whose families have lived in Japan for generations must continue to register as foreigners (and, as such, to be fingerprinted). They are despised for being Korean while also, for all practical purposes, being forbidden to assimilate. The physically and mentally handicapped are also not always treated kindly by society at large. There is at least one curiosity. Unlike the Mafia, the *yakusa*, the organized Japanese underworld, is an equal opportunity employer: Koreans and burakumin are found in organized crime in numbers disproportionate to their numbers in society. It is certainly not surprising that some of those who are rejected by the larger society should turn to crime, but Japanese gangsterdom, for its part, while yielding to none in patriotism and attachment to Japanese traditions, seems also to provide careers open to talent.

This general exclusivity is one of the less attractive features of Japanese society. Yet grasping it may be critical to an understanding of Japan. Throughout recorded history Japanese have known that their civilization—or what they would have considered civilization pure and simple—comes from China. In traditional times Chinese identity was more cultural than ethnic: the world was divided between civilized people and barbarians, with the Chinese being civilized and anyone else who accepted civilization also being civilized regardless of ethnic background. The Japanese knew that they were not barbarians—they had, after all, taken on civilization—and they knew equally well that they were not Chinese. When the new world order imposed itself on East Asia in the 1800s, it was perhaps easier for the Japanese to adopt foreign ways—after all, they had done the same thing before. Probably more important, it was easier for the Japanese to see themselves as one people or nation among a plurality of nations. For China, the highest social values were identified with a particular form of culture or civilization. The Japanese could more easily see themselves as a nation and take whatever steps were required for the strength and integrity of the nation.

3

✦

Intellectual Background

Geography at most sets limits or suggests predispositions for culture. This chapter looks at the intellectual heritage of East Asian society, with a particular emphasis on that part of it bearing on politics and government. Most of the discussion centers on China, which was the font of the East Asian worldviews; the last part of the chapter, however, examines Japanese thought and the adaptations of Chinese thinking to the Japanese environment. The ideas outlined in this chapter do not always have a direct, mechanical relationship with political action today. Ways of thinking change all the time and have been modified by modernizing tendencies; most people in China and Japan would consider many of the ideas presented here outmoded (although they would not necessarily agree about which these are). In fact, to some extent these systems are worth studying if only to understand what the modernizers in China and Japan were reacting against. At the same time, these systems have helped shape and define the East Asian civilization.

The East Asian Background

There are different systems of thought in East Asia, and some are incompatible with others.

Behind the differences, however, are certain common features that, in their combinations with each other, make a distinctive East Asian style. These may be compared (obviously on a very general level) with the intellectual heritage of the West, since that congeries of ideas has been most influential in shaping the modern world, and since this was the system that in recent times presented the most serious challenge to the East Asian one.

To give a feel for what is distinctive about East Asian thought, it is probably useful to emphasize its differences with certain Western assumptions. To put it in what is no doubt an overly simple way, premodern Western higher-intellectual culture was an uneasy mixture and synthesis of Athens and Jerusalem (combined, of course, with the local cultures of the various historical periods). Jewish monotheism and Greek philosophy are compatible with each other, but they come from separate traditions and represent very different ways of interpreting the world. In this sense, the structure of Chinese and Japanese thought is simpler than that of the West. There are certainly different tendencies in Chinese thinking (as there are in Greek thinking and, for that matter, the Bible), but they are variations within the same overall tradition. The major outside intellectual influence in East Asia prior to modern times was Buddhism, but its social importance and significance are not quite comparable with that of Christianity in the West.

A central question in premodern Western thought, and perhaps in modern thought as well, is the question of God. Chinese thought is not necessarily atheistic, and its mainstream is certainly not impious. The Confucian and pre-Confucian concepts of Heaven or God on High share some of the attributes of the God of the Judeo-Christian tradition. Rather, the question of theism and atheism, whether there is or is not a God, how one might rationally prove or refute the existence of God, has not been a central theme in East Asian thinking. There has also been less of a propensity to try to ground assertions about the world or morals in the existence or nature of God.

Chinese philosophy focuses overwhelmingly on questions of personal morality and the proper ordering of society. This is also, of course, a major concern in the West. Western thought, however, has been strongly centered on explaining the natural world. Greek theorists before Socrates, for example, were given to arguing about whether reality was one or many, whether all things were ultimately water or ultimately fire. The Chinese did have opinions about the nature of the universe, but in comparison with Western thinkers did not tend to argue about them.

Greek philosophy developed in conjunction with the unfolding discovery of laws of logic. There were analogous tendencies in ancient Chinese thinking, but these were not carried through in a systematic way, and formal rigor and argumentation are less characteristic of Chinese thinking than of Greek. In China as in Greece early logic dealt with paradoxes. Both the Greek Zeno and the Chinese Gongsun Long, for example, demonstrated that a journey could never be completed (because first you must go halfway, and before that half of that, and half of that, so on forever). Gongsun Long also developed a demonstration that a white horse is not a horse (because if you want a horse, the color doesn't matter, whereas if you want a white horse, not any old horse will do; therefore, a white horse is not the same thing as a horse). The older Chinese thinkers, however, seem to have associated systematic logic with paradoxes of this nature, and to have dismissed it as something frivolous and irrelevant to real problems. The Legalist philosopher Han Feizi commented that when Gongsun Long rode a white horse up to the toll booth, the guard was not able to refute his argument, but Gongsun still had to pay the toll for a horse.

In logic, everything is either A or not-A. Everything in the universe is either a horse—or, if it comes to that, a given horse—or it is not. The normal Indo-European pattern may encourage thinking in these terms, and thinking in terms of essences. Linguistic considerations may influence Chinese ontology (that is, concepts about the nature of things). The Western concept of the universe is, perhaps, that of a collection of everything that is. The Chinese see the universe as a kind of organic flux, with all the discreet things in a continuous process of change. In the ancient Greek view (prevalent in Europe until late into the Renaissance) all things were compounds of the four elements—air, earth, fire, water. An *element* is the most basic form of matter, the substance that cannot itself be broken down into more primitive substances (a usage that survives in the modern concept of the chemical elements). China had a comparable list of five material constituents of all things—water, fire, wood, metal, earth. These, however, are not *elements*—they constitute the basic forms of matter, but they also change into and give rise to each other in systematic ways; they are perhaps more accurately called agents.

Thus, there is a creative cycle: wood produces fire, which produces earth (ashes), which produces metal, which produces water (condensation), which produces wood. There is a simultaneously operating destructive cycle: wood overcomes earth, which overcomes water, which overcomes fire, which overcomes metal, which overcomes wood. There are additional, less intuitively obvious cycles, in which each agent is "controlled" by another, and in which each is "masked" by another.[1] The physical universe is a constant process of change, with all the cycles operating simultaneously and interacting with the others. Analogous processes operate within the human body, the human personality, and human society.[2]

---

1. Laurence C. Wu, *Fundamentals of Chinese Philosophy* (Lanham, 1988), pp. 166–170, gives a useful discussion of the cycles, although he refers to the substances as elements.

2. A systematic outline of the workings of the cosmos is found in the *Book of Changes* (*Yi Jing*—or what is probably a more familiar spelling, the *I Ching*), a work traditionally considered to have been compiled by Confucius, but which may actually date from a few generations after his time. *Changes* enjoyed a certain vogue in the Western counterculture of the 1960s and also among Chinese youth following the sad events of June 1989. It may be appreciated as a work of profound philosophical and psychological insight, or it may be treated as a fortuneteller's manual.

A simplified idea of the workings of the system may be derived from considering the workings of the cosmic forces of yin and yang. The character *yin* referred, originally, to the shady side of a hill, and *yang* to its sunny side—the origin showing the complementary interdependence of the forces (if a hill has a sunny side, it must also have a shady side; and what is in the sun now will be in the shade a few hours hence). Yang is masculine, hard, bright, dry, active; yin is feminine, soft, dark, wet, passive. Yang is creative, yin is productive. All things in the universe, and the universe itself, display the interaction of yin and yang. The two are always found together and can be seen or understood only in relation to each other. Each contains the other: all yang has some yin, all yin some yang. Once each reaches its ultimate development, the other begins to increase (so at midsummer, the longest day of the year, yang is at its height, but immediately the days grow shorter—yin is asserting itself, even as the days continue to grow hotter; at the mid-fall festival, what the West calls the harvest moon, the moon, the clearest symbol of yin, is at its most yang).

The yin–yang pairing is sometimes confused with the similar-seeming Manichean or gnostic dualism in the West (heretical by Christian standards), in which the universe is the arena for the eternal battle of good and evil, the forces of darkness and the forces of light. If good and evil are considered as a paired relationship, good is certainly yang and evil is yin. But yin as such is in no way evil. Rather, good is normally found in the proper balance of yin and yang, with evil reflecting an unnatural surplus of one or the other. Yin and yang do not clash, but blend harmoniously. Since they always exist in a relationship, neither is absolute. Whether something is predominantly yin or predominantly yang depends on how it stands paired with something else. A man is yang relative to his wife, but yin relative to his mother.

The yin–yang framework exemplifies the East Asian tendency to see the world not in terms of isolated things but as relationships. In human affairs the difference is perhaps greater with the modern than with the traditional West. Modern Western thought has tended to focus on the individual—the abstract human entity encased in its own skin, considered in isolation from specific settings or specific characteristics. The mainstream of Chinese thought, like the older mainstream of Western thought, looks instead at the person, the individual enmeshed in and partly defined by a set of relationships with other persons, each relationship carrying different obligations and expectations. Modern liberal thinking treats organized society as an artifact invented to serve the interests of previously isolated individuals. In the classical Western concept, however, humans are by nature social—or, as Aristotle put it, political—animals. For Aristotle the basic social unit is the politically organized society (since smaller groupings were not economically self-sufficient). In China and, in a modified form, Japan the "natural" human unit is, instead, the family. This may be another reflection of the yin–yang thinking—the assumption that fully human life is possible only through the union of the complementary opposites of male and female and the generation of other humans.

Some people find that the traditional Chinese worldview has something in common with those interpretations associated with contemporary physics. The Chinese interpretation of nature may, in fact, be more compelling than it should be to encourage the development of physical science. Virtually any natural or human event can be interpreted in terms of the yin–yang format. But the interpretation is not analytic, and is after the fact; it does not allow for prediction and control, nor is it clear how statements about yin and yang should be tested.[3] The ready availability of a persuasive theory of the nature of the universe, coupled with the generally humanistic bent of Chinese scholarship (and the social and political prestige attached to humanistic learning) may have given the Chinese relatively little incentive for developing theoretical scientific explanations.[4]

The traditional Western view (here from Jerusalem, not Athens) is that the universe came into being, created by God. This was another set of ideas the Chinese did not give systematic thought to, but their assumption seems to be that the universe is self-existent: it always has been and always will be. The Chinese do have stories about the origin of the cosmos. They tell, however, how the "ten thousand things" were generated from the original undifferentiated chaos, without any hint of the Jewish-Christian notion of creation from nothing. One story has a certain Pan Gu splitting the cosmic egg with a blow of an axe, separating heaven and earth (it does not say what he was standing on when he did it). Such tales were used, mainly by the Daoists, to make points about the ultimate nature of things, and among more sophisticated people were probably not intended as as-it-were historical accounts of something that once actually happened.

The Chinese cosmological view is cyclical and so, in part, is the Chinese interpretation of society. One of the most famous opening sentences in Chinese literature is that of the classic novel *Romance of the Three Kingdoms*: "The Great Circumstances under heaven, having been long united, must divide; having been long divided, must unite." Society is given to periodic alternations of order and chaos. Behind the cycle, however, is a picture of social evolution. All East Asian schools hold civilization to be the product of a lengthy development. In the olden days people were few and resources many; there was no government and, according to one text, people knew their mothers but not their fathers (either because the family had not yet been invented—Confucians consider the family a natural unit, but that does not

---

3. This may be an overly negative evaluation. In China a physician may practice either "western" or traditional medicine (or some combination of the two), and those who belong to one tendency will, in school, be taught at least a little of the other. It seems that traditional Chinese medicine (herbal theories, acupuncture, and the like) is still taught in accord with the theory of the human body based on the five agents and yin and yang.

4. See Joseph Needham, *Science and Civilization in China*, Vol. II (Cambridge University Press, 1956).

mean that everyone does—or because the primitive people did not quite understand the facts of life). With increasing population came the division of labor and political society. For the Daoist school, civilization is a mark of degeneration. The Confucians were more ambivalent: civilization is a condition for a fully human life, but it also brings temptations and occasions for corruption, irresponsibility, and cruelty. The Western view tends, perhaps, to identify the origin of the state in conquest or superior force. Chinese theorists, even the most tough-minded, stress instead consent and contract. Political status was originally given to those who benefited the people: the first to make fire, the first to build houses, Yu the Great, who controlled the waters. All Chinese thinkers, even the most tender-minded, would agree that in these later days, political authority, no matter how virtuous, is founded on force and requires superiority of force if it is to persist.

This section has dealt with the opinions of the educated. A few general comments about popular religion are also in order, to give a fuller idea of how the world looked to the ordinary person. Japanese popular religion, Shinto, is discussed in the section on Japan. Chinese popular religion is a mixture of Daoist and Buddhist beliefs and practices, and these, too, are discussed below. But in Chinese religion there are also some elements that do not seem to have anything to do explicitly with Daoism.

A general preliminary comment must refer to the nonexclusive nature of popular religion. In the West, one is a Christian or a Moslem or a Jew; one is a Protestant or a Catholic; one is a Pentecostal or an Evangelical; one is a believer or an agnostic or an atheist. This is not the indigenous East Asian approach. The Daoists and Buddhists (and Shintoists) have their own clergy who practice and propagate particular kinds of rituals and ideas. The ordinary person does not discriminate, but, rather, worships in those ways that are the most effective for the particular purposes at hand.

In Chinese thinking there has been since ancient times a notion of a supreme being, although there has not been much speculation on the character or properties of this being. The most ancient name is *Shang Di*, "High God." The most popular is probably *Tian*, Heaven. Tian also means sky, but the character for it depicts a person wearing a hat or crown. It may refer to a personal God; it may also refer to a vaguer moral force pervading the universe; it may even be a synonym for natural processes pure and simple. Early Catholic missionaries used Tian to translate God, but later decided that the Chinese term had too many unsatisfactory connotations and coined their own term, *Tianzhu*, Lord of Heaven or Heavenly Lord. Protestant translations of the Bible used the term *Shang Di*. In traditional China only the emperor could formally sacrifice to Heaven, but in daily life appeals to Heaven are common—and may be as pious or as profane as similar appeals to God in the West.

Ancient writings speak of "altars of the spirits of land and grain," presumably altars to the guardian spirits of a locality. The Confucian philosopher

Mencius says that these spirits are the most important things in a country—the next most important are the people, with the ruler coming last. It may not be too much a modern rationalization of Mencius to identify these spirits with the community itself or with the social order—although this does not preclude Mencius from thinking there were actually such beings. Similar spiritual beings survive to this day: there are guardian spirits of fields, for example, and of the household. Every New Year the kitchen god reports to Heaven (or the Jade Emperor, the chief Daoist divinity) about the doings of the family, and it is prudent to give him a good meal before he leaves.

The Chinese have various kinds of nonmaterial beings. The good ones are called spirits. These may be local guardians, or mountain deities, or fairies. Dragons, I guess, are animal spirits. Although themselves yang, they are associated with water. In the West, dragons are considered evil: the dragon even figures as a metaphor for Satan himself. Chinese dragons are on the whole benign, although one shouldn't be too casual about messing with them.

There are also malevolent spiritual entities, called ghosts or demons. Some figure in romances: fox spirits, for example, may appear in the guise of beautiful young women, to seduce and destroy credulous, weak-willed young men. Fox spirits may be quite clever, but demons in general are not credited with a great deal of intelligence. Demons are thought to travel only in straight lines, so traditional Chinese houses have a screen placed directly behind the front entrance to keep them out.

The spirits and demons are popularly held to be organized into a heavenly hierarchy, remarkably similar to the political hierarchy of the Chinese Empire—complete even to the graft. This model of the spirit world still prevails on Taiwan and has been revived on the mainland since the 1980s, even though the political world no longer has an emperor or the other old-fashioned officials. The concept of the spiritual world, then, is not simply an extrapolation of the earthly bureaucratic apparatus; it also serves as a symbol of popular religious consciousness.[5]

In a somewhat separate category are ancestors. Ancestor worship (or, probably better, veneration) is the most widespread manifestation of Chinese religion. Traditional households all held tablets inscribed with the names of dead ancestors, and these were objects of daily prayers and offerings. In principle all ancestors were venerated; in practice the tablets were confined to those of ancestors in the living memory of someone in the household. The ancestors guarded the fortunes of the family, but also, like the other spirits, required offerings and service from the living. Thus, it is of crucial importance that the family line continue. As Mencius said, of the three unfilial acts, the worst is to have no posterity. Normally the family line is carried only

---

5. For an interesting elaboration of this, see P. Steven Sangren, *History and Magical Power in a Chinese Community* (Stanford University Press, 1987).

through the males. Girls become, after marriage, members of their husbands' families and venerate their husbands' ancestors. The need for male heirs is one of many reasons for the unpopularity of the Chinese government's single-child policy, and one reaction to that policy in the 1980s was, reportedly, in some places the systematic killing of newborn baby girls. Persons who die without posterity (or who for some reason are not served after death) become "hungry ghosts," wandering the world causing mischief. At least in southern China, these are propitiated once a year by a special festival held in the early fall. The Confucian virtue of filial piety (the not very satisfactory but probably unavoidable translation of *xiao*—the honoring of your father and your mother) is the inner moral meaning of the cult of ancestors.

The cult of ancestors and the general attitudes toward ghosts and spirits imply a popular belief in personal immortality. Among the educated in China there has perhaps been the same range of opinion on this as is found among the educated elsewhere: some accept it, some see no reason to doubt it, some deny it, some don't know what to think. A Confucian scholar who does not believe in personal immortality would still practice the rituals of ancestor veneration, taking these to be the expression of natural human sentiments, whether the ancestors are able personally to experience anything or not.

The educated would also have a similar range of opinions about the spiritual world generally. Confucius is perhaps typical of the orthodox educated view of such things. Confucius said: Serve the spirits, but keep them at a distance. Serve the spirits as if they were actually present. When asked about spirits, Confucius said: I don't understand people yet; how can I understand spirits? When asked about death, the Master said: I don't understand life yet; how can I understand death? This is sometimes taken to show Confucius to be a skeptic: Serve the spirits as if they were present—that is, there are no such things as spirits, but it's good for you, or it sets a good example, to act as if there were. This interpretation is arbitrary, however. And to all indications Confucius did seem to think of Heaven not merely as a moral force but also as an active, conscious one. It is fair to say, however, that the general Confucian opinion is that too much concern with the nonhuman world is pointless, possibly unhealthy, and a distraction from our real duty.

The Formative Period

Around 1122 B.C. (or, perhaps, 1027 B.C.) a people from the west, the Zhou, conquered the city-states along the Yellow River that constituted the Shang (or Yin) kingdom. The Zhou king died prematurely, and during his son's minority, actual rule was exercised by the founding king's younger brother, the Duke of Zhou. The Duke, in Confucius's view the greatest man who ever lived, designed the Zhou institutions. The Zhou justified their conquest on the grounds that the later Shang kings, especially the last one, were personally wicked and politically incompetent. The world belongs to Heaven and Heaven establishes rule to benefit the people. Heaven gives its Mandate to the virtuous and able, and this Mandate is the only justification for rule. If a ruler abuses his authority or is incapable of ruling justly, Heaven withdraws the Mandate and finds a more worthy holder. For example, centuries earlier the world had been ruled by the Xia; but the Xia degenerated, and Heaven transferred the Mandate to the Shang. And now it has come to Zhou. Archaeologists have not yet found any direct evidence that there was a Xia state, and some scholars speculate it was invented by the Zhou for propaganda purposes. At any rate, the idea that political power is responsible for (if not necessarily to) the people and that authority is legitimate to the extent that it benefits the people is an ancient one in China.

The Duke of Zhou supposedly set up a feudal system. In principle the king controlled all the land (as the agent of Heaven) and entrusted portions of it in fief to his followers. The early Confucians saw this system (or, rather, their idealized conception of it) as centralized enough to prevent bloody conflict and decentralized enough to allow a personal relationship between the king and his vassals and his vassals and the common people.

Farming was (supposedly) organized on the principle of the "well-field" system (so called either because the fields were irrigated by a single well, or, more probably, because they were organized on a tic-tac-toe type grid similar in shape to the character for well, 井). The large field would be divided into nine smaller ones and would support eight families; the families would jointly farm the field in the middle, whose produce would go to the overlord. He would feed himself from this and use the surplus for the common good (so *gong*, which means duke, also, at a rather early stage, acquired what is now its primary meaning, public). Although this system, what we would consider a kind of serfdom, may not have existed in precisely the traditional form, it reflects certain general Chinese social concepts: wealth should be evenly distributed; taxes should be relatively low and used for the public benefit.

It is not clear how much of this is more or less how things were and how much is a Confucian idealization (Confucius, after all, lived about 500 years after the Zhou founding). There may never even have been a real "system" other than a collection of independent warlords giving nominal loyalty to a feeble king. The Zhou elite were a hereditary warrior aristocracy, each aristocrat jealous of the others and of his own prerogatives. In 770 B.C., bullied by the powerful lords, the Zhou king moved his capital to the east—so the earlier period is now called the western Zhou. The early part of the eastern Zhou is called the Spring and Fall (technically this refers to the period 722 to 481 B.C.—it is named for a book allegedly compiled by Confucius, a documentary history of his native state for the period in question). The various warlords continued in theory to render homage to the Zhou Son of Heaven, but in practice China was divided into dozens of warring principalities. From time to time one warlord could establish a modicum of temporary peace by achieving hegemony (*ba*) over the others. Confucian scholars tended to disparage the hegemons, as their power was based on force rather than virtue. Confucius himself, however, professed a grudging admiration for the prime minister of the first hegemon (the man who was actually the brains of that outfit): the hegemon may not have had the Mandate of Heaven, but at least he brought about a little peace and security.

The period following the Spring and Fall is known as the Warring States (technically the term refers to the period 403 to 221 B.C., but transformations to the new system were well under way by 500 B.C.). This was a major social change.[6] The little principalities were reduced in number, as large swallowed up small, leaving, by the end of the period, seven large states. The idea of unity under the Zhou king became ever more remote. Previously the title "king" (*wang*) had been reserved for the Zhou Son of Heaven, but in Warring States times the rulers of the states took that title for themselves. In 256 B.C. the small territory directly under the Zhou king was taken over by the state of Qin. There continued to be a hereditary nobility, but its power declined as the old families died off or were killed in war, feuds, and intrigues. A new social elite developed alongside the nobility and was sometimes absorbed into it, based on wealth or ability—prowess in war, technology, administration, communication, business, or crime. The old feudalism was giving way to despotism: strong, tightly organized states governed by administrators serving at the pleasure of the king.

Iron tools allowed increased productivity in agriculture and, hence, increased capacities for the state. Iron weapons made war more destructive. Technological change encouraged social change. Previously the rulers presumably derived their income from feudal dues. In the Warring States, land came for all practical purposes into private ownership, and the land tax became the main source of revenue for the state. This gave the population at large at least one (clumsy) check on tyranny: there was still a lot of undeveloped land, and if rule became overly extortionate, the people could move elsewhere, and by opening up new lands for cultivation increase the food reserves, tax base, and supply of soldiers of rival states. Warfare had earlier been an aristocratic hobby, conducted according to rules of chivalry, fought from cumbersome war chariots. In the Warring States, professional or conscript mass armies were organized into infantry and cavalry. The rules of war changed, too. Chairman Mao once retold the story of a Spring and Fall general who came upon the enemy army while it was crossing the river. He refused to attack the enemy while he was vulnerable, but gallantly allowed him to cross and get his troops deployed, and so turned a sure win into a defeat.

---

6. See Hsu Cho-yun, *Ancient China in Transition* (Stanford: University Press, 1965).

Mao commented: We are not like that general. But, then, neither was any Warring States commander.

The general level of wealth increased, but the Warring States period was also a time of political, social, cultural, and moral confusion. The old ways no longer fit and there were no new ways available. Confucius, the first of the great Chinese philosophers,[7] lived around the time of transition from the Spring and Fall to the Warring States, and the other seminal works, those of his disciples or rivals, reflect the Warring States background. They can be interpreted as a search for true order in a time of chaos.

Confucianism

Confucius (Kong Fuzi, or Kongzi—his surname was Kong; *Fuzi* or *zi* are honorific titles meaning Master or Teacher; his personal name was Kong Qiu) lived, it is generally thought, from 551 to 479 B.C. He was a native of the state of Lu, in what is now Shandong province. His family may have been descended from the Shang aristocracy. He aspired to political office, but was not well received by the gangster cliques that held power in Lu. He may have held several minor positions dealing with ritual affairs, and he also may have been, even then, a professional teacher, taking in pupils and charging tuition. According to the tradition, when he was in his early 50s he was appointed police chief in Lu, doing an outstanding job (sections of one of the more utopian books said to have been edited by Confucius are usually cited to describe his achievements—everyone kept proper order, people would return lost property, so forth and so on), but after a few months he was forced from office. He wandered with his pupils through the various petty principalities, returning home at the age of 70. He said he neither complained to Heaven nor blamed man. Yet he sometimes felt abandoned by Heaven, and once sighed it had been a long time since he had dreamed of his hero, the Duke of Zhou. Even if he was not given to grumbling, he probably died thinking his life had been a waste.

Like Socrates, his younger contemporary, Confucius left no written exposition of his views, although he is traditionally alleged to have edited the set of works known as the Classics (the *Spring and Fall*, the *Book of Poetry*, and other works). The closest we have to Confucius's own words is the *Analects*—as its name implies, a collection of sayings by or about Confucius, along with some anecdotes of his life, arranged in no particular order and with a minimum of context. The oldest stratum of sayings was probably compiled within

---

7. Laozi, the supposed Daoist founder, would actually have been the first, were he a real person. I am assuming, perhaps arbitrarily, that the book that bears Laozi's name did not take its familiar shape until after Confucius's time.

a few years of his death. The beginning student may wonder what all the fuss is about, as superficially the *Analects* seems a compilation of commonsense platitudes, "Confucius says…" fortune cookie slips. Longer immersion in the work gives a sense of its profundity. Perhaps the best way to read the *Analects* is to use an index or concordance, to see the different ways in which Confucius employed his words and their relations to each other. In the same way, Confucius's disciples emerge as distinct personalities—some bold and impulsive, some suave and diplomatic, some modest and childlike. We also get a sense of Confucius's personality: dignified without being solemn, with a quiet sense of humor; serious about his sense of mission but not overly serious about himself; generally poised but sometimes flustered; discouraged and bemused by the folly of the world.

Even if he had written down his ideas, Confucius would probably not have had a fully systematic philosophy. One reason he did not write down his opinions (for it is certain that he could read and write) may be precisely that, in his own eyes, he had no system of his own. He claimed he invented nothing: he merely transmitted the ways of antiquity. He wished to restore the ways of the early Zhou, even the authority and dignity of the Zhou Son of Heaven. In one trend of current communist interpretation, Confucius was a reactionary or, at least, a conservative, stubbornly resisting the tide of the times. Confucius would have agreed with this interpretation, but not the value judgment it implies. Yet in the process of trying to apply the ancient concepts to his own time Confucius transformed them, giving them universal meaning—or, as he would probably prefer to have it, making their universal meaning explicit.

A starting point might be his concept of ritual (*li*). The term refers originally to religious ceremonies. It also referred to manners and etiquette, particularly the code of behavior of the aristocracy. Confucius expanded the meaning to encompass the way human beings properly behave toward each other—and even toward themselves and toward nature. Religious ritual and aristocratic manners become in effect specific instances of a more general proper human behavior, adjusted for the particular circumstances.

Ritual is the outward expression of human feelings—not just any feelings we happen to have, but the proper feelings for the particular occasion. The concept of ritual focuses attention on the specific, concrete, "situational" nature of proper action. Human beings constantly interact with others in the family and society at large. Except for the relation between friends, all of these interactions are between people of different status, between superior and inferior. Ritual meets the obligations of status differences while preserving human feelings and dignity. The soldier salutes the officer and the officer returns the salute: the dignity of each and of their relationship is acknowledged. There are, of course, different degrees of politeness. Toward strangers or acquaintances one is *keqi* (in the modern colloquial)—one has the "air of a guest." Among close friends and inside the family one practices *limao*—still a kind of politeness, but warmer and looser than implied in *keqi*.

A modern romantic or an ancient Daoist might find all of this perversely stuffy. Shouldn't one forget about these artificial forms and ceremonies and follow one's spontaneous, natural, authentic feelings? For the Confucians, ritual arises from and expresses spontaneous feelings. Mencius speculates that primitive people had no funerals. When their parents died, they would simply throw the bodies into a ditch. But passing by the place a few days later, they would feel inner anguish at the sight of the bodies decaying and being eaten by animals. Hence, funeral ceremonies evolved. The ritual both expresses and channels our natural feelings. Abstracted from custom, society, or circumstance it is not obvious that we have any "natural" way to express authentic feelings. Even when being spontaneous is not arrogant, slothful, or self-indulgent disregard for the expectations of others, it means we are without any guide to action. Ritual gives our feelings form.

Ritual also exercises power and leads to virtue. The Chinese word here, *de*, like the English word (as it happens) has a double meaning, both a valued quality and a power to produce an effect (as when we speak of the virtue of a medicine, or an official says, perhaps redundantly, by virtue of the power vested in me). Ritual is outward expression, but outward expression can induce the proper inner feelings. You and I quarrel, and as things are getting bitter you yield and smile. In reaction I also smile, and yield in my turn. Our feelings are harmonized and form has produced the content. Another implication of ritual is that virtue or morality can be found only in concrete situations; they are not and cannot be reduced to the mechanical carrying out of a set of rules.[8]

Confucius was not one to depreciate mere outward observances. He had a generally dim view of how religious and civic (to make a distinction probably not valid for his society) ceremonies were carried out in his time, but would go along with current convention where that did not violate the spirit of the ceremony. More generally, though, Confucius realized the relative, contingent nature of any particular ritual form. He admitted he could say nothing about the ritual of Xia or Shang, because there were no longer any records. But he speculates the Zhou ritual is of such high quality because it was built upon the achievements of the Xia and Shang. Confucius says, "We follow Zhou." He no doubt means we—or he himself and his disciples—adhere to the Zhou patterns, but he can also mean that we succeed to and build upon the rites of Zhou, just as Zhou built upon those who had gone before. Ritual is a means to bring order to society, but it is relative to time and place and can even be entirely lost, so it is not the ultimate foundation for order.

---

8. This interpretation is suggested by Herbert Fingarette, *Confucius: The Secular as Sacred* (New York, 1972), an interesting and original but also somewhat controversial analysis.

Ritual expresses human feelings. Most fundamentally it is the outward expression of the defining human virtue, *ren*. Ren is pronounced exactly like the same word for human being and is written 仁 , the character for person with the number 2 beside it. The popular and obvious (but apparently incorrect) interpretation is that the character represents the feelings two persons should have toward each other, or how two persons should relate to each other. It is often translated humaneness or benevolence, although unfortunately these may sound stilted or pompous. It may also be translated love. Confucius said: Ren is to love people. He also said it means not doing to others what you don't want done to yourself—the Golden Rule, albeit stated negatively. It can also be translated goodness. Perhaps the best translation, but one not easy to use regularly, is "humankindness," incorporating a pun: the kindness human beings owe to each other, and the character we share in common with each other as part of humankind.

Confucius also talked about the rectification of names. By this he did not mean, like Socrates, the search for the right definition of terms (although some Warring States philosophers were interested in this). Rather, through love and ritual we bring what we are into conformity with the name, role, or position that we hold. The denotation and the connotation of a word must coincide. A father must be a father, a son a son; a king must be a king, a minister a minister. A father must be a father—and everything that word implies. A father who abuses or neglects his children is not truly a father. The rectification of names highlights the ethical definition of the status distinctions Confucius affirmed. For a king to be a king means that he rules for the good of the people. To be a minister, the minister must be loyal, but this does not mean unquestioning obedience to the whims of the king. Rather, it means to act in the best interests of the ruler and the people. The political relationship has limits—in the Confucian tradition, a king who does not act the way a king should is in danger of losing the Mandate of Heaven and may be ousted by the people or by rivals. Unworthy parents, of course, may not be similarly deposed: the filial child must put up with things as best he can.

Confucius expounded on the virtues of the *junzi*, the person representing proper human virtues. Literally the term means the child of a ruler, a prince. The best translation is probably gentleman, a word that once underwent an analogous evolution of meaning.⁹ The term shows the workings of the Confucian rectification of names. A gentleman is a nobleman, and nobility is governed by birth. But the true meaning of nobility is in character. A born

---

9. In contemporary culture, *gentleman* may no longer carry quite the punch it once did, and in any case *junzi* may always have had a somewhat higher moral connotation. Some may object to the English term as "sexist." It is certainly masculine. The feminine versions, lady or gentlewoman, do not have quite the same connotations. Chinese has no gender, and while Confucius probably had mainly men in mind when he used the term, junzi can be and has been applied to either sex.

aristocrat may or may not be a real gentleman—as may a born commoner. A true gentleman is one who has cultivated his character through education and behaves in accord with love and ritual. Only such a person can be entrusted with authority over others.

One attains this status by hard work and study. Confucius said: At 15 I set my heart on study; at 30 I stood firm; at 40 I was no longer confused; at 50 I knew the order of Heaven; at 60 I could accept it; at 70 I could follow my heart's desire and not depart from the track. Virtue is cultivated by study, and intellectual grasp of the way is only a part of it: we can know Heaven's will without quite accepting it (as Confucius implies was the case with himself up to his sixtieth year). If we persist in cultivation, our own will and desires are merged with what is truly good and right. The function of cultivation is not merely personal growth, for our personal growth in its turn is to be used for improving the world. As a Confucian passage (not necessarily uttered by Confucius himself) has it, from the cultivation of the person we go to the regulation of the family, to bringing order to the state, to bringing peace to the world. In Confucianism the progression is from the personal and immediate to the more distant, abstract, and general.

The gentleman is not the highest type of human development. That would be the sage—someone like the ancient culture heroes or the Duke of Zhou, one so attuned to the Way of Heaven that his very existence leads the world to right order. Confucius believed he had ample evidence that he was not himself a sage. Later generations have disagreed: Confucius is the greatest of the sages, if also the least fulfilled. He is the uncrowned king, an unrectified name.

The Second Sage is Mencius (Mengzi or Meng Qi), who lived about 372 to 289 B.C. He lived at the height of the Warring States period, and Confucians[10] (and, presumably, proponents of the other schools as well) were in demand by the growingly complex new bureaucratic kingdoms for their ritual, administrative, and diplomatic skills. The more influential among the scholars and intellectuals, apparently, were treated as real celebrities. The long book that bears Mencius's name is a subtle, profound, even imposing work of moral philosophy.

It opens with Mencius visiting King Hui of Liang. The king greets him respectfully and asks, innocently enough, if perhaps Mencius has some advice to benefit his country. Mencius jumps all over the poor monarch: Why does the king speak of benefit? If the king wants to benefit the state, the vassals will

---

10. They were called *Ru*, which acquired the meaning of scholars but originally probably meant cowards or weaklings. Maybe the term was used, first in a derogatory fashion, to distinguish the increasingly important civil officials from the *shi* or knights, the hereditary warrior aristocracy. Confucius, on his part, used the term *knight* to designate the stage below the gentleman on his moral hierarchy. The knight is a person of courage and breeding, manifesting common decency and respect for convention.

think only of benefiting their territories and the common people will think only of benefiting their families. Rather, the king should think about what is Right. Whether or not Mencius is being priggish, his point is that a focus on benefits or what we may call utility leads everyone to center on his own good, and that this will yield disorder. What is objectively right or good should guide our concept of what is advantageous.

Mencius has a moralistic approach to government and life generally, but it is not a narrow or simple moralism. Mencius said (in a statement a famous British analytic philosopher found "rather sinister"[11]), The great man need not always stand by his word, nor need his actions always bear fruit, as long as he acts according to what is Right. This is probably the standard Confucian notion that morality is always embedded in context and cannot be reduced to a mechanical application of rules. It does not mean the end justifies the means. Mencius was asked if one should violate the Way of Heaven in order to save the world. He says no. And yet, his questioner persists, it is immoral to have physical contact with your brother's wife, but if your sister-in-law is drowning, you would surely stick out a hand to help her. Mencius replies, in effect, that the world is saved only through the Way and so cannot be saved by violating the Way. Incest taboos no doubt accord with the Way, but it would violate the Way to allow someone to die in order to avoid a technical violation of an incest taboo. Good and evil, right and wrong, depend on context, and it takes judgment to see when which is which. But we are never justified in doing evil for the sake of good.

We make this judgment by consulting our own nature. Mencius's central teaching is that human nature is good. He argues with one Gaozi, who has a naturalistic concept: "Nature is food and sex." This, says Mencius, does not distinguish specifically human nature from animal nature in general. Human nature is manifest in our sense of compassion, an inborn empathy for the suffering of others. Even the most depraved scoundrel, he says, will feel at least some stirring of anxiety when he sees a baby about to fall into a well—a rather apt example if we reflect on the worldwide media attention babies who actually do fall down wells sometimes receive. Someone who does not feel compassion, Mencius says, is not human.[12] His argument is circular, but it takes into account the possibility that we may become dehumanized; that is, our original human nature may be perverted to the point of destruction.

Mencius would not be bothered if people criticized his concept of morality as sentimental. We recognize morality by our sentiments and make moral judgments by examining the basis of and generalizing from our sentiments.

---

11. I. A. Richards, *Mencius on the Mind: Experiments in Multiple Definitions* (New York, 1932), p. 36.
12. This reasoning has recently reemerged in moral philosophy. James Q. Wilson, *The Moral Sense* (New York, 1993).

He has some fun with a king who substituted a sheep for a bull at a ritual sacrifice. The people think it is because I am cheap, the king complains, but actually I felt sorry for the bull. It will be just as hard on the sheep, Mencius comments. But, the king says, I saw how uncomfortable and afraid the bull was; I didn't see the sheep. Exactly, says Mencius, adding sardonically: That's why a gentleman stays away from the kitchen.

Mencius does not have a fatuous trust that left to our own we'll always do the right thing. We are born good, but our good nature needs to be developed through study and cultivation, in a constant struggle against forces in the world that corrode and erode it. Mencius uses the analogy of Bull Mountain, apparently a well-known ecological disaster of his day. It was originally covered with thick forests, but the woods were cut down and cattle grazed upon it and now it's a barren waste. People who see it now have no idea of what it was once like, just as it is hard to realize that a wicked man was actually born good. An implication of Mencius's concept of nature is that people are equal—since everyone has the same nature. We are no different from the sages, and everyone has in himself or herself the potential to become a sage.

Because people are good, they must be ruled in a benevolent fashion. A good ruler knows what is good for his people because he knows his own likes and dislikes. A king who lives in luxury with a huge harem knows, from his own desires, that everyone else has the same desire for food and sex, and when he reflects on his duty will know that he must provide his people with the means to support themselves and raise their families. A ruler whose selfishness or misgovernment brings disaster to the people is a murderer: to kill by policy is no different from killing with a knife.

Mencius did not give much thought to a restoration of the Zhou. He hoped some ruler would be able to bring order to the world. This required virtue, and could not be accomplished by conquest. One may gain a state by force, he says, but not the world. On one level this probably means that one might take over one of the various warring states by force but would not be able to conquer what we would now call China. The deeper meaning is that violence may be sufficient to set up a system of political rule but it can't bring true order and a decent life.

Like Confucius, Mencius applied the rectification of names. When asked whether it was ever right to kill a king, Mencius said no. Well, then, what of the last wicked king of the Shang dynasty? Mencius said: I have heard that a gangster was executed; I've never heard of anyone killing a king. Mencius is sometimes credited with developing a right of revolution. However, the king's authority comes from Heaven, not from the people. But Mencius also quotes an ancient poem: Heaven hears as my people hear; Heaven sees as my people see.

There is a certain democratic spirit in Mencius, but also strong elitism. He certainly believes in government for the people and maybe even of the people, but not by the people. Mencius says: Those who work with their hands feed those who work with their brains; those who work with their brains rule those who work with their hands (an attitude not entirely foreign to Chinese intellectuals today). Some defend Mencius by suggesting he was simply saying how things are, not giving an opinion on the merits of the situation. There is no hint, however, that Mencius saw this as anything but proper. In fact, he accords the duty or privilege of rule to those with intelligence and education, not birth, luck, connections, money, or force. Also, those who are fed by the physical labor of others also work—they must exert themselves for the benefit of those who feed them.

The third great Confucian of the formative period was Xunzi (Xun Qing; he does not sport a Latin soubriquet). He lived from about 300 to 237 B.C. Against the older Mencius, he believed human nature is evil. As a police official in the state of Qi he may have had a cop's eye view of the human condition. He lived at the tail end of the Warring States period, when international turmoil and general moral confusion had reached their climax. He had the best analytic mind of the ancient Chinese philosophers, rivaled only by his sometime pupil, the Legalist Han Feizi.

Human nature is evil, Xunzi says, with good the result of acquired training. We are evil by nature because left to ourselves we will follow our passions and desires, seeking our own benefit regardless of right and wrong.

In Confucius and Mencius there is not the distinction we find in the Greeks between reason and emotion. Both are aware that we can be swayed by passion and desire, but we are also parts of a morally coherent universe, however incoherent our own lives or society may be, and our feelings are one way of getting in touch with the moral order. For Xunzi there is no morally coherent universe. For him Heaven is only the natural world and natural processes.[13] Morality is grounded in the human condition and human conventions. Xunzi agrees with Mencius about the natural equality of persons, but equality means constant strife. The sages, then, devised ritual, distinctions, morality to bring harmony among persons and create the conditions for human life. For Confucius and especially Mencius the sages are exemplars of moral virtue. For Xunzi they become, in effect, its inventors.

Xunzi gives a utilitarian interpretation of Confucian morality, but it is not a narrow utilitarianism. He has no patience with those who would eliminate music and ritual as unproductive wastes of time and money. Funerals, to be sure, are neither here nor there to the dead. They are held for the living who need to express and sublimate their sorrow for the loss of someone they have loved and their fears about their own mortality. Music puts food on the table of only the musician, but it regulates, pacifies, brings harmony to the human soul.

---

13. In China both the term and the concept here are entirely different from that referring to human nature.

Xunzi eloquently defends what would now be considered a liberal education. Education is not for the sake of acquiring skills that may be applied for profit, but for cultivating and developing the person. Education becomes a treasure inherent to our being, something we cannot lose. If we have it, we may look down upon kings and princes. Unfortunately, later in Chinese history the liberal education did in practice become, in a directly utilitarian fashion, a tool for getting a government job, itself the way to power and wealth.

Later Confucians took Mencius as the valid continuator of the Master's tradition. The authoritarianism and classicism of later Confucian practice, however, may reflect the influence of Xunzi.

Daoism

Confucianism came to dominate Chinese thought after 200 B.C., but it is not the whole of it. In politics it has been balanced by Legalism and as a general philosophy of life by Daoism (or, in the more familiar spelling, Taoism). *Dao* means way or path; by a happy coincidence it also means to speak. From this it comes to mean the way of things, the inherent principle of things. Its usage is somewhat analogous to the ancient Greek concept *logos*, word, from which we get logic. The Gospel of John begins: In the beginning was the word (the logos), and the word was with God, and the word was God. The Chinese translation of this runs: In the beginning was Dao…. In Confucian usage Dao means the Way of Heaven, the moral order of the universe. Daoists say that you can't talk about the Dao, so it is hard to say what they mean by it; it seems at bottom to mean the Way things are.

Daoism derives from two works, each named for its author: the *Laozi* and the *Zhuangzi*. The *Laozi* is also known as the *Dao De Jing*, the Classic of the Way and Virtue. Laozi may mean either Old Philosopher or Old Boy; his actual name was Li Dan, and he is supposed to have lived (to an extremely great old age) around 600 B.C., with his life overlapping that of Confucius. He came from Chu, in what is now Hubei and Hunan provinces, then the southern part of the Chinese culture area, known to the staid northerners as a region of "strange ceremonies and obscene rites." Confucius is sometimes supposed to have visited Laozi, and Zhuangzi has many humorous stories of the stuffy, conventional, humorless Confucius being put in his place by his more profound and nimble-minded elder. It is pleasant to think that a callow young Confucius did indeed meet Laozi, to be shocked into seeing through the conventional wisdom and pieties of the world—and, on more mature reflection, in Zen Buddhist fashion to see through the seeing through. On the other hand, Zhuangzi (or Zhuang Zhou), who lived about the same time as Mencius, tells many stories about Laozi, leaving the impression that he was a figure his readers would recognize, but does not quote from Laozi's book—leading some to think that the *Dao De Jing* must have been written about the same time or later than the *Zhuangzi*.

The *Laozi* begins: The Way that can be spoken of is not the real (or eternal, or constant) Way—or: The Dao that can be daoed is not the real Dao. The second line runs more smoothly in English: The names that can be named are not the real names. Whatever we can say or, presumably, think about rationally is not the full reality of the world. Nor can the Confucians rectify their names: the names they give, the concepts they formulate, cannot capture the truth of things. If this is the case it seems perverse to try to explain Daoism or the Dao. Perhaps we should approach it negatively, interpreting it as an attempt, like Confucianism, to make sense of a disordered world but also as a polemic against Confucianism as a futile and fruitless attempt.

The Confucians thought the world had deteriorated from a high level of civilization and wanted to restore that civilization. For the Daoists the trouble is civilization itself, which imposes artificial values and distinctions. If there is happiness to be recovered, it is found in following nature, going with the flow, not in striving to improve oneself or one's society. A key Daoist metaphor is water, always passive, always seeking the lowest point, always overcoming all obstacles, wearing down what is hard and resistant.

People are part of nature, but Confucianism (and maybe people in general) takes humanity (in either sense of the word) as the standard of nature. Confucian virtues are artificial standards irrelevant to the Dao. At best they are second best. When the Dao was lost, Laozi says, love and justice came into the world. Morality is an invention of a fallen age.[14] Zhuangzi (in an uncharacteristically bitter passage) tells a story of an attempt by Confucius to convert a notorious robber. The robber turns on Confucius: Confucius eats food others have grown and spends his time currying favor with the mighty. If he would talk about ghosts and monsters (the kind of thing Confucius never spoke of), he might be of some count, since people are interested in that kind of thing; instead he pours forth empty words whose main theme is that people, as if their lives were not short and troubled enough already, should deny their natural desires. Confucius is the biggest robber of them all, thwarting his natural inclinations and trying to bring others to his own twisted ways.

The Confucian mentality rests on the drawing of distinctions, and there are no distinctions in the Dao. Zhuangzi tells how the primal chaos, Mr. Hundun, once entertained his friends. They noticed he was all one undifferentiated block—he lacked sense organs. To repay his hospitality they decided to give him the means to perceive the world, boring holes in him for his eyes, ears, nose, and mouth. They bored one hole a day, and on the seventh day Mr. Hundun died.

Confucians judge by human standards, but in the Dao there are no standards, or, rather, each thing has its own standards. People look down on a

---

14. In the Bible, Adam and Eve know good and evil only when they have chosen evil.

gnarled, twisted tree as useless—but that is the tree that won't be cut down, so its uselessness is what preserves its life, the most useful thing of all. If use-lessness is the most useful thing, so the best course of action is no action at all—we move passively with the Dao. Zhuangzi tells of the butcher who has not had to sharpen his knife for 18 years. At first, the butcher explains, he saw only bone, muscle, and sinew, and he needed a new knife every few days. But eventually his "eyes saw the whole cow" (this has become a proverbial expression). At its very edge the blade has no depth at all and where bones or muscle meet there is always empty space. When what has no breadth moves through empty space, nothing is cut but the cow is dismembered. This example implies, however, that Daoist effortlessness comes only after a great deal of practice and effort.

Politically Daoism advises "rule by nonaction." According to Laozi, the worst rulers are those the people hate, while the second worst are those they praise. The best are those the people never notice at all. All things are accomplished but the people seem to have done it themselves. Laozi also advises: Fill the bellies and empty the minds. This could be a good formula for successful despotism. In its intention, however, it probably was an expression of a desire for a primitive utopia—for a world, Laozi elsewhere says, where people hear the dogs and chickens in the next village but have never had an inclination to go there. One problem may be that to keep the minds empty requires a mighty thrusting against the Dao—this supposed simple natural-ness is really neither simple nor natural—and that the longings for it are products of highly civilized and sophisticated minds.[15]

Within the Chinese context Confucianism and Daoism are opposites, but from an outside view they share a family resemblance. While neither Zhuangzi nor Mencius ever mentions the other, some scholars believe that parts of the work of each are implicitly directed against the other. Yet they have a certain similarity of temperament. Mencius also talks of the effortless following of nature. For the Confucians, except for Xunzi, following the moral Way is something natural, not a distortion of our natural desires. For the Daoists, human morality has no foundation in nature, but is only convention.

Daoism has become inextricably merged with Chinese folk religion—perhaps it has always been so. It decisively conditioned the form Buddhism assumed when that religion made its way to China and Japan. It is common to distinguish (a non-Daoist activity) religious from philosophical Daoism, although the differences may often be exaggerated. Religious Daoism and even some of the post–Warring States philosophic Daoism is identified with magic and superstition, alchemy and a search for physical immortality. This kind of thing was part of the heritage leading to the development of science in the West—much more so, say, than the highly rationalistic Aristotelianism of

---

15. A recent analogy might be the movie *Dances with Wolves*.

Catholic scholasticism. Confucianism, like other forms of rationalism, may be too quick to identify what is rational with what is currently real, and the low prestige accorded popular Daoism by the Confucian elite may have been one more cause of China's failure to evolve theoretical science.

Religious Daoism is also associated with rebel ideologies, promising to abolish all distinctions, to make all things new, to turn heaven and earth upside down. On the few occasions when the rebellions succeeded, either they had been co-opted by the Confucian elite or their leadership had come over to Confucianism. More recently, many of the attitudes and much of the symbolism of radical Maoism (total transformation, Chairman Mao as the red, red sun in our hearts, the rejection of conventional attitudes) show, probably inadvertently, Daoist influence.[16]

Mohism

A passage in the *Analects* concerns "things about which the Master did not speak"—ghosts, strange phenomena, and the like. Confucius's silence also tells us something about Confucius. Similarly, ideas considered in China but not accepted into the mainstream tell us something about Chinese culture.

Mozi, or Mo Di, is thought to have lived from about 480 to 390 B.C. He may have been, like Confucius, a native of Lu, and he may have studied in Confucius's school under the first generation of disciples. His own thinking seems to have developed in critical reaction to Confucianism, especially its elitist implications. He himself may have come from a low social class or have had firsthand experience with the harder side of life. *Mo* means ink, and the name the philosopher is known by may indicate that he was tattooed as a criminal—or it may simply be his family name.[17]

Against the Confucian focus on distinctions, Mohism advocated universal love. God loves everyone without distinction and, therefore, people should love each other in the same way. The Daoists also denied the validity of distinctions, but the Mohists agreed with the Confucians on the objective validity of the moral pattern.

Mozi, however, traced this pattern directly to God (while for the Confucians the path would be indirect). Morality is valid because it is willed by God, and God backs his will by rewarding the good and punishing the wicked.

Mozi was not only a theist but a utilitarian, a combination that gives his thought a flavor somewhat like that popularly associated with the Puritans. Mencius (probably reacting against the Mohists) insists on a distinction

---

16. Wolfgang Bauer, *China and the Search for Happiness* (New York, 1976).

17. In English discussions of the school it is common to insert an *h* into the middle of the word—so that Mohist is pronounced Mo-ist, two syllables, not moist.

between what is right and what is expedient. For the Mohists the two are the same: the right thing is whatever benefits other people. People require food, shelter, and clothing, and the way to show love for people is to help them provide for these needs. Music, ritual, poetry, all the other frills the Confucians set so much store by, are a waste of precious resources, diverting material away from meeting urgent human needs.

Like the Confucians the Mohists believed in a political or social hierarchy—again, like the Confucians, one founded on virtue. Mozi talked of "identification with the superior." We each identify with and pattern ourselves after the person who is morally our superior, and the one at the top identifies with God.

In their arguments with other schools the Mohists felt compelled to develop a logical style, backing their love without distinction with distinctions in the use of words. Opponents could argue, for example, that if you love people you don't kill them; neither do you allow others to kill or plunder them. To protect people from robbers you sometimes have to kill robbers, but robbers are people, too. The Mohists (who may have been softhearted but were not softheaded) tried to demonstrate that to kill robbers does not mean the same thing as to kill people—another version of the paradox that a white horse is not a horse (in yet another version, the Mohists show that even if your younger brother is a handsome man, when you say you love your little brother you are not asserting that you love a handsome man).

Confucians were scandalized at the idea that we should love strangers as much as we love our own parents. They placed themselves in the middle ground, between the extremes of the Mohists on the one side and, on the other, one Yang Zhu (about whom nothing else is known), who supposedly would not sacrifice a hair even if that would save the whole world. On a deeper level, the Confucians felt the Mohist concept of universal love was too abstract. Universal love may be implicit in Confucianism, but it grows from the actual practice of love of those we are in contact with (even Jesus, after all, says we should love our neighbor, not humanity). From the Confucian perspective the Mohists are a little like the 1960s hippy who always talks about love, love, love, but who cannot stand his own parents.

In the Warring States time, Mohism rivaled Confucianism in influence, both intellectual and cultural. The Mohists were organized into a disciplined, cohesive corps. They were much in demand by rulers, for although they were pacifists they believed that good defenses would make war unprofitable, and so became famous as experts in defensive warfare.

The school as such died out soon after the Warring States. Mozi's writings continued to be studied as interesting but biased perceptions of a partial truth. In the nineteenth century, Christian missionaries helped revive interest in Mozi, and more recently some leftist Chinese intellectuals found in him populistic and universalistic principles, a sort of modern mentality, to set against the elitist particularism of Confucianism.

Legalism and the Unification of China

The West has historically placed a high value on the rule of law, but in China law has been feared as mechanical, impersonal, and amoral. Rather, there should be rule by the virtuous, by those who know what is appropriate under all circumstances. The problem, of course, is how to assure that those with power will also have virtue.

The Western notion of the rule of law is a moral one: traditionally law was conceived as the will of God or the order of nature. In the modern concept of positive law, the sovereign (whether king or people) makes the law. In the traditional view law is not made but discovered and applied, and binds the sovereign along with everyone else. The equivalent in China would be ritual or the Way of Heaven. Law in Spring and Fall times referred to regulations by which the nobility governed their subjects (the relations among themselves being regulated by ritual), and in China, law always had a positive-law connotation. Certain Warring States political thinkers and practitioners, known as the Legalists, recognized that positive law might be a surer path to order than ritual, benevolent government, or the rule of virtue.

The origins of Legalism go back at least to the Spring and Fall: the hegemons of that period are sometimes considered precursors of Legalism. It is mostly associated, however, with Qin, the most backward of the Warring States, and with the reforms initiated by the Qin prime minister Lord Shang (or Shang Yang; died 338 B.C.). Qin was on the western border of the Chinese culture area (in present day Shaanxi province) and was not fully assimilated into Chinese culture until relatively late.[18] Perhaps as a consequence of its poverty, to assure the state's survival Qin's rulers (like those later of Prussia) concentrated on developing its military prowess.

Shang Yang believed the power of the state depended on the centralization of all authority in the person of the king. The salvation of the state lies in agriculture (which is the source of wealth) and war (which allows the state to survive in a world of other states). All that contributes to success in agriculture and war should be encouraged; everything else is at best superfluous, probably pernicious. Standards of behavior should be set forth clearly in law and the law should be strictly and impartially enforced. Both military and civil offices should be assigned according to merit, merit here meaning not Confucian virtue but the ability to do a particular job. Those who do well should be rewarded; those who do not should be punished.

Although an advocate of despotism, Lord Shang also believed in equality before the law. He broke the power of the feudal nobility in Qin, since birth is not necessarily related to ability and since nobles, even when they do not set themselves as rivals to the king, are not always the most docile of subjects.

---

18. As the saying goes, in his journeys to the west, Confucius never reached Qin.

Lord Shang promoted private farming so that the best farmers could become rich, increasing both the food surplus and the tax base. The commitment to equality is one of the few elements of Legalism that the Confucians admired, if grudgingly. The law was enforced equally on all. Once when the crown prince committed some kind of trespass, Lord Shang ordered the boy punished. When the old king died, Lord Shang thought it prudent to go on the lam. The new king sent thugs to hunt him down and murder him: the Legalists did not typically have happy ends.

Probably the most systematic exposition of Legalism is the *Han Feizi*. Han Fei (died 233 B.C.) was a member of the ruling house of the state of Han—ironically, in view of his principles, the only real aristocrat among the Warring States thinkers. He was not, apparently, close to the king of Han, and several of his essays seem to be diatribes against the frivolous and incompetent way his native state was being governed. He seems to have had a speech impediment, or at least not to have been good at public speaking; but he writes in a clear, logical style, touched with sarcasm.

As a young man Han Fei studied with Xunzi, and it is generally taken for granted that he was influenced by Xunzi's thought. They share the same general perception of what people are like, but there is no evidence of direct influence. Xunzi is mentioned only two or three times in Han Fei's writings, and then only as the proponent of one school of Confucianism among many.

Han Fei speaks of "universal human feelings," but not of human nature. This perhaps indicates a very different perspective from that of Xunzi. Han Fei would probably not assert that human nature is evil, because (in modern terms) he spoke to the human condition rather than to human nature and, in any case, in his system value judgments about human nature or anything else would be beside the point. Universal human feelings dictate that we seek safety and comfort and avoid danger and pain. All human action is self-seeking adjustment to the conditions we find ourselves in. Adam Smith says it is not the benevolence of the baker that gives us our bread—rather, it's the baker's own interests. Han Fei has a similar metaphor: if the undertaker rejoices in times of famine, it's not because he is cruel but because business is good.

We seek always in all things our own ends; often we can achieve these only at the expense of another's good. Therefore, there is disorder in the world. Since all our behavior is a response to circumstances, order is assured when circumstances are brought under control. This means in effect under the control of the ruler, although there are hints in Han Fei that in the end the problem of order is unsolvable.

The ruler controls circumstances by stipulating and enforcing the law. Law fixes rules of behavior and absolves subjects from the effort of figuring out what to do in specific circumstances, particularly if the law is clear and mechanically enforced. It reconciles the private and public good. It is in my private interest to steal your money rather than work to earn my own, but it ceases to be in my interest if there is a high chance that I will be caught and punished if I steal (Han Fei is something of a "rational choice" theorist). In conjunction with specifying and enforcing the law the ruler governs through "technique," methods producing effective results and requiring little, if any, judgment for their exercise. Technique basically reduces to reward and punishment: behavior that accords with the law is rewarded and that which violates the law is punished. The ruler also exercises as part of technique a little elementary prudence. Since control over circumstances must rest with the ruler, he must keep to himself sole power to reward and punish (although, for the sake of efficiency he normally delegates this power, taking care to keep his agents in check).

The ruler must control and not be controlled. This means he must also control his personal desires, for otherwise he will be vulnerable to those able to satisfy him. He must be especially wary of those closest to him: his relatives, his women, his immediate subordinates. As Han Fei puts it, "Superior and inferior fight a hundred battles a day." The interests of the ruler and his agents can be made to coincide superficially by rewards and punishments—reward for carrying out duty, punishment for any use of power for private benefit. The ruler must conceal his own biases, preferences, and opinions concerning policy and personnel, because if the officials can figure out what the ruler wants to hear, that is what they will tell him. For Han Fei the public good reduces on one level to the good of the ruler—although the ruler himself does not gain much satisfaction, beyond power itself. In effect, the public good is whatever contributes to the power of the ruler or, even better, the strength of the state.

Han Fei has no place for morality or virtue (other than prudence or political sagacity). He finds the political morality preached by the Confucians and the Mohists to be downright pernicious. Order is assured through law, but morality sets up standards independently of the law. Han Fei almost uniformly assumes that assertions of morality are and can be nothing but rationalizations of self-interest. Morality, in fact, is subversive. Confucians told of the ancient sage rulers who, instead of giving the throne to their own sons, sought out the most worthy and turned the rule over to him. For Han Fei it goes without saying that such legends originated as propaganda for the usurpation of power and to repeat such stories is an incitement to rebellion. To measure law by morality is to set one's self up as judge of the law and is tantamount to loss of control by the ruler.

Moral discourse is dangerous because it can persuade the ruler himself. Rulers are human, too, and want to be thought well of; they want to win reputations for benevolence and mercy. This may be harmless in itself, but it might also divert the ruler from the necessities of the exercise of power. When children go out to play they make mud pies. But at supper time, when they are hungry, they go home for real food. Rulers may frivolously flaunt their benevolence and righteousness, but the intelligent ruler, when real business is at hand, relies on law and technique.

Han Fei's most profound critique of virtue turns on the possibility that morality might in fact be authentic. It may be the case, he notes, that some sage or hero (he mentions specifically Confucius) may act as a true moral agent, not merely in response to circumstances. By the same token, a really bold villain will not be deterred by a harsh law. But most of us are neither sages, heroes, nor villains. We are mediocrities and the law is sufficient to control us and assure general order. But to tolerate the sage or hero setting standards independently of the law undermines the position of the law itself.

While Han Fei's theory calls for concentrating power in the ruler, several of his chapters clearly show he knows actual rulers to be as shallow, weak, and mediocre as anyone else. The unresolved, not even explicitly acknowledged, paradox in Han Fei's system is that while the ruler must be the cause of all that happens, he must also himself be caused to do what is proper. One essay in Han Fei's book provides techniques whereby the honest official induces the ruler to do what a good ruler should, despite himself, do. But, of course, if this kind of manipulation is successful, there would not really be any Legalist rule (and where does Han Fei think we are going to find these honest officials?). Had Han Fei been aware of the concept, he perhaps would really have preferred an automaton to a real king. His goal, in fact, was the Daoist one of "rule by nonaction"—the law should rule while the ruler does nothing.

Han Fei contributed to the development of Chinese logic. He was the first to explicitly formulate in China the principle of contradiction. He told of an arms dealer who boasted he had a spear that could pierce anything and a shield that nothing could pierce. "And what happens," he was asked, "if someone tries to use your spear to pierce your shield?" Shield and spear, *maodun*, remains the Chinese term for contradiction. As this example implies, Han Fei was something of a wit, and he compiled what amounts to China's first joke book, a collection of anecdotes to illustrate principles of effective politics.[19]

Around 233 B.C. Han Fei went on a diplomatic mission to Qin, behaving, if the existing documents are to be credited, in a highly ambiguous manner. He made a presentation to the Qin king outlining a strategy whereby Qin could conquer the entire world. He made another presentation arguing it was against Qin's interest to destroy Han. The prime minister of Qin was Li Si, who had been Han Fei's schoolmate when they both studied with Xunzi. Li Si was jealous of Han Fei's ability and afraid he would gain influence with the

---

19. A couple of examples: A man wanted to buy some new shoes and made a tracing of his feet. When he got to the store, however, he found he had left the tracing at home. Never mind, said the cobbler, all we have to do is measure your feet. No, the man said: I trust the diagram, not my feet. A man of Song (a small state, the territory that remained under the direct control of the Zhou king; its inhabitants frequently figure as the butts of Warring States–era jokes) was plowing his field when a rabbit ran by, crashed into a tree, and broke his neck. Thereafter the man gave up plowing, to spend all his days sitting under that tree waiting for another rabbit to crash into it.

king. He persuaded the king that Han Fei could not be trusted and managed to get Han Fei arrested. Before the king could have a change of heart Li Si issued orders in the name of the king for Han Fei to take poison (had Han Fei not complied, presumably his death would have been even more unpleasant).

A little more than a decade later, by 220 B.C., Qin had destroyed all the other states. The state structures were abolished and replaced by administrative districts whose civil and military governors were appointed directly by the new emperor. Li Si organized a general standardization of weights, measures, cart axle lengths, and the written language. Li Si and the Qin emperor also supervised the first completion of the Great Wall. On Li Si's advice the Qin ruler ordered the burning of all histories of states other than Qin's, as well as most other written material available, sparing only technical manuals on agriculture, warfare, medicine, and divination—all in order to discourage subversive thought. When various scholars protested the new world order, on Li Si's advice the Qin ruler had some 300 of them buried alive.

The Zhou rulers had been called king, but this title had passed into general use by all rulers of the various Warring States. The Qin ruler after he had unified the realm thought he needed something grander. He (or Li Si) devised *Huangdi*, "august god"—but conventionally translated emperor. He styled himself the First Emperor, figuring there would be another 10 thousand to come. Later historians somewhat sarcastically call him the First Qin Emperor: there were in all only two Qin emperors.

Following the sudden death of the First Emperor in 212 B.C., the new political system fell into turmoil. Intrigue broke out at court while rebellion spread among the general population. Li Si and several of the abler Qin generals were murdered by political rivals. The central government could not hold and in 208 B.C. the Qin capital was destroyed by rebel armies. Like Hitler's Thousand Year Reich, the Qin dynasty lasted only 12 years.

The Traditional Period

The reforms instituted by the First Emperor and Li Si were logical continuations of processes that had been going on in all the Warring States, but the final changes perhaps came too quickly and produced too much social dislocation. The rebellions were set off when a work gang, unable to get to its assigned destination on time and fearful of the consequences of violating the regime's strict Legalist order, mutinied. Basic order was reestablished in 206 B.C. with the victory of the Han dynasty.[20] The Han founder had been born a peasant and had served as a local official under the Qin. His main rival during

---

20. The dynasty takes its name from a river in central China and is not the same word as, and has nothing to do with, Han Feizi or the earlier state of Han.

the rebellion was an aristocrat from central China. Had the aristocrat come out on top there might have been an attempt to restore the old multistate system. The Han founder had no attachment to that system and instead adapted, with some modifications, the institutional structure of Qin, moderating the harsh Qin policies.

Part of this moderation was an end to the Qin persecution of the educated and its drive to destroy higher culture. The Han founder himself was perhaps even more an anti-intellectual than the First Emperor. I conquered the world on horseback, he once boasted—why do I need these bookworms? True, was the reply, but can you rule it from horseback? At another time the Han founder observed a scholarly conference. Here are the heroes of the world, he mused, all within the range of my bow. These stories form a model of the relationship between intellectuals and the Chinese state. The state needed educated officials and so had to cater to educated sensibilities, but the state also co-opted the educated class, making it dependent upon and vulnerable to the state. Within a couple of generations the Han state gave its sole official patronage to Confucianism.

Han Confucianism

Han Confucianism, however, was a little different from that of the Warring States period. Early Confucianism lacked metaphysical ramifications. Han Confucianists tied Confucian ethics to the general cosmological system of yin and yang, seasonal cycles, and the five agents. Confucianism took on a religious coloration along with its new cosmological scaffolding. The new elements were asserted through analysis of the Confucian classics (such as the *Spring and Fall*), which were alleged to contain hidden allegorical meanings that could be discovered by proper reading.

The central Han concept was the Mandate of Heaven. The emperor was the Son of Heaven, the agent of Heaven on earth, chosen for his virtue and kept in office by his virtue.[21] Heaven desires to reward good and punish evil, and the emperor is Heaven's instrument for this. The ruler is also the guarantor of order under Heaven. But since all things are connected, his actions also influence the general order of the universe. The ruler is the thread linking Heaven, earth, and man. Misrule on earth reverberates in the universe at large. Natural disasters—earthquakes, famines, hermaphrodite chickens—are evidence of disordered rule and are either warnings from Heaven to the emperor to amend his ways or signs that Heaven has withdrawn the Mandate.

The ideology certainly gives the emperor an exalted status: to work against the ruler is not merely treason but blasphemy. The overall effect of

---

21. In principle the Mandate should have rested with individuals, but in practice it was deemed to pass on through the family line unless there was some reason it should not.

the ideology, however, was as much to limit imperial power as to glorify it. The emperor holds a unique position in the cosmos as well as the state, but he keeps this position only by acting as a good emperor should. This was a moral check on despotic power. It also served certain social interests. A good emperor was one who ruled in accord with Confucian norms—which in practical terms meant in accord with the opinions and interests of the Confucian bureaucracy and the powerful families from which, in Han times, the bureaucracy tended to be recruited. The Han compromise, as it might be called, shaped Chinese political culture for the entire dynastic period. Confucianism, somewhat against its nature, became the ideology of a despotic Legalist state and (in tension with this) a privileged social elite, but at the same time Confucianism helped humanize the state and induce into the elite a sense of responsibility. It also helped guarantee that elite status at least in principle had some grounding in objectively measurable merit.

Later Confucians perhaps tended to take the cosmological elements less literally than had the early Han scholars—judging whether a ruler had the Mandate of Heaven more by his virtue and ability, say, and less by whether his reign coincided with the birth of a two-headed calf. The cosmological model retained some influence among the elite and also among the general population. In the summer of 1976, when Chairman Mao was sickening to his death and Chinese political life was at one of its historic low points, there was a terrible earthquake in northern China. The newspapers felt it necessary to explain that earthquakes were purely natural phenomena, trying not very convincingly to show there is no such thing as the Mandate of Heaven.

Buddhism

By the official record, the Han dynasty collapsed in A.D. 221, although it had become moribund decades before. Its last years were marked by incompetent rule and corrupt government. Armies raised to defeat a rebellion by a Daoist sect, the Yellow Turbans, became private forces for their generals. Central Asian nomads raided unmolested south of the wall. Government revenue fell and personal security declined. China was divided into three separate kingdoms and then was reunified briefly when one of those swallowed the other two. After that the political system fragmented completely. Unity was finally restored under the Sui dynasty (A.D. 581–618), like the Qin a harsh, brief transitional regime. One of the Sui generals organized a coup against the ruler, setting up the Tang dynasty (A.D. 618–907), another golden age of Chinese civilization.

By the fall of Han, Confucianism had stagnated. Daoism was manifested among the people in magical practices and in ineffective revolts; among the elite it appeared as an escape from duty and responsibility into effete abstraction. These were the conditions for the introduction of Buddhism to China.

Some Western commentators, perhaps reflecting and reacting against earlier missionary impressions, assert that Chinese lack a sense of sin. Mencius says that human nature is good, the argument goes, so the Chinese have no feel for the Christian concept of humanity's fallen nature. Taken as a general interpretation this is probably false: Chinese are as aware as anyone else of the dark side of life and the extent of human depravity and frailty. Yet it is true that both Confucianism and Daoism are this-worldly and find this world on the whole a pleasant place. There is little allowance for the sense we sometimes have that our own mundane surroundings do not exhaust the meaning of our lives. In East Asia, Buddhism has helped supply this.

The original Buddha was a prince in India. In spite of the ease of his own happy circumstances he was acutely aware of the void within himself and, it seemed, everyone else. This void was not filled by normal social interaction, by pleasure, by learning, or by religion. By and by he came to realize that to live is to suffer. Life means desire and desires are never satisfied; the search for satisfaction leads to endless frustration. To live is to struggle, and survival is at the expense of other beings struggling themselves to survive. Sometimes we do attain satisfaction and even joy—but as soon as we have it, it is gone, and we are thrust back into our normal unease, discontent, and fretfulness. There can be lasting good only by the extinction of desire (which amounts to the extinction of life). The extinction of desire leads to compassion for all living things, while the practice of compassion helps to extinguish personal desire. The end is Nirvana, which seems very much like nothing, nonbeing.

Perhaps everyone identifies with this vision of the world (if it has been fairly presented) some of the time. The general Indian background, with the belief in reincarnation, might make it more universally appealing. Into each life some rain must fall and we must take the bitter with the sweet—but if life is an endless, meaningless repetition of bitter rain, then maybe the platitudes carry even less conviction than they normally do. Another implication of reincarnation is that our own individuality is an illusion—there is no such thing as our selves as such, but only temporary manifestations of a more general surging, discontented life force.

Although Buddhism came to China in bad times, it had to adapt to the generally sunnier East Asian temperament. Buddhism in China, Korea, and Japan is of the so-called Mahayana or "Greater Vehicle" variety, one that makes salvation[22] easier and more accessible for the ordinary person. In the original teaching, Nirvana comes from extinguishing desire, and for most of us this is the work of many lifetimes, if that. In the Mahayana tradition there is a sharp distinction between clergy and laity. By their own prayers, austerities, devotions, and good works the monks and nuns may accumulate merit for the rest of us, while we may accumulate merit not only by general good works and worship but also by supporting the clergy. In Chinese and Japanese

---

22. Specialists in Buddhism may object to the use of this Christian term, but it seems that it corresponds with what Buddhism means, at least in its popular form, in China and Japan.

Buddhism there is a veneration of bodhisattvas, beings who themselves have achieved the merit necessary for Nirvana but refuse to enter until all living things have been saved. The most prominent include Amitaba Buddha, who bestows grace upon those who merely repeat his name. Another is Guanyin, in India a male figure but in East Asia the goddess of mercy, who intercedes for and protects those who are in trouble. In East Asia, Nirvana itself is sometimes fleshed out. Thus, the devout need not aspire to personal extinction but may hope instead to be reborn in the Western Paradise. For those who do not behave there is the chance of being reborn in hell—although the damnation, while it may endure for aeons, is no more eternal than anything else in this bitter sea. In ritual practice Buddhism and Daoism have taken over much from each other, and commonly the temples of each religion contain images of deities associated with the other.[23]

The most influential variety of East Asian Buddhism has been *Zen* (as it is usually called; this is the Japanese pronunciation—the Chinese term is *chan*). Zen emerged as a reaction against what some of the religious considered the superstitious excesses of popular Buddhism and the overly elaborate intellectual speculations of the educated. It shows traces of the incorporation of Daoist philosophical approaches into Buddhist thinking. For the Zen practitioner, scripture, prayer, or reason are all obstacles to enlightenment, manifestations of the illusory life in the red dust.[24] One must, rather, empty one's self of one's self by quiet sitting. Some popular Zen spin-offs, such as the tea ceremony in Japan and the martial arts in both China and Japan, show the marks of the Daoist concept of emptiness and nonaction, in ways reminiscent of Zhuangzi's parable of the butcher and his knife. Although Zen leads to detachment from the world, it does not imply abandoning the world. Enlightenment implies not just seeing through the vanity of our existence, but also seeing through the seeing through. Seeing our worldly duties in their true perspective, we are better able to meet them.[25]

---

23. For the flavor of Chinese Buddhism, the best source is perhaps the Ming dynasty comic allegory, *Journey to the West*. It details how a Tang dynasty monk fetched some of the sacred scripture from India, and how he was helped on his mission by his companions, including a monkey of brilliant if untamed intelligence and a pig of truly preternatural earthiness. The entire work has been translated by Anthony Yu (four volumes; University of Chicago Press, 1973), but the older abridged translation by Arthur Waley, under the title *Monkey*, (New York, 1943) remains more accessible.

24. This is perhaps more true in principle than in fact. Contemporary Zen monks, at any rate, do conduct ceremonies, study scripture, and perform works of mercy.

25. See on this Robert Pirsig, *Zen and the Art of Motorcycle Maintenance* (New York, 1974). This may be a little too 1970s for some people's taste, and its general spirit is closer to Mark Twain than any alleged wisdom of the East. Yet there is a valid point that one cannot fix motors or do much of anything else properly with a flustered, distracted, self-filled mind. Pirsig's tacit analogy, of course, is the traditional association of Zen with skills such as archery. These same techniques, I understand, are generally used in the training of competitive rifle target shooters.

Buddhism has not had the political influence of Confucianism. During the period of disunity some of the petty rulers sponsored Buddhism, but Confucians always resisted such support for both principled and political reasons. When a Tang emperor tried to bring from India as a relic one of the Buddha's finger bones, a famous Confucian statesman and writer scolded him for squandering taxpayers' money on a piece of the rotting carcass of a dead barbarian. With Daoism, Buddhism has sometimes figured as a rebel ideology, carrying a promise to make all things even, to turn heaven and earth upside down. The cult of Mitraya Buddha (known in China as Miluo), the Buddha of the future, was particularly potent here (although Mitraya is probably now better known in his tamed form: the fat, jolly, relaxed Smiling Buddha). For a time Buddhism was China's intellectual vanguard, and it has been enormously influential in Chinese and Japanese art, in both painting and literature. The Buddhist monk became, with the Daoist hermit, a symbol of withdrawal from both the responsibilities and vanities of the workaday world (symbolized by Confucianism). Buddhism provides the sense we sometimes find in Chinese lyric poetry of the sorrow of things, of the need to cherish our pleasures and joys as we find them, for they are insubstantial and are certain not to last.

Buddhism also permeates Chinese popular culture generally. Some analysts even postulate a distinct Buddhist-Daoist popular culture in opposition to the Confucian culture of the elite. These subcultures are at best abstractions and do not demarcate either intellectual or social divisions. Both are part of the mental and moral universe of the entire society. They interpenetrate: just as Confucianism has taken in Daoist and Buddhist elements, so Chinese Buddhism has become highly Confucian in its ethics. Yet if the differences are kept in perspective, they do tell us things about Chinese culture. The East Asian system is not monolithic; it contains tensions and even contradictions. A cultural analysis cannot be a mechanical generalization from philosophical or moral principles to the actual beliefs or behavior of persons. Culture provides the context and syntax of people's actions, and the sometimes contradictory ways in which they perceive the world.

Neo-Confucianism

By the end of the Han, Confucianism had lost much of its intellectual appeal. It was simply the official ideology, the value system promoted by the state and the morality one had to give verbal assent to if one wanted to hold state office. Advanced thought at the time was in Buddhism and variations on Daoism. By the end of the Tang, however, the educated had renewed their interest in Confucianism as a guide to personal and social action. Confucian thinkers worried about the decay of public morality (a recurring theme in China as well as the world at large) and the allegedly pernicious effects of Buddhism on public life. Some also had patriotic motives, a desire to show China had as respectable a system of thought as the barbaric Indians.

The major Confucian revival came during the Song dynasty (960–1279), which followed the Tang after a brief period of anarchy. The thought of this period is known in the West as neo-Confucianism (in China it is called Song Learning or the School of Principle). Confucian ethics comes to be embedded in philosophical categories rooted in Buddhism—although the content is often explicitly anti-Buddhist. A rough analogy might be the Catholic philosophy of the European Middle Ages, combining the revealed religion of the Bible with the philosophy of Aristotle. The greatest of the Song neo-Confucians was Zhu Xi (1130–1200), who brought together the various strands of neo-Confucianism into a general synthesis. Shortly after his death his interpretations became the state orthodoxy, a sort of textbook Confucianism used as a standard in evaluating answers to the state civil service examinations.[26]

In the neo-Confucian system the universe consists of *qi*, which can probably be rendered as substance or matter—or maybe even matter and energy, since qi has its own inherent dynamism and is active rather than passive. The original meaning of the term is breath or vapor. In some Daoist practice it refers to a kind of vital force (a type of Chinese physical exercise is known as *qi gong*, "qi work"; it helps us nourish our vital forces through controlled breathing). Mencius spoke of his "surging qi." The neo-Confucian usage combines these senses together with that of the stuff everything is made of.

We never see qi in general, matter as such. Rather, we see and know particular things. All matter is informed by *li*, which can be rendered as principle, reason, or pattern. This is not the same li that means ritual or propriety, but a different character whose original meaning is the veins in a piece of jade. In modern Chinese the word for reason is *daoli*, "way-pattern." Every particular thing is qi with a particular li. A dog is qi informed by the principle of dogness. All dogs share the same principle (although, not to labor this, each breed would presumably have its own principle as well); each dog is himself because his qi is not that of other dogs.

A general metaphysical and ethical assumption of neo-Confucianism, contrary to that of Buddhism, is that existence is real and that being is good—that is, everything that is, is good to the extent that it is, and evil is not an active force itself but is an absence or deficiency of being. The ultimate of being is Heaven (which is also the ultimate of nonbeing, a Buddhist-Daoist term the neo-Confucians kept, however uncomfortably; in the Confucian usage it does not mean absence of being, but, rather, that Heaven is no particular

---

26. The following explication can only give a flavor of a very elaborate system, looking at key terms and relationships. The relevant terms are sometimes used in different ways by different writers, or even by the same writer on different occasions—partly because of different interpretations but more, I think, because as in East Asian philosophy generally terms are understood less through set definitions than as relationships with other terms.

thing, and in that sense "no thing"). Heaven is the substance of the Dao, and the Dao is the principle of Heaven. Reflected in human beings, this principle is human nature (*xing*). Since our nature is what we receive directly from Heaven, it must, as Mencius says, be good.

Another pair of concepts is *ti* and *yong*, structure and function, what a thing is and what a thing does. The function of Heaven is the Mandate (*ming*). This is the word used for the emperor's ground of legitimacy, but that usage is only one instance of a more general concept. Ming also means the life of an individual; it also means fate or destiny—that which is given in our lives, over which we have no control (although Confucianism is not fatalistic—it is up to us to make what we can of what we are given). Most generally, it is the order of Heaven in the universe: both what Heaven orders, decrees, and also the source of regularity and meaning. On the human level, our nature functions through our heart or mind (*xin*—the Chinese term refers to both or either). Through our mind we perceive the order of Heaven and also experience those feelings that underlie our moral experience.

Since principle operates through qi, our perception of it is sometimes clouded. We are swayed by private passions, preferring what seems to be our own personal good to the objective good. The central ethical concept in neo-Confucianism is selflessness. There may be a Buddhist inspiration behind this, although the interpretation is not quite Buddhist. To be selfless is to act in accord with the order of Heaven rather than to try to impose our personal desires; it is not, with the Buddhists, to renounce the world, but to act according to nature. There is nothing unnatural, for example, in wanting to eat when hungry or even to want to eat food that tastes good. But there is nothing natural about gluttony or being overly particular about what we will or will not eat. Selflessness does not mean we deny our appetites, but only that we satisfy them in the appropriate way.

A certain political conservatism—more, perhaps, a pessimism about politics—is related to the neo-Confucian ethical system. A generation before, Zhu Xi political reformers had tried to bring about a more nearly perfect Confucian society by increasing the power of the government bureaucracy. The reforms were intended to benefit the poor and were opposed by the rich and powerful. In the end, however, the reforms hurt the poor as well as the rich and led to general confusion and inefficiency. The argument over the reforms turned partly on the question of how Confucianism should be implemented, and in the aftermath the conservatives seemed vindicated. Thereafter, perhaps until modern times, there was a certain skepticism about the ability of politics to achieve positive good, however necessary it may be to prevent evil. Zhu Xi and other neo-Confucians take for granted the gentleman's sense of social and political responsibility, but stress the internal cultivation necessary to become a gentleman rather than the kind of social order the gentleman should seek to produce. Zhu Xi agrees government should rest on virtue, but also acknowledges that actual rule, at least since the Qin, has been based on force. Unlike the Qin, the Han and Tang were legitimate and not purely coercive, but even they relied ultimately on power. This implies, probably, that in these later days government must be imperfect; the imperfection, since it is general, cannot by itself be an excuse for disobedience. But neither is politics an instrument for achieving the good society, and political expediency cannot be a standard of morality.

Moral cultivation entails an increased awareness of the inner principle of things. Principle can be observed only through matter and the operations of matter, however. For Zhu Xi, then, the path of cultivation is through the "investigation of things." This may imply a certain scientific spirit. Zhu Xi did not really mean experiments to discover natural laws, however; the things worth investigating are human things, and the term implies the study of the classics, of history, and of the ways of government.

Although Zhu Xi's interpretations became the official standard, his was not the only neo-Confucian system. In the Ming dynasty Wang Yangming (1472–1529) developed something like a "Zen" Confucianism. He became disenchanted with Zhu Xi's investigation of things, although, by his own account, he may not have approached it in the most constructive spirit (he says he spent a whole day investigating bamboo—that is, staring at a stand of bamboo plants—and knew no more at the end than at the beginning). He decided instead that truth is not something external to us. The principle of Heaven is embodied in human nature and operates through the mind. The way to grasp the principle of Heaven, then, is in the cultivation of the mind. He uses a metaphor of Mencius's: the mind is a mirror that may become tarnished; we must, therefore, constantly polish the mirror. One implication of Wang's view is the identity of knowledge and action. To know something is not merely to grasp it intellectually but to be able to act upon it. We know love and justice not when we are able to define them and discuss them abstractly, but when we behave in a loving and just manner. Wang emphasized as well Mencius's concept of human equality. We all share the same human nature, but become different through experience: "The streets are full of sages."

Wang's ideas had a wide influence despite their lack of official sanction. Japanese *samurai* liked his emphasis on action. For the same reason early Chinese revolutionaries like Sun Yat-sen and Chiang Kai-shek found his thought attractive. His thinking also has affinities with the Marxian doctrine of the unity of theory and practice, a key concept for Chairman Mao.

During Wang's lifetime China was undergoing economic and social change. Wealth was becoming more widely distributed, trade was increasing, cities were growing. We might speculate that Wang's thought could have provided a philosophical basis for a spontaneous Chinese modernization (although one that would probably have been quite different from the process in the West). Wang stressed the ability of every mind to perceive the truth contained within itself, and there was a potential break here with the classicism and conservatism of the Zhu Xi orthodoxy. Wang's followers could be quite antiauthoritarian. Some advocated the education of women. Some of the more radical argued that if truth inheres to the mind, there is no need for external guidance from any source—not teachers, nor Zhu Xi, nor the classics, nor Confucius himself. All we need to do is follow our heart's desire.

If there is a relationship between systems of thinking and modernization, however, it is probably a complicated and indirect one. Whether or not the Wang Yangming style encouraged modernization, it is common to assert that the Zhu Xi style discouraged it. Yet it may be that there is nothing inherently antimodern in Zhu Xi, either. The system may have discouraged modernization not because of its content but because it was a state-sponsored orthodoxy. Since mastery of Zhu Xi led to wealth and power, there was no social incentive to take anything else seriously. Perhaps any system of thought—logical positivism, Marxism, existentialism, Quakerism, Daoism—would have similar conservative consequences if it served a similar function.

Wang's thought was fashionable among the advanced intelligentsia during the last decades of the Ming. In those same years political incompetence and corruption led first to popular rebellion and, in 1644, to a new dynasty ruled by the conquering Manchus. Critics at that time and later did not believe Wang's ideas encouraged social reform but, rather, they were one more symptom of general decadence. Instead of concerning themselves with serious social and political problems, the critics claimed, Wang's devotees spent their time cultivating their minds—or, as we might say, contemplating their navels—in self-indulgent disregard for morals, tradition, and the good opinion of their fellows.

During the Qing dynasty (as the Manchu system was called) Zhu Xi continued to set the official standard. The more creative Confucian thought was a reaction against the whole neo-Confucian metaphysical elaboration, whether by Zhu or Wang. A typical line of argument was that since principle is not directly observable and, in any case, operates only through matter, it is an unnecessary complication; it is sufficient to know about qi and the changes in qi. Instead of the neo-Confucian Song learning, the more radical Qing thinkers hoped to recover the Han learning—that of the time of the earliest existing texts. The scholars developed a scientific methodology for recovering the authentic versions of the classics (although this had also been one of Zhu Xi's interests as well), inadvertently preparing the way for the critical treatment of the entire Confucian tradition in the modern and contemporary periods.

Japanese Adaptations

Most of this long chapter is devoted to China: the "higher culture" of both countries is that of China, and the matters discussed so far are the heritage of both. Yet Japan did not mechanically appropriate Chinese ideas, and Japan also reformulated some of its native culture on the basis of the Chinese influence.

Shinto

Shinto is Japan's folk religion. Many Japanese thinkers have considered it to represent the essence of Japan. Shinto may in fact be so much a part of what is meant by being Japanese that there is no real Japanese name for it. Until Japan's exposure to China, Shinto was not a religion, but simply religion itself. The word is Chinese-Japanese. *Shin* (in Mandarin, *shen*) means god or spirit or sacred; *to* is dao, as in Daoism.[27] Shinto is the sacred way, the way of the gods.

Shinto centers on the worship or veneration of the *kami*, the sacred or divine (kami is the native Japanese pronunciation of *shin*). The kami is generally an object or force of nature—mountains, trees, streams, the ocean. The kami is anything especially powerful, beautiful, good, perhaps even evil. People may be kami—the emperor, of course, but other great ones as well, including (for you, anyway) your parents.

Like Chinese Daoism, as a popular cult Shinto has become intermingled with Buddhism. Shinto shrines more or less resemble Buddhist temples and contain Buddhist images. Organizationally and in their clergy the religions remain distinct but (with some exceptions) neither makes exclusive claim to the devotion of ordinary people. Whether one worships in a Buddhist or Shinto manner depends on circumstances and objectives rather than creed or conscience. The Shinto wedding ceremony is commonly held to be the superior, but the Buddhists give a better funeral. In the early twentieth century, even though Shinto was the official state cult, the official registry of births and deaths was kept, as it traditionally had been, by local Buddhist temples.

Shinto legends detail the origins of the Japanese islands and people. Japan, the "root of the sun," is the pearl of creation, the land especially favored by the gods. The Japanese imperial line is descended in unbroken succession from time immemorial from the sun goddess herself. Shinto has been a source of symbolism and identity when the Japanese people (or individuals among them) wished to distinguish themselves from others—first from the Chinese, later from Westerners. Chinese identity was cultural: to be Chinese meant to be civilized. The Japanese knew their civilization came from China, but they were never politically subject to China. It was perhaps intuitively easier for them to think of themselves as a nation among others (to be sure, a particularly excellent one), thereby easing the adaptation to the nineteenth-century world order. Shinto provided a ready-made definition of national identity.

We tend to associate religion with a set of beliefs—a creed—and with a moral system. Shinto has neither. There is no specific set of Shinto beliefs, nor does it imply any specific notions of right and wrong. Shinto ritual

---

27. The term also appears in other familiar Japanese terms: *bushido*, the way of the warrior; *judo*, the gentle way.

centers on cleansing and purification (there is probably some deep connection here with the ancient Japanese custom of daily hot baths), and Shinto worship may be more an aesthetic experience than anything else. This lack of moral content may encourage a certain flexibility in Japanese culture, since Shinto is consistent with whatever moral code that culture might adopt.

The closest approach to a Shinto morality is Japanese patriotism—an attachment to and identification with the land, people, and traditions of Japan. This has sometimes taken the form of nationalism, an exaltation of Japan above other nations and a desire for its glory even at the expense of others. Japanese patriotism in the past centered on the role of the emperor. The emperor, remember, is kami, divine. He is sacred and inviolable, heir to the lineage that has ruled Japan from time immemorial, descended directly from the sun goddess. China also had something like a sacred emperor, but the Son of Heaven was sacred by courtesy, as it were. He held the Mandate because in Heaven's eyes he was doing a good job. The Japanese emperor is unconditionally sacred, sacred by his very being.

From rather early times—from at the latest A.D. 700 or so—Japanese emperors have not wielded actual power. Political control in Japan gravitated first to strong families at court and later to various rural warlords. From the beginning, however, there was a kind of cultural decision—perhaps influenced by Shinto but also contributing to it—that the imperial institution and the imperial family would be left in place. A political science rule of thumb is that in any system, no matter how despotic or arbitrary, there cannot long be a separation of power and responsibility. If the emperor was so "inviolable" that he could not be held accountable for his actions, there was a political need to be sure that the emperor could not take any actions that mattered.[28] At one point in history political power did revert to the Japanese imperial family, but at that time the reigning emperors would be little boys. Upon maturity the emperor would abdicate in favor of his infant son and retire—and from retirement (and sometimes in conjunction with his father and grandfather) exercise actual power.

The Japanese concept of an emperor who is literally divine seems less modern than the Chinese notion of an emperor responsible to the people (through the mediation of Heaven). The Japanese way, however, may be more hospitable to *modernization*. The Chinese ruler holds his position by his virtue. The measure of his virtue is his success in preserving Confucian society, which must mean in part his success in meeting the needs and desires of a Confucian elite. The Chinese throne had a difficult time promoting those aspects of modernity adverse to the dominant Confucian interests, and could do so only at the risk of some legitimacy. The Japanese emperor, however, is legitimate in

---

28. As the English say, the Queen can do no wrong. Neither can she do anything right: political responsibility is carried by the Queen's ministers, not by the Queen herself.

his own person, and does not depend upon any particular social or political order. The emperor could rule directly or be the front for powerful court or warlord families; in the nineteenth and early twentieth centuries he could be the head of state in a conservative constitutional monarchy; since 1945 he can be a "symbol of the state" in a democratic system. Imperial continuity is an assurance that no matter how much Japan changes, Japan remains Japan.

Japanese Confucianism

At its most basic the Japanese value system is different from that of the Chinese. Chinese morality is founded on the family, with the most important social tie being that of parent and child. The Japanese system is perhaps more military or "tribal," with the primary tie being that between leader and follower. Confucianism stresses particular relationships, but it is also a universal moral code. Japanese ethics are more radically situational than Chinese, with proper behavior varying according to the relative status and connections. This is reflected even in the language, where usage differs according to the relative ages, social standing, and sex of the speaker and spoken to, as well as according to their relative closeness to each other. The particularistic features of Confucianism made it suitable for adaptation to Japan, but to a certain degree Confucian terms are applied to relationships carrying a different meaning from those in China.

An example is the paired concepts of loyalty and filial piety (*zhong* and *xiao* in Chinese, *chu* and *ko* in Japanese). They are related: both are the duties we owe our superiors. Loyalty is our duty to our ruler, and filial piety is our duty to our parents. In China there is also a tension and sometimes even a contradiction between them. For example, the ruler may demand our service as a soldier, and this may require us to leave our aged parents with no way to support themselves. The general Chinese prejudice (for each instance must be decided on its own merits) is that our duty to our parents outweighs that to the ruler. In Japan, on one level loyalty takes precedence over filial piety, but, more deeply, the Japanese do not acknowledge the tension: one is a filial child only if one gives loyal service to one's superior. In China loyalty implies acting in the ruler's best interest, not necessarily in obeying the ruler's commands.[29] In Japan loyalty is expressed primarily in unquestioning obedience and implies total selfless devotion to one's overlord.[30]

---

29. Thus, the contemporary Chinese Marxian dissident Liu Binyan wrote an essay, "The Second Kind of Loyalty," describing how one hero who thought of himself as a good communist stood against the party for the sake of what the party was supposed to stand for.

30. Michio Morishima, *Why Has Japan "Succeeded"? Western Technology and the Japanese Ethos* (Cambridge University Press, 1982).

The author Michio Morishima compares Chinese and Japanese rankings of various Confucian virtues. A typical Chinese ranking might run: love (ren), justice, propriety (li—ritual), wisdom, sincerity. The twentieth-century Nationalist leader Chiang Kai-shek once spoke of wisdom, sincerity, love, courage, and strictness (with oneself). The 1889 Japanese imperial rescript on education, however, ranks: loyalty, propriety, courage, sincerity, frugality. In general, Morishima says, the Japanese neglect ren, love.[31] Japanese Confucianism stresses reciprocity less than Chinese, putting more weight on unconditional subordination to the superior.

Japanese Confucianism is another expression of Japanese cultural flexibility. Taken in itself Confucianism is a guide to personal morality and life in society. In China it became overwhelmingly identified with public office and the quest for office, the examination system and the social and political elite produced by that system. China was a relatively open society without hereditary status distinctions. A person could in principle and often enough in fact improve his position by passing the exams, and the greatest social prestige as well as access to wealth and power were enjoyed by those who had achieved the academic degrees conferred by success in the exams. Confucianism's function as the route to success in life tended to overwhelm Confucian content.

Japan in early modern (or late traditional) times was a closed society, with a rigid social hierarchy and hereditary class distinctions. If you were born into a family of farmers, soldiers, workers, or merchants, that is what you would remain, as would your children. You might, of course, improve your lot by being a good farmer, soldier, worker, or merchant—and to the extent that Confucianism might help you do so (by inculcating a proper attitude perhaps) there may have been an incentive in Japan to apply Confucianism more broadly and in some ways even more seriously.

Chinese Confucianism is civilian in tone, even pacifistic. The Japanese cult of *bushido* (the way of the warrior—an analog in Japan of the Western cult of chivalry) is a military adaptation of Confucianism, albeit strongly infused with the more basic Japanese spirit (including a romanticization of violent death that Chinese Confucians would find irrational and puzzling). In the 1700s there were also Confucian academies established to train the sons of merchants, where students would learn that the accumulation of wealth had to be justified by service to the country, society, and humanity.[32]

This may give a clue to the solution of a paradox. Observers used to argue that Confucian values stood in the way of modernization in China, but more recent experience shows that Confucian societies—not just Japan, but also Korea and Chinese societies or communities outside the rule of the central

---

31. *Ibid.*, p. 6.
32. Tetsuo Najita, *Visions of Virtue in Tokugawa Japan* (University of Chicago Press, 1987).

Chinese state—modernize quite successfully. There is perhaps nothing inherently antimodern in Confucianism as such. The crucial element may be the social and political functions of Confucianism, and how those functions are exercised.

Later Shinto

Shinto lost whatever intellectual appeal it may have had after the introduction of Confucianism and Buddhism. Yet the Japanese were always aware that while their higher culture was patterned on that of China, they were not part of the Chinese system. In the 1200s China was ruled by the Mongol Khans, whose ambitions extended to the whole wide world. The emperor Khubilai Khan twice attempted to invade Japan, and each time his armada was sunk by providential typhoons—the first divine winds (*shimpu* or *kamikaze*), evidence that Japan enjoyed the special protection of the gods.

In the 1700s there was an intellectual revival of Shinto, directed toward purging Japan of Chinese influence. The Shinto scholar Motoori Nobinaga (1730–1801) argued that while Confucius, the classics, the sages, and so on might be just the thing for the benighted Chinese, they were superfluous in Japan, where people were naturally good and had no need to be instructed in morality (he seems not to have reflected that he had absorbed these notions from Mencius along with his mother's milk, and probably through the influence of Wang Yangming). Motoori convincingly refuted those who doubted the literal truth of the Shinto legends: "Some may say that the records are the fabrications of later sovereigns, but who would fabricate such shallow-sounding, incredible things? This is a point you should reflect upon seriously."[33]

The Shinto revival had a domestic political significance. Japan was then ruled by the Tokugawa family, whose head had the title of *shogun*, general. Tokugawa ideology was based upon Zhu Xi Confucianism, in part because that system lends itself to an easy misconstruction to the effect that the current social or political order is part of the natural order of the universe. Also, the Tokugawa lacked the emperor's sacred status and so had to base their legitimacy on something like the Mandate of Heaven, a claim to superior ability or virtue. Some of the Tokugawa's court philosophers were even prepared to argue that the emperor himself was accountable to Heaven.[34] The shoguns themselves would not go that far, but accepted the emperor's sacredness and his ultimate (and irrelevant) authority. Shinto became, then, a relatively safe

33. *Sources of the Japanese Tradition*, Vol. II, compiled by Ryunake Tsunoda, Wm. Theodore deBary, and Donald Keene (Columbia University Press, 1988), p. 19.

34. Kate Waldman Nakai, *Shogunal Politics: Arai Hokusaki and the Premise of Tokugawa Rule* (Harvard University Press, 1988), p. 255.

way of dissenting against Tokugawa rule, and over the long term its revival helped undermine Tokugawa legitimacy.

The Tokugawa regime was overthrown in 1868 by a coalition of young samurai (warriors) who "restored" direct imperial rule. In fact they established a conservative, authoritarian modern state in the form of a constitutional monarchy. The concentration of power in the emperor meant a strong executive and a free hand for those in control of the institutions of the state. Shinto, with a pronounced emphasis on the divinity and inviolability of the emperor, became the official state religion. For the founders the state religion served an overtly instrumental function: it symbolized basic continuity in a world of radical change. In the 1930s, however, this state Shinto became part of a fascist-type extreme nationalism among elements of the military, who led Japan into repression at home and reckless adventure abroad.

After its defeat in 1945 Japan came under American military occupation. The Occupation authorities were convinced that Japanese traditional culture was the cause of the country's domestic and foreign misbehavior, and set out to remake that culture. The emperor prudently renounced his divinity, although some with an ear for nuance claim that he did it in such a way as to deny himself attributes no one ever claimed he had—as if, say, he were denying that he could fly or walk through walls. The Shinto religion was disestablished and is not allowed to receive state support.

As Japan regained national self-confidence the public role of Shinto became a matter of controversy. The funeral of the Showa emperor in 1989 and the enthronement of his son, the Heisei emperor in 1991, are unalterably affairs of state and also unalterably involved with Shinto ritual. Part of the enthronement ceremony requires the new emperor to hold a solitary midnight vigil, in the course of which he acquires his divinity. The solution was to divide the ceremonies, naming those parts of them centering on Shinto to be private observances, not public acts. A more lasting problem is how to honor Japan's war dead. The souls of all Japanese soldiers killed in battle reside in the Yasukuni shrine in Tokyo, a Shinto temple. Its function is analogous to that of Arlington National Cemetery in the United States. Because of its Shinto associations, however, there is always controversy about how ministers of state should treat it. The usual practice is for a cabinet minister to pay homage to the dead, but to say he is doing so in his personal rather than official capacity. This kind of public homage frequently becomes a matter of diplomatic controversy as well, since Japan's Asian neighbors see in it reflections of state Shinto and associate state Shinto with Japanese aggression and a revival of militarism. These controversies over Shinto do not engage much of the interest or attention of ordinary Japanese. They are important symbolically, however, as an indication of the division between those whose vision of modernity is secular and universalistic and those who credit Japan's wealth and power to its cultural traditions and believe that Japan must publicly assert its pride in those traditions.

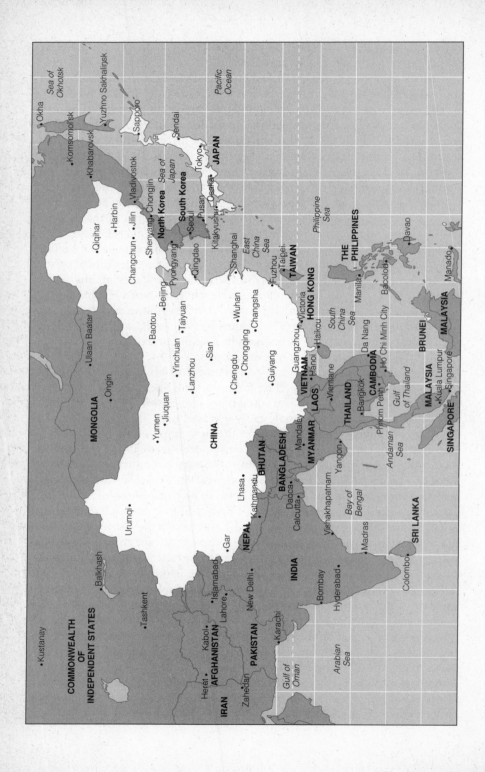

Intellectual background, along with geography, provides the context for East Asian politics. This chapter looks at the actual social and political structures in the advanced agrarian societies of China and Japan prior to their contact with the modern industrial West.

Chinese Society

Traditional China was a society of small peasant landholders, with the tax on land providing the financial foundation of the state.[1] This peasant society was ruled by an educated bureaucracy not based on heredity or, strictly considered, wealth. The peasant landholders did not all have the same economic status, and there were always many peasants who had no land of their own but had to rent it (on better or worse terms) from others. Economically more secure than these landless were peasants who owned their land but not enough of it to survive and feed their families; to supplement their own holdings they would have to rent additional land from someone who had a surplus. Chinese peasants typically live in villages rather than on isolated farms, as is common in the United States. The Chinese village, however,

---

1. Ray Huang, *China: A Macrohistory* (Armonk, 1988), p. 41.

is not normally a highly organized unit. The main unit in society is the family, with family membership (normally) determined by the male line. In some parts of China large extended families, usually called clans, have been quite powerful, but historically most Chinese families meant the mother, father, little children, married sons and their wives and children, and unmarried daughters. The ideal was to have four generations living under one roof, but this was rarely attained. Ordinarily family property was divided among the children after the death of the parents. The oldest son might become family head for ceremonial purposes, but for practical purposes the family would be broken up. Daughters became upon marriage ritually part of their husband's family, although they kept, of course, ties of sentiment with their own parents and siblings. The village itself was a collection of families or households. Villagers would get along or not as neighbors, where necessary working out common problems, such as the conservation of irrigation water and priorities for its use. The lack of strong social ties within villages as such may be one reason for the recent failure of collectivized agriculture in China. By contrast, the Japanese village is much more of a social unit. In China, cohesion among unrelated neighbors may come about through cooperation on set tasks, such as upkeep of a local temple whose resident deity looks after the local area.

Social and political connections within and beyond the family are summed up in the term *guanxi*, which simply means relationship; it refers to an affinity between two or more persons based on some shared attribute. People from the same village have guanxi with each other, especially when they are away from home. The same is true, to a lesser degree, for people from the same province when outside that province. Even the same surname can, in a pinch, serve as a guanxi base. Some guanxi is hierarchical—that between a landlord and a tenant, or between a teacher and a pupil; some of it is among equals, as among schoolmates. The general idea is that if two people have some basis, however tenuous, for a relationship, either may make demands upon the other, and, true to Confucian ethics, the one who has received a favor is morally bound to do favors in return.

Guanxi is sometimes taken to be a general explanation for patterns of association among Chinese. It does not explain much in *particular*, however, since there are innumerable bases for guanxi and there is no automatic way to tell which will operate in a particular circumstance. Guanxi is activated, as it were, by *ganqing*, "feelings." In general, ganqing is greater for closer connections—and here it must be made plain that ganqing need not refer to actual feelings, but to an idealized view of what the feelings should be. You are more bound to do the bidding of your brother, say, than of a schoolmate, even if you should happen to like your brother less. Ganqing may be deliberately cultivated: you may seek the favor of a superior or show concern for inferiors, or court the friendship of someone in an influential position. This may be motivated by genuine attachment, or by calculation.

This may sound much like the way things work anywhere in the world. The point is that in Chinese culture common action, for whatever "real" reasons, is easier to achieve if it can be presented as the outgrowth of a genuine personal connection backed by genuine mutual sympathy—a reflection, probably, of the Confucian view of the way in which human beings should relate to each other. In their actual operations, guanxi and ganqing often smack of corruption, the use of human relationships for your own selfish purposes—although this would be a perversion or malformation of Confucian values, not their expression. Confucianism proper, as much as Legalism, holds that public obligations override private ones,[2] although Confucians define public more in social than in political terms. Confucian morality does stress the particular and specific rather than the general or abstract, and Confucianism is strong on reciprocity: if I do something for you, you are morally (not legally) bound to do something for me. In fact, Confucius articulated his version of the Golden Rule (do not do to others what you don't want done to yourself) as a definition of reciprocity. Tensions surrounding the concept, or abuses of it, may result in corruption. If I am a public official and do for you what you have a right to expect under the laws, I might act as if I'm doing you a special favor (and expect favors in return). Or, if it turns out we have some kind of "relationship" and you are solicitous enough of my "feelings," I might do for you what I have no right to do for anyone.

The structures and institutions of Chinese government, whether Legalist, Confucian, Nationalist, or Communist, have been designed deliberately to counteract this cultural tendency. Yet these personalistic connections have been a perennial part of informal Chinese politics, whether at the village or national level. Chinese popular interpretations of politics (as found, for example, in Hong Kong magazines giving the inside story of what's going on in Peking or Taipei) have the liveliness, tone, and perhaps accuracy of Hollywood gossip, focusing on shifting personal alliances and rivalries. In contrast, Western interpretations tend to look at policies, principles, ideology, bureaucratic structures, class relations, and so on. Reducing politics to personal rivalries is no doubt oversimplification but may sometimes be more to the point than the fancier Western visions.

Guanxi does not just imply corruption. It may also seem to imply that the weak or the poorly connected will be at an even greater than normal disadvantage. This is not necessarily the case, however. The working of guanxi may mean instead that anyone, however poor or friendless, has a claim to the attention and possibly the help of someone, as long as some objective relationship can be found. Chinese are as quick as anyone to see the disadvantages of guanxi as a social institution, but they also may miss it in its absence. American society certainly falls short of its own ideals, but relatively speaking the United States

---

2. Remember, however, that in Confucianism, obligations to parents are morally superior to those to the ruler or the state. This would probably not entail doing an active injustice to someone else in order to benefit one's parents, but it would mean shielding, if necessary, one's parents from the demands of strict legal justice.

operates according to impersonal, universal rules. Chinese visitors sometimes find American society to be impersonal to the point of cold indifference. Americans, they say, are very friendly to strangers, but this friendliness is superficial, and at bottom Americans do not really care. Friendliness may not translate into support, help, or protection.

Guanxi is part of the "micro" workings of the culture, that part of the culture that has perhaps changed least over the centuries. The larger social institutions have certainly changed much more, although, even there, there may be continuities under the surface. Marxian analysis usually takes landlords to be the ruling class. In traditional China most of the social and political elite probably were landlords of one sort or another, but most landlords were not part of the social and political elite. Typically the road to status was more through education than wealth. Education in its turn could give a person (or family) some access to political power or influence, and access to political power was the surest way to acquire and safeguard wealth.

Unlike many other traditional societies, including those of western Europe and Japan, China had no important hereditary elite.[3] From Qin times, China has been a bureaucratic society, ruled by officials serving at the pleasure of the ruler. The bureaucracy was recruited from the social elite, and the social elite was formed by civil service examinations open in principle, at least since Tang times, to anyone. A hereditary nobility often limits the power of the central ruler, since nobility carries a prestige and authority of its own, independent of the power of the king. In western Europe, kings fought for centuries to curb the power of the nobles; bureaucracy, recruited from the clergy and from among educated commoners, was one of the king's weapons in this fight. This was also one of the functions of bureaucracy in Chinese Legalist thought. The post-Qin bureaucracy, however, was recruited from among persons acquainted with Confucian principles, and actual practice had to make concessions to those principles. Bureaucracy came to carry some of the prestige of nobility.

Chinese society obviously did not remain unchanged for 2,000 years. There was a general tendency toward a more nearly equal distribution of wealth (never, of course, reaching anything like absolute equality) and toward greater centralization of state power in the throne. The Han founder, despite his Legalist predilections, awarded his major followers large grants of land, and big landholdings remained a feature of Han society. Han officials were almost universally recruited from this big landholding stratum, although they also had to show some knowledge of Confucianism. Sometimes

---

3. As always, there are exceptions. The ruling family, within several degrees of relationship, was a hereditary aristocracy, although aristocratic rank did not always imply any political influence. Sometimes emperors would honor someone by granting hereditary titles (which would give privileges but not formal authority), the titles lapsing after the passing of two or more generations.

the landlords were wealthy enough to maintain large numbers of "guests," that is, small private armies. In outward form the Han elite was much like a hereditary aristocracy, except that it did not constitute a distinct social order. In Tang and Song times (618–1279) family background remained an element in determining elite status, but examinations were increasingly important. By Ming and Qing times, from 1366 on, examinations were the major determinant of status.

The examination system had several layers, with tests given at the county, province, and central levels. To be eligible for the higher levels a candidate had to first pass the lower exams, and the attrition rate increased drastically at each level. Perhaps 10 percent of those who took the county-level exam would pass, but maybe only 2 or 3 percent of those taking the tests would pass at the provincial and central levels. Only those who passed at the central level were normally eligible for public office, but those who passed at any level were part of a recognized social elite. The examinations themselves were a Confucian concession to Legalist reality: Confucianism holds that authority should come from virtue, but virtue is notoriously hard to measure on a large scale in an objective manner. The next best thing, then, was to test people on their ability to discourse on virtue. Question topics were taken from the Confucian classics. They might concern arcane matters of textual analysis, although frequently the candidate would be asked to apply a particular passage in the classics to a problem of current public concern. In some periods the candidates would also be tested on their ability to compose poetry.

There were always many more candidates than could be permitted to pass, and since all the candidates had prepared themselves in about the same way and to the same degree, the problem for the examiner was to find reasons to fail them. These were not hard to come by: a single miswritten character would suffice. In later centuries the examination essays had to be written in a set "eight-legged" format: the argument had to be developed in eight paragraphs, each with its own set function in the overall structure of the essay, with rules on the exact number of characters allowed in each paragraph. Any deviation from the formula would be cause for failure. The eight-legged essay has become a proverbial symbol of brainless, stilted, boring writing. The format, taken in itself, was possibly a good discipline for developing a theme in a logical, concise manner. But it became an end in itself, no doubt stifling creativity and originality.

A Legalist feature of the examinations was the manner of their administration. The examiners took great precautions, of course, to prevent cheating, but also to prevent any bias or partiality in the grading. Thus, professional scribes would recopy each answer, with the graders seeing only the copy (on the off-chance that a grader might be familiar with a candidate's handwriting). Although the tests were administered and graded impartially, after you had passed you had formed a personal relationship with the official who had graded you—you had become, in effect, his client; you had to honor him as a teacher, and he could call on you for favors.

The perennial Chinese criticism of the exam system was that it did not accomplish its objective, the selection of the able to public office. In principle the exams measured virtue, but in practice they measured ability to write about virtue. The study of the Confucian classics may possibly have led to moral cultivation, but the system rewarded study of the classics less than study of Zhu Xi's interpretations of the classics, or others' simplifications of Zhu Xi. Booksellers found it profitable to collect examples of successful eight-legged essays and print them up as study aids. Students were motivated to put more effort into studying model eight-legged essays and practicing their own than into giving thought to the substance of what they were supposed to be learning. When all is said, the exams may have measured nothing except the ability to pass the exams. This, however, is probably a danger inherent in any attempt to get an objective measure of merit. Despite its defects and abuses, the Chinese system in its time was among the more rational ways of allocating political authority.

Only a few examination passers could hold public office. The incentive for so many to make the effort was that passing even the lowest level conferred status. The Chinese social elite is often called in English the gentry, a translation of *shenshi*. The term is a vague one, and there may never have been an overly precise meaning to it; a frequent usage, however, was to apply it to all who had passed an examination, with the status spilling over to the close relatives of examination passers. The gentry constituted the elite of their home areas. They were exempt from physical punishment[4] and from certain kinds of taxes. Since those who had failed an examination could keep on trying, the government gave a modest stipend to persons who had passed the lowest level, to allow them leisure to keep up with their studies.[5] The gentry enjoyed guaranteed access to local officialdom, and officials had to consult with the gentry on local projects and other matters of local interest.

The Chinese liked to think that the examination system allowed for equality of opportunity—any peasant boy could hope, with brains, hard work, and luck, to grow up to be prime minister. This was not completely false, but the evidence indicates fairly low levels of actual social mobility. Most examination passers came themselves from gentry families, although over the generations new families would enter the gentry and old families would drop out. On the whole the examination system, like education systems generally, favored the wealthy.

Granting this, education remained more nearly decisive than wealth as such in determining status. Since family property was divided evenly among all the heirs, families had a difficult time preserving large fortunes over

---

4. If they were guilty of a crime they first had to be deprived of their gentry status before punishment could be applied.

5. To maintain gentry status, those who had passed only the lowest-level examinations had to take an easy retest every few years.

several generations. Rich families could sometimes get around the inheritance customs by turning lands over to an ancestral temple—setting up what amounted to a family corporation run by the more influential members of the family. The state gave only poor protection to property, and wealth became most secure when backed by the kind of access to political authority that came from gentry status. This same success was itself a source of wealth. The Qing dynasty satirical novel *The Scholars* must certainly exaggerate, but one chapter tells how an old scholar, after years and years of failure in the examinations, finally does pass; he becomes rich overnight as friends, neighbors, relatives, and casual acquaintances flock to bestow presents on him, seeking his goodwill.

China did not only lack a hereditary nobility; it was also without another familiar feature of the early modern West, an independent urban middle class or bourgeoisie. Here, too, however, the situation is complicated. The Western cities were outside the feudal system and provided the foundation for the commercial and industrial growth that produced modern society. The lack of such a bourgeoisie would help explain why China failed to modernize. The older Western view of China, exemplified in the work of the great German sociologist Max Weber,[6] treats Chinese cities as primarily administrative centers, with commercial activity too much under the disdainful gaze of Confucian bureaucrats to achieve real vitality. More recent scholarship shows (at least for the cases studied) that not only did commerce flourish in "late imperial China" (the Qing dynasty and perhaps the Ming) but also merchants were active in regulating their own affairs and in general civic concerns, independently of the official state structure.[7] Confucianism looks down upon a life devoted to profit and often treats mercantile life as exactly that; yet the early Confucian texts are not particularly disdainful of commerce as such, and at least since Song times there has been much overlap between gentry and merchant families, with both groups sharing a common way of life. Some writers, Marxists but also others, speculate about the "sprouts of capitalism" in Chinese society, sprouts unhappily stamped into the dirt by Western imperialism.

Yet China did not have a bourgeoisie in a Western sense—and it is probably an example of ethnocentrism to think that China should have evolved anything like Western capitalism or modernization in the Western form. The difference is not so much in the character of economic activity in China as in the more general social and political environment.

China's relatively open society, itself seemingly modern, may have inhibited the kind of "development" we associate with the West. The examination system allowed in principle and occasionally in fact for social mobility, and

---

6. Max Weber, *The Religion of China: Confucianism and Taoism* (New York, 1968).

7. William T. Rowe, *Hankow: Commerce and Society in a Chinese City, 1796–1889* (Stanford University Press, 1984), and *Hankow: Conflict and Community in a Chinese City, 1796–1895* (Stanford University Press, 1989).

in any case it held out a practical hope for mobility. Rapid changes of status over one person's lifetime were probably quite rare, but change could take place over generations. A peasant, say, might have some surplus from farming, and invest it in setting up a pawnshop or in buying knickknacks to resell door-to-door. By his death his sons might inherit a small but thriving business, which might expand over the next generation. The family would reinvest in the business, of course, but much of the profit would be diverted to the purchase of land, a generally more secure way to hold wealth. The sons of the third or fourth generation would be encouraged to study for the examinations, both because that is where the glory was and because gentry status would really secure the family fortune. Later generations growing up in luxury and perhaps in a snobby, bookish atmosphere might lose any business sense and find the fortune dissipated, particularly if the family's status was not reinforced by sufficiently frequent success in the examinations.[8]

This kind of open society should also be a stable one. Limited economic opportunity and the exams gave hope to those of ability or drive who were unhappy with their station in life, and in ordinary times there was a better chance of improving your lot within the system than by fighting against it. The system may, in fact, have been too stable for its own good. Certainly much talent that otherwise might have contributed to art, literature, science, or business was diverted into the exams. The West has had a stereotype of a stagnant China: "Better a decade of Europe than a cycle of Cathay." While inaccurate, there may be a germ of truth in the caricature. Contemporary Chinese reformers—for example, the authors of "River Elegy"—fault what they take to be stagnation: this was a society that could not change. One provocative analysis places Ming and Qing China in a "high level equilibrium trap." The country was about as rich as an agrarian society could be; with a high standard of living, plentiful human labor, and weak foreign enemies, there was no incentive to push into industrialization.[9]

It is also interesting to speculate that late traditional China was involved, somehow, in some kind of moral crisis. Possible evidence of this would be

---

8. This little story describes the decline, if not the rise, of the family in *The Dream of the Red Chamber*, a Qing dynasty novel generally taken to be the masterwork of Chinese fiction. The family in the novel made its fortune (well before the novel begins) through its connections with the imperial family and its operations in the state-dominated silk industry in the lower Yangtze valley.

9. Mark Elvin, *The Pattern of the Chinese Past* (Stanford University Press, 1973). The analogy is with what developmental economists call a low level equilibrium trap: in a poor country at subsistence level, small increases in productivity will supposedly only cause a matching rise in population, keeping the level of income the same. More recently some students of China have elaborated the concept of the "involuted society," where general output grows along with population, but the marginal contribution of each additional person drops. Philip C. C. Huang, *The Peasant Family and Rural Development in the Yangzi Delta, 1750–1988* (Stanford University Press, 1990), p. 18.

the endemic opium addiction of the 1800s. Popular fiction of that time and earlier shows some disaffection from Confucian values, although not a great deal of disaffection. It does show, in perhaps grossly exaggerated forms, a society in which these values do not operate—a society rife with corruption, cruelty, hypocrisy. The darkness of the picture is probably overdrawn, but the works reflect a mood: this is the kind of thing that people wanted to read. There may have been a need for change in the traditional society, but no mechanism or forces to generate change.

The Traditional Chinese State

In the liberal tradition we are inclined to see the state as an organization (or collection of organizations) reflecting the interests of groups or categories in society. Even Marxists think of the state as an instrument for enforcing the will of the ruling social class. It makes more sense to think of the Chinese state as the reverse of this: the traditional Chinese social order was shaped by the state, by means of the examination system. But there is a paradox here. Athough the Chinese state was in some ways autonomous from society (or, to use what may be a more accurate formulation, the political order was prior to the social order), it was not necessarily always a strong state or one that intruded much on society. Since the state was so central to the Chinese order, questions of social change, including modernization, have been inextricably bound with questions of political cohesion and political efficacy.

Emperor and Bureaucracy

The Chinese emperor goes by two titles. On one level he is the Son of Heaven (*Tianzi*), the holder of the Mandate of Heaven, Heaven's agent for carrying out the Way. His other title, *Huangdi*, which literally means something like "august god," but is best translated simply as emperor, refers to the emperor in his "secular" function as actual ruler not of the entire world but only of the civilized portion of it. The two roles were sometimes in tension, in that things a secular chief executive might want to do might not be appropriate for a Son of Heaven. In principle the emperor's power and authority were absolute; in practice they were less than that. In effect the Son of Heaven function checked the function of the emperor. As Son of Heaven the emperor had to act in a moral fashion, meaning he had to conform to the values of the dominant Confucian elite, and the source of the emperor's authority came from his position as Son of Heaven. An emperor who wanted to disregard Confucian values could do so, but only at the risk of incurring at the least passive resistance and merely mechanical compliance with his wishes from the bureaucracy. Courageous officials would criticize him to his face, and he might be written down in history as a tyrant. Except, perhaps, for some dynastic founders, emperors were instructed from their infancy in the attitudes and behavior appropriate to a Confucian ruler, so rulers who did not comply were likely to feel pangs of conscience and to lack easy ways to rationalize their deviations. In this way Confucianism served as a bureaucratic check on imperial rule, the role of the Son of Heaven fitting the world picture of the bureaucracy, perhaps better than it fit that of the Son of Heaven himself. Individual officials served at the emperor's pleasure and could be easily removed, sometimes even tortured or put to death at the emperor's whim. But the bureaucracy as a whole remained and maintained its own standards and its own criteria for entry. The emperor could not rule without the bureaucracy, while the bureaucracy required the emperor, or someone like him, to make the final decisions and provide policy guidance and coherence.

Over the long run, power became increasingly centralized in the person of the emperor. Up through the Song dynasty, emperors had been helped by powerful prime ministers recruited from the bureaucracy. The prime ministers sometimes even had the legal authority to block the implementation of an imperial command. This office was abolished by the Ming founder after some unhappy experiences with several of his own prime ministers (experiences ending with the prime ministers' violent deaths for treason). The Ming founder was something of a tyrant and may have been imitating the despotic ways of the Mongols who had ruled China for the previous century and a quarter. At the time, however, there was also sentiment among Confucian scholars that strong centralized rule was needed to bring order from the change-of-dynasty chaos. The problem, of course, was that not only giving all power to the emperor but also making the emperor personally responsible for exercising it did not guarantee that the emperor had the ability or character to use that power. When emperors were personally weak the consequence was corruption, factionalism, irresponsibility, and drift.

The emperor presided over a complex bureaucracy. The traditional Chinese central government may be divided into two "courts," the inner and the outer, so called by their location in the imperial palace. The outer, southern front areas of the palace served as the formal offices of the central government, while the emperor lived in the recesses of the inner palace. The central government was administered through a series of boards, roughly equivalent to modern ministries—the board of works, for example, or revenue, or punishment, or ritual (which also was charged with the administration of the examinations).

The outer court was the apex of the formal government machinery. The inner court served the emperor's personal and household needs. A small staff of Confucian officials served in the inner court to help the emperor with his official duties—arranging schedules, reading over and making summaries of incoming documents, drafting replies and imperial orders. In Ming and Qing times this was headed by a grand secretary, a position roughly equivalent to the White House chief of staff in the American government. The grand secretary was, of course, a very powerful official, as he controlled the flow of information to and from the emperor and was also able to decide who would get to see the emperor and when they could see him.

In Ming times especially, the great majority of males serving in the inner court were eunuchs. During that dynasty the imperial harem was inordinately large, with the women numbering in the thousands. This does not imply that the Ming emperors were superhumanly lustful, although the numbers may have carried vague implications concerning the potency thought appropriate for the Son of Heaven. The major reason was probably political. In the Han and Tang dynasties political power tended to gravitate toward the families of empresses. In later dynasties, to prevent this, palace women were recruited from the families of commoners, and to dilute the impact of the influence any one family might have, huge numbers were recruited. To be selected for the palace was no doubt an honor, although one most women and families would just as soon forego. A girl taken into the palace was to all purposes lost to her family. If she bore a son and had an engaging personality she might be able to make a pleasant life for herself (assuming the emperor's company was personally agreeable). For most of the wives contact with the emperor was a one-night stand, if that. They lived out in obscurity comfortable but lonely and, perhaps, from their perspective rather meaningless lives, if they were lucky with the companionship of a sympathetic eunuch. Since all boys born in the palace were potential heirs to the throne, there could be no grounds for doubt about their paternity. Thus, eunuchs were the only adult males allowed access to the imperial living quarters.

The eunuchs did not simply take care of the palace women, but also acted as a kind of private staff for the emperor, providing for both his personal and political needs, and sometimes even acting as companions and confidants. Chinese eunuchs typically had been castrated after puberty, and castration was one method of punishment for crime. Palace eunuchs were probably for the most part voluntarily castrated, although it is not everyone who would choose to seek his fortune in this way. The eunuchs definitely were not part of the Confucian bureaucracy, which tended to regard them with disdain, both because of their frequently unsavory background and because their inability to leave posterity showed their contempt for their ancestors. By their personal relationship with the emperor or the emperor's mother (or, probably less frequently, with one of the emperor's wives) eunuchs could sometimes become quite powerful, but this power had no institutional basis and rested entirely upon the emperor's wish. Because they depended upon the emperor's personal favor, they could be used by the emperor to do things the Confucian bureaucracy would not do, and so could serve as an imperial check on the power of the bureaucracy. The infamous Yellow Portal, for example, was a secret police agency staffed by eunuchs.

Eunuch influence was not always sinister. In the early Ming, large Chinese fleets sailed in voyages of exploration into the South Pacific and around India— at about the same time that Spanish and Portuguese sailors were beginning their own great voyages of exploration. This was not the Confucian establishment's notion of proper use of tax money, and the commander of the fleets, Zheng He, was a eunuch. Zheng He's imperial sponsor died and was succeeded by a young emperor more under the thumb of the bureaucracy. The funds for the voyages were cut off and the fleet disbanded. China moved into relative isolation from the rest of the world. The episode shows a contrast between imperial and bureaucratic ideas of proper rule—the tension between the emperor and the Son of Heaven.

As far as I know there have been no aspersions on the character or ability of Zheng He. Nonetheless, eunuch influence was normally associated by the Confucian establishment with corruption and abuse. While eunuchs could help the emperor assert himself against the bureaucracy, a strong-minded eunuch could dominate a weak-willed emperor. Since there was no legal or moral basis for eunuch power and since there was no mechanism for holding eunuchs outside the practical control of the emperor responsible to any vision of the public good, eunuch influence was corrupt almost by definition, and too much of it raised questions about the dynasty's legitimacy. The Confucian version blamed eunuch influence, probably to some degree correctly, for the collapse of the Ming. The Qing dynasty was more successful in curbing eunuch influence. In that period many of the political and administrative (as opposed to household) functions of the inner court were performed by Manchu bannermen, ethnic Manchu soldiers whose technical status was that of slaves to the emperor in his capacity as ruler of the Manchus.[10]

Eunuchs or bannermen served as extrabureaucratic checks on bureaucratic power. There were internal checks as well. One interesting institution is known in English as the censorate. Censors were officials with the duty to investigate suspected cases of official misconduct and to bring accusations against officials believed guilty of misbehavior. To do the job properly required courage, since censors were usually younger, relatively low-ranking bureaucrats, and they themselves did not have any kind of official immunity. If their charge of malfeasance was found to be without foundation or if the person they accused had too much political influence, the censors would themselves be degraded, humiliated, and punished.

The emperor was expected to be a real chief executive. He probably did not normally initiate policy, but was expected to hear reports from officials and to make the final decisions on programs and appointments. On top of his administrative duties he had ceremonial functions. He had to hold court

---

10. In Qing times a Chinese bureaucrat, addressing the emperor, would refer to himself as "your official." A Manchu official would call himself "your slave." There was reverse snobbery at work, since the title "slave" implied a warmer and closer personal relationship with the ruler (and the lifestyle of those Manchus who had access to the emperor was very far from that usually implied by the term *slave*).

each day at dawn—the sun being a symbol of imperial virtue. In later dynasties the overconcentration of power in the emperor became a source of weakness. Officials would try to shift as much responsibility as possible onto the emperor, drowning the emperor in petty detail. At the same time, potential heirs to the throne were indoctrinated from birth to show deference to their Confucian advisors and to not assert themselves in a capricious or tyrannical fashion, while their upbringing kept them isolated from much contact with the real world. Chinese emperors were probably less commonly cruel than slothful, indecisive, and passive.

Local Government

"Heaven is high, the emperor far away"—little of palace life affected ordinary people, except as material for gossip and drama. The ordinary person rarely saw even the lowest level of officials, the county magistrates.

The magistrate was the only regular member of the civil service in a county. Above him was a prefectural government and above that the province. The magistrate's office combined all local governmental functions: law enforcement, civil and criminal justice, tax assessment and collection, superintending local public works. Magistrates could refer to detailed lists of laws and regulations for direction, but as proper Confucian gentlemen they were expected to use the law only as a general guide, using judgment to reach a proper and just solution to problems in accord with the particular facts. Decisions by the magistrate, especially in criminal cases, could be appealed to higher authority, and a magistrate could himself be punished if that authority decided that he had been in error.

The concentration of local power in the person of the magistrate made him an awesome figure, and his isolation from the rest of the bureaucracy meant that he had the opportunity to abuse his power if he were so inclined. The superior authorities did not want the magistrate to become a corrupt tyrant; neither did they want him to become so entrenched in local society that he could ignore orders from above. One measure of control was the "law of avoidance," which prevented any official from holding office in his native province. In that way he would not be part of the local network of connections (guanxi) and, in principle, would be better able to act impartially in carrying out his duties. Another measure was frequent rotation in office—the tenure of a county magistrate would typically be for two or three years. That meant there was little chance of his becoming too much a part of the local guanxi network over time. These practices also guaranteed, however, that the magistrate was a stranger to the area and that he would be gone at just about the time he might begin to figure things out.

The magistrate was supposed to meet both household and many official expenses from his not exorbitant salary, which might be taken as a slice from the local tax collection. The position provided both opportunity and temptations for graft, and a limited amount of corruption (the imposition of technically unauthorized fees for government service, the acceptance of gifts from both parties—to be fair—to a lawsuit) may have been virtually customary. At the same time, the magistrate was supposed to be, and would often see himself as, the "father and mother" of his people, and there is no reason to think that most magistrates most of the time did not try to live up to the ideal.

There were physical limits to what a magistrate could do, and much local government was informal, carried out by the local gentry. The magistrate was supposed to consult with the gentry on local projects, and the gentry's access to the magistrate was a major element in their social influence. The traditional Chinese system shows a paradox: although the state seems in many ways autonomous from society, neither was the state necessarily very strong. The lack of power of the state at the base level certainly helped temper what was in principle a despotic system, but it also meant the state was not always effective in protecting ordinary people from the exactions of the rich and powerful. Government functions might be farmed out to the local elite, or even to outside entrepreneurs.

Another set of local government workers existed outside the official civil service—the local clerks and policemen attached to the magistrate's office. This was a permanent staff made up of local residents, often of an unsavory sort. Their popular reputation is summed up in their nickname, the government's "claws and teeth." They knew the area better than the magistrate and were in more frequent and direct contact with the people. They were well placed to carry out graft and extortion, if not closely supervised. The ordinary person preferred to have as little to do with the state as possible. To render a piece of Chinese doggerel into English doggerel:

The portals of the county court
lie open like an eight:[11]
If you're rich or if you're poor,
don't go through that gate.

To enhance social control and check the power of the gentry the state sometimes tried to organize commoners, grouping households to enforce collective responsibility for law enforcement and tax collection. It was difficult to get respectable persons to hold office in these organizations, which meant they tended to become instruments of rogues and thugs. The organizations do not seem to have been very effective. On the whole, as long as the state was strong enough to provide stability and a modicum of personal security, Chinese society was able to take care of itself.

---

11. The character for eight (八) looks a little like an open gate. The Chinese original goes: *Yamen damen bazi kai; you qian mei qian bu jinlai.*

Politics

As in all other societies there was competition for power, office, and policy in China, but the prevailing ethos inhibited open competition. Confucian morality dictated that one not push one's own advantage. People certainly did so anyway, but could not openly admit that was what they were doing. There could be relatively civil and open debates among the bureaucracy on matters of specific policy and even high principle. A famous round of debates during the Han dynasty centered on how much control the state should exercise over the economy, and this was also a great controversy in the Song dynasty. In each case, discussions of principle were amalgamated with personal and factional rivalries. Confucianism treats morality as the standard for politics and judgment. This sometimes serves as a healthy reminder that political expediency is always subject to moral judgment. Tainted by ambition and heated by competition, however, this moral focus could degenerate into moralism—a self-righteous identification of oneself and one's side with all that is good and one's rivals not merely with error or different interests but with evil.

Scholars of Chinese affairs sometimes assert that China has no tradition of legal opposition, that political opposition is equated with treason and subversion. In fact, one of the sternest duties of a good Confucian official was loyal opposition, to tell the truth to power. The function of loyal opposition was to correct errors and shortcomings of superiors, however, not self-advancement at their expense. In liberal democracies the opposition uses loyal criticism as an instrument to suggest they could do a better job of governing than the current power-holders. In the Confucian order the loyal dissenter may also opine that certain officials be dismissed and hint (it would not be proper to say so directly) that he himself could do a better job. But if these powerful wicked officials were able to make a case that the criticism was motivated by conceit, envy, or ambition (as, of course, it may well have been), there was nothing to protect the critic from the wrath of the powerful. Loyal criticism could also be directed against the emperor himself, without, of course, implying the emperor should step aside or be overthrown. The good Confucian emperor was supposed not merely to tolerate but to welcome loyal criticism, although some emperors were clearly better about this than others. Given the moralistic tenor of Confucian analysis, criticism of the emperor's public acts could slip over into criticism of his character and personal habits, a move not always encouraging open-minded self-examination. Once again, there was nothing to protect the bold or imprudent critic from imperial anger.

The Confucian ethos was more comfortable with an individual acting alone politically, since groups acting together, or cliques, as they were called, were more effective and, therefore, more dangerous. In the Song dynasty some of the conservative opponents of a reform prime minister argued for the propriety of factions on roughly the same grounds used later in England by Edmund Burke: if good people do not band together, the field is left open to the bad. This view never gained much following in China, although in practice cliques were pervasive. Since in many dynasties there was no automatic succession (the reigning emperor would designate one of his sons as heir, with the choice sometimes kept secret until after the old emperor had died), as an emperor aged various factions formed around plausible heirs, with major purges following the new emperor's accession.

Most politics took place among bureaucrats or those eligible for bureaucratic appointment. No mechanism held the government responsible to public opinion. The gentry, however, sometimes voiced opinions on matters of state, claiming to speak in the name of the people (even when a neutral observer might wonder whether instead they were more nearly speaking in the name of privilege). There was a general acknowledgment of the importance of the opinions of subjects at large. The *Book of Songs*, said to have been edited by Confucius, includes poems from the Spring and Fall period that are (or are interpreted by Confucians to be) protests against bad government. In subsequent centuries officials continued to look for new folk songs, children's chants, or street songs indicating popular grievances. Some of these songs may not really have been the work of "folk" or children but of educated gentry malcontents or even, for that matter, bureaucratic factions. Nevertheless, they were taken seriously as pointers on what might need to be changed, and the practice of citing such songs or chants continues in the People's Republic.

The most radical (and also most dangerous) way for the ordinary person to express dissent was rebellion. Rebellion itself was often an outgrowth of banditry, banditry becoming rebellion when a gang leader came to believe for whatever reason that the Mandate of Heaven had passed to him. Even ordinary outlawry could have political implications. A common theme of popular fiction concerned honest fellows forced by wicked government to become bandits,[12] and even nonpolitical criminals sometimes consoled themselves by thinking that this, indeed, was the case with them too. From the other side, what began as political activism could degenerate into mere racketeering. Secret societies formed in the early Qing to resist Manchu rule sometimes became, within a generation or so, criminal organizations, and some of these remain today active in the drug trade and other international crime.[13] Some rebel movements took on a radical anti-Confucian ideology based on Daoism or Buddhism, although many had no ideology other than the replacement of the existing dynasty (in the process, of course, promising

---

12. The best and most famous example of this theme is the Ming dynasty novel *Shui Hu Zhuan* (translated as *Water Margin* or as *All Men Are Brothers*).

13. Not all secret societies or all branches of secret societies are criminal. It is possible that most individual lodges are concerned with fellowship, charity, and mutual aid among members—similar, say, to the Masons in the West. No doubt more research should be done on secret societies, but given the nature of the organizations information is obviously not going to be easy to come by.

everyone a better deal). By the time any movement had come within striking distance of success, it had made peace with the established Confucian order.

The most dramatic political changes in traditional China were the rise and fall of dynasties, often thought of in cyclical terms, order alternating with chaos. The Confucian stereotype was that the Mandate of Heaven was given to good and capable rulers and taken away from wicked and incompetent ones. This is no doubt unfair to many last, allegedly bad emperors, although there may be some objective foundation to the traditional way of thinking. The founders of dynasties may not always have been men of virtue, but they were all intelligent, politically astute, and tough. A new regime could make a clean sweep, putting in needed reforms. Over the decades, however, abuses accumulated, and, as noted before, the upbringing of potential heirs did not always equip them to rule.

Dynastic collapse was rarely sudden. It usually came after a long period of decay marked by weakening capacity of government, both military and fiscal, and social unrest. Natural disasters, which might be interpreted as signs of Heaven's displeasure, put strains on the government's dwindling resources, and disasters might possibly become more severe than they would otherwise be when the state was unable to provide disaster aid. Unrest might lead to rebellion and the state would find itself unable to meet the expenses of the armies raised to suppress the rebellion, who would then take to living off the local area, with their generals forming their own power bases. A dynastic change might come when one of these autonomous warlords vanquished his rivals. Qin (in a way), Sui, and Song are dynasties formed in this fashion. Another method could be a coup organized by a powerful minister or general of the old emperor: the most important example is the Tang. The Han and Ming dynasties were formed when the leader of a popular rebellion managed to make his claim to the Mandate stick. The (Mongol) Yuan dynasty and (Manchu) Qing dynasty resulted from foreign conquest. The Qing founding is especially complicated. A popular rebellion had taken control of Peking, and its leader had proclaimed himself emperor. The rebels either killed the Ming ruler or that unfortunate killed himself in despair after the occupation. Officials loyal to the Ming requested help from the Manchus, who had been building their own base on the Chinese border for a generation or so, to suppress the rebellion. The Manchus defeated the rebels and decided that the Mandate had come to them. In the meantime, members of the Ming ruling family had fled south, and loyalist officials organized resistance against the Manchus. The Qing spent the next generation in a bloody war of conquest of the south.

Japanese Society

Our usual impression of the continuity of Chinese society is a little misleading. It comes from the superficial similarity of the institutions of the various dynasties and the long association of elite status and Confucian education. Japan gives a greater impression of change. Japan adopted Chinese culture but did not copy it mechanically, and Japan did not develop the gentry society characteristic of China in the later centuries.

The ancestors of the modern Japanese came to the islands probably by way of Korea, probably as warrior bands known as uji, a term usually translated as clan. The clans were hierarchically organized and membership was, of course, hereditary (with at least fictitious kinship being one of the elements holding the bands together). One of the clans, the Yamato, centered in Nara, near Kyoto, achieved supremacy over the others, and the imperial family presumably is descended from the head of the Yamato clan (Yamato is now a poetic name for Japan). By about A.D. 600 the Japanese elite had become literate in Chinese and the islands were ruled by an imperial system patterned superficially on the Chinese, but with the subordinate bureaucratic functions performed by a hereditary court nobility rather than a civil service recruited by examination.

The imperial family did not rule directly for long. In time real power in court and country had passed to the Fujiwara family, who maintained their influence by marrying their daughters into the imperial family. The tradition of Fujiwara brides for future emperors lasted well beyond actual Fujiwara control of the government: in Japan, forms tend to remain after the content has changed.

Around A.D. 1000 or so the court itself no longer had much direct political power. The new ruling group were the samurai, at first coarse rustic warlords, although over time they acquired a little Confucian and chivalric polish. In 1185 the warlord Minamoto Yoritomo became supreme ruler of the country, proclaiming himself *shogun*, or general, and his form of government the *bakufu*—"tent government," but, by extension, military government. The bakufu did not abolish the court or eliminate the emperor, nor did the shogun make any attempt to become emperor himself. The imperial court remained, even though it had become politically irrelevant.

The following centuries saw the rise and fall of different shogunal regimes, sometimes in competition with each other. By the 1500s overall political order had collapsed, and Japan was in its "Warring States" period (the term copied from the Chinese era prior to the Qin unification), with various warlords struggling for supremacy. Order was restored in 1603 by Tokugawa Ieyasu, who established the most impressive and successful of the bakufu. A key part of his policy was to freeze the social order in such a way as to maintain the Tokugawa system indefinitely. This system, or its eventual decay, is the context for Japan's modernization.

Before examining the overall social structure of "traditional" Japan in its later phases, however, we might look first at some of the more basic and enduring principles of Japanese social organization. Like traditional China, Japan was an agrarian society organized into peasant villages, the principal economic activity being wet rice cultivation. Rural organization in Japan seems to have been tighter than in China, with the village functioning more as a social unit under a chief. In earlier centuries Japanese peasants had the status of serfs, working on estates owned by the nobility. By Warring States times the estate system was weaker and Japanese villages were tending toward becoming self-governing units, with the various families held together by bonds of obligation derived from expediency and reciprocity.

Like Chinese social structure, Japanese society is built on personal relationships. The Japanese also emphasize guanxi, or *kankei*, as it is pronounced in that language. Chinese guanxi entails an extended network of relationships, some among equals, some among superiors and inferiors, with family ties tending to take priority over all others. In Japan the most important connection, at least among men, tends to be a patron–client tie rooted in the workplace. A popular term for this relationship is *oyabun–kobun*, which literally means parents–children but more accurately might be rendered as big shots–little shots. When the term became popularized in the years following World War II it had something of a gangster connotation, but it describes a common and recurring social pattern: the tie between lord and samurai, between chief and villager, between landlord and tenant, between boss and employee, between faction head and follower.[14]

The sociologist Chie Nakane compares the oyabun–kobun relation to an upside-down V (Figure 1). A is the boss and there is a personal tie between him and his followers B and C (of course, in real life a boss is apt to have more than two followers). The group coheres because of the bond between the leader and each of his followers. There is no direct tie between B and C, only the indirect one of their common allegiance to A. They act together as part of A's group (company, conglomerate, faction, office, gang) in dealing with outsiders; within the group they are apt to be rivals. A reflection of this structure on behavior is that Japanese are often not comfortable with relations among equals or where relative status is not clear. In any group (or drinking party) things go most smoothly and spontaneously when there is a clear if subtle recognition of status differences, based on, if nothing else, age or seniority.

Relatively lower status does not imply humiliation for subordinates. Rather, status differences give a framework that allows people to know how to interact with each other.[15] This acceptance of hierarchy is, paradoxically, one

---

14. For an interesting analysis of how oyabun–kobun works, see Chie Nakane, *Japanese Society* (University of California Press, 1971).

15. Where there is no framework—say on a subway at rush hour—the normally polite Japanese may become openly rude. This same logic has been used to explain the propensity of Japanese soldiers in World War II to commit atrocities when away from home, although it is probably not a full explanation for that kind of behavior, nor is that behavior confined to Japanese.

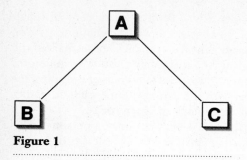

Figure 1

of the reasons for the much-praised egalitarianism of the Japanese management style. American society has an egalitarian ethos, but in spite of this there are still relations of power and authority. Bosses may feel a need to flaunt their superior status by arrogating petty privileges to themselves and fear that too intense interaction with underlings may lead to a dangerous overfamiliarity. Japanese bosses may share lunchrooms, bathrooms, and even office space with those who work for them without having to worry about undermining their status; by acting as one of the boys[16] they foster cohesion in the unit.

A possibly related paradox is that while the boss or big shot is the source for what cohesion the group may have, he does not typically lord it over his subordinates. Rather than providing policy leadership or direction, the boss's function more often is to symbolize the entire group, listen to advice from subordinates in the fashion of a good, modest Confucian leader, smooth over jealousies among subordinates, stroking fragile egos. A boss's prestige will depend in part on his ability to satisfy both the material needs and the vanities of his followers. In a sense, probably, we can say the clients serve the interests of the patrons, but equally both patron and clients serve the interests of the group they form.

Clients may have clients of their own, in which case the group can become a complicated hierarchy. A simplified model is diagrammed in Figure 2. In this example, A's group (faction) holds together against the faction headed by D, or any other outside force. However, within A's faction there will be conflict between the subgroups headed by B and C, and the faction as a whole may fragment into separate segments when A retires or dies. In a historical example, Tokugawa Ieyasu betrayed the young heir of his former patron.

The terms *oyabun* and *kobun* treat the group as analogous to the family. The usage shows Confucian influence. In practice, for Japanese males on a day-to-day basis, the working group is a more important social unit than the

---

16. The masculine gender is probably appropriate here. This same kind of consideration helps explain the weakness of feminism in Japan.

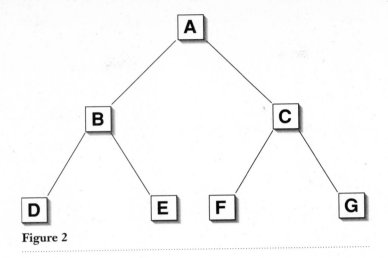

Figure 2

family (although in agrarian society the two may largely coincide). The family (*ie*) is somewhat apart from this group structure, although its organization shows the influence of the same operating principles. The Chinese family is in principle an extended unit embracing all ancestors and all descendants. In Japan the family line is transmitted through the oldest son, who also gets (or gets trusteeship over) the bulk of the family property. Younger sons are expected to go out and form families of their own. Despite the family's relative lack of social importance, family background has typically been more important in Japan than in China. There is less emphasis on biological relationships, however, and boys are relatively easily adopted into different families for reasons of expediency or convenience.

Japanese class and status systems were probably always more rigid and closed than those of China, but the Tokugawa social system was artificially so. The rulers' idea was to keep the social system exactly as it was when the bakufu was consolidated. The law mandated a strict distinction of four hereditary statuses: warrior, peasant, artisan, and merchant (a classification derived originally from Zhou dynasty China). Prior to the Tokugawa the system had been relatively more fluid. Tokugawa Ieyasu had himself carved his way to the top from relatively humble beginnings, but, understandably, he did not want anyone else to be able to do the same thing again.

Warriors constituted the ruling class. They were divided among themselves into a series of hierarchical hereditary distinctions, from the great lords (*daimyo*) to ordinary samurai. Prior to the Tokugawa, Japan had one of the world's most advanced infantries, and warfare was one way a peasant or worker lad might hope to advance himself in life. The Tokugawa feared large, efficient armies. They disarmed the commoners (a policy that actually began prior to the Tokugawa consolidation), and samurai were allowed to keep only weapons good for personal combat—one long sword and one short sword. In order to assure the social prestige of samurai, they were allowed to "cut down" any commoner who seemed to show disrespect (although one hopes they did not lightly take advantage of this privilege). Samurai were forbidden to engage in trade or remunerative labor. They lived on stipends paid them (usually in the form of rice) by their overlords, while the daimyo lived on the income from taxes on their fiefs (*han*) entrusted them by the shogun. Unlike European knights, who usually lived on their own estates in their own castles, samurai mostly lived together in the castle of their overlord. Although war was their reason for being, the Tokugawa period was an extended era of peace. The samurai who did not give themselves over to idleness or hobbies became a core of civilian bureaucrats working in the central government or the government of their han, with jobs much like those of the Confucian bureaucracy in China and even more humble positions than those held by the Chinese elite—policemen, for example. If an overlord became too strapped for funds he might be forced to let his samurai go. If there were too many of these masterless samurai, known as *ronin* ("wave men"), there could be a social problem: unemployed intellectuals, disinclined to do useful work, filled with personal grievances and a sense of duty to right the wrongs of the world, highly skilled at hand-to-hand combat.

In Confucian thinking agriculture is the root of the state, and in principle farming, next to war, was the second most honorable profession in Japan. As the British scholar and diplomat George Sansom once remarked, however, the Japanese elite's esteem for agriculture was not necessarily matched by esteem for agriculturalists. On the whole peasants were probably among the more miserable elements in Tokugawa society, facing lives of low income, low prestige, and arduous labor.

On the other hand, things were not uniformly bad. Toward the beginning of the Tokugawa period the lower ranks of samurai were given the choice of taking warrior or peasant status, and many chose to become peasants, seeing in farming greater economic opportunity and probably greater freedom. Many of the village heads in the Tokugawa period were descended from these former samurai.

The surplus produced by the peasants fed the warrior elite and supported the state. If a peasant, whether from bad luck or lack of skill, was unable to meet the lord's obligations, he might be obliged to borrow from his more fortunate neighbor, illegally putting up his land (which was technically held in fief by the daimyo from the shogun, not the private property of the peasant) as collateral. A rich enough peasant might be able to set himself up as a pawnbroker, with luck or work acquiring land and more liquid forms of capital. Speaking of liquid wealth, rural *sake* (rice wine) brewers seem to have been especially well placed to branch out into lending and land speculation, perhaps because they could use the extra grain on hand as capital. Over the decades, independently of and even in opposition to the policies of the bakufu, there developed a thriving class of landlords and rural entrepreneurs among the peasantry. Agriculture itself became more commercial, feeding an expanding urban population.

Agricultural productivity rose during the Tokugawa period, but so did economic pressure on the general mass of peasants, partly because of increased population, partly because of exactions from above. The warrior class came more and more to need funds, squeezing the peasants harder to meet their own expenses, while landlords and moneylenders contributed their own forms of exploitation. By the late Tokugawa period there was chronic agrarian distress in Japan, a situation persisting into the early twentieth century.

Technically below the peasants in prestige were artisans, skilled workers—carpenters, masons, blacksmiths, brewers, and the like. Their standard of living was probably on the whole higher than that of the peasantry.

Farmers produced goods necessary to sustain human life while artisans made life more comfortable and happy. The honorable warriors guaranteed the fabric of the social order. Merchants, however, produced nothing. They bought cheap and sold dear. They did help assure that goods were generally available and this was a useful and necessary thing, but they contributed nothing to the value of the goods and were motivated by the least honorable of human passions, a desire for gain; they did not mind making this gain at the expense of honest workers and warriors.

This bigoted upper-class (and probably peasant and artisan) view of merchants may have been unfair; not surprisingly, the consequent low social status of merchants did not last for long, if it had ever been all that low anyway. The Tokugawa peace provided the background for expanding commerce. The merchants had money they could lend to help warriors meet expenses, so that while a merchant had to keep a humble—even servile—demeanor in the face of warriors, in actuality he might have held the upper position in the relationship. There was even some mixing of classes. One way for a samurai to climb out of debt might be to adopt the son of a merchant or to marry one of his children into a merchant's family (illegal as all of this was). Urban life grew along with commerce, and the urban economy was outside the feudal system and the urban way of living common to all classes—samurai, artisans, merchants—with the differences based more on wealth than on status. Japanese society in 1800 was not what it had been in 1600, regardless of the way the Tokugawa had designed their institutions. But those institutions were unable to legitimate the new social order.

The Tokugawa State

The Tokugawa social structure might as easily be considered part of the political system, since it was stipulated by law and was designed to assure perpetual Tokugawa supremacy. Society changed despite political efforts to freeze it, and by the end of the bakufu the lack of fit between institutions and the social order was one of its prime weaknesses. The new social forces by themselves, however, may not have been strong enough to cause a change of regime.

The Tokugawa system is often described as centralized feudalism. The concept of feudalism is taken from European history, but the Japanese arrangement resembles that of Europe (and, of course, of early Zhou dynasty China—the Chinese descriptions of feudalism were partial models for Japan). The closer analogy for the Tokugawa, however, would probably be early modern Europe in the age of absolutism (France under Louis XIV, say) rather than the more classically feudal Europe of the Middle Ages.

Lord Tokugawa distributed land as fiefs to the other great lords, or daimyo. The Tokugawa capital was Edo, today's Tokyo,[17] a beautiful harbor in the middle of Japan's most productive farmland. The lands near Edo were held by the various branches of the Tokugawa family itself. Another ring of fiefs was held by the *fudai* lords, followers of Ieyasu prior to his final victory—his kobun, as it were. Lands farther away were the *tozama* or outer han, allocated to lords equal in rank to Ieyasu. Some of these had been his allies, but whether from magnanimity or a disinclination to push his luck, Ieyasu also gave fiefs to lords who had opposed him to the very end. In some of these han a tradition of hostility to the bakufu persisted, although those who shared that tradition curbed their overt expressions of it until the very end. The han, especially the outer ones, enjoyed autonomy in internal affairs and were expected to support themselves by taxes on the peasantry. In Chinese and European feudalism, as well as in earlier Japanese attempts, vassals in time could become more powerful than their nominal overlord, and feudal systems are generally characterized by constant internal warfare. The Tokugawa prevented this by the policy of disarmament and by police and financial controls over the daimyo.

Along with disarming the population, freezing the social structure, and feudalism, the "closed country" was another basic Tokugawa policy. During the Warring States period Japanese pirates raided at will along the China coast. One of the major warlords had tried to conquer Korea and even dreamed of taking on the Ming dynasty. At the same time Europeans, then on the crest of their first great age of exploration, were active in Japan as traders and missionaries. The bakufu, however, saw this openness to the outside as a source of instability. It expelled all foreigners (with exceptions noted below) from Japan and forbade Japanese from leaving the islands. The Tokugawa were afraid mostly of Spain, then the most dynamically powerful country in the world; in the late 1500s Spain had conquered the Philippines. The

---

17. The actual capital of Japan then was Kyoto, where the emperor's court was (the word *Kyoto* means "capital city"). After the overthrow of the Tokugawa the court was transferred to Edo, whose name was then changed to Tokyo ("eastern capital"). What is now the imperial palace was originally the shogun's castle.

Tokugawa outlawed Christianity, which had won a considerable following in Japan, interpreting it as the ideological expression of Spanish ambition. They crucified thousands of Japanese converts who did not recant and, by a clever piece of logic, made those who claimed to have given up the religion swear by Jesus, Mary, and Joseph that they really had renounced it.

The country was not absolutely closed. Limited trade was conducted with China and with Holland. The Dutch, who maintained a small trading post on an artificial island in Nagasaki harbor, were favored over other Europeans because they were Protestant and at that time had no interest in missionary activities.[18] The bakufu also had a small staff of public officials specialize in "Dutch learning," translating works from that language into Japanese. By this means, despite its isolation Japan was able to keep abreast of developments in the wider world.

The Central Government

The shogun (either in person or as a front man for a dominant clique or coalition of cliques of councillors) ruled from his castle in Edo. Attached to the shogun's court was a bureaucracy in most ways like that of the Chinese central government, but staffed by samurai loyal to the Tokugawa family or the fudai han. The major government revenue came from land taxes on the Tokugawa holdings, although each han also had obligations toward meeting certain government expenses, such as water works or repairs of fortifications. Many bakufu officials were relatively low-ranking samurai, rank here being determined by birth, and they came over time to feel that their contribution to the state was not rewarded with commensurate status. They found Mencius's idea of rule by those with ability persuasive. Although the central bureaucracy was not a major mover in the eventual overthrow of the bakufu, its members accepted the downfall with good grace and formed the core of the civil service in the first generation of the modern state.[19]

Most governmental functions were performed at the local level, by the han, with the shogun keeping controls over the han. The shogun could take fiefs away from the daimyo virtually at will—if the daimyo was suspected of opposition to the bakufu, if the daimyo in the opinion of the shogun was not running his fief well, if the daimyo did not produce a male heir. The bakufu also maintained a secret police with agents spread throughout the islands eager to nose out disloyalty.

---

18. The Irish satirist Jonathan Swift, who resented Holland's commercial and military rivalry with England, says that Dutch traders would readily trample on a crucifix to ingratiate themselves with the Japanese rulers. This may be a calumny, but it is true that the Japanese regularly exposed the Dutch to various humiliations and indignities.

19. Thomas M. Huber, *The Revolutionary Origins of Modern Japan* (Stanford University Press, 1981).

Toward the end of the bakufu's course there developed a spate of localized agrarian riots, with farmers protesting their increasingly hard lot. Japan, unlike China, had no tradition of broad-based social rebellion. Perhaps the oyabun–kobun structure inhibits the development of the "horizontal" links among persons that facilitate social movements. The shogun had to worry, then, much more about opposition from the elite than from society at large.

The daimyo were most effectively kept in line by the practice of *sankinkotai*, or "alternate attendance." The wife and children of each daimyo had to live in Edo, and each daimyo had to spend half of each year in Edo himself. The families of the daimyo were permanent hostages, and half the time the daimyo, too, was within reach of the shogun's sword. The practice required the lords to keep up two households, both at a level sufficient to their station—and over the decades the expense began to drive daimyo into bankruptcy.[20] The prolonged absence of the lord from his fief meant that his control over local government came to be nominal, with the real work done by the bureaucratized samurai acting without much supervision from above.

Local Government

The han took responsibility for most problems of law enforcement and tax collection. Even public works programs mandated by the bakufu were generally implemented and financed by the han. Within the han the government organizations were staffed by samurai, with the han governments being smaller versions of the bakufu.

The outer han enjoyed more internal autonomy than the inner, but the samurai serving those han were not eligible for office in the bakufu government. By the 1800s these fiefs contained a store of skilled administrators with little scope for their considerable talents, and no pro-bakufu incentive to counter their hereditary hostility to the Tokugawa family. Tozama warriors became the main political force behind the fall of the Tokugawa and the major architects of the modern Japanese state.

Politics

The bakufu was designed to concentrate power in the person of the shogun, and, therefore, had no toleration for competition for power or influence; that is, there was no room in the system for politics. Political action, then, tended to be covert—probably more so in Tokugawa Japan than in Ming and Qing China, both because the Japanese state was more tightly organized and because Japanese political culture was less tolerant of dissent and opposition.

---

20. Toshio G. Tsukahira, *Feudal Control in Tokugawa Japan: The Sankin Kotai System* (East Asia Research Center, Harvard University, 1966).

Chinese rulers may not always have given the tradition of loyal dissent the respect due it, but in Japan the tradition did not exist: loyalty meant obedience.

There was, of course, maneuvering among bureaucratic cliques, both at the bakufu and han levels. Most of these no doubt concerned personal power and privileges and had no long-lasting significance. There were two areas of higher politics, however, places where the bakufu was vulnerable, not to direct attack but to implications and insinuations. The first centered on the grounds of legitimacy of the bakufu system; the second was the policy of the closed country and the perception, especially after 1800, of threats to Japan from abroad.

Both Japan and China valued rule by virtue, but, as noted in Chapter 3, despite the shogun's adherence to Zhu Xi's version of Confucianism, his power was generally held to rest on force. The emperor, although politically impotent, remained the ultimate font of legitimacy. Shinto and the primacy of the emperor created alternative sources of legitimacy to those of the Tokugawa, sources the bakufu might try to ignore but could not suppress.

The head of a branch of the Tokugawa family, headquartered in the town of Mito, had a falling out with the dominant branch at Edo and began to sponsor a series of Japanese "national studies," rescuing the Shinto tradition from intellectual oblivion and denigrating the alleged decadence resulting from Chinese influence. The Shinto revival, tacitly subversive of the bakufu system, gained the attention of, among others, retainers at the imperial court at Kyoto (who had their own ambitions) and of samurai from the tozama han. When the bakufu in the mid-1800s proved unable to cope with the modern world system, Japan, unlike China, had available to it an alternative traditional foundation for authority.

The issue of the closed country also became a focus of political attack on the bakufu. The policy had been imposed by the Tokugawa, but by the 1800s dissidents were criticizing the bakufu for its supposed inability to enforce the policy. The Tokugawa's earlier concern had been to counter the influence of Catholicism. By the 1800s, however, patriots were worried that the shogun was unwilling and unable to resist the even more mighty Western powers who, if given the chance, would reduce Japan to a colony. These fears combined with the Shinto revival, giving rise to images of foul barbarians polluting the sacred land of Yamato. In 1854 the shogun was in effect compelled to open to the outside, and this departure from his house's basic policy precipitated a drop in the bakufu's legitimacy.

The long-term social change during the Tokugawa period gave both the opening of the country and the Shinto revival their political effect. By the 1800s the bakufu's institutions no longer described Japanese reality. Social pressures were building up inside a rigid institutional container. Perhaps they could have continued to build for a longer time, or perhaps the bakufu would have made adjustments in the shape of the institutions or provided outlets. The international situation, however, brought the chronic crisis of the regime to a head.

China and Japan

Traditional China and traditional Japan may both have been faced with social crisis, but the old orders did not in fact change radically until faced with
the modern world order, then based on the West and its industrial revolution. We might pause for a moment to consider what might have hindered a
spontaneous modernization of China and Japan, looking at features common
to both societies but different from those of early modern Europe. When the
modern world order did intrude upon Asia, Japan seemed rather better able
to cope with it—and this raises the question of whether there might also have
been relevant differences between the two systems.

To ask, in effect, why China and Japan did not modernize on their own
may not be a fair question. The process of modernization may have been a
historical event unique to the West or, to put it even more narrowly, to England. The question of why it did not happen elsewhere may not be a relevant
one. On the other hand, given the worldwide importance of modernization
as a process, the question may be worth at least speculation—especially since
Chinese and Japanese society did have so many elements that might be taken
as prerequisites for modernization.

Marxian theory may provide a beginning, if not necessarily a conclusion.
According to that school, the social structure reflects the "forces of production"—the technology available for the production of wealth and the manner
in which that technology is used.[21] The advances in science and technology in
Europe from about 1500 furthered the modernization of European society,
economy, and politics. China and Japan were technologically on a par with
Europe in 1500, and there are no obvious physical or mental reasons why the
scientific and technological revolution could not have occurred there as well.[22]

The Chinese elite owed its position to Confucian learning, and the Confucian monopoly of learned prestige was reinforced by its political centrality.
There was no incentive to devote mental energy elsewhere—say, to scientific
discovery. Japan did not have the same kind of Confucian elite. The Tokugawa regime, however, actively discouraged technological innovation, considering it, no doubt correctly, a source of social instability.

---

21. Even to state the general idea, however, hints at its limitations. The forces of produc-
    tion in premodern China and Japan were not all that different from those in premod-
    ern Europe, but the social structures are alike, if at all, only at a very general and
    abstract level.

22. The previous chapter, however, outlines a certain bias in Confucian elite culture
    against an exploration of nature, but a similar bias was characteristic, perhaps, of me-
    dieval Christianity. The question is why the bias was more effective in one environ-
    ment than in the other.

A complementary line of explanation focuses on the high level equilibrium trap.[23] China and Japan were about as wealthy as agrarian societies could be, and there was no social incentive to go beyond the agrarian modes of organization. A predecessor to the industrial revolution in Europe was the agricultural revolution. New foods (such as potatoes) introduced from the Americas and new technologies applied to the growing of food allowed a surplus to accumulate, and this could be converted to capital for the development of industry. In China the new foods, combined with a more intensive exploitation of existing resources using existing methods, brought about dramatic increases in population while keeping the standard of living at about the same level century after century.[24] China's population grew from about 60 million in 1400 to about 400 million in 1900 to about one billion in 1980, with per capita food consumption remaining fairly constant.[25] The large population kept labor costs cheap, obviating any incentive to switch to machinery.

The modernization of the West is associated with the bourgeoisie, the urban middle class not comfortably confined within the structure of the older feudal system built on relations of lords and vassals and lords and peasants. Both China and Japan had social groups similar to the European bourgeoisie, but their position and function were not the same. Here we may add a political approach to the Marxian one.

The European bourgeoisie (or some of them) were encouraged to develop commerce and then industry because they provided a source of income for kings and other state rulers; the kings could use this wealth to consolidate their own power against recalcitrant nobles and to fight with other kings. The bourgeoisie, for their part, on the whole liked the kings because the kings provided unified laws and regulations and protected business from the exactions of local tyrants. China by the Qin and Han dynasties was a centralized state of a kind not achieved in Europe until the early modern period, while the Japanese shoguns devised less expensive methods than those used by the European kings for keeping their rivals down. Both the Chinese and the Japanese states depended more on agricultural than commercial taxes for their revenues. The Chinese state may have been more active than the Japanese in attempting to

---

23. Elvin, *The Pattern of the Chinese Past.*

24. The effect seems to have been less dramatic in Japan, perhaps because existing resources were more limited. Rather than devoting technology to handling an increased population, Japan practiced more rigorous and ruthless population control measures than China, with infanticide apparently being not at all uncommon even among respectable, relatively well-to-do families.

25. Dwight L. Perkins, *Agricultural Development in China, 1368–1968* (Chicago, 1969). I am, of course, extrapolating from Perkins's findings, but in fact the first real increases in income seem to have come only in the 1980s.

get money from the commercial sector, but the efforts did as much to stifle enterprise as to foster it.

European culture was a multistate one, with the states constantly at war with each other. As the old saying has it: war made the state and the state made war. The Asian states were probably stronger relative to society than were the European ones, but they were also less activist and intrusive. Constant warfare gave the European rulers an incentive to encourage technological and economic development. China, however, was sufficiently large and wealthy compared with its neighbors that as long as it kept a passably competent and unified government at the center it did not have to worry seriously about outside threats. In Japan the Tokugawa handled the international challenge by opting out. Had the Tokugawa not closed the country, Japanese technology would perhaps have developed more rapidly—and Tokugawa rule would probably have been less stable.

Each of these possible elements of an explanation can be argued with, and others could be suggested. No single one is likely to be an adequate account of the differences between the Asian and European experiences. Some combination of these or similar reasons, however, may approximate the truth.

China and Japan did not react in the same way once they were exposed to the modern world. To explain this we should not look at how China and Japan were alike, but how they were different.

A start here might be to note that China was a Confucian society, while Japan was a society in which Confucianism was probably the most important element, but still only an element. China, of course, also had other systems of thought, but the social and political structure was built upon a version of Confucianism. The Confucian stress on rule by virtue and ability (however they might be measured) encouraged an open society and elite. The structure of Chinese society as a whole was quite stable—some would even say stagnant—but there was opportunity for movement within the structure. The social and economic problems of the late Tokugawa period—increasing mercantile wealth, increasing landlordism, and the like—would have been handled as matters of course in China. In Japan, by contrast, there was no incentive for anyone disaffected with the Tokugawa to wish to preserve the system. This lack of social mobility (in itself a nonmodern trait) may have encouraged the development of ideas and practices appropriate to modernization. A Chinese merchant could invest in land and urge his sons to study for the exams. The best a Japanese merchant could do was to plow his profits back into the business and maybe try to think of ways in which Confucianism might justify and enhance a career in business.

Paradoxically, traditional China's relative modernity stood in the way of its later modernization, while Japan's nonmodern practices may have been a positive help. In China, status was based, as it supposedly is in modern societies, on education and personal achievement. But the education and achievements were of a particular type—mastery of the Confucian classics—not highly valued in the modern world order. In Japan, status was hereditary, a condition considered not very rational at best, maybe even primitive or backward. Yet, perhaps, because a samurai was born a samurai, he was not required to show any special characteristics or achievements to enjoy the perquisites that went with the status, and so could adapt to new roles while relying on the glamour bestowed by the traditional system. By the 1870s certain farsighted samurai came to believe that Japan's survival as a nation demanded the abolition of the feudal system and all it implied, including hereditary distinctions. They could impose such radical changes partly because even after the legal nullification of aristocratic privileges their birth gave them the social prestige that could be translated into authority. Because China was built on Confucianism, however, its elite had to adhere to Confucian ways and could not abandon them without abandoning their claim to elite status. China was flexible internally but overall rigid, even brittle. It was supremely adapted to its environment prior to the 1800s, but close to helpless after that environment had changed. Japan was internally rigid, but its lower level of what might be called political and social development made it more resilient, better able to cope with challenges from the outside.

Neither traditional China nor traditional Japan were static. Both societies were undergoing social change in the late traditional period; both may well have been in a condition of social crisis, although how that crisis might have been resolved had there been no outside intervention will always be an open question. We might assume (without ever being able to prove) that further change in China would have been some adaptation of the Confucian system, with many features associated with modernity but not necessarily resembling the modern systems growing in Europe. The collapse of the bakufu would probably have amounted to more than the equivalent of a Chinese change of dynasty, since it is unlikely that the social system decreed by the Tokugawa would have survived their demise. But there is, again, no reason to think that the outcome would have been the same as in Europe. In any case, to understand the process of modernization in East Asia, we must look not only at the characteristics of the state and society, but also at what actually happened.

5
✦

Traditional
Societies and the
New World Order

There have been at least two ways of understanding the modernization of non-Western societies. One treats individual societies as more or less independent units, attempting to discover whether they go through processes similar to those of Europe during the industrial revolution, whether they have what are thought to be the prerequisite qualities for modernization, or whether their rulers carry out policies appropriate to modernization. Another approach sees modernization as the result of a worldwide process beginning in Europe in the 1500s and resulting in the forcible incorporation of the entire world into a single system organized to the benefit of the technologically advanced societies, or the centers of wealth within those societies. The first approach seeks to discover how poor societies become rich, and may be baffled by the persistence of poverty in most of the world. The second explains poverty as the result of the exploitation of the "peripheral" societies by those at the "core" of the world capitalist system.

Japan, which in 1850 was about as peripheral as any society could be and by 1900 was a major world power, shows the limitations of the second mode. But it must be admitted that modernization as we know it did in fact come to the non-Western world as part of a series of events that might legitimately be called imperialism. This chapter looks at the modernization of East Asia in concrete historical terms, investigating what happened when the technologically advanced modern Western culture imposed itself on the traditional societies of China and Japan.

Early Contacts

The cultural conflict that began in the 1800s contrasts with the earlier interchanges between Europe and East Asia. There had long been a movement of artifacts and inventions from China to the West. Gunpowder and paper came first from China. There was not, however, much influence on the intangible elements of culture.

The most famous early Western visitor to China was, of course, Marco Polo. A merchant of Venice, he came to China in the late 1200s, during the Yuan dynasty, when the Mongols ruled China. Most of Eurasia, in fact, had been pacified by Mongol rule, and it was relatively safe to cross the continent. Marco served in the Chinese government, the Mongols being prone to give administrative office to foreigners. Returning to Europe, he wrote an account of his travels and the fantastic things he had seen and done in the enormously wealthy, civilized, sophisticated empire of Cathay.[1] His stories were treated with considerable skepticism, properly so, since Marco was an inveterate liar,[2] and what was truthful in his account was no more believable than his fabrications.

The story was sufficiently compelling, however, to cause some Europeans to wish to find a cheaper, safer way to East Asia by water. This was a motive for the great voyages of discovery by Christopher Columbus. By the early 1500s European traders, mainly Spanish and Portuguese, were doing business in China and Japan. They were known to their hosts by various names— Franks (a term the Chinese learned from the Arabs), red-haired barbarians, ocean devils (still an impolite term for Westerners), southern barbarians (the Chinese and Japanese had only vague ideas about Western geography but knew that the new visitors approached land from the southern direction).

The most interesting of the early cultural contacts is the experience of Christian missionaries in East Asia, especially the experience of the Society of Jesus, or Jesuits, an order of Catholic priests formed around 1550 originally

---

1. Cathay is a form of the word *Khitai*, the name of a northern tribe that had conquered parts of northern China before themselves being conquered by the Mongols. Khitai or Cathay remains the Russian word for China.
2. Some scholars even doubt whether he really reached China proper, although this may be carrying skepticism too far.

to reclaim Christendom from the Protestant threat.[3] Zealous and well-educated, the Jesuits carried on missions in North and South America, too, as well as in India, China, and Japan. The major early missionary to Japan was a first-generation Jesuit, Francis Xavier, who held friendly but not very productive theological debates with Buddhist monks and scholars and who made many converts among the people and nobility.

The Jesuit experience in China is of greater cultural interest. Father Matteo Ricci, who served in China from 1589 until his death in 1610, concluded that the way to convert the Chinese was to appeal first to the educated. He tried to convince them that Christianity was not a crude superstition but a faith accepted by persons from a highly developed, sophisticated civilization. To this end, he did not concentrate solely on telling the Chinese about religion but also told them about new European developments in math, astronomy, and other early fruits of the burgeoning scientific revolution. From the other side, Ricci argued that conversion to Christianity did not mean giving up China's culture and morality. He asserted that there was nothing in Confucianism (properly understood) inconsistent with the true faith. Confucianism was not erroneous but only incomplete, and Confucius ranked with the "virtuous pagans" of ancient times, such as Socrates, Plato, and Aristotle. Ricci encouraged the development of Chinese forms of Catholic ceremonies and permitted the continued observances of practices and rituals that seemed to be either beneficial to or harmless toward faith and morals.[4]

Ricci and, especially, his successors were criticized by Catholics outside the Jesuit order. Whether from jealousy or conviction, rival missionaries accused the Jesuits of diluting and misrepresenting the faith for the sake of their own worldly power (and it must be admitted that the Jesuits at that time did sometimes—but not in China—play fast and loose with doctrine and ethics in order to gain access to or influence over libertines or unbelievers). The Jesuits considered certain points of Chinese ritual, such as ancestor veneration (or what their opponents called ancestor worship) and veneration of Confucius and the emperor to be expressions of legitimate filial and civic duty; their rivals considered the practices idolatrous. At one point during this "rites controversy" the Jesuits prevailed upon the emperor to write to the pope supporting the Jesuit position—a tactical error, since the pope resented

---

3. For good summary accounts of these early missions, see George Sansom, *The Western World and Japan* (New York, 1949), Chapters 6 and 8; Wolfgang Franke, *China and the West* (Oxford University Press, 1967), Ch. IV; and Donald Treadgold, *The West in Russia and China, 1582–1949* (Cambridge University Press, 1973), Vol. 2.

4. Ricci definitely did not teach that anything goes. Converts were forbidden, for example, to engage in concubinage. Husbands remained responsible for the upkeep and comfort of what secondary wives they may have had, but their more private conjugal duties were limited to the first wife.

the Son of Heaven's presumption to teach him theology. The emperor was equally irritated by the pope's presumption to interfere in his business. Over the long run the Jesuits lost, and in 1742 their concessions to Chinese culture were condemned. The emperor around the same time forbade active missionary work in China. Jesuit priests continued to be sent to Peking to serve the court as advisors on astronomy and, of all things, artillery, until 1773, when the pope abolished the order (it was restored in 1815). The last of the old Peking Jesuits died in the early 1800s, only a few years before China would again be open to Christian missionary activity, this time under very different conditions.

The early episodes hint that the major cultural divide may not have been between East and West, but between the traditional and the modern. Before the 1800s the two cultures were roughly equivalent in technology and similar in moral outlook. While there was much incomprehension, people of goodwill in each culture were able at least to appreciate aspects of the other. The two societies met as equals—a big contrast to the experience after 1800.

Japan went into seclusion in the early 1600s, but China and Europe kept up a steady commerce. There was more demand in Europe for Chinese goods—such as tea and porcelain (whence our word for dishes and the like, china)—than for European goods in China. Chinese porcelain factories even took to decorating their cups and plates with romantic vulgarizations catering to European notions of what a true Chinese style was like, and allegedly Chinese styles in building and furniture—*chinoiserie*—were the rage in fashionable European circles in the 1700s.

The intellectual balance of payments also remained in China's favor. Some assert that Thomas Jefferson's phrasing in the Declaration of Independence was at least indirectly influenced by Mencius's "right of rebellion." Jesuit propaganda had described an idealized China, a magnificent, rational civilization ruled by true philosophers whose people were doomed to eternal damnation simply for want of knowledge of the true faith. The more impious products of Jesuit education, such as the sarcastic philosophe Voltaire, could turn the picture around, using China to demonstrate that the Christian faith was not necessary for either good government or good morals. An interpretation of the significance of traditional China became one of the streams feeding the river of secular Western modernity.

The Opium War and What Came After

In 1793 the British diplomat Lord McCartney approached the Chinese government hoping to establish normal foreign relations. After some dithering and posturing on each side, including a debate about whether McCartney should have to kowtow to the emperor (it was finally agreed that he would genuflect on his left knee—the same courtesy that he would accord the king of England—but that it would be entered into the records as a full kowtow), McCartney was able to present his requests in an audience with the Son of Heaven. After due consideration, the Qianlong emperor replied in a graciously worded, condescending memorial to his good-hearted but obtuse vassal, King George III. The emperor reminded the king that his request was unprecedented, unreasonable, impossible. The Chinese, from their humanity, did not grudge foreigners access to Chinese goods, but China already had everything it needed and had no use for the strange and ingenious gadgets of foreign lands.[5] By 1793 England was technologically ahead of China, but China was still rich and powerful and beyond British military reach. If George was offended by Qianlong's answer or tone, there was not much he could do about it.

Within a generation the balance had shifted. England had certainly grown stronger and its technology more sophisticated, but China had also declined. The Quianlong emperor was a great ruler, but in his old age, lethargy and corruption had taken root in the central government and rebellion was growing in the provinces. The emperor's claim that there was nothing China wanted from abroad also ceased to be valid. By the early 1800s opium addiction was endemic to China, affecting (like the perhaps analogous narcotics plague in the contemporary United States) people from all social levels. Most of the opium came from the new British acquisitions in the Bengal region of India, and British traders (with some participation by Americans) controlled most of the opium traffic. As far as I know, the spread of opium addiction in China still awaits scholarly description and explanation. The new availability of a drug that had been known for a long time is surely only part of the story. In any event, it was unfortunate for China that its encounter with the industrial West took place at a time of dynastic decline and social and moral crisis.

The Opium War

By the 1830s the government had become alarmed by the opium problem. It was concerned, of course, about the moral issue. The illegal trade also affected China's balance of payments, which previously had always been in China's favor. The country was buying more opium than it was selling tea or porcelain, and the difference had to be made up in cash. The flow of silver coins into the coffers of British smugglers worsened the Qing's already bad financial condition.

The court sent an able and honest official, Lin Zexu, to Canton (or Guangzhou, as the town is now often spelled), the British trading outpost, to

5. For an abbreviated version of this famous document, see Ssu-yu Teng and John King Fairbank, *China's Response to the West: A Documentary Survey, 1831–1923* (New York, 1965).

suppress opium smuggling. Lin and the merchants entered into a series of abrasive negotiations. He also wrote a moving, if patronizing, letter (in the Qianlong vein) to Queen Victoria, urging upon her the evils of narcotics traffic. Despairing of a settlement based on goodwill and reason, Lin finally seized and destroyed the stocks of opium in British warehouses.

The merchant interests persuaded the British Parliament to respond with a declaration of war. The government in London was not particularly proud of this pretext, but it was also determined that China, like the rest of the world, should be open to British commerce—which the British genuinely believed to be a necessary instrument of progress and civilization. They consoled themselves with the reflection that the Lord in his unfathomable ways works to bring good from evil.[6]

The Opium War lasted from 1839 to 1842, a series of relatively small battles ending in an easy British victory. This was the first of a number of losing wars the Chinese fought with England and, later, France, during the 1800s. Its settlement, the Treaty of Nanking (or Nanjing) in 1842 was the first of the "unequal treaties" giving foreigners special privileges in China.

Without worrying about the specifics (although some, of course, are rather important: the Treaty of Nanking gave Hong Kong to the British as a colony), it may be more useful to list the general sorts of privileges resulting from the unequal treaties. They opened both the interior and coast of China to foreign commerce. They also opened China to Christian missionary activity. Missionary-sponsored modern Western education increasingly came to rival the Confucian education that was the foundation of the traditional social and political order. Foreign powers or the international community generally gained "concession" areas in various cities along the coast and the Yangtze River, areas outside the jurisdiction of the central Chinese government. The most impressive of these was Shanghai, in 1842 a scattering of villages on mudflats near the mouth of the Yangtze, a few years later a major world metropolis. Foreigners enjoyed "extraterritoriality"—they could be tried or sued only in their own special courts or by international tribunals, not in Chinese courts.[7] After the opening of the country the court continued to try to limit trade by imposing high tariffs. As a result the foreign powers eventually took away the power of the government to set its own tariff rates, giving the authority to an independent international commission.

The United States did not participate directly in the general bullying of China, but after the Opium War proposed instead a most-favored nation treaty, automatically giving the United States the same rights as the foreign power enjoying the currently most favorable treaty relations. The Chinese

---

6. In fairness to the British, it is unlikely that they realized how corrupting and demoralizing a narcotics epidemic really is.

7. Fairness again requires pointing out that a major reason for extraterritoriality was that Chinese court procedure still permitted judicial torture.

were happy enough to agree, hoping this might be a way to pursue the traditional policy of "using a barbarian to check a barbarian." The other Western countries also established most-favored nation status, meaning, then, that everyone enjoyed as a matter of course whatever the most recent aggressor could gouge from the Chinese Empire.

Chinese nationalist and communist historians stress the exploitation of their country by foreign imperialists. It is not certain whether on balance the Western interest in China did more economic damage than it did good. There must have been some harm. It is often argued, for example, that cheap cotton textiles produced in the mechanized mills of England or the United States or the new mills built in Shanghai took away the market for the homespun cloth produced by peasant women in their spare time, so radically reducing the incomes of rural households. The mills of Shanghai and Tianjin, however, also employed these same women or their young daughters, presumably to the women's economic advantage if not their moral or social well-being.

The main damage of the treaties may have been political and cultural rather than economic. The coastal cities became enclaves for the modern industrial world, oriented toward the outside, for most purposes beyond the reach of the central government. Along the coast there developed new paths to status, either through participation in the modern economy or education in the Western missionary colleges. Chinese culture had become bifurcated. The Confucian order of the interior had no control over the new society along the coast, while this unassimilated coast thwarted the operation of that order even in the interior.

The Taiping Rebellion

The Qing dynasty's weakness toward the outside was partly a consequence of China's relative technological backwardness, but also a reflection of the dynasty's internal decline. In the late 1700s and early 1800s the Qing defeated with great difficulty a set of popular rebellions in the northern provinces inspired by a utopian version of Buddhism. Shortly after the Opium War the dynasty faced its greatest challenge: a rebellion by the Taiping Tianguo, the Heavenly Kingdom of Great Peace. The Taiping Rebellion (1850–1864) was the bloodiest conflict of the nineteenth century, killing perhaps 20 million people and devastating whole areas of central China (the American Civil War was a distant second in that relatively peaceful century's record of slaughter). Taiping ideology was Christian, and in this and other ways the movement reflects at least indirectly China's new exposure to the West.

The Taiping founder, Hong Xiuquan, was a scholar from a Hakka family from Guangxi province, in the southwest. After repeatedly failing the civil service examination he had a nervous breakdown and lay abed for months. He had once visited Hong Kong, and there read some missionary literature translated into Chinese. In his deep depression he dreamed he had risen up to Heaven, where he met God, God's wife, and their son Jesus.[8] He learned he was Jesus' younger brother, and learned, too, that he had the mission of expelling the demons—meaning both the Manchus and Confucius—from China, establishing the Heavenly Kingdom of Great Peace.

Hong made converts among his family and neighbors. The authorities feared the sect's subversive implications, provoking it to militancy. The Taipings grew rapidly into a major military and political force, within a few years controlling cities and scattered territory south of the Yangtze and waging military campaigns north of that river.

There is still no clear explanation of the appeal of the Taipings. The rebellion itself was probably a symptom of cultural and social unease, as was the endemic opium addiction. Christianity as such may have been a relatively minor element in the appeal. Taiping Christianity is often dismissed as an ignorant caricature of the real thing, but it is probably no more unorthodox or strange than the contemporaneous Mormon movement in North America. The Taipings also made repeated efforts to instruct themselves in the more mainline versions of the religion. Yet it may well be that the Taiping teachings lacked spiritual depth and were too closely connected with the personalities of a too obviously flawed leadership. In any case, Taiping Christianity vanished without a trace following the final defeat of the rebellion.

The movement's leadership was Hakka. The Hakka are a subgroup of the Han people who migrated south centuries ago. They have customs and language different from their "native" southern neighbors. They have a reputation of being tough, resourceful, and independent, and have also been targets of discrimination from those around them. It is understandable that the Hakka as a whole might be less attached to the way things were than the ordinary Chinese—yet the appeal of the Taiping was hardly restricted to the Hakka. The Hakka, possibly, were overrepresented in the movement, but were still only a minority within it.

Southern China had been brutally subdued by the Manchus two centuries earlier, where the invaders met strong resistance from both gentry and the common people. The southern provinces were also disadvantaged by the quotas set by the Qing dynasty on the number of possible civil service exam passers. The Taipings appealed to residual anti-Manchu sentiment in the south, or, since it is unlikely that the average southerner ever saw a Manchu, the rebellion may instead have reactivated that sentiment. The Taiping had a

---

8. The Chinese rendering of Jehovah or Yahweh, the forbidden Hebrew name of God, is *Yehewa* or, to give it a Chinese form, *Ye Hewa*. Jesus is *Yesu*, or *Ye Su*. Thus, it can easily be made to seem that they are father and son in the Ye family. The similarity is, of course, not a coincidence, since Yahweh is the root of the word *Jesus* (that is, Yeshua, a variant on Joshuah, "the Lord saves").

radical program of land redistribution, although they did not control sufficient tracts of rural territory to give their program a fair try. They advocated sexual equality and even recruited women soldiers.[9] Strict celibacy was enforced on the troops, backed by the death penalty, although the leaders did not apply the rule to themselves.

The Taiping are sometimes considered proto-nationalists, although the movement was not particularly hostile to foreigners and even aspired to foreign support. In general the movement seems without specific cause, but to be a product of a disordered society, a reflection of free-floating resentments against the order of things and diminishing capacity of the existing order to defend itself. The Chinese communists claim the Taiping among their precursors.

The Taiping long occupied Nanking and a few other cities south of the Yangtze. There they set up their own civil service examinations, based on the Bible rather than the Confucian classics. With time, however, they did begin to refer to some of the more utopian elements in the Confucian canon. Like other radical populist Chinese social movements, by the time of their defeat the Taiping seem to have been in the process of coming to terms with the mainstream Chinese tradition.

While Taiping ideology may not have had strong staying power, the gravest weakness may have been the quality of the leadership. Some of its practices seem hypocritical. Although they imposed strict sexual morality on their followers, the Taiping leaders, or princes, as they were called, accumulated impressive harems for themselves. Some of the behavior of the princes smacks of charlatanry. One of Hong Xiuquan's relatives, for example, took to claiming that while Hong was Jesus' younger brother, he himself was a manifestation of the Holy Ghost, using this to boost his status within the hierarchy. Hong was apparently unwilling to call him on this claim for fear that to do so might bring his own revelation into question. Rivalry and jealousy among the princes disrupted the movement, especially after Hong's death, with capable military leaders becoming targets of intrigue by their less-talented colleagues. A visitor to Taiping-held Nanking commented that the whole affair was without the slightest hint of the kingly way.

The character of the movement caused much of the more capable and honest of the gentry to rally to the Qing dynasty. It was not so much that they loved Manchu rule: the Manchus, however, were at least civilized—they embodied and protected Confucian civilization; the Taiping, on the other hand, with their outlandish beliefs and assaults upon true values, may have been Chinese in birth, but were barbarian in their souls. The Qing military establishment had been organized around "banners," hereditary regiments of

---

9. Hakka women did not bind their feet and generally enjoyed greater social freedoms than their sisters in other Chinese communities.

Manchus and Chinese who had allied with the Manchus at the time of the conquest. The soft and inexperienced heirs to a proud military tradition proved ineffective against both Westerners and Taipings. As the rebellion spread through the central provinces, a Hunanese official, Zeng Guofan, returned to his hometown and persuaded his relatives and the other gentry to put up money for a peasant militia to fight the Taipings. Zeng's force and others like it became the nucleus of China's first modern armies. In the short term they saved the dynasty from the Taipings, but over the longer run they proved to be another symptom of its decay. The new armies were held together by the personal relationships among their commanders, the loyalty of officers to their superiors rather than to the state or dynasty as such; given the poor state of the central government's finances, most of the funding for the new armies came from local or provincial sources.

A second key reason for the dynasty's survival was the rallying to it of foreign opinion. The foreign powers also had no particular use for the Manchus, and in the beginning some Westerners expressed considerable sympathy for the Taipings. From a colder point of view, however, Western statesmen and merchants calculated that no one would predict what a China under Taiping rule would be like. The Manchus, of course, were stubborn, xenophobic, corrupt, and reactionary, but at least you could push them around.

With the defeat of the Taipings, Zeng Guofan became the main figure in the Chinese government and for a short time the Qing followed a constructive policy of conservative reform.[10] This program fell apart after Zeng's death. His lieutenant, Li Hongzhang, was not his equal either in ability or character. Power at the court gravitated to the Empress Dowager, the mother, aunt, and great aunt of the dynasty's remaining emperors. She could dominate the emperors by virtue of her status as a parent, but her sex prevented her from holding legal power, and she maintained her position by playing court factions off against each other, preventing China from following a consistent policy of either conservative or radical reform.

In retrospect, the defeat of the Taipings may have been a tragedy for China, despite all their deficiencies. A new regime would have been able to deal with the new challenges in new ways. The Qing, on their part, may have been more unimaginatively conservative than a native Chinese dynasty would have been. Because the rulers were Manchus, they could not automatically call on Chinese patriotic or nationalist sentiment; their legitimacy rested on their commitment to the Confucian order, and their situation may have forced them to interpret this order in a rigid, mechanical way. A new dynasty may have been better able to deal with the modern world in a way consistent with China's traditions, in a manner analogous to what happened in Japan.

---

10. Mary C. Wright, *The Last Stand of Chinese Conservatism: The T'ung-chih Restoration, 1862–1874* (New York, 1966).

As things were, the dynasty survived for more than half a century after the end of the Taiping Rebellion—but on artificial life support, as it were, unable to reform itself but with no force strong enough to overthrow it.

A Crisis of Civilization

By the end of the 1800s it seemed that the civilization that had served the society so well for 2,000 years no longer worked. The most traumatic event was the loss of a war with Japan in 1894–95, in which Japan took away China's traditional influence over Korea and also appropriated to itself the province of Taiwan. By that time the Chinese were used to losing to Western powers, but they had known the Japanese for centuries, considering them a people who with greater or lesser success aspired to the kind of civilization China enjoyed. Conservatives could previously console themselves by thinking that Western technological superiority was based on a devilish knowledge of barbarian techniques unworthy of humane and decent people. In logic the Japanese mastery of such techniques should not have mattered, but psychologically it certainly made the Chinese wonder why the Japanese were able to do what they themselves seemed incapable of.

Part of the problem was simple in principle: China would do better against the outside if the government were more competent, honest, and efficient. One joke was that the funds allocated for the Chinese navy had gone instead to building a marble pavilion in the shape of a boat in the lake at the Empress Dowager's summer palace on the outskirts of Peking. But thoughtful people also increasingly recognized that competence and honesty alone were not enough. Western superiority lay in modern technology, and modern technology could not be adopted in isolation from comprehensive social change. Yet if social change meant that China should lose its distinctive civilization, then conservatives for both moral and practical reasons might be wary of such change: China might gain the world but lose its soul.

The statesman Zhang Zhidong popularized a slogan: Chinese learning as the essence, Western learning for practical use. China should take on Western technology in industry, military affairs, business, and the like, but the moral and political system should remain Confucian.

Essence and use are technical neo-Confucian terms. *Ti*, substance or essence, indicates what a thing is; *yong*, use or function, points to what it does or how it works. Critics, both radical and conservative, were quick to point out Zhang's abuse of philosophical concepts. Yan Fu, a radical westernizer, pointed out: a horse has the ti of a horse, an ox the ti of an ox; the ti of each is clearly related to its yong. The function of a horse (that is, what a horse can do) is to run long distances; the function of an ox is to pull great loads. It is nonsensical to talk about putting the yong of a horse into the ti of an ox. Wo Ren, a very conservative Manchu official, made the same argument: We cannot say that the West is function and China is essence. China has its essence and its function; the West has its essence and its function. To function like the West, China must become Western in essence. For Wo Ren, the way to remain Chinese was to remain Chinese.

This being admitted, the slogan can be construed in a nonabsurd, commonsensical way. Japan had, after all, achieved something very much like what Zhang Zhitong advocated, and Japanese publicists even used an equivalent slogan: Eastern essence, Western use. There is no reason to believe that Confucian morality is inappropriate to modern society.

The problem is more concrete than abstract. As Yan Fu and Wo Ren pointed out, Chinese learning had its function: crassly, the production of a social and political elite. If it lost this function, practically speaking there would be little incentive to continue the Chinese essence, at least as it was known (or operated—the philosophical discussion continues to intrude) at the time. If rewards and status continued to accrue primarily to Confucian studies, who would want to study engineering or commerce or military science? To reward modern learning would require a decision by the elite to eliminate the foundations of its own status. In effect, the essence–use distinction led to an empty slogan, not a real program.[11]

Another approach involved a reinterpretation of what Confucianism and, hence, Chinese culture, really meant. The philosopher Kang Youwei (1858–1927) asserted that far from being incompatible with modernity, Confucianism was really a program for it. A properly esoteric interpretation of the Confucian classics shows a projection of all human history, a forecast of its fate. Confucius long ago predicted the evolution of the world toward the Great Harmony, an age in which people would be able to fly. They would live in an even more than normally repellent utopia, with all distinctions of status and sex abolished, with the hospitals conveniently adjacent to the potash plants.

Kang's views had a limited appeal. They were too forced and strange for orthodox Confucians and irrelevant to the radicals who were ready to abandon Confucianism itself as the main obstacle to China's modernization. Yet, however fantastical in the long run, Kang's theory had sensible, pragmatic implications for the short term. Kang believed that a Chinese, Confucius, had discovered the truth of human affairs, but that China had systematically misinterpreted Confucius and so had fallen behind the rest of the world, where Confucius's vision was on the way to being implemented—although without proper moral direction, since the modern West was also ignorant of Confucius. A proper understanding of Confucianism required economic, cultural, and political modernization.

---

11. This discussion is strongly influenced by Levinson, *Confucian China and Its Modern Fate.*

In 1898 Kang was granted an audience with the young emperor. Kang proposed a program of thoroughgoing political reform, including the adoption of a written constitution, a modern civil service, and elected representative assemblies. Kang urged in effect that China should take measures similar to those already adopted in Japan. His ideas made sense to the emperor, who over a period of about 100 days issued an appropriate series of decrees, pushing China into rapid political change.

The reforms, however, cut at the sources of the power of the Empress Dowager and the more conservative Manchu courtiers. After gaining the support of Yuan Shikai, the commander of the modern army stationed around Peking, a man previously considered a strong reformer, the Empress Dowager ordered the emperor into seclusion in the inner palace and caused the suicide of his favorite wife, who had been an enthusiast for reform. She ordered the arrest of Kang and his disciples. Kang himself with some of his friends was able to escape to Japan, but those who could not get away were executed.

China continued to weaken domestically, and international pressures increased. By the end of the century there was genuine fear that China would be "carved up like a melon." The Empress Dowager's solution was to turn for help to a secret society, the Boxers.[12] They had originally been anti-Manchu, with the aim of restoring the Ming dynasty. Somehow, agents of the court managed to turn the organization around, so that the Boxers now supported the Qing and wanted to rid China of Christianity and the barbarians. They raged through northern China in 1900, killing foreign missionaries and Chinese converts. They entered Peking and laid siege to the foreign diplomatic legations in the capital.

The foreign powers put together an eight-nation[13] expeditionary force to fight the Boxers and rescue the diplomats. As the foreign troops moved on Peking the Qing court declared war against the powers. The military governors of the southern provinces, however, announced that they did not consider themselves at war. The southern soldiers were taking the only realistic course; their ability to disobey the government, however, is evidence of how much central authority had come to rest on local consent.

Despite surprisingly effective resistance the foreign armies entered the capital. Peking was occupied and the Empress Dowager forced, temporarily, to flee. Huge indemnities were imposed on China, along with further foreign control over the country's internal affairs. Foreign troops were stationed permanently at locations throughout China. China had reached the depth of its humiliation.

---

12. They are so-called for their practice of *gongfu* (kung-fu) or the martial arts. The Chinese name is *Yihequan*. This translates literally as "righteous harmonious fists," and is probably too awkward and unusual a term to use in English. The nickname Boxer also probably tends to trivialize the movement, but it is well established.

13. Britain, France, Germany, Japan, the United States, Russia, Austria, Italy.

Now even the Empress Dowager knew that something had to be done. She began to wear a Western dress and invite the ladies of the diplomatic corps to tea in the palace. The government began again to implement reforms. In 1905 the examination system was abolished and a modern educational system established (on paper). The Empress Dowager died in 1908, a few hours after the unfortunate emperor (it is assumed she had him poisoned), and a baby emperor took the throne. The reforms continued their course, with preparations for first provincial and then national legislative elections. During their last decade the Manchus tried to achieve what had been projected in 1898, and which conceivably might have worked then. But by the 1900s the only thing keeping the Qing dynasty up was the lack of a force sufficiently powerful to knock it down.

Japan

Although smaller than China, Japan had several advantages over it in dealing with the West. Because it had fewer resources, it was a less-tempting target and so was able to make a certain psychological preparation for the onslaught from the outside. The Japanese were able to see what the British had done first to India and then to China. They knew that Japan was not going to be able to keep the foreigners out forever, and also that when the opening did come, without change Japan would be powerless in the face of superior Western technology.

In the early 1800s Japan rebuffed attempts by Britain, Russia, and the United States to open the islands to foreign commerce. The United States was particularly interested in the opening of Japan. America at that time had the world's largest whaling fleet, and the oceans around Japan were particularly rich in that animal. The Americans wanted to be able to go ashore to get fresh water and buy pine trunks to replace broken masts.

In 1853 Commodore Matthew Perry, America's highest-ranking sailor, steamed into Edo harbor with his squadron of "black ships." This time the bakufu officials decided it would be expedient at least to talk to the intrusive foreigners. Perry treated them to a mixture of diplomacy, threats, and bluff. He then sailed away for a season to give the Japanese time to think about his offers, with the implication that if they did not do what he wanted he might turn to stronger methods. Knowing they could not put up effective military resistance, the bakufu yielded to the inevitable, and when Perry returned agreed in principle to a commercial treaty with the United States.

The End of the Bakufu

The opening to America was followed, as a matter of course, by the opening to everyone else. This was a violation of basic bakufu policy and made clear how weak that government had become. The shogun made things worse by convening the daimyo together to consult with them on what should be done next. There was nothing wrong with consultation in itself, of course, and it might have been a good idea from the beginning for the bakufu to have had such a practice. But by asking advice from his inferiors at a time of acute crisis, the shogun left the impression that he was no longer sure of his authority to command and to be obeyed.

Opponents of the bakufu coined a slogan: Revere the emperor, expel the barbarian. Both aspects of the slogan were subversive: it implied that the shogun had usurped the legitimate power of the emperor and had also sold out to foreigners. But the bakufu could only make itself look bad by trying to suppress the sentiment the slogan expressed. Educated public opinion in general increasingly distanced itself from the bakufu. The main organized forces included factions in the imperial court in Kyoto and samurai from the tozama han, especially the powerful southern fiefdoms of Satsuma and Choshu. Satsuma and Choshu were as rivalrous with each other as they were with the bakufu, so the result was a complex political quadrille, with Satsuma sometimes allied with the bakufu against Choshu, Choshu sometimes allied with the bakufu against Satsuma, in a rather small-scale civil war.

In 1868 things came to a head. The old emperor, who had a reputation of being extremely antiforeign, died or, some say, was poisoned and his son, a 14-year-old boy, took the throne. At about the same time, Satsuma and Choshu managed to form a coalition, joining against the bakufu and forcing the shogun to resign. The shogun was given a generous pension and the Tokugawa remain a highly respected and respectable Tokyo family to this day. The victors declared the restoration of direct imperial rule.

The Meiji Restoration

Although in principle power had been "restored" to the emperor, in practice policy was set by the young samurai from Satsuma and Choshu, colloquially known as the Satcho clique (although the clique also had factional divisions within itself). The Satcho group's anti-bakufu program called for expelling the barbarian, but having come to power they knew this could not be done literally. The program was reinterpreted to mean that Japan should strengthen itself so as to deal on equal terms with the barbarians. This implied a thoroughgoing modernization, the adoption of Western technology and industry and the social and political structure necessary to sustain that technological and industrial base. At the same time they wanted to keep as much of the traditional system of authority as they could, both because they believed in it and because it made their hold on power more secure. The emperor was developed as a symbol of this structure of authority, with that authority identified with the *kokutai*, the "essence of the state."[14] The new

---

14. The *tai* here is the same as the Chinese *ti*, as in ti and yong.

emperor took the reign name Meiji, "bright rule."[15] The guiding theme of the Meiji Restoration was "eastern learning as the essence, western learning for use."

The modernization program was outlined in a "charter oath" the Satcho samurai wrote for the young emperor. The emperor promised to consult with both nobility and commons on matters of reform and the best policy for Japan. Japan would seek enlightenment from foreign lands and abandon the "absurd customs of former times."

In short order the new government abolished the feudal system, giving the daimyo generous pensions and markedly less generous ones to ordinary samurai. Legal inequalities of status were abolished. The han were replaced by a system of prefectures, modeled on French local government, with magistrates appointed by Tokyo ("eastern capital"—formerly Edo; with the Restoration the emperor moved into what had been the shogun's castle). Japan built a modern army and navy, based upon what were thought to be the best foreign models. The model for the navy, of course, was British. The army was first based upon that of France, but this was rapidly changed to Prussia after that country easily defeated France in a war in 1871. The army required an economic base, so the government invested in the construction of factories, selling them to private entrepreneurs once they began to run a profit. It was understood that the businessmen would continue to take direction from the government in return for being allowed to make profits—a relationship between government and business that has persisted for more than a century. At first Japan concentrated on light industry, especially textiles, with many of the very earliest textile workers being the wives and daughters of the newly impoverished samurai; the women approached their tasks with patriotic dedication. Industry required an educated labor force, so the government enforced compulsory education, at first up to the third grade for both girls and boys; by 1900 the population was almost totally literate. The government was unwilling to allow much foreign investment—another perennial Japanese official attitude—so the capital for economic development was raised internally, gouged from the peasantry through land taxes and other exactions, with poor farmers paying most of the cost of Japan's modernization.

While Japan's adjustment to modernity was clearly easier than China's, it was not without psychological and other stress. In the first flush of enthusiasm, some Japanese tended to identify everything Western as civilized and

---

15. His personal name was Mutsuhito, but the name was too sacred to be used by anyone. The reign name technically refers to the *period* during which the emperor holds the throne; thus, he is the Meiji emperor, as if we were to call Franklin D. Roosevelt the "New Deal president." (Note that China had a similar system; thus, we say the Qianlong emperor, technically, the emperor of the Qianlong period.) The reign name becomes the emperor's posthumous name, so after his death we can say the Emperor Meiji.

everything Japanese as crude and backward. Many Japanese had a pervasive fear that foreigners would laugh at them. The new attitudes extended even to food. Sukyaki, a grilled beef dish, is not traditionally Japanese but an invention of the Meiji period, developed because Westerners liked beef and thus a liking for beef must have something to do with wealth and power. Men took to wearing Western clothes in public and cutting their hair in the Western fashion.

In 1877, the Satsuma samurai Saigo Takamori, one of the original reformers, had become thoroughly disgusted with how far his colleagues were willing to go and organized an antigovernment revolt. He was joined by large numbers of former samurai unhappy with what they saw as their loss of status and way of life. In the Satsuma rebellion the hereditary warriors were handily defeated by the new modern army of conscripted peasant kids.

The Meiji State

In 1789 the United States became the first country to adopt a written constitution. A century later Japan became the first non-Western state to do so. The constitution was drafted by the Satcho oligarchy. It is surprising at first that they would want one, since any constitution in principle limits state power, while the Satcho group in principle wanted that authority to do anything they thought proper.

The oligarchy had several motives. The most shallow was, probably, to humor the foreigners. The Western powers had imposed unequal treaties on Japan as on China, although not to as severe a degree. They would not renegotiate the treaties until Japan had what they considered a "civilized" set of laws. A written constitution would remove the pretext for the unequal treaties.

Satcho policies had produced a great deal of discontent in society, both from conservatives attached to the old ways and from radicals resentful of the clique's authoritarian ways. A written constitution would provide an institutional framework for the expression of public opinion without necessarily allowing it to make policy. A constitution would also regularize the system of rule generally.

Although it was not officially adopted until 1889, the constitution was long in the making. Its main designer, Ito Hirobumi, an ex-samurai from Choshu, took a trip around the world, studying various systems of government and consulting with constitutional scholars in different countries. He decided that just as Prussia had the best army, so it also had the constitution most appropriate to Japanese conditions—particularly in the scope it allowed to executive power.

The American constitution begins: "We, the People..." This is a formulation the Meiji constitution deliberately avoids. It explicitly rejects any idea of popular sovereignty. Rather, the emperor is and remains sovereign. The emperor retains all executive, legislative, and judicial authority. The constitution, which prescribes how that authority will be exercised, is a free gift of the emperor to his people, bestowed from his boundless grace.

The executive power is exercised by a cabinet, headed by a prime minister appointed by the emperor. The prime minister appoints other cabinet ministers—except for the ministers of the army and navy, who are also appointed directly by the emperor (and so not directly responsible to the civilian head of government).[16] The cabinet ministers were the political, responsible heads of the various government agencies, which were staffed at lower levels by a permanent civil service, recruited first from the Tokugawa civil service, later primarily from among graduates of the more prestigious universities.

Legislative power was vested in a parliament, or Diet, as the Japanese body has always been called in English.[17] The Diet consisted of two houses. The upper house was the House of Peers. Although the hereditary nobility had been abolished early in the Meiji period, it was partly restored. The new peerage consisted of much of the old court and upper daimyo nobility, along with meritorious persons the government wished to honor. The new nobles did not have the feudal privileges that went with their status under the Tokugawa. The powers of the upper house were, however, in principle the same as those of the lower, and in that way it served as a check on possible popular passions. The lower house, the House of Representatives, was elected by the people—but not, at first, by very many of them. In the early years there were stringent property qualifications for voting, although the franchise was gradually expanded until 1925, when it was extended to all male subjects aged 25 and over.

Historically the main power a legislature has had over the executive has been control of the purse. If the British Parliament or the American Congress does not approve and appropriate money for a project, that project cannot go forth. The Meiji framers avoided this inconvenience. The Diet had to approve changes in taxing and spending, but in the absence of such approval the government and its various ministries could continue to operate on the same level as in the previous year. It was certainly convenient for the government to have the consent of the Diet, but the Diet could not bring government to a halt.

The constitution also provided for a judicial system, modeled on the continental rather than the Anglo-Saxon model. Judges were charged with

---

16. Although not part of the constitution, at various times there were laws stipulating that the military ministers had to be active-duty officers; this made the military even more autonomous from civilian control.

17. The word is not Japanese but is taken from the German. Presumably it reflects the Prussian origins of the Meiji constitution, although the term continues in use today when that constitution is no longer in effect.

interpreting the laws and the constitution, and there seems to have been no general problem with the working of the courts. There was no question of a court's ever declaring a law or an administrative act unconstitutional.

The emphasis on the power of the emperor should not be misunderstood. The emperor was the source of all authority, but he was not supposed to be an actual ruler, much less a personal despot. He was for all purposes a constitutional monarch. He had no authority to issue commands. Laws and orders were promulgated in his name, but had no legal effect unless countersigned by the appropriate cabinet minister. The Meiji founders wanted in fact to curb any exercise of personal power by the emperor: the emperor was sacred and inviolable, meaning he could not be blamed when things went wrong. All responsibility and, therefore, all power for real decisions, remained with the political leadership. The emperor was supposed to be above the political process, not a part of it. The emperor might from time to time, when asked, offer his personal opinion on matters of policy, but even this was generally considered improper.[18] The reason for making the prime minister responsible to the emperor was not to allow the emperor to choose the person closest to his own heart but to give the government the greatest possible freedom of action, insulated from the will of the Diet.

Here, however, was a weakness in the constitution. Even though the emperor was supposed to abstain from politics, according to the constitution he also appointed the prime minister (and the ministers of the army and navy). Had the emperor actually exercised the appointment power and the other powers given to him, he would have had to make political decisions. The emperor did not make such decisions, but this left the actual source of overall decision making undefined.

This vagueness allowed the Meiji constitution to evolve in a democratic direction. By the 1920s prime ministers were generally chosen from the leadership of the political party holding a majority in the lower house of the Diet. But nothing in the constitution *guaranteed* democracy, and by the end of the 1930s power had shifted to a collection of military cliques—without violating either the letter or the spirit of the constitution.

The first solution to the general problem of where political authority should be lodged was probably the most effective. During the last part of the Meiji period basic political decisions were made by a semiofficial agency, the *genro-in*, "council of original elders" or founding fathers. During the last decade of the nineteenth century the Satcho samurai who had brought about the Restoration ceased to hold active government or political office,

---

18. This seems to be the constitutional rule. A minority of historians in Japan and abroad assert that informally both the Meiji and the Showa (1926–1989) emperors had a great deal of personal influence on policy.

but continued to meet behind the scenes to decide on basic questions of personnel and policy. While the genro survived the Japanese system functioned in an exemplary fashion. As they died off the country entered a period of chronic constitutional crisis.

The Meiji emperor died in 1912. When he had taken the throne Japan was a medieval society and economy bullied by the powers of the world. At his relatively early death Japan was a major industrial and military power, itself something of a bully on the world scene.

China, Japan, and the West

China and Japan began from roughly the same base and faced roughly the same challenges from the modern world system. It seems fair to say that as a society Japan handled the challenge more successfully, despite Japan's relative lack of resources.

Part of the explanation must lie in specific historical conditions and events: Japan had a longer time to prepare for the challenge, and could profit from China's (bad) example. Here Japan's relative lack of resources was probably an advantage. The outside world put less pressure on Japan and was slower in getting to it. In Japan the old order was rapidly replaced by reformers, who had a clear field of action. In China the old order lingered, and there was no political opportunity to implement radical change. Although the Qing government proved to be more resilient than the Tokugawa, it probably had a weaker hold on its society. Japan's relatively small size probably meant, all else being equal, that it was easier to govern, and therefore easier to enforce reforms upon.

There is a dramatic difference in the way the two societies were able to resolve the issue of "eastern essence and western use." Japan's modernization seems to have included salvaging a great deal of the traditional culture, especially its moral elements. In China at that time modernization seems to have been at the expense of tradition. Although the two societies are part of the larger Confucian tradition, that tradition meant different things for each.

In effect, each society had its own traditional "essence." There is nothing in the Confucian tradition as such that precludes modernization, but that tradition as embodied in Qing China may have been a grave obstacle to modernization.

Status and power in China rested on education, but on education of a very specific sort: immersion in the Confucian classics. By 1900 there was also a small but growing number who had received a modern, Western-style education, but there was no place for such persons in the Qing system. Those who might have had the power to change the system could do so only by undercutting the basis of their own power and status at the cost of everything that gave meaning to their lives.[19]

The way of life of the samurai of the Tokugawa period was much like that of the Chinese gentry and officialdom. Their status, however, was based on birth rather than achievement. Although less modern than the Chinese system, the Japanese way was more hospitable to modernization. Since one was a samurai by birth, one did not have to do any particular thing to be a samurai or enjoy the status that went along with it. To be sure, the Meiji reformers abolished the old system of hereditary privilege. This was much more a legal reality than a social one, however, and the glamour of noble status remained after its legal basis was gone. In fact, Japan did not have a "commoner" as prime minister until 1919, and that gentleman had been born into a quite noble family but chose not to resume the status officially when the peerage was restored. By contrast, gentry status in China could be attained only in the context of the existing Chinese order. To modernize would have destroyed the status entirely (as, of course, eventually happened).

By about 1850 neither the Qing nor the Tokugawa necessarily enjoyed great support within the societies they ruled. But to act against the Tokugawa did not mean to tear down Japanese culture. Parts of that culture could even be used against the Tokugawa: Shinto and the cult of the emperor, for example. Given the pressures of the outside world, after the Opium War no new set of Chinese rulers could have hoped to base their title on the old claim to be the Son of Heaven, holder of the Mandate, legitimate ruler of everything under Heaven. The claim was hardly credible for the Qing, either, but at least they had the advantage of inertia. Those who valued the tradition even as it was becoming obsolete had reason to keep silent about any distaste they might have held for the Qing. Increasingly, from the perspective of those committed to Chinese culture, the alternative to the Manchus was chaos and barbarism.

The less modern Japanese theory of legitimacy was also more favorable to modernization than that of the Chinese. The Chinese emperor's right to rule rested on ability and achievement. He ruled because his rule benefited the people. Benefit to the people, however, was defined in terms of the current

---

19. England in the 1800s and afterward was ruled through a civil service educated mainly in the Greek and Latin classics, and this civil service is sometimes compared with the Chinese mandarinate. In fact, the British system of civil service examinations, adopted in the late 1800s, was based in part upon the Chinese example. (The American civil service system, adopted a little bit later, was copied from the Chinese as well as the British system; the Americans, however, geared the examination to the recruitment of specialists, while the Chinese and the British stressed general knowledge and skills.) In England, however, the state did not dominate society to the extent that it did in China, and the civil service was hardly the only completely respectable path to wealth and power.

Confucian vision. Reforms that might disrupt Confucian society could be construed, at best, as amoral Legalist interference—things that possibly might make the state more effective but would also destroy its moral foundation. The Japanese emperor was sacred in his very being, regardless of any personal qualities or behavior he might show. His position was not tied to any particular social or political order, and he could serve as a symbol of continuity in an era of rapid change.

Given the world environment they found themselves in, to modernize successfully China and Japan had to learn to act as states like any other in a world of states, in an era in which the nation, the sense of being a special people, was becoming the major legitimizing element in the state. The Chinese had seen themselves not as a nation, but as persons participating in civilization, culture. By 1900 it was evident, however, that Chinese civilization or culture was itself only one among many. The Japanese had always seen themselves as something like a nation—a special people within the general civilization defined by Chinese standards. It was not that difficult for them to see themselves next as a special people within the general civilization defined by the modern West. The ground had already been prepared for the political modernization of Japan. Chinese modernization required substantial numbers of persons in positions that counted to value the wealth and power of a Chinese nation more than they valued the survival of Chinese culture as they knew it. Yet even the most radical of modernizers would sometimes have ambivalent feelings about Chinese culture: perhaps it was backward, but it was also magnificent. Modernization in China meant a revolutionary collapse of the old order, and that revolution has probably not yet fully played itself out.

6

✦

Change and Decay

In 1911 the Qing dynasty finally collapsed, more from its own decrepitude than from the strength of those who pushed it. The old social and political order was no longer viable, but there was nothing at hand to replace it. China entered a period of near-anarchy lasting almost 40 years. The revolution resulted first in a personal dictatorship and later in warfare among ambitious military chieftains, "warlords." The Kuomintang (KMT) or Nationalist party seemed by the 1930s to be about to consolidate its own rule and institutionalize a new and effective system. This emerging order, however, was destroyed by war with Japan and later civil war with the Communist Party of China (CPC). In 1949 the Communists were able to impose their own rule, although after more than 40 years this rule has probably not been fully institutionalized.

Japan entered its own period of crisis after the Meiji period. In most ways the crisis was less serious than in China, although someone judging from the perspective of 1945 might have thought its consequences worse. In the 1910s and 1920s the political system evolved in a democratic direction, although the democracy was rather corrupt and did not enjoy respect or support from the ordinary person. During the 1930s Japan came to be ruled by soldiers committed to a harshly fanatical nationalism, leading to a police state at home and aggression abroad. The foreign policies, especially, led to the virtual physical destruction of the country and to the only occupation by a foreign army the islands have ever known.

The Chinese Revolution

The Revolution of 1911 was a genuine historical turning point, even if its immediate effects were superficial and the event itself mostly the outward sign of changes that had long been taking place. The Qing attempted constructive reforms in the 1900s, but these only helped weaken the dynasty further. The dynasty experimented with local self-government and democracy at the provincial level, encouraging the formation of provincial assemblies, so giving the local gentry one more opportunity to assert autonomy from the center. Most of the gentry believed, to be sure, that there should be a strong and effective central government, but they were far from confident that the Qing court could provide one.

In 1905 the dynasty abolished the traditional examinations in favor of a modern educational and civil service system. This symbolized and reinforced a trend already taking place. As Mencius said, those who labor with their minds rule others: ability to use one's mind justified authority over others. The old gentry may have sometimes exploited the people, but there was a sense that they had earned their status by their mastery of the dominant values of the society. After 1905 power relations in the countryside remained perhaps in substance what they had long been, but the rationalization was gone. Power was increasingly seen to rest upon fortune, fraud, and force, with cunning, luck, crime, and warfare becoming more obviously the routes to local and national power.

When the old order collapsed there was nothing to replace it. At the base, at the level of the family and face-to-face groups, there were certainly strains, but perhaps the society remained basically healthy. There was nothing to hold the society together at the top.

Sun Yat-sen and the Revolution of 1911

In 1894 Sun Yat-sen (1866–1925), a native of the region between Hong Kong and Canton, organized a revolutionary group in Honolulu. This organization, after various name changes, evolved into the Kuomintang (KMT), Nationalist party. Sun and his comrades wanted not merely to overthrow the Manchus but to replace the whole dynastic system with a modern republic founded on the principles of liberal democracy.

Sun may be a good example of a marginal man—a person living between worlds, partaking of all but not completely integrated into any. His native area was not rich, and for generations many natives of the region had left to sojourn, as overseas Chinese, in Southeast Asia, America, or Europe. Sun was thus exposed to Western influences, although necessarily of a shallow kind, from his early years. As a boy he listened to war stories of old Taiping soldiers, much as boys of his generation in the American South listened to the tales of aging ex-Confederates. He picked up hostility to the Manchus from them, although China's far south had a long anti-Manchu tradition anyway. As a teenager Sun went to live with an older brother who had a sugar plantation in Hawaii, and there he attended an Episcopal high school. At some point he converted to Christianity. Hawaii was by then already under predominant American influence, and it may have been there that Sun came to his high opinion of American democracy. He valued democracy for its own sake and also because it was then associated with economic prosperity and national strength. He later studied (Western-style) medicine in Hong Kong and became a doctor, although his main interest was always politics.

Sun's political fortune was made in 1896. While living in London he somehow, whether through his own foolishness or a ruse, entered the Chinese embassy. He was detained and held in a room in the attic, pending his return to China for execution. The "kidnapping" became known to the English doctor who had taught him medicine, who had in the meantime also returned to London to live, and that gentleman organized a vigorous campaign in the press and among British officialdom to have Sun released. The Chinese were forced to let him go. As a result of this adventure he became world famous, the best-known and most glamorous spokesman for Chinese modernization and democracy.

Sun's associates carried out various "uprisings" in southern and coastal China in the 1900s, for the most part acts of terror against local officials. This brought distress to the victims, the perpetrators (most of whom were caught and executed), and their families, but did not seriously inconvenience the Qing dynasty. Sun did not have much mass support. His following was among the more or less westernized intellectuals and business people in the treaty ports. The overseas Chinese, not tied into the traditional system, disdainful of the Manchus, patriotically concerned, at a distance, with the well-being of their homeland, and relatively wealthy, were a source of income for the movement. Sun also attracted the support of Chinese students in Japanese universities and military academies. There he competed for influence with the followers of Kang Youwei. Both reformers and revolutionaries supported some kind of constitutional democracy, but the reformers hoped to achieve this in the framework of the Qing dynasty. Despite being a revolutionary, Sun kept a very high regard for traditional Chinese culture, although his understanding of it was less deep than that of the scholarly reformers.

He tried, without success, to interest the American and British governments in his revolution. He had slightly better luck in Japan, getting funding from various political and industrial combinations, some motivated by idealism, some figuring that after the fall of the Qing Japan could get a better deal for itself in China.

The decisive event came on October 10, 1911. Some Japan-trained young officers in the army stationed in Wuchang, a strategic industrial city inland on the Yangtze in central China, staged a mutiny. They dragged their poor commanding officer from under his bed, where he was hiding from them, put a pistol to his head, and offered him the choice of leading the revolution or being shot. Hubei, the province Wuchang is part of, declared its independence from the dynasty. Within a few days the military in other central and southern provinces also declared independence.

Sun Yat-sen had nothing to do directly with all this. He was on a fund-raising trip among overseas Chinese communities at the time, and learned about the revolution from a newspaper in Denver, Colorado. He did start back home—although he took his time about it, going by way of London, where he made further attempts to get official British support. Back in China, he became "provisional president" of the proposed Republic.

The court turned for help to Yuan Shikai. Yuan had been the commander of the army stationed around Peking, China's most modern armed force, tracing its lineage back to the militias raised by Zeng Guofan to fight the Taipings. Yuan was the Chinese military commander in Korea during the war against Japan. Although he had lost that fight, he was still considered China's most capable and progressive soldier. In 1898 he seemed to back reform, but then sided with the Empress Dowager and led the purge and killing of the reformers.

Later he himself fell from grace and in 1911 was in retirement. He made the court officials come beg him to resume command. He led his army to the Yangtze, fought some desultory battles, and opened negotiations with the rebels. By the early spring he and the revolutionaries had made a deal: in return for selling out the Manchus, Yuan would become the first regular president of the new Republic of China. Sun, motivated more by patriotism than thirst for power, agreed to step aside. Yuan returned to Peking to give his former masters the news.

The Aftermath of the Revolution

Following the change of regime there were elections to a national legislature. Sun had hoped that the KMT would act as a kind of parliamentary opposition. Yuan Shikai had at best an elementary concept of what this meant and little liking for what he did understand. His goons gunned down a couple of KMT legislative leaders, and Sun Yat-sen once again fled to Japan.

The revolution made little difference to the ordinary person. One view is provided by the famous short novel, *The True Story of Ah Q*, by Lu Xun, this century's best-known writer of vernacular Chinese prose. Writing in 1919, Lu Xun presents Ah Q, a cowardly village bully, as the epitome of what he considered to be defects in China's national character. He is vulgar and violently abusive toward women, whom he regards as impure because they arouse his lust. Whenever he is beaten up by the local ne'er-do-wells, Ah Q proclaims that he has won a spiritual victory—in this allegedly similar to Qing dynasty China, priding itself on its cultural and spiritual superiority to the materialistic West. When the thugs hear of Ah Q's boasting they return to beat him some more, giving him even more pride in just how abject he can be. Ah Q has constant run-ins with the local gentry and with the "fake foreign devil," a village intellectual who cut off his pigtail (a Manchu hairstyle forced on all the emperor's subjects during the Qing period) while studying in Japan—back home he deems it prudent to have a hairpiece to conceal his lost tresses. Ah Q envies and despises these local worthies, and they treat him with brutality and contempt.

Comes the Revolution, and Ah Q thinks his fortune is made. The main result, however, is that where previously the sign in front of the government office had read Great Qing, now it says Republic of China. The magistrate is the same, as is the local power structure—except now, perhaps, the fake foreign devil has a little more prestige than he used to. Fearing the spread of banditry in the wake of the possible breakdown of order, the local elite decide they need an example, and latch on to poor Ah Q, who has, after all, been rather noisy in sounding off about the revolution. The story ends with Ah Q's execution. It is a bitter work and the caricature is not completely fair. On the whole, however, while the revolution may have met some of the political interests of the more westernized and urban Chinese, it did not mean much change for the ordinary person.

The longer-term effect was the deterioration of order that Ah Q's nemeses feared. Yuan Shikai ruled as a not very oppressive but neither very effective military dictator. He was able to handle without much trouble an attempt, joined in by some veterans of the 1898 reform, to put the Manchu emperor back on the throne. He had no principled objection to monarchy, however. In fact, one of his advisors, a somewhat unworldly American professor of political science, opined that China would do better as a constitutional monarchy than as a republic. In 1916 Yuan (and especially his son) intrigued for the establishment of a new dynasty. After everything seemed to be all set, adverse public opinion forced Yuan to back down. He died a few months later, perhaps of disappointment.

Yuan's death made visible the consequences of the localized militarism that had been growing since the Taiping Rebellion (and which had been a decisive factor in precipitating the 1911 revolution). When Yuan's desire to become emperor became known, the military governor of remote, prosperous Sichuan province rose in rebellion, and had not been suppressed by the time Yuan died. Elsewhere Yuan had been able to place his own subordinates in command of the provincial military. These soldiers, however, were not prepared to give each other the deference they gave Yuan. China fell into a decade of warlord anarchy as military leaders competed with each other for national power.

The warlords always needed money and did not scruple to get it from foreigners. They all aspired to restore unified, effective government to China. None had much of an idea of how to go about this—especially with all of those other warlords in the picture. The main object of warlord policy was the occupation of Peking. This had symbolic value as the national capital. Also, anyone who could claim, however tenuously, to be in control of the central government would get the funds collected by the international board in charge of administering China's tariffs. The money could buy weapons and pay soldiers.

Warlord politics is characterized by a bewildering series of alliances, counteralliances, and betrayals. Scholars have tried to make sense of the chaos by applying multi-person zero-sum game theory—a game especially structured so as not to reward at all any sentiments of loyalty or sense of shame. At a distance it seems promising material for farce. By the 1920s, however, thousands of soldiers were being killed in pointless battles and between battles wreaking destruction on helpless populations, and it was not funny at the time.

There was also during this period a visible change in cultural consciousness. The symbolic event is the May Fourth movement. China had joined the victorious allies in World War I, but Japan had also been an ally in that fight, a more significant ally than China. As an inducement to Japan to join the war, that country had been secretly promised all of the German concessions and privileges in China, especially those in Shandong province. At the Versailles conference, where the peace was hammered out, Japan claimed its due and the other allies, some more reluctantly than others, had to make good on their promise.

When news of this reached China, on May 4, 1919, students in Peking and other cities staged massive demonstrations directed both against Japan and against the weak and ineffective warlord government that made China helpless before Japan. These demonstrations were the first in a continuing tradition of student activism.[1]

The May Fourth incident gave its name to an entire period—roughly from 1915 to 1925. The students on May 4 believed that the warlord government kept China weak, but the deeper source of China's weakness was the traditional culture. A cultural revolution had to supplement and guarantee the

---

1. The warlords of May 4, 1919, showed more restraint than those of June 4, 1989. Despite some outrageous provocations by the students in 1919, none were killed by the authorities.

so-far disappointing political revolution of 1911. The young philosopher Hu Shi, a student of the American pragmatist John Dewey, successfully urged the replacement of the classical written language with the vernacular. He argued that the literary language was itself dead and no longer capable of producing anything worth reading or thinking. The young radicals summed up China's glorious past in terms of foot-binding, opium smoking, and eight-legged essays. The May Fourth generation would smash the shop of Confucius and Sons and take their business instead to Mr. Science and Mr. Democracy. Among the changes in customs dictated by these two gentlemen were equality for women and a dismantling of the authority of the traditional family system. By democracy the May Fourth generation meant at first liberal democracy, but the more advanced elements among them soon came to advocate socialism, conceived less as an alternative to liberalism than as an improvement on it. At least until 1949 Chinese democrats were in an ambiguous position. In the West, modern democracy was originally a method to limit the power of the state. Chinese democrats wanted more humane and rational rule, but they also wanted effective rule, and were not primarily concerned with limiting state power.

This intellectual ferment remained remote from the concerns of the ordinary person and obnoxious to the mind of the average warlord. But the movement and what it represented set new parameters for political activity. May Fourth intellectuals provided leadership and ideas for a revitalized KMT and, later, especially for the new Communist Party of China (CPC). Otherwise, by about 1920 China was without a coherent state or a coherent set of ideas upon which to build one.

The Search for Order: The Political Parties

Political power—according to one of the most famous aphorisms of Chinese Communist leader Mao Zedong—grows out of the barrel of a gun. If this is not always valid as a general political principle, it is certainly an accurate appreciation of how things worked in early twentieth-century China. As Mao also realized, an effective political order was the key to resolving the social, economic, and cultural problems plaguing China.

Guns by themselves, of course, could not bring this order. The warlords had plenty of guns, but lacked a program. The programs were formulated by the two major political parties, the KMT and the CPC. The parties, however, were impotent until each acquired its own private army. By the end of the 1920s these groups had become the main contenders for power over China.

For almost two decades the fates of the two parties were intertwined. They always competed with each other, but sometimes cooperated as well. Even after the Communists won complete control of the mainland in 1949 the two parties remained rivals, alternative focuses of legitimacy.

Rebuilding the KMT

In 1919 Sun Yat-sen came to an arrangement with the warlord who controlled Canton, near Sun's hometown. Sun was able to return to the area and use Canton as his base of operations. He had a stormy relationship with this gentleman, who after a few months expelled him. Later Sun was able to build his own military force and expel his warlord friend. He tightened his personal control over the KMT, demanding that each member swear personal allegiance to himself: the experience of post-1911 China had added some fiber to his idealism. After his return to China he received aid from the Comintern (the Communist International), the headquarters for the world Communist movement established in Moscow by Lenin after the 1917 Bolshevik Revolution. Sun was no communist and the Comintern was under no illusion that he was. Rather, Sun was considered a "bourgeois" anti-imperialist nationalist. China was held to be too backward for a socialist revolution, but was ready for bourgeois democracy and capitalism to replace feudalism.

The Comintern gave Sun organizational help, encouraging him to organize the KMT on the Leninist principle of democratic centralism, a pattern alleged to allow a combination of tactical flexibility with adherence to strict party discipline, and that tends to increase the ability of the central leadership to control the activities of the party. While the KMT took on Leninist forms, it remained in reality organized more on personalistic factions and personal loyalties. The Comintern also gave the KMT money for weapons and sent military advisors to teach party soldiers how to use them. In 1924 the KMT established a military academy at Whampoa, an island near Canton. Its commandant, Chiang Kai-shek, was a former Shanghai stockbroker who had studied military science in Japan. Chiang trained an officers' corps to lead a KMT army.

Sun Yat-sen took the occasion to develop the party's ideology along with its organization and military capacity. Sun's philosophy is known as the Three Principles of the People (*San Min Zhuyi*). These are nationalism, democracy, and welfare. In Chinese each of the principles contains the word for people, *min* (although the only place where the term translates neatly into English is democracy, *minzhuzhuyi*, or people's sovereignty). Sun compared his ideas to Abraham Lincoln's government of the people, by the people, for the people.

Nationalism (*minzuzhuyi* or "people's ethnicity") was sometimes early in the twentieth century translated as racism—although that term has come to have vicious connotations not appropriate for Sun's use of it. The term refers above all to the Chinese as an ethnic group. Originally it had anti-Manchu connotations: one nationality, the Manchus, had conquered the Han and other nationalities and reduced them all to inferiority. In the modern world, however, the state is an expression of the nation, and it is not fitting for a national minority to rule the state. Sun did not believe the Han should lord it over the Manchus, either—the Manchus, along with the Tibetans, Mongols, and others, were also a Chinese nationality. Sun seems to have taken for granted the general primacy of the Han, however, both because of their numerical preponderance and because of their cultural influence. Nationalism also emphasizes those qualities all Chinese share, rather than those that may divide them, such as family, partisan affiliation, or social class.

In the 1920s, disillusioned with Britain, the United States, and, increasingly, Japan, Sun interpreted nationalism in an anti-imperialistic sense. Nationalism implied a strong Chinese state, able to control its borders, subjecting foreigners within those borders to the jurisdiction of the laws, and participating on an equal basis in a world of other states.

Democracy, for Sun, was on the whole standard, liberal, "bourgeois" democracy. He admired the American political system and modeled the political system he would like to build upon it. However, to the American separation of government functions into three branches—executive, legislative, and judicial— Sun added two more, derived from his interpretation of Chinese tradition. There would be a control (or investigation) branch, based on the old censorate, empowered to bring impeachments against officials suspected of wrongdoing; and there would be a separate examination branch, charged with conducting civil service examinations and recruiting government officers. While the question is not completely clear, there is a possibly radical difference between Sun's system and the American: the American system is one of separation of *powers* and checks and balances, whereas Sun's may be only a division of *functions*.[2] In order to give power to the people, Sun believed in the practices of initiative, referendum, and recall—institutions popular in progressive American circles at the turn of the century.

Sun at first had thought that China's political culture was inherently democratic. The only thing necessary for China to become a democracy was the overthrow of the despotism. This is one reason he so complacently stepped aside in favor of Yuan Shikai. After 1920 Sun had become more hardheaded. He then argued that democracy could be achieved only in stages. The first stage would be military rule—military force was required to defeat the warlords and bring basic unity to the country. This would be followed by a period of "tutelage." The KMT would exercise one-party rule while training the people in the civic responsibilities required to preserve democracy. Once the people had become adequately educated the country would enter the final phase, constitutional rule. Sun's opinions on how to achieve democracy are reasonable but were not always persuasive to those outside the KMT. The period of tutelage began in 1929 and lasted until 1947. There was no obvious point during those years when it would have been safe to move to the constitutional stage (and, abstractly speaking, you could make a good argument that 1947 was too early). Yet the longer the KMT kept its single-party dictator-

---

2. For additional discussion of the five-power constitution, see the chapter on Taiwan.

ship, the more it alienated liberal public opinion. It did not help matters that during this same period the party became increasingly corrupt.

The principle of welfare or people's livelihood is a vague one. At one point Sun said: People's livelihood is communism. It is likely, however, that here he was trying to be polite to his Soviet sponsors. Sun was no Marxist and he did not approve of class warfare: all Chinese, regardless of social class, should try to get along harmoniously. He desired economic development, and after 1911 he originally thought his next great contribution would be the design of a railway system for the country. He also believed in a free economy, but not in uninhibited capitalism; rather, the state should regulate the market and intervene to protect people from real distress. Sun wanted to eliminate landlordism and to make sure that all land belonged to those who actually tilled it. He proposed to do away with the landlord stratum by putting high taxes on rent, adapting economic theories developed by Populists in the United States.

The Three Principles of the People is a sensible, moderate political program. It may still be, as some on Taiwan contend, the best guide to a unified, prosperous, democratic China. After Sun's death the KMT built a cult around him and his ideas, presenting him as perhaps the greatest political thinker since Confucius and Plato. The Three Principles became the basis for the indoctrination of school children and party leaders. It is probably not really much of a political philosophy—or, if it is, it is broad enough to tolerate within itself a virtually limitless diversity of opinion, conviction, and policy.

The Communist Party of China

The CPC was founded in Shanghai in July 1921, with the help of representatives of the Comintern. This first party congress was attended by 12 Chinese delegates, representing about 60 members. One of the founding members was Mao Zedong, later to become the party's supreme leader, although it was to be several years after the founding before he would again figure prominently in the history of the party. Several other founders also later played major roles, but about half the founders simply faded into obscurity. Neither of the party's top leaders, a couple of Peking University professors, attended the first congress. A little later the Comintern set up a separate branch of the CPC in France, among Chinese students on a work-study program in that country. A founding member there was Zhou Enlai, later first premier of the People's Republic and contemporary China's foremost diplomat. Deng Xiaoping, while not a founding member, also joined the party's European branch.

Before 1917 Marxism, although known in China, did not have much of a following. The most popular radical ideology was anarchism, which combined a critique of the alleged restrictions of the traditional family and social systems with an affinity for the more antistatist implications of Daoism and some strains of Confucianism. Marxism did not seem relevant to the concerns of Chinese radicals (and could not be expected in any case to have much of an appeal to nonradicals). It purported to be not merely a political program but a scientific elaboration of the laws governing history and society. Marxism predicted a socialist revolution led by the proletariat (factory workers),[3] but this revolution could occur only under conditions of advanced capitalism. China, however, was at best only in the very early stages of capitalism, and even still in what the Marxists would consider the feudal stage. A fervent revolutionary would not be attracted to doctrines whose practical implication seemed to be that China should develop capitalism. Alternatively, revolutionaries who might want to develop a form of capitalism, such as Sun Yat-sen, were not eager to encourage class struggle, which for Marxists is the motive force of human history.

The Bolshevik Revolution of 1917 changed Marxism's image. While Russia could, by stretching things, be considered a capitalist society, it was certainly not the most advanced one, and the revolution there demonstrated the possibility of socialism in a relatively "backward" country. The Bolshevik leader V. I. Lenin had elaborated a theory of the party that encouraged a flexible interpretation of Marxism. Lenin concluded that the proletariat, if left entirely to itself, would not "spontaneously" develop the kind of class consciousness inclining them to revolution. The revolution would require, rather, a disciplined party of professional revolutionaries, persons who had trained themselves to a true understanding of the forces of history, who would act as the "vanguard of the proletariat." This allowed for the formation of organizations of persons who felt they had achieved proletarian consciousness even in societies where there were not many real proletarians around. They could prepare the way for the eventual revolution.

One of the first acts of the new Soviet state was to renounce all the unequal treaties tsarist Russia had wrested from China. This could only encourage good feelings toward the new regime, especially when, at Versailles, the liberal democracies showed themselves ready to endorse Japan's imperial claims.

Lenin also had a theory about imperialism. He had wondered why the Revolution predicted by Marx was not taking place in the advanced capitalist countries. Part of the answer, he decided, was imperialism. The mature capitalist societies should be generating the kind of contradictions that would lead to their revolutionary overthrow. By expanding into what Lenin called the empty areas of the world (empty of capital, of course, not of people), these societies postponed the day of reckoning. Eventually all the empty areas

---

3. The term (from the Latin *proles*, offspring) originally referred to the lowest stratum in the Roman republic, those whose contribution to the common good was to bear children to serve as soldiers. Marx, something of a classics scholar, used the word to mean persons whose only economic resource was their labor power. The Chinese translation is *wuchanjieji*, "propertyless class."

would be filled up, and capitalism would become a worldwide system. At that point one capitalist country could expand only at the expense of another. Lenin thought this was a major cause of the First World War. At the same time, imperialism introduced capitalism into the traditional agrarian ("feudal") societies, breeding a native modernizing bourgeoisie hostile to the traditional pre-imperial leadership and eager to drive out the foreign exploiters so they could exploit the workers by themselves. Driven from the colonies and exhausted by war, the capitalist powers would no longer be able to avoid the crisis. Lenin has been cited as saying that the road to Paris leads through Peking. He apparently never really uttered that aphorism, but it does capture his general drift.

The policy implication of Lenin's analysis, however, is what has been discussed before, that the international Communist movement should support bourgeois nationalists in the colonial countries—a policy the communists in those countries were not uniformly enthusiastic about. In China this meant supporting the KMT (although the party's bourgeois nationalist status may have been more the product of Lenin's ideologizing than of social or political reality). Ideology aside, it was in the interests of the new Soviet state to have a friendly China as a neighbor, a China strong and united enough to contain the ambitions of the British and, especially, the Japanese. Lenin and his collaborators judged the KMT the force best able to achieve this, at least in the short run. They persuaded the CPC, very much against the better judgment of the party leadership, to form a united front with the KMT.

That leadership did not, perhaps, have a very mature political judgment in any case. The top leaders were two professors at Peking University, China's leading modern institution of higher education. One, Chen Duxiu (1879–1949), had actually won an examination degree under the Qing. An intellectual trendsetter, he had advocated the use of vernacular writing; he was a strong critic of the traditional social and family systems and a proponent of political democracy. One suspects part of the appeal of communism to him was that it was the latest new thing. His younger partner, Li Dazhao (1888–1927), believed communism would save the Chinese people, whom he identified at least as much with the peasantry as with the proletariat. He held the probably un-Marxian notion that China as a whole was a proletarian nation, picked on by the privileged nations of the world. In Italy at about the same time, the Fascist Mussolini was developing a similar appraisal of the position of his own nation, making the idea central to his ideology.[4] The other party members were mostly students and young intellectuals, at home in the Western-style universities of the big cities and treaty ports.

---

4. The communist soldier Lin Biao in 1965, speaking as a disciple of Mao Zedong, elaborated a similar theory: the revolutionary movement was centered in the exploited Third World countries, the world countryside, which would encircle and overcome the world city—mainly North America and western Europe.

According to the agreement setting up the united front, Communists would join the KMT as individuals while keeping membership in the CPC. Part of the strategy, of course, was to infiltrate the KMT, to influence its policy and, with luck, to eventually take it over. The KMT had itself been reorganized on Leninist principles, and while this did not eliminate factional struggle in the party, it did hinder the Communists from taking the party's higher posts.

There was considerable communist influence at the lower levels, however. Young Zhou Enlai became a political instructor in Chiang Kai-shek's Whampoa military academy. Mao Zedong at one point worked in the KMT peasant affairs department, which was headed by a right-wing member of the KMT. At the grass roots the two parties were practically indistinguishable, with the Communists perhaps being on the whole more skilled and better motivated than the regular KMT members, and more involved in day-to-day work in organizing workers and peasants. Again, the Communists did retain their own organization and discipline, and there was always more than an element of mutual mistrust in the relationship.

The Kuomintang Under Chiang Kai-shek

Sun Yat-sen's death in 1925 precipitated a power struggle within the KMT. The party was divided into various factions around leaders who ranged in ideology from leftist to traditionalist. The ultimate victor was a relatively nonideological figure, Chiang Kai-shek (1886–1975). Chiang was an orphan from a well-to-do family in Zhejiang province in the southeast. He studied military affairs in Japan and worked as a stockbroker in Shanghai. He formed connections with the Green Gang, an underworld secret society originally organized by boatmen on the Grand Canal, an artificial waterway that runs along most of China's eastern coast. Chiang joined with Sun Yat-sen around the time of the Revolution of 1911 and soon became Sun's major military advisor. In 1924 he became commandant of the new Whampoa military academy. His control over the KMT army was the decisive element in the party's internal struggles.

Chiang's preferred method was to isolate his rivals and then co-opt them. This did not work well against the Communists. Chiang had reason not to like the Communists anyway. Although a strong Chinese patriot, he had no major problems with the traditional social order, at least insofar as it was consistent with national power. At the time of the formation of the alliance of the KMT with the Comintern he had visited the Soviet Union to study the latest military techniques. Although he kept his opinions to himself, he did not like what he had seen, and he considered the CPC to be an agent of Soviet influence.

From the time of Sun's death Chiang acted to limit the influence and activities of the Soviet advisors, although he was not then ready to break the alliance. Chinese Communists sent warnings to Stalin, who by then was in control of Comintern affairs, saying that Chiang could not be trusted. Stalin, however, considered Chiang to be more of an asset than the CPC, and counseled his Chinese comrades to be patient, to use Chiang to full advantage. As he put it, Chiang should be squeezed like a lemon and then thrown away.

At this point it is conventional to say: Chiang squeezed first. In 1926 he organized the long-awaited Northern Expedition, mobilizing the KMT army and party organization to defeat the warlords. By April 1927, KMT forces were outside of Shanghai. Communist-led labor unions took control of the city and welcomed Chiang in. Chiang congratulated his progressive comrades and urged them to put down their weapons. The Green Gang then went into action, killing every Communist it could find and almost destroying the party.

Even after this, Stalin was not completely ready to break with the KMT. He had the remaining Communists make an alliance with a left-wing faction of that party, led by Wang Jingwei, an old crony of Sun's and a rival of Chiang's. Wang soon decided, however, that in the circumstances it made more sense for him to make his own peace with Chiang.

In addition to satisfying his own predilections and eliminating rivals for power, this "cleansing of the party" solved other problems for Chiang. Communist organizers had been agitating among peasants as the Northern Expedition got under way, and the young agitators seem to have had a special eye for redistributing land belonging to the families of KMT officers. The suppression of the Communists helped consolidate the KMT and also reassured local elites, whose support was obviously useful, about the consequences of reunification under KMT control. Foreigners in China, meanwhile, had been very upset by Chiang, the "Red General." Chiang was happy the foreigners felt a little intimidated, but he was not strong enough to defeat them if they brought their full pressure against him. The purge of the Communists helped reassure the foreign community and allowed Chiang to work slowly for the full elimination of special privileges by the imperial powers.

Nor was Chiang strong enough to defeat the warlords outright. His style was to fight a few battles and then offer to negotiate either with the warlord or with the warlord's less scrupulous lieutenants who might be tempted to betray him. Chiang allowed the warlords to keep local power as long as they joined the KMT, ceased to make war on their neighbors, and accepted the overall authority of the new National government. Thus, Chiang won over to his side the Manchurian warlord Zhang Zuolin, who in 1927 had conducted his own antiradical purge, invading the Soviet legation in Peking and putting to death Chinese Communists who had sought refuge there (one of his victims was party founder Li Dazhao). Zhang had been close to the Japanese, but with the new signs of patriotism the Japanese decided he was no longer reliable, and in 1929 they organized his assassination—one of the first acts leading toward the Second World War. Chiang also defeated and then

made peace with a coalition led by the warlords Yan Xishan and Feng Yuxi-
ang. By 1930 the major internal war in China was that against the guerrilla
armies organized by a reviving Communist party. Chiang had not really eliminated warlordism, but, rather, had confined it to the provincial level.

Chiang further extended the range of his influence by marrying Soong
Meiling, the beautiful American-educated youngest daughter of one of
Shanghai's richest capitalists.[5] Meiling was a Christian, and Chiang converted to that religion (after divorcing his previous wife), so gaining support
from the influential missionary community, especially the Americans in it.
His connection with the Soongs gave him greater access to the Shanghai
business world, and he could continue to count on the Green Gang to keep
that same business world docile and amenable to his interests.

Chiang's methods brought a unity that was more superficial than real, although it is not clear that other methods would have worked better. In Chinese society generally and the KMT particularly he practiced divide and rule.
The party remained factionalized, the glue holding the factions together
being the personal loyalty of each of the faction leaders to Chiang. Given the
disintegration of China's institutions, Chiang may have had little choice
other than to rely on personal connections, but relying on these connections
hindered his ability to build effective institutions.

To enhance KMT control over China and to further its mission of tute-
lage Chiang enforced ideological indoctrination within the party and within
China's schools. The ideology, of course, was the Three Principles of the
People, now interpreted mainly as an affirmation of Chinese patriotism, of
Sun Yat-sen as perhaps the greatest political mind ever, and of Chiang as
Sun's worthy heir and successor. Chiang also urged a return to Confucian
values. Western scholars have criticized this as traditionalistic rather than
truly traditional, an artificial attempt to revive an ethical system that had lost
its social function, a perversion of the universalistic Confucian ethic into an
instrument of Chinese nationalism and of the power of a particular Chinese
regime. The criticism, however, may be more a reaction to the scholars' interpretation of what Chiang was doing than what he actually did; it implies a
kind of value relativism, and not everyone will find honor to parents, loyalty
to the nation, self-sacrifice, and personal honesty to be absurd, irrelevant, or
immoral notions. On the other hand, it must be admitted that Chiang's traditionalism was not very persuasive to its targets in the schools, even among
the increasing number who felt the May Fourth attacks on the cultural heritage had gone too far.

One KMT faction had an as-it-were fascist ideology. This was the Blue
Shirts, a youth group that had connections with the army and with the par-

---

5. Meiling's older sister, Chingling, almost as pretty, equally political, and with more
   progressive social views, had been married to Sun Yat-sen. Another sister was married
   into the Kongs, a wealthy banking family from Shanxi.

ty's secret police. The Blue Shirts believed that China needed to be toughened up under Chiang's supreme leadership. Their ideology was anticommunist, anticapitalist, anti-imperialist, and antiliberal. KMT fascism did not advocate the aggrandizement of China at the expense of other countries, nor did it gratuitously glorify violence; in these respects it was somewhat different from its European and Japanese contemporaries. There was also room for liberal elements within the KMT, such as the Political Science clique, whose core was Shanghai academics and business people with connections with the Soongs.

The period 1927–1937 is sometimes called the Nanking decade: Chiang moved the national capital from Peking (Beijing, or northern capital; he then changed the city's name to Peiping, "northern peace") to Nanking (that is, Nanjing, "southern capital"), which had been the country's main or secondary capital at various times in the Ming and Qing dynasties. The decade was a generally hopeful, prosperous, and progressive one. Chiang and his government gradually consolidated their authority, limiting the residual power of the warlords. By the end of the decade the communist insurgency had been almost totally defeated. The government developed educational, social, and political institutions and even sponsored experiments in land reform. All this promise, however, came undone after 1937, with the full-scale Japanese invasion of China.

The KMT regime still has a rather poor reputation, both in China and abroad. Toward the end of its course on the mainland, especially, it increasingly manifested police state behavior without any hint of police state efficiency. The main problem was not that Chiang and his party were tyrannical, but that they were weak—the tyrannical behavior being an indication of weakness, with incompetent exercises of force and power serving as substitutes for authority. The overall social and political order had deteriorated after 1911, and before a new order could be developed the country had to be pasted together—and this is as much as Chiang was able to achieve. He established connections with various elites, but this did not count for as much as it might have, since the various elites were not necessarily compatible with each other and the traditional sources of elite authority had collapsed without being replaced by alternatives. Had Chiang done differently he probably would have perpetuated chaos and come to failure even earlier; by acting as he did he left it to his enemies to mobilize forces unhappy with the structure of the weakened elite.

The Revival of the CPC

Chiang's purge of the CPC crippled the party, but, obviously, some members survived. The general character of the survivors was perhaps different from the general character of the membership before the purge. Previously most party members had been young, maybe naïve intellectuals. After 1927 the party rapidly became a considerably tougher group. The party had also learned the key lesson of Chinese politics in a time of political decay: political power grows from the barrel of a gun.

In late summer, 1927, as the left wing of the KMT was coming over to Chiang Kai-shek, a group of communist officers in the KMT army, along with Zhou Enlai, staged a mutiny in the town of Nanchang in southeastern China. This is considered to be the founding of what was first known as the Red Army and now as the People's Liberation Army (PLA). At about the same time Mao Zedong tried to organize a peasant uprising in his native province of Hunan. This was defeated, and Mao and perhaps 700 followers took to the hills. They were later joined by a military force led by one of the Nanchang rebels, Zhu De, a one-time warlord and opium addict who had amended his ways and converted to communism while studying in Germany. The Zhu–Mao forces, as they were called, later gained control of several counties in the mountainous Jiangxi–Fujian border, establishing what they called a soviet zone. Mao, the head of the soviet government, at first followed a rather brutal policy of land reform, killing landlords and rich peasants. He discovered this tended to alienate people and so moderated his policy. Other communist leaders set up similar soviet areas in other parts of the country.

In the meantime the central organization of the party reestablished itself, semicovertly, in the concession areas of Shanghai, where it was relatively safe from Chiang's government, if not from the Green Gang or the KMT secret police. At Moscow's initiative but with the enthusiastic support of young ambitious party members, Chen Duxiu was removed as the party head, accused (accurately enough) of sympathy with Stalin's rival, Leon Trotsky. A succession of leaders and groups headed the central organization over the next few years without having much control over the party beyond the boundaries of Shanghai. Throughout the period, no matter who held the top position in the party, Zhou Enlai consistently was the number two or number three man.

The party leader in 1929 was Li Lisan, an associate of Zhou's from their time in France. He ordered Mao and other party bosses in the soviet areas to organize attacks on large cities. The ideological motive was that a communist party required a mass base in the urban working class. A more concrete reason was probably Li's desire to assert central party control over what might have looked like emerging party warlords. Mao tried one attack and was severely beaten, reinforcing his perception that if the party was to have any mass base at all it would have to be in the countryside.

The failure of his "line" led to Li Lisan's ouster. He was replaced by a group known collectively and rather sarcastically as the "28 Bolsheviks," a cohort of very young Chinese intellectuals returned from study in the Soviet Union, their heads full of Marxist-Leninist theory. They had little experience with politics at all, much less Chinese politics, but had, at least, the very able Zhou Enlai to help them out.

The Shanghai CPC headquarters engaged in a vicious underground struggle against the KMT secret police and against defectors in its own ranks.

As things grew too hot in Shanghai, party leaders moved out into the countryside, and in 1933 the party headquarters reestablished itself in Mao's Jiangxi soviet.

Mao, on his part, had been fighting the KMT, warlords, and rivals in the party. The inner party struggle became more fierce with the arrival of the headquarters onto his own turf. The main issue was, no doubt, power, but the Bolsheviks accused Mao of being too soft on landlords and rich peasants. They also tended to accept the opinions of their Comintern-supplied German military advisor, who wanted to defend the soviet area from the various "bandit extermination campaigns" launched by Chiang Kai-shek by holding onto territory. Mao and many of the party soldiers thought mobile warfare a more prudent policy, avoiding direct confrontations with superior forces and not worrying too much about holding territory for its own sake.

Mao may have been losing this argument by the fall of 1934. Deng Xiaoping suffered the first of his several falls from grace for taking Mao's side. Mao's salvation may well have been the defeat of the communist armies. In October Chiang's forces overwhelmed the defense of the soviet area and the party decided to evacuate the area. This was the beginning of the epic Long March, a fighting retreat of about 2,000 miles, with the Red Army moving from southeast to southwest China and then up to the northwest, to the remote safety of Shaanxi province. Perhaps 5,000 of the 100,000 soldiers who started the march kept with it all the way. During the march Mao's forces were joined by and sometimes quarreled with military forces under other communist leaders. The march lasted into the early months of 1936 and was, of course, the definitive event in the evolution of Chinese communism. Along the way they fought the KMT, local warlords, and hostile minority nationalities.

In January of 1935 the main column of the Long March reached the town of Zunyi in Guizhou province. The party leadership convened a meeting to evaluate past errors and decide what to do next. Military commanders criticized the Bolsheviks' military strategy. Liu Shaoqi, a young labor organizer whose hometown was close to Mao's and who had himself studied in the Soviet Union, although not a member of the Soviet faction, defended Mao's military and political line. Zhou Enlai, who had been in overall political charge of the Red Army, cinched the matter by making a self-criticism and coming over to Mao's side—where he was to remain for the rest of his life.

The effects of the Zunyi meeting were probably not as immediately dramatic as the older Maoist historiography used to make out. It was, none the less, a decisive moment. It took place when the Red Army was out of radio contact with Moscow. Mao was never overtly hostile to Stalin and may even on some occasions later have deferred to Stalin against his better judgment, yet he achieved party leadership without Stalin's explicit endorsement. The meeting was not a victory of a Maoist group over the Bolshevik faction. Rather, the Bolsheviks seem to have been divided among themselves and disillusioned with their Comintern military advisor (who was to take the blame for the failed strategy) and without a very high opinion of the member of their faction most favored by the Russians, Wang Ming (who was not at the Zunyi meeting). Many former Bolsheviks were to work comfortably with Mao up until the Cultural Revolution, more than 30 years after Zunyi.[6] After Zunyi, Mao became first among equals, and not even that as far as some party leaders not present at the meeting were concerned. He did not really consolidate his control over the party until the early 1940s, when a Rectification movement imposed Mao's vision on the party as a whole.

Mao in his person and his leadership style can be taken, however, to symbolize the nature of the change in the Communist party as it adapted to its environment. He was born in 1893 in Hunan province in central China (and from the 1940s into at least the 1970s a disproportionate number of party leaders came from Hunan and adjacent provinces, perhaps a consequence of the workings of guanxi). His father was a rich peasant. In 1937, when he told his life story to the American journalist Edgar Snow, Mao claimed to have had a stormy childhood and said that he had learned to hate his father. This may actually have been an overstatement, but the two do seem to have had trouble getting along. As is often the case in families, the reason may have been that they were so much alike: both were willful, self-centered, and intelligent. One of old man Mao's complaints was that the boy wanted to lounge around reading books rather than working on the farm—more or less the same problem old Zedong was later to find with the youth of China generally. In fact, Zedong was able to badger his father into sending him through school, although it's not clear that Zedong ever showed any gratitude—but what child ever does?

Mao graduated from normal school, the equivalent of an American junior college. One of his professors was a rather impressive authority on modern German philosophy, and Mao married the daughter of that professor. When the KMT shot her in 1930, however, he was already living with the woman who was to be his second wife. Mao taught primary school for a time and in 1919, in the wake of the May Fourth movement, drifted to Peking. He got a job in the periodical room of the Peking University library. There he tried to engage in philosophical conversation the famous figures associated with that movement. These gentlemen were perhaps inclined to snobbishness and seem not to have treated the hulking young lout (Mao was six feet tall, very large for a Chinese of his generation) with his hick Hunanese accent with the tact and courtesy they should have. Yet Mao was not badly educated, at least in the humanities. He had a broad general knowledge of modern Western history and thought (he read whatever was available in Chinese translation) and a deeper if unsystematic knowledge of Chinese culture.

---

6. The last surviving Bolshevik was Yang Shangkun, a personal friend of Deng Xiaoping's and head of state in 1989, held by analysts to be one of the hard-liners most responsible for the massacre of democrats that year.

Mao had always been patriotic and interested in public affairs. As a boy he had admired Zeng Guofan, his fellow provincial, and the Qing reformers. He was physically powerful and (another unusual trait among Chinese of his generation) a strong swimmer. He and a friend once took a walking tour of some weeks' duration through the mountains and villages of Hunan. His first published work was an essay arguing that China's salvation lay in strenuous physical activity. He flirted with anarchism and other fashionable ideologies, and in Peking became a Marxist, presumably influenced by Li Dazhao, who was the director of the Peking University library and perhaps (for while Mao's ideas show affinities with those of Li, there seems to be no information on their personal relationship) one of the few big-shot intellectuals to be nice to him.

Mao, in sum, was knowledgeable about the modern world but a pure product of China. He knew no foreign languages. He once had an opportunity to participate in the work-study program in France, but at the last minute decided not to go. His followers were later to present him as the greatest thinker who ever lived—somewhat in the way the other side presented Sun Yat-sen, although Sun did not connive in his own cult. Mao was, rather, a man of action, but by no means contemptible as a man of thought. He was a skilled calligrapher and a talented minor poet.

During the Rectification movement of the early 1940s he consolidated his leadership over the party. The party's secret police helped the movement along by intimidating and terrorizing those insufficiently susceptible to Mao's charm, but by that time most Communists were ready voluntarily to accept his primacy. The Thought of Mao Zedong became the party's guiding ideology. This was defined as the application of the universal truths of Marxism-Leninism to the concrete practice of the Chinese revolution. Part of the idea had been that Mao's strategy and tactics, whether political or military, had been proven correct while everyone else had been wrong. Its polemical point was directed against the Soviets' darling, Wang Ming, who might have known chapter and verse of Marx and Lenin but allegedly knew nothing of China. The broadest meaning of the Thought is that abstract theory by itself means nothing. Revolution requires the ability to apply theory to practice and to use practice to correct and develop theory. This means that one must know local conditions and have the skill to analyze their implications.

The imperialist intrusion divided Chinese society. Schematically, there was the coast and the hinterland, with the coast tied into the world economy and the hinterland stagnant. Both the KMT and the CPC were products of the coast and the treaty ports. The KMT had great difficulty coming to terms with the hinterland. The CPC, expelled from the coast, had to come to terms in order to survive. The Maoist tendency might be considered a synthesis of coast and hinterland, of tradition and modernity. This, anyway, is the older interpretation. An alternative interpretation favored by many Chinese intellectuals is that Maoism over the long term proved to be not a synthesis but the triumph of what was most regressive in the tradition over the forces of modernization from abroad—the more humane elements of the tradition having earlier been overwhelmed by the modernizing forces introduced by imperialism.

The Sian Incident

Even after the Long March the Communists were not exactly safe on base. Indeed, Chiang continued to seek their destruction throughout 1936. He also had other things to worry about, however. The Japanese had been aggressively pushing their interests in China, and Chinese public opinion was becoming increasingly impatient with the government's inability or disinclination to put up effective resistance.

In 1929 the Japanese murdered the Manchurian warlord Zhang Zuolin. There was already a Japanese army stationed in Manchuria to protect Japan's railway investments there, and in 1931 this army took control of the region, expelled the Chinese forces, and in 1932 set up a nominally independent state, really a Japanese colony, called Manchukuo ("Manchu country"), with the last Qing emperor as their puppet head of state. Also in 1932 the Japanese helped themselves to part of Shanghai; they remained in control over those areas that prior to World War I had been part of the German sphere of influence in China.

Chiang Kai-shek resisted Japan covertly, through his intelligence organizations and his Blue Shirts, and he protested Japanese aggression to the League of Nations. He was not ready to do more. He argued that China was still too weak and that war with Japan would destroy the country. This was true enough, but not entirely convincing when Chiang showed himself more than eager to carry out large-scale military operations against his fellow Chinese, the communists. Chiang's response to that was that the Japanese were a disease of the skin (an irritation, but not deadly, and not significant in the long run), while communism was a disease of the viscera. From his own perspective this was probably true, but did not impress a public taught to believe that its government represented the force of Chinese nationalism.

The Communists, for their part, had long been announcing their desire to fight Japan, both from patriotic and ideological conviction and to distract the KMT from themselves. In December 1935, Liu Shaoqi, who had broken off from the Long March to do party work elsewhere, helped organize a series of mass anti-Japanese demonstrations among students in Peking. Many student activists from this movement were to become important party leaders later on.

Chiang, however, continued to try to organize a final battle of annihilation against the Communists. The generals charged with the execution of this plan were Yang Husheng, who commanded forces in the northwest, and Zhang Xueliang, who commanded troops from Manchuria. Their headquarters was in the ancient northwest town of Sian (Xi'an in pinyin), close to the Communist base at Yan'an. During much of 1936 they had been in communication with the Communists. Zhang, known as the Young Marshal, was the son of Zhang Zuolin, murdered by the Japanese in 1929. His army, which he had inherited from his father, had been expelled from the soldiers' homeland in 1931. Zhang longed to avenge his father, his troops pined for home, and all were eager to restore honor to the nation. None were particularly eager, in the circumstances, to fight the Communists.

In December 1936, Chiang flew to Sian to try to get some action out of his subordinates. After some frustrating negotiation, he was placed under arrest by Zhang Xueliang.[7] Zhang and Yang notified the Communists about what they had done.

Obviously, this could not but precipitate a major crisis, one that no one really knew how to deal with and whose details, not reflecting very well on anyone involved, remain obscure. Some Communists, possibly including Mao Zedong, thought Chiang should be shot; others thought this would only mean more trouble. The Nationalists in Nanking did not know how to react either. Some KMT generals wanted to attack Sian, but other party leaders, including Soong Meiling, Chiang's wife, thought this would not be the most prudent thing to do. She herself flew to Sian to join her husband. Chiang had been losing popularity steadily for many years, but with the news of his kidnapping came a great rallying of popular support behind him. In Moscow, Stalin worried about Japan's unchecked expansion and believed that Chiang was the only Chinese leader with sufficient prestige and ability to unite the country. He sent word to the CPC to make a deal, but the Chinese comrades may already have come to that decision themselves.

The well-spoken Zhou Enlai headed a Communist negotiating team to Sian. The Nationalists still insist that no deal was made, but it seems likely that there was at least tacit agreement on what was to become the second KMT–CPC united front. Military campaigns against the Communists ceased. When the united front took official form the following summer, with the outbreak of full-scale war with Japan, the Communists agreed to accept the National government, to place their armies under the nominal authority of the National government, and to treat Chiang Kai-shek as the commander in chief. However the armies would keep their own officers and men, and the Communists would continue to rule the territory already under their jurisdiction—in effect, they accepted the same kind of conditions Chiang had earlier imposed on the warlords. Both parties agreed to cooperate to fight Japan. This agreement and the war with Japan probably saved the Communists from extinction.

---

7. The story is that Zhang's soldiers broke into Chiang's bedroom in the middle of the night. Chiang escaped out a window, leaving his teeth behind in a jar in the room. He was found a few hours later, shivering in his nightgown in the snow.

Zhang Xueliang allowed himself to be brought back to Nanking under arrest, to show he had acted in good faith from loyalty and patriotism, not from personal ambition. In 1949 he was taken to Taiwan (Yang Husheng that year was shot) to be kept under what soon became a very lenient house arrest. In 1989, after the death of Chiang Ching-kuo, Chiang Kai-shek's son and successor, all restrictions were removed from the 90-year-old Young Marshal. He continued to refuse to say anything bad about Chiang Kai-shek.

Taisho Democracy

The Meiji emperor died in 1912 and was succeeded by his son, known to posterity as the Emperor Taisho.[8] For Japanese it is psychologically natural to treat a change of imperial reign as signifying a more general change of historical era (the years are numbered according to imperial reign, and with each new emperor the count begins again), and for the Taisho transition this may be historically valid, too. From the Taisho period on, Japan was, like China at the same time, in a condition of crisis. In Japan overall public order was not endangered (despite many dramatic instances of political lawlessness), but as in China the forces of modernization were proving to be more than the existing institutions could easily cope with.

By the end of the Meiji era voices in the Diet and in society at large were demanding an end to the *hambatsu*, the "han cliques" of Satsuma and Choshu. The number of the original Satcho founders was shrinking anyway. Japan was a modern industrial country, and progressive public opinion wanted a more democratic political system, one more in keeping with the new social and economic order. Most of the Satcho genro and conservatives generally argued instead for "transcendental government," a concept less arcane than it sounds. The idea (which is found also in some of the older forms of European conservatism) is that political parties are fine for representing different strands of public opinion, but each party can represent (by definition) only part of the nation and has (again by definition) a partisan concept of the general good. Final authority, then, should not rest with the parties and the special interests they represent, but, rather, should transcend all these divisions to represent the true essence of the nation, the kokutai.

These different concepts met in an early skirmish right at the beginning of the Taisho period, in an episode known as the Taisho political crisis or political change. To simplify somewhat: even before the Meiji constitution

---

8. The Taisho emperor suffered from some kind of mental disorder, and in 1921 Japan was placed under the regency of the crown prince Hirohito, who, after his father's death in 1926, became the Showa emperor.

was adopted, opponents of the Satcho clique had organized themselves into a political party, the Jiyuto, Liberal party. In the 1890s the Satcho oligarchs, especially Ito Hirobumi, concluded that if they had their own rule it would be easier if they sponsored their own political party to contest elections for the Diet. This organization was called the Seiyukai, "friends of the government association." In 1912 the prime minister was Saionji Kimmochi, one of the founders of the Seiyukai and also head of the Privy Council, an organization attached to the imperial household, independent of the cabinet, which could act as a voice of the emperor. The Seiyukai controlled a majority in the Diet and supported Saionji. Saionji and the Seiyukai wanted to cut the military budget, but the army and the major military genro were opposed. The minister of the army, therefore, resigned from the cabinet without consulting the prime minister (for, remember, the ministers of the army and navy in principle were responsible directly to the emperor, not to the prime minister). The army refused to approve a replacement, and the cabinet collapsed. Saionji resigned and the military genro caused the appointment of a prime minister favorable to them. The Seiyukai then began to prepare a motion of no confidence against the new prime minister. When challenged to name the source of his appointment, the prime minister said this was too sacred to talk about. Seiyukai politicians then accused him of cynical abuse of the emperor's authority and the imperial institution. After some negotiation, Saionji agreed to ask his party, in his capacity as head of the Privy Council and as if in the name of the emperor, to withdraw the motion of no confidence. The Seiyukai, however, refused. In the end, the military genro were forced to back down.

The Taisho political change did not mean the immediate democratization of Japanese politics. In fact, little happened for the next few years. By the 1920s, however, party government became increasingly common. The Taisho period shows the potential for democratic evolution under the Meiji constitution.

The Democratization of Japanese Politics

Japan fought on the Allied side in World War I, a consequence both of an alliance with Great Britain and of Japan's desire to help itself to Germany's imperial spoil in China and elsewhere in the Pacific region. Public opinion came under the influence of the liberalism and the (so soon to be tarnished) idealism of the victors. In the late 1910s and early 1920s there was considerable liberal and radical ferment in Japan, similar to that of the May Fourth movement in China. As in China there was a sense that the traditional past was synonymous with darkness and repression and that the future lay with the West. In China this cultural ferment came at a time of national disunity, weakness, and humiliation, and soon merged with nationalist resentments. The Japanese political and international situations were quite different. Liberalism in Japan was associated instead with a distaste for what liberals took to be overly aggressive assertions of Japanese patriotism. The Japanese liberals may have been good patriots themselves, but they also thought of themselves as cosmopolitans, identifying with the wider modern international society. Since the Japanese state remained strong and cohesive, Japanese conservatives, more convincingly than the Chinese, could reconcile tradition with whatever in modernity contributed to the wealth and power of the state. Although there are exceptions, and although one must make all kinds of qualifications, in China nationalism tended to be critical of the tradition. In Japan nationalism and tradition were at odds with liberalism.

Many who came to maturity in the early Taisho period were in political and cultural opposition to the system built by the Satcho oligarchy, just as the Satcho oligarchs, in their younger days, had opposed the decadent bakufu. As in China, the dominant opposition trend was political and cultural liberalism, with liberalism sometimes taking a socialist coloration. Another tendency was feminism, a demand for equality between the sexes. This combined easily with attacks on the traditional family system and on what some considered the arbitrary and repressive morality associated with the old order.

There was more aggressive agitation by and on behalf of certain victims of modernization. The main burden of growth had been carried by the peasantry, which was squeezed of its surplus to provide capital and labor for the modern sector. The peasants, however, remained too unorganized and too much under the influence of local elites to cause much trouble, beyond localized riots. Factory workers were more restless. In those days Japanese businesses did not practice the paternalistic "Japanese management system" characteristic of big firms after World War II. Rather, they adhered to the classic capitalist style in its most ruthless version: employ labor at the lowest possible cost, work it as hard as it can sustain, fire it whenever convenient. Unions tried to organize in the late Meiji and early Taisho period, although always under legal disabilities and police harassment. The union organizers often had some variety of anarchist or socialist ideology, making the establishment even more worried.

Rapid cultural change often creates a generation gap, and the Japanese experience shows a continuity of change. By the 1990s worried parents and social conservatives fussed about a *shinjinrui*, a "new human race," a younger generation that seemed to care nothing about hard work and conventional morality, but lived only to amuse itself in the indulgence of private pleasures. The great grandparents of the shinjinrui, back in the Roaring Twenties, were the *mobo* and *moga*, the "modern boys" and "modern girls," who played all day and all night in the coffeehouses and cabarets, indifferent to the opinions of elders, Confucius, and the ancient gods of Yamato.

The most active political movement was for the extension of the suffrage, which had been restricted by property-owning qualifications to a small proportion of the population. All else being equal, this expansion of the electorate should also increase the influence of the Diet, as the representative of the popular will.

The major breakthrough for democratization came in 1918, when the military-backed wartime government found itself too out of touch with the prevailing trends in society for reform. The prime minister was dismissed and replaced by Hara Kei (1856–1921), the president of the Seiyukai, the first prime minister to be chosen from the House of Representatives, the first not to be of noble status.[9] Although known as the Great Commoner, Hara should not be confused with some prairie populist. His family, in fact, was rather higher in noble rank than the typical Meiji oligarch. He was not from Satsuma or Choshu, however and, not being part of that inner circle, was limited in how high he could climb through bureaucratic politics. With the restoration of the peerage in the 1880s he chose not to resume noble status. He worked in the bureaucracy but made most of his career in partisan politics. He was quite conservative in his social and economic views, but he did think the government should be responsible to the majority in the Diet. He perhaps had mixed views about the desirability of a broad franchise, but in 1920 did cause to be passed a law lowering the property qualifications for the vote.

Hara was murdered by a nationalist fanatic—the kind of event that was to become increasingly common over the next decade and more. Japan reverted for a time to transcendental governments, over the loud opposition of the press, labor unions, and the parties. The transcendental cabinets proved unable to govern effectively, and in 1924 the parties formed a common front and forced the dissolution of the Diet. The elections were won by a coalition of parties whose ancestry can be traced back to the Jiyuto and the opposition of the early Meiji period. This victorious coalition formed itself into a single party, known after 1927 as the Minseito, or the people's government party; the leader of this coalition became prime minister.

In 1925 this Minseito government (as I shall call it[10]) passed a universal manhood suffrage law, giving the vote to all male Japanese subjects aged 25 and over—no women and no kids, but also no restrictions based upon wealth. This was the high tide of democratization under the Meiji constitution. At almost the same time the Diet passed a strong Peace Preservation law, giving the police even more power to query not only the behavior but also the thought of those the establishment might consider subversive. This was a conscious attempt to counter the threat conservatives (including many Minseito Diet representatives) thought universal suffrage might present to the existing power structure.

---

9. Saionji had also been president of the Seiyukai, but he was a member of the House of Peers.

10. The official name of the party then was *Kaishinto*, Reform party.

Japan enjoyed responsible party government, at least in the formal sense, for the remainder of the 1920s. The Seiyukai won the 1927 elections (disconcerting the Minseito, who hoped the public would be more grateful) but lost to the Minseito in 1931. The parties lacked the institutional strength and the base in popular support to ride out the military indiscipline, economic distress, and social crisis of the 1930s.

Some Characteristics of Taisho Democracy

During the 1920s Japan evolved a two-party system. Two parties competed for and alternated in power, and the party with the majority in the lower house of the Diet organized the government. As in other two-party systems, both parties tended to be similar in ideology and policy orientation. In Japan it may be fair to say they were close to identical, although, for what it is worth, the Seiyukai was reputedly more conservative than the Minseito.

This similarity in other two-party systems is usually explained in terms of electoral strategy. To control the government a party needs a majority in the legislature, and this quest for majority means both parties have to compete for the favor of the same voters. On a left–right or other continuum the parties may have somewhat different centers of gravity. But if we assume that the opinion of the general population clusters toward the center, with few people at either extreme, both parties must converge toward that center to maximize the number of votes they may receive.[11] Two-party systems are fairly rare, and probably work well only when public opinion is in fact distributed in this centrist manner. A two-party system would obviously be very divisive if the population were severely polarized on economic, ideological, religious, ethnic, or racial lines—it would guarantee that the government of the winners would be intolerable to the losers.

Although Japan is ethnically and religiously fairly homogeneous, there was not necessarily a consensus on policy in the 1920s among the general population.[12] As in "classic" two-party systems, both parties did try to appeal to the same constituency—but it was a constituency of the elite. The structure of political power in Japan at that time may be described as a triangle between the bureaucracy, the big business combines (*zaibatsu*, or finance cliques), and the two major political parties. The dominant partner was the bureaucracy, which set basic policy, largely in the interest of business. Business accepted guidance from the state in return for the opportunity to make money. The parties passed the laws desired by bureaucracy and business, and

---

11. For a classic statement of this logic, see Anthony Downs, *An Economic Theory of Democracy* (New York, 1957).

12. For an analysis of the potential and problems of democracy at this time, see Peter Duus, *Party Rivalry and Political Change in Taisho Japan* (Harvard University Press, 1968).

were financed by business, either as parties, or as factions in parties, or as individual politicians.

Such a system might work well when the electorate consists of a wealthy minority, but it is not so appealing to the mass public. Here we should introduce an institutional explanation for the two-party system to supplement and even partly displace the earlier sociological explanation. Japan's electoral system—the way in which Diet seats were divided and the votes counted—helped assure a two-party system regardless of the content of the party programs. Japan until 1925 elected its lower house by a system of single-member districts (one representative for each voting district) in which a plurality (more votes than any other candidate, as opposed to a majority, where the winner has to have more than half the votes cast) sufficed for victory.[13] This system is the same as used in U.S. Congressional elections and elections to the British Parliament, and in practice (if not strictly in theory) it virtually guarantees a two-party system. In each district the party or candidate with even slightly more support than anyone else wins total victory, and technically speaking all voters who supported anyone else might as well have stayed home. The system greatly overrepresents the party that wins the most votes generally, and virtually drives third and lower-ranking parties out of existence.[14]

Because this kind of electoral system virtually guarantees that only two parties will prosper, it has been little used outside the Anglo-American cultural milieu. In countries with less political consensus than has traditionally prevailed in Great Britain or the United States, that kind of electoral system would leave important trends of social interest and opinion without any representation, aggravating discontent and perhaps leading those excluded to believe they had no stake in democracy. This is part of what happened in Japan in the 1920s.

This Anglo-American system, it should be noted, does not guarantee that the *same* two parties will always predominate. The party system sometimes also responds to changes in the social composition of the electorate. Great Britain is a classic example. In the nineteenth century the dominant groupings were the Tories, or Conservatives, and the Whigs, or Liberals. The Tories (to the extent they were other than a parliamentary clique) represented the traditional rural ruling class (and the religious and social values

---

13. After universal suffrage the system was changed so that each district elected two or more representatives, but each voter voted for only one candidate. It was hoped that this system would encourage the formation of smaller parties to compete with the Seiyukai. This arrangement, which is analyzed more thoroughly in the discussion of contemporary Japanese politics, is still biased toward the larger parties.

14. This assumes that the votes for all the parties are distributed fairly evenly throughout the country. A third party that is highly concentrated geographically may also survive. In Britain the Liberal party was almost eliminated as a national contender earlier in the twentieth century, but continued to enjoy representation in Parliament partly because of strong local support for it in Wales.

associated with that class), while the Whigs represented new commercial and industrial elites. During the late 1800s both parties, hoping for electoral advantage, broadened the franchise. A coalition that later formed itself into the Labour party pushed a socialist program, also hoping to attract the newly enfranchised working poor. They were successful in doing so, and by the 1930s the Liberals had shrunk to a small third party.[15] The Conservatives were more flexible than the Liberals, co-opting much of the working class vote by adopting welfare state policies beneficial to the workers. As representatives of the traditional elite, with a heritage of paternalism and a sense (in principle) of the obligations of nobility and privilege, the Conservatives had more room to maneuver than the Liberals, who were more closely tied to business interests and free enterprise. Today, typically, the bulk of the Labour party vote comes from the working class, but half the Conservative vote is also from that same stratum.

There is no reason in principle that the Seiyukai or Minseito could not have emulated the British Conservatives. The Liberal Democratic Party (LDP), which dominated Japanese politics until 1993, is in effect a merger of the two older parties, and the LDP not only survived but prospered in an age of mass democracy. In the abstract, it seems either party, or both, would have had much to gain by trying to broaden its appeal to the general public—this was the main motive for expanding the size of the electorate in the first place.

There were, of course, differences between Japan and England. The nearest equivalent to the Conservatives as the preferred spokesman for the ruling class would have been the Seiyukai. But while the Conservatives represented a rural elite against a modernizing business class, the Seiyukai represented (again, to the extent that they represented anything other than themselves) what had been part of the traditional ruling stratum (the warrior nobility), which was also sponsoring the growth of business and modernization. The Minseito traced its heritage to wealthy rural elites uneasy about the Meiji-era modernization drive (although this whole analysis may imply a greater programmatic basis for both parties than is really justified). Neither was predisposed to make the kind of populist appeal to traditional values that the Conservatives accomplished. Populist traditionalism in Japan found only a perverted expression in numerous small groups of as-it-were fascist extremists.

At the same time, neither party depended overwhelmingly on popular appeal in order to win votes, paradoxical as that may sound. Both parties were coalitions of personalistic factions of Diet representatives. The party organi-

---

15. Since that time a reform of the electoral system has been a typical plank in the Liberal (and, later, the Social Democratic) platform: the party receives a greater proportion of votes in the electorate at large than it wins in seats in Parliament, and so argues for a system of proportional representation.

zation hardly existed at the grass-roots level. There, especially in the country-side, the vote was delivered by local notables connected by ties of sentiment, expediency, or obligation to the politician. These notables could control the votes of clients who owed them favors or were otherwise beholden to them. Issues, opinions, programs, and probably even interests were beside the point.

We still might wonder whether the parties might have improved their electoral chances by more systematically cultivating links with voters. To have done so would have strained the establishment triangle described above, as programs to benefit the working poor might have displeased big bureau-crats or businessmen. The parties might have met this criticism as it has been met in other countries, by arguing that change was necessary in any case and it would be better to have change come about through friendly agencies rather than by radicals who might be voted into office if the representatives of the current structure of power and privilege did nothing.

In Japan, however, this was not as much a concern as in, for example, Great Britain. The state was sufficiently strong that the establishment did not have to worry about radicals being voted into power. The Peace Preservation law and similar legislation protected the powers that were from socialists and other leftists. In the late 1930s these same laws gave a legal basis to a near-totalitarian police state. Since the Seiyukai and Minseito had to worry only about each other, not about radical opposition, they had no incentive to disac-commodate their original bases of support to seek favor from the wider public.

This lack of interest in the opinions or sensibilities of the electorate was reciprocated. The ordinary person did not have much obvious reason to see his interests served by the parties, nor was he edified by the normal means of electioneering—lavish distributions of bribes and the sending of goon squads to disrupt opponents' rallies. Newspapers, which operated fairly freely, con-centrated heavily on the many scandals, giving the impression that electoral politics was inherently dishonest, shameless, sleazy.

Japanese democracy collapsed in the 1930s, as did democracy in other countries where democratic institutions were weak. In Japan, however, there was no antidemocratic mass movement. Neither was there effective or vocal resistance to the antidemocratic forces, or any expression of mass regret that democracy had failed.

Militarism and Fascism

The Japanese left wing and Japan's enemies at the time consider that coun-try's prewar and wartime system to have been fascist. This is partly because Japan was allied with the fascist powers in Europe, Germany, and Italy. There were similarities in political structure and ideology between Japan and its allies, but major differences as well.

The term *fascism* does not encourage easy or precise definition. Since the Second World War it has become associated with evil, and few political movements will call themselves fascist, although many postwar movements seem quite similar to those before the war. In very general terms, and admitting that each generalization has exceptions, we may consider fascism a totalitarian political movement that typically develops in late modernizing societies, particularly those where substantial segments of opinion believe their country has not been treated fairly by the prevailing international system. The movements generally glorify the Nation, with the nation often conceived in racial—or even racist—terms. The movements typically aspire to bring about effective social, economic, and political modernization while recapturing a perhaps mythical sense of community that has been destroyed by the bad effects of modernization imposed either by foreigners or by evil and alien elements within. Fascism often glorifies war or violence and the virtues of toughness and ruthlessness: fascist thinking was influenced by a vulgar Darwinism, in which only the fittest survive and nations or races test their fitness in struggles against others. Fascism typically finds expression in the cult of a Leader, who embodies the spirit of the race or nation. The people are organized into a mass movement led by a political party headed by the Leader. Fascism is both elitist and democratic: the Leader and the activist true believers around him are better qualified to rule than are ordinary people, but the Leader and his following derive their legitimacy as representatives of the people. Fascism is often considered a right-wing totalitarianism. This is valid historically if right wing simply means anticommunist. Fascists, unlike communists, do not believe in class warfare—rather, it is nations or races who should be fighting each other. But fascists usually favor welfare state measures, if not to help the disadvantaged, then in order to impose political control over all areas of life. Fascist regimes have treated the working class at least as decently as communist regimes have, and in the 1930s both movements were quick and eager to learn from each other, even while professing mutual hatred.

This syndrome, taken as a whole, describes the Blue Shirts movement within the KMT and, with some modifications, Cultural Revolution Maoism. The process of modernization in China and Japan produced similar symptoms, although in different combinations. In Japan the fascist trend consolidated itself in the power of the state more effectively than in China. By the end of the 1930s Japan had taken on an official fascist ideology, under the coloration of state Shinto. It had also set up a thoroughgoing police state that attempted to control not only the actions but also the thinking of its subjects—although, it must be said, the Japanese state practiced less terror toward its own people than did its European counterparts.

Japan, however, lacked a Great Leader. Fascism was imposed in the name of the sacred emperor, who was personally probably not in sympathy with the tone or behavior of his more ardent supporters. There was no Japanese fascist party, nor was there even a unified fascist movement. There were many little fascist and nationalist movements, politically opposed to what they took to be a corrupt, incompetent, repressive, unpatriotic ruling establishment. In the end, however, it was this establishment that imposed the fascist regime—largely as part of a process of suppressing the undisciplined fascist movements. Fascism was imposed legally, violating neither the letter nor the spirit of the Meiji constitution. Its consolidation did not require random terror against or systematic intimidation of the general population.

Decay of Democracy

The main institutional antagonist to the democratic system was the military, although the military was divided ideologically and factionally and Japan experienced no successful military coup. The democratic regime had been undermined by the economic collapse occasioned by the Great Depression. The main structural weakness of the system was the autonomy of the military from the political leadership, which translated in practice not merely to lack of civilian control but even to the autonomy of certain field armies from military headquarters. Economic distress brought demoralization at home and temptations to expansion abroad, especially in China, and both of these trends helped radicalize the military.

Japan had come late to the imperialist game, but it learned fast. As early as the 1870s Japan had designs on China's island of Taiwan, and in 1895, following a victorious war with China, it made that island a colony. In the following years it also acquired Korea. After the Boxer Rebellion Japan, along with other countries, was given the right to station troops in parts of China. During World War I Japan took over Germany's privileges in China and even attempted, through the "21 demands" voiced in 1915, to get control of China's foreign policy. In the meantime, the elite Kwantung army[16] was stationed in Manchuria to protect Japan's railway interests there.

In the liberal 1920s there was a pause in Japan's expansionist drive. The Depression renewed Japan's sense of vulnerability. Since the islands were so poor in natural resources and depended upon the outside world not merely for prosperity but even for survival, Japan needed to secure control over its sources of supply and its markets. Because Japan was a new imperial power, it was likely to come into conflict with the early arrivals, especially Britain—and Japan had the misfortune to come to its full imperial glory at a time when imperialism was losing its moral standing among public opinion in the older imperialist powers. The United States was especially inclined to moral

---

16. *Kwantung* (in pinyin, *Guandong*) means "east of the pass" (that is, east of the Great Wall), and refers to Manchuria. It should not be confused with the southern province of Kwangtung (Guangdong), whose name means the "broad east."

condemnation of Japanese expansion, although Japanese commentators—not only rabid superpatriots—could point out with reason that Japan's behavior in China was quite analogous to that of the United States in Latin America. Japan's ambitions in China clashed directly with emerging Chinese nationalism, which enjoyed the sympathy of enlightened public opinion in the West. Japanese behavior earned ineffective but still irritating condemnation from world opinion and the League of Nations. This reinforced a sense by some radical nationalists that Japan was hated and envied by a hostile world determined to deprive it of its proper place, and encouraged the notion that Japanese who entertained liberal opinions were probably not completely loyal and patriotic children of the emperor.

In earlier years the prestige of the genro kept the army in line, but the civilian party cabinets had no such charm. The Kwantung army, particularly, was given to swashbuckling independence. In 1929, apparently without the approval either of the cabinet or of military headquarters in Tokyo, and to the personal consternation of the emperor, its officers arranged for the murder of warlord Zhang Zuolin. In 1931 and 1932 it engineered a takeover of Manchuria, setting up "Manchukuo" under the nominal rule of the last Qing emperor. For all practical purposes this was a Japanese colony. The economic crisis and new problems in China combined with the ineffectiveness and incompetence of the party governments to cause the appointment of a military cabinet, headed, however, by a moderate, conservative admiral: the navy was less given to nationalistic excesses than the army.

Part of the background atmosphere of the time was resentment in the military, particularly among junior officers, over some of the consequences of Japan's modernization. The soldiers had been taught in the military academies that they were true samurai, the purest bearers of the spirit of Japan. In the 1920s military values were out of fashion, and the social prestige of the military career declined. The economic collapse was evidence for some of the moral hollowness of the materialism, hedonism, and worship of foreign things characteristic of the liberal period; it showed the need to return to the sterner virtues.

Military resentments were sometimes linked with rural grievances. The peasantry had benefited perhaps less than any other sector of society from the country's modernization. Many army officers were children of poor peasants: the military was the most accessible opportunity of upward mobility for an intelligent and energetic farm boy. Even officers from nonrural or privileged backgrounds worked up indignation at the hardship of the farmers, the soul of Japan, compared with the useless westernized mobos and mogas in the cities.

Along with the military nationalists were a variety of social organizations devoted to China policy or to the special nature of Japan. These groupings had various connections with the military, with business, and with the underworld. Like other imperialisms, Japan's included a large measure of idealism.

Japanese sympathized with revolutionary China's aspirations, happy that that ancient civilization seemed ready to follow the path Japan had so successfully blazed. Many nationalists also believed that China should stick to Japan's path, and were, of course, not blind to the material and political gains that China's subordination to Japan might bring. One of the most famous of these nationalist groups was the Black Dragon Society, although its aims were not as mysterious, romantic, or sinister as the name implies: what Westerners know as the Amur River, dividing Manchuria from Siberia, is called the Black Dragon River in Chinese and Japanese, and the group's objective was to project Japan's influence to the banks of that river.

Nationalistic groups proliferated in the 1930s, as did ideological diatribes against democracy and liberalism. The best-known case is the persecution of Professor Minobe Tatsukishi, a constitutional theorist who argued that the emperor was an "organ of the state." To the extreme nationalists, this implied there was a state superior to the emperor, of which the emperor was a mere part. Rather, in their view, the state was the creature of the emperor, and Minobe's theory allegedly called into question the absolute, unconditional sovereignty of the emperor. Minobe's thesis might in fact have helped convert the Japanese state into one limited by and subject to law and may even have had democratic implications. He intended no disrespect to the emperor, nor did he aspire to limit the emperor's theoretical prerogatives.[17] In private conversation with his advisors the emperor himself said that this "organ theory" made sense to him. Nevertheless, an orchestrated campaign of vilification forced Minobe out of his university position and out of the House of Peers. It reinforced a dominant attitude that anything whatsoever was permissible, even honorable, as long as it was done in the name of the emperor.

The opinions of Kita Ikki (1883–1937), a one-time socialist with an interest in the Chinese revolution, epitomize important trends in Japanese radical nationalist thought. Renouncing socialism, he came to believe that the Japanese tradition (in his interpretation of it) was the answer to the people's spiritual and material needs. On the international level, he decided, the world today was like Warring States Japan, in grave need of a Tokugawa shogun to bring about order and stability. In Asia, at least, this role should obviously go to Japan.

But Japan's supremacy is not founded in a selfish desire to dominate. Rather, Japan would conquer only to serve. The major task was to expel Western influence from Asia, to return Asia to the Asians, to allow all Asians to prosper together (the idea translated into government policy as the East

---

17. In the postwar period he argued that the new American-inspired (or dictated) constitution, which reduced the emperor to a symbol, destroyed Japan's kokutai, the essence of the state.

Asian Co-Prosperity Sphere). The key here was China, which should join with Japan to eliminate the imperialists. Unfortunately, China's soul was no longer its own. It was dominated by the Communists—stooges of Moscow—and Chiang Kai-shek, a stooge of the United States and Britain. China is like your stupid little brother, who sometimes might need to be slapped around a bit to be made to do the right thing. It may be necessary, with a heavy heart, to wage war against China to make China recognize its own true interest in throwing in as Japan's ally.

Domestically, Japan had to purify itself of greed and materialism imposed on society by the big capitalists and bureaucrats. The political system was especially corrupt, and it might be necessary to use violence to remove all the corrupt people around the emperor, replacing them with true patriots who would act according to the kokutai. Purged of foreign corruptions, the true Japanese spirit could then shine forth. Japan, in Kita's estimation, remained a relatively backward, weak country. But if Japan's spiritual values could be mobilized, this would more than compensate for any material inferiority.

The exact role of the emperor in all this is unclear. After the war it became expedient both for the American conquerors and for the Japanese establishment to depict the emperor as a harmless nonentity, thereby justifying keeping him on the throne and avoiding the troubles that might come by trying to assess his responsibility for the war and for war crimes. It is clear that the Showa emperor was in fact an intelligent, well-informed man, with strong opinions on public affairs—although one of the strongest of those opinions was that he should stay out of politics. Several times he expressed dismay at the illegal or undisciplined behavior of the radicals. But he was himself a Japanese patriot, perhaps not opposed in principle to his country's expansionist policies. He showed himself able to act decisively in times of crisis, especially after a major coup attempt in 1936 and again in 1945, at the time of the surrender. He possibly could have done more, had he chosen, to preserve democracy. For many radicals, however, the emperor's personal opinions were beside the point. His sacredness was in his role or position, not necessarily in the possibly unworthy temporary occupant of that position, and some radicals contemplated the possibility of deposing or even killing the emperor should he try to thwart their plans.

Assassination had become a popular political tactic from the 1920s and into the 1930s. The murderers were often junior army officers and the victims high-level politicians, businessmen, bureaucrats, or generals. The vocal segment of public opinion influenced the way these cases were treated by the courts. The prevailing sentiment was somewhat to the effect that these young idealists should probably not have done what they did, but they were pure and sincere while their victims were selfish and corrupt. Outrageously violent and illegal actions were treated with inappropriate leniency.

The attention of the authorities, using the Peace Preservation law, was directed more against the less obviously threatening political left. An interesting government agency, the Thought Police, attempted by persuasion and psychological coercion to convert communist and other radical political prisoners back into good children of the emperor. Exported to China, these techniques were used a little by the KMT but became most notorious in the early 1950s in the Chinese Communists' "brainwashing." Even while Japan remained a relatively liberal state, it had developed the apparatus of totalitarian repression.

The Triumph of Radical Nationalism

On February 26, 1936, a group of radical soldiers influenced by the writings of Kita Ikki killed some high-ranking military and civilian officials, occupied downtown Tokyo, and attempted but failed to take over the imperial palace. This group, organized as the Young Officers' movement, demanded a Showa restoration to match the Meiji one. They wanted a better deal for farmers, a fairer distribution of wealth, and the assertion of the glory and spirit of Japan.

For the military high command this was the last straw. After the February 26 incident it was no longer inclined to coddle viciously idealistic hotheads. The Young Officers were court-martialed and shot. Kita Ikki, who had probably not been directly involved in the incident itself, was hanged. The generals reimposed discipline over the officers' corps.

Yet, an indirect result of the incident was an adoption of the repressive and aggressive—if not the populist—elements of the Young Officers' program. The army urged that to restore social discipline the influence of the political parties must be curbed and the military budget increased. Elections in April 1937 favored both the Seiyukai and the Minseito, who had taken an antimilitary posture, over some smaller military-sponsored parties. The time for party government had passed, but it was clear that the military-backed cabinet could not stand, either. Prince Konoe Fumimaro, a well-spoken aristocrat with connections in all the different factions and tendencies, became prime minister. He proved to be too weak to check military influence, however, especially after the summer of 1937, when Japan drifted into full-scale if only partly acknowledged war with China. Wartime conditions encouraged greater state control of the economy, increased military influence in the cabinet, and more mental and physical control over the population. Social control was exercised mainly by traditional neighborhood associations, not a totalitarian party or faceless agencies of the state. There was little if any random terror against the general population.

Japanese politics became largely a matter of intrigue and bickering among cliques in the armed forces. The cliques were largely based on personal relationships, although there was fighting over policy as well. The army as a whole tended to be more militant and expansionist than the navy, and less realistic about Japan's physical limitations; it was also the politically more powerful service. After the war in China drew to a stalemate there developed an argument over what Japan's next step should be. A "strike north" faction advocated expansion into Siberia, while a "strike south" faction wanted to invade Southeast Asia, a strategy that would mean war with Britain and the United States. Withdrawal from China was not an option to be seriously considered. Poor showing in a battle lasting several weeks against Soviet forces in Mongolia and, later, the accommodation between Japan's ally, Hitler, and Soviet dictator Stalin made the strike north the less attractive option.

In July 1941, the most rabidly militant of the generals, Tojo Hideki, became prime minister. He was to figure, inaccurately, in wartime Allied propaganda as Japan's equivalent of Hitler or Mussolini. In the meantime, practice for the surprise attack on Pearl Harbor had already begun.

China and Japan at War

By the end of 1936 both Japan and China were ready for war against each other, psychologically if not materially. After the February 26 incident no force in Japan was prepared to resist the pressures for expansion in China. After the Sian incident the Chinese National government could no longer temporize with Japanese aggression.

On the night of July 7, 1937, Japanese and Chinese army units held exercises on the outskirts of Peiping. The two forces ran into each other at the Lugouqiao or Marco Polo bridge, an ancient structure near that city. The two sides exchanged fire. The Japanese government made outrageous demands for concessions, but Chiang Kai-shek had to draw the line. Later that month the second united front between the KMT and the CPC took effect. Japan sent an expeditionary force to China, attacking at Shanghai and moving up the Yangtze. The Japanese call this whole set of events, one of the major feeder streams leading to World War II, the China incident (originally, presumably, because they were not prepared to call the chastising of their stupid little brother a war). The Chinese call it the War of Resistance Against Japan.

In December the Japanese captured the National capital, Nanking, and for two weeks the victorious armies slaughtered and raped at will. Chiang Kai-shek retreated upriver first to Wuhan and then to remote Chungking in Sichuan province, beyond the Yangtze falls. With only a few exceptions, each time the Nationalists confronted the Japanese army they were badly defeated (as Chiang had known would happen), and after 1939 or so the two sides fought few large-scale battles. The Communists for the most part confined themselves to guerrilla operations. In 1940 they launched a successful but costly offensive, the Hundred Regiments campaign, which helped them secure their major base areas, but after that reverted to more low-scale tactics. The myth persists that the Communists were more serious about fighting

Japan than was the KMT. If seriousness of purpose in war can be measured by casualties, the Nationalists suffered more at each rank. The Nationalists like to point out that they lost 70-some generals, while the highest-ranking Communist casualty was a colonel. The resistance Chiang Kai-shek put up in the first year or more of the war exhausted his forces. Given Chiang's inability to defeat the Japanese in pitched battles, it would seem that the Communists' strategy of conserving strength and expanding political organization was the wiser course.

The Japanese persuaded the leftist KMT leader Wang Jingwei, one of Chiang's main rivals in the party, to come over to their side. They hoped this would legitimize their aggression and give some substance to their altruistic claims. They set Wang up in Nanking, where he claimed the heritage of Sun Yat-sen, flew the National flag, called his government the Republic of China, and dressed his troops in the uniform of the National army. The Japanese no doubt considered Wang a pawn to be sacrificed once Chiang Kai-shek could be induced himself to join them. This is not something Chiang could seriously consider, although after the United States entered the war he did like to hint that if the Americans did not give him more supplies he might be forced to make peace—a ploy that helped alienate him and his regime from those American officials working most closely with him.

By the time of Pearl Harbor, China was effectively divided. The northeast was under Japanese control, especially in the cities; Communist guerrillas operated in much of the countryside. In the southeast and central regions Wang Jingwei's forces, with Japanese help, fought Communist and KMT guerrillas. The Communists had fairly good control of the northwest. Chiang Kai-shek's government, uprooted from what social base it had in the coastal cities, reigned in the southwest, sharing power with truculent local warlords.

The united front endured in form throughout the war, although it had always been rather superficial and by 1940 no longer had much substance. The Communists were never really prepared to subordinate either their government or their army to Chiang Kai-shek, and Chiang was not willing to tolerate an ideologically hostile autonomous military force. In 1940 KMT troops in east China viciously attacked a Communist army operating in what had been designated a KMT sphere. After Pearl Harbor it became apparent that Japan's defeat was only a matter of time. Neither side had an incentive to exert itself against Japan, especially given America's war priorities: it would fight in Europe first while holding to the defensive in the Pacific region, and when it did fight it would fight on the Pacific islands rather than on the China mainland. Both sides made plausible claims about how much more they would do would they only get more American money and equipment. The Americans tended to believe the Communists more on this than they did the Nationalists, but Chiang was not eager to see the United States arm his rivals. Both sides nursed their strength for the showdown that each knew would come.

The war drained the KMT of what energy it had left. The regime was cut off, as indicated earlier, from its major base of support. The inability or disinclination of the government to take a more active part in the war after 1940 demoralized the party and army. Defeatism, cynicism, and blatant corruption permeated the party. Given the few resources at his disposal, more than ever Chiang emphasized loyalty to himself over ability or merit.

The Communists took the war as an opportunity to increase the size of their army and expand the scope of their political control. The party spread its influence through the rural areas of the north, in those areas where the local elites had either collaborated with the Japanese or fled from the Japanese invader. The party conducted a rectification drive, consolidating Mao's control over party ideology and organization and establishing Mao not only as the party's top leader but also his Thought—defined as the application of the universal truths of Marxism-Leninism to the concrete practice of the Chinese revolution—as the party's guiding ideology. The rectification campaign sometimes entailed very rough measures against dissidents, but its repressive aspect was not visible to outsiders. These outsiders, whether Chinese or Western, tended rather to idealize the Communists, who seemed so much more honest, competent, and upbeat than the KMT. Yan'an attracted students from all over the country, eager both to fight Japan and to reform society. The party also recruited large numbers of peasants as soldiers and cadres and brought larger and larger populations under its jurisdiction. It appealed opportunistically both to anti-Japanese and patriotic sentiments and to economic and social discontent, in whatever combination would be most effective in the prevailing circumstances. On the whole, Communist social policy during the war was moderate: the party did not want to make enemies unnecessarily. Thus, instead of exterminating anti-Japanese landlords, it was content to limit the amount of rent they could charge.

The Japanese attack on Pearl Harbor, like the war with China, is an example of what has later been glorified as the Japanese decision-making style. The decision was made incrementally, on a step-by-step basis. Much of the initiative came from lower ranks. The decision involved endless consultations, from which a general consensus emerged, with no one asserting a strong personal opinion and no one clearly personally responsible for the outcome. The decisions were not made but, rather, were formed or came about. There was only the most tenuous distinction between making the decision and implementing it. This style is excellent for its tactical flexibility in coping with problems that come up in the course of everyday business. It is not quite so good if there is a need to examine critically the basic premises of the policy or to make radical changes in it.

Japan blundered into surrender in about the same way it had drifted into war. After the fall of the island of Saipan, the first part of Japan's prewar empire to be conquered, in the summer of 1944 the Japanese elite knew in their hearts that the war was lost. Statesmen might drop hints to each other about the need to think of surrendering, but to make surrender come about would require that everyone simultaneously conclude that now was the time to make one's own sentiments public. Anyone who explicitly pointed out what everyone was thinking risked losing credibility in decision-making circles, since this knowledge, however obvious, had not yet become part of the accepted consensus. Such a blunt soul would even have been in danger of being murdered. It was easier and safer to boast about the Yamato spirit and to urge all men, women, and children to cut themselves spears of bamboo to resist the materially superior but morally debauched American invaders. In the end, after the destruction of all Japan's major cities, two atom bombs, and the Soviet entry into the war, it took the personal intervention of the emperor—who could with relative safety point out his own nakedness—to produce the consensus necessary to end the war.

The war between China and Japan was part of the pathology of the modernization of the two societies. Modernization weakened the Chinese state and strengthened the Japanese, and Japan was ready to fill the resulting vacuum. The different outcomes of the modernization process are related to differences in the traditional societies. The more hierarchical character of Japanese society must have made the building of a strong state easier. This hierarchy was quite compatible with a flourishing personalistic factionalism, but not with the centrifugal factionalism more characteristic of China, as in warlord politics. Japanese hierarchy discouraged the formation of strong social movements such as the Communist Party of China: in Japan social bonds tend to be between superiors and inferiors, with no connections as such between equals. A social movement, however, probably requires that connections be established among persons on the same level. These social movements might temporarily provide a basis for social and political cohesion, once they are triumphant, but until they are triumphant they will hinder anyone else from consolidating authority.

In spite of many differences, the development of China and Japan in the early twentieth century shares at least one major theme: whether it is possible or desirable to reconcile the highly complex and sophisticated traditional culture with the need to modernize. This theme is related to what should be considered a puzzle; that is, facts show that the ideas of democracy and liberty had great appeal to many persons in both China and Japan, but facts also show a close-to-uniform failure to put these ideas into practice. A beginning consideration is that psychologically both modernity and democracy were identified with the predatory West. The Western powers imposed themselves on China and subverted the traditional order. The Western powers were not so successful in Japan, and it was not long before Japan was making its own victims. But fear of the West was the major motive inducing Japan to modernize.

The identification of modernity with the barbarian West made the traditional Chinese elites reluctant even to attempt to modernize. For those who did want change in both countries, it discouraged attempts to find resonances between the more humane elements of the modern Western and traditional Confucian civilizations. Rather, liberals tended to equate tradition as a whole with darkness, backwardness, and repression, while those attached to tradition tended to dismiss the liberals as running dogs of imperialism.

The overall problem was simpler in Japan than in China. Japanese elites could more easily construe their country as one nation among many in a world of nations (even while also construing it as the best). They had, after all, always recognized China as the font of civilization while also realizing that Japan was both civilized and not Chinese. The Meiji elites were able to take selectively from the Japanese tradition whatever contributed to the power of the state. Liberals could be dismissed or persecuted as non-Japanese, unpatriotic. Japanese traditionalism and nationalism took a fascist coloration in the 1930s, and many among those who defeated Japan in 1945 considered the tradition to be itself inveterately fascistic. It is more likely, however, that tradition helped humanize, moderate, and temper fascism.

In China, by contrast, the traditional culture was defined as the criterion of civilization itself, with national considerations at best secondary. There was, then, more of a tension in China between tradition and nationalism, and in China there is even some linkage between nationalism and democracy. More generally, however, there has been a three-way tension among liberalism, nationalism, and tradition: none fits easily with either of the others.

Liberals wanted the strengthening of the Chinese state and the self-affirmation of the Chinese nation. But unconnected with tradition, liberalism was hollow. In the 1920s some liberals proposed that China should undergo "full-scale westernization," and others gingerly returned to this theme in the 1980s. This allowed persons wary of liberalism to portray its proponents as sycophantic to China's oppressors.

The KMT under Chiang Kai-shek tried to make its own version of the Chinese tradition the ideological foundation of nationalism, aspiring to the Satcho achievement in Japan. Although the point can be overstated, this required a distortion of the Confucian heritage, turning a universal ethical system into a rationalization for a particular political regime in a particular country, making what had been a moral check on state power into an instrument of the state. As in Japan, this led to an identification of tradition with repression, and the Chinese combination of tradition with nationalism, like the Japanese, sometimes congealed into a form of fascism.

The Communists achieved the most nearly successful synthesis of the various cultural trends. Rejecting full-scale westernization, they claimed the real Chinese tradition was that of the people, not the "feudal ruling class." Since there was in fact only a vague and arbitrary distinction between the elite and popular elements of tradition, this allowed the party to select those elements that would suit its purpose, so it could present itself as anti-imperialist, antifeudal, modernizing, and truly Chinese. In principle, however, Confucianism, at least, is probably harder to reconcile with Marxism-Leninism than it is with liberalism. Confucianism assumes the objective reality of moral categories, while Marxism denies morality any independent standing. Pragmatically, no doubt, Confucianism of some sort could provide a moral filling to Marxism, although such a combination would be difficult to justify logically. In practice, the result was often that those in power behaved according to rules associated with the Confucian heritage but without the moral awareness provided by traditional Confucianism. Alternatively, the Marxian critique of morality could tacitly join with the anti-Confucian trends in the Chinese heritage to produce a nihilistic rejection of all limits and restraints, as in the Cultural Revolution.

In Japan probably the most workable synthesis, should conditions be right, was the configuration of the 1920s, in some ways reproduced in the postwar order. This reflects more the mercantile culture of Tokugawa-era Osaka than the military and bureaucratic ambience of Edo. It combines a business ethos with a Confucian code of personal conduct. This synthesis, too, has its problems: Confucianism is certainly compatible with a life of business, but not so easily compatible as a general guide to conduct when the business ethic pervades the entire society rather than characterizing one segment of it. The liberal order in Japan, whether in the 1920s or 1990s, is plagued with pervasive corruption and questions about the ultimate meaning of the whole thing.

The Second World War and its aftermath mark a "critical juncture" for both societies. The war and the U.S. Occupation destroyed the physical basis of the Meiji order and discredited the mentality behind it; they also eliminated for an indefinite period the military as a major institutional interest in Japan. The 1949 Communist victory in China was the near-total triumph of a revolutionary movement that finally took effective control of the country and was determined to bring about total change.

COMMONWEALTH
OF
INDEPENDENT STATES

Lake
Baikal

Lake
Balkhash

MONGOLIA

Heilongjiang

Xinjiang

Jilin

Inner Mongolia

Liaoning NORTH
KOREA

Peking

Tianjin

SOUTH
KOREA

Hebei

Ningxia

Shanxi

Shandong

Gansu

Qinghai

Shaanxi

Henan

Jiangsu

Yellow
Sea

Tibet

Sichuan

Hubei

Anhui

Shanghai

Zhejiang

East China
Sea

NEPAL

BHUTAN

Guizhou

Hunan

Jiangxi

Fujian

Taipei

INDIA

BANGLADESH

Yunnan

Guangxi

Guangdong

TAIWAN

MYANMAR

Hong Kong

VIETNAM

LAOS

Hainan

South China
Sea

PHILIPPINES

THAILAND

China

⊙ National Capital
━━ International Boundary
── Provincial Boundary
Hunan Province Name
- - - Disputed Boundary

0   Miles   500

7

◆

China's Political and Social Structure

As World War II wound down, the United States attempted to mediate between the two Chinese parties, the CPC and KMT, hoping to avoid civil war by means of a coalition government. Both parties were armed and neither, with good reason, trusted the other. By 1947 they were in full-scale war with each other. By the end of 1949 the CPC had achieved almost total victory over a surprisingly weak KMT. The Communists had a strong base of popular support among the peasantry, reinforced during the civil war period by a violent land reform program. They also had the goodwill, ranging from ardent to wary, of intellectuals and anti-Chiang politicians inside and outside the KMT, and even support among business interests. Many Chinese unenthusiastic about communism believed that the Communists, unlike the KMT, could provide a stable order, with effective, competent government.

Historically, the 1911–1949 period in China resembles earlier eras of disunity between strong dynasties. But even less than the Nationalists, the Communists did not think of themselves as just another dynasty. They were determined, like the Nationalists, to restore China's place in the world and end poverty, but also to end all exploitation and contribute to the ultimate liberation of the entire human race. The ambitious nature of their program required an attempt at total control and the building of a system of totalitarian rule. After the passing of several decades this enterprise seemed to be strangled in its own contradictions. Without a major reorientation the Communists seemed unlikely to build an enduring order, although there was no obvious alternative to their continued rule.

Ideological Foundations

The official ideology of the People's Republic is Marxism-Leninism, Mao Zedong Thought. Its role is similar in some respects to that of Confucianism in traditional China, but in important ways it is different. Confucianism, overall if not always in its details, was the distillation of the moral consensus of society. Marxism-Leninism, Mao's Thought is, rather, the guiding thought of the Communist party, what the Party would like to make the moral consensus of society.

According to Franz Schurmann, an ideology is the way of thinking of an organization.[1] In this formula, Marxism-Leninism, Mao's Thought is the manner of thinking of the Communist Party of China. On one level, the ideology embodies the truths of history and social development and the Party exists to put these truths into effect, to serve the ideology. On another level, the ideology justifies and rationalizes the ruling position of the Party and its actions. Without the ideology the Party would have no claim to legitimacy. The ideology is likely to hold official status, therefore, as long as the Party rules the country, even if the ideology is no longer very persuasive in its claims to truth.

Western writers sometimes call Chinese communist ideology Maoism, a practice also used in this book. *Maoism*, however, is not a term the Chinese themselves use: it is always the *Thought* of Mao. Schurmann explains that *thought* here refers to practical ideology, while *-isms* mean general truths. One common Chinese definition of the Thought of Mao is that it is the "application of the universal truths of Marxism-Leninism to the concrete practice of the Chinese revolution." A somewhat different formulation has occasionally been used: the Thought is the universal truth of Marxism-Leninism applied to the concrete practice of the Chinese revolution.[2] The distinction is a subtle one, but may indicate varying appreciations of Mao

---

1. Franz Schurmann, *Ideology and Organization in Communist China* (University of California Press, 1966).
2. Raymond F. Wylie, *The Emergence of Maoism: Mao Tse-tung, Ch'en Po-ta, and the Search for Chinese Theory, 1935–1945* (Stanford University Press, 1980).

within the Party. The first, more common formula makes the Thought the application of a universal truth, while the second has the Thought as itself part of that universal truth—a rather higher appraisal than the first. During the period of the Cultural Revolution (1966–1976) the Thought was sometimes defined as Marxism-Leninism itself: Marxism-Leninism in the age when imperialism is headed for collapse and the proletarian revolution is marching toward total victory. Around that time the Thought of Mao was even called the "peak" of Marxism, although bolder souls objected that this implied Marxism could never develop any further. In any case, whatever its precise estimation of Mao, the official line always asserts that the Thought of Mao is a creative development of Marxism-Leninism, and Mao himself a great Marxist theorist.

This leaves Marxism-Leninism as the universal truth, although it is also possible to consider Leninism an application of Marxism. These elements may be considered separately.

Karl Marx (1818–1883) described the transition of the traditional agrarian European system to the modern industrial one. He was impressed by the material gains of the process but appalled by the human costs. Not particularly a sentimentalist, Marx was not content to scold the evils of early industrial society; he tried to understand why things were as they were, figuring this understanding would provide a basis for changing things. He conceived of social and historical developments in terms of impersonal laws operating independently of human will, analogous to the laws of nature. Human understanding of these laws, however, can contribute to social progress, just as, say, knowledge of the properties of gravity helps people figure out how to fly—and also reveals the limitations of what kind of flight is possible.

A key theoretical principle in Marxism is materialism, the proposition that ultimate reality is material. For Marx the main implication was that economics—the way in which we feed, clothe, and shelter ourselves, and meet our other physical needs, is the foundation of social life. Everything else—politics, religion, literature, kinship structures, other elements of culture[3]—are ultimately expressions of the economic base. In any society beyond the most primitive there is a division of labor, and this division gives rise to social classes. Some persons will own more of the means necessary to produce wealth than others, and those who own more become the economically dominant class. The dominant ethical, religious, and general cultural systems in a society are those of the dominant class, and their function

---

3. An exception may be language, since different social classes in a society speak about the same language (although, of course, there may be differences of accent and usage). In any case, this is a problem Stalin somewhat maliciously amused himself with in his last years.

is to show that the interests of that class conform to universal principles of justice and right. The state is the executive committee of the ruling class, the means by which the dominant force their will on those subject to their domination.[4]

Marx was not a "mechanical" materialist; he believed in the "dialectic." This originally referred to a mode of argumentation: I say one thing, you say the opposite, we reason it out. The philosopher G. W. F. Hegel applied the dialectic to the movement of ideas in history, and Marx applied it to social processes.[5] The idea is that things change according to their internal logic. The internal logic of history is class struggle: those who have try to hold, those who have not try to get. Class struggle reveals the *contradictions* inherent in any social order, and the resolution of those contradictions makes for historical and social progress. So, merchants and industrialists replace nobles and landowners as the dominant class, and the new social order soon manifests the contradiction between those owners of capital and the proletariat, those who own nothing but their labor.

Another Marxist premise is the labor theory of value: the value of an object is the amount of human labor put into making it. Those who own the means of production—land, capital, or whatever else it may be—employ labor, paying it the going price. The difference between a worker's wages and what that worker produces is the surplus value, which is taken by the boss. It may be used for luxury consumption, of course, but in capitalism most of it is reinvested. The size of the surplus value is also a measure of exploitation, giving this moral term the color of an objective definition.

In capitalist society labor works by means of machinery and generates enormous wealth. Wages, however, remain about the same or, Marx would say, tend to go down over time, as the demand for skilled labor diminishes. This means the society is producing more goods than the members of society are able to buy. The consequences include plant closings, bankruptcies, and frequent depressions. Over time the proletariat becomes larger and poorer. Ultimately the process results in social revolution, which removes the contradiction (and the fetters on increasing prosperity) by removing the ownership of the means of production from private persons and giving it to society as a whole.

---

4. A possible objection is that in, say, western Europe and China in the 1400s land was the main source of wealth, but the two societies were otherwise very different. However, there are certain similarities in their moral systems.

5. Marx's collaborator and friend, Friedrich Engels, even applied the dialectic to the material universe. Chairman Mao, perhaps unconsciously influenced by yin–yang theory, also liked this line of reasoning. One difference between the dialectic and yin–yang theorizing is that yin and yang move in a cycle, ending where they begin, while the dialectic produces ever higher and more advanced forms.

Marx did not go into great detail about the consequences of revolution. Marxists have identified separate stages. The first, in the wake of the revolution, is dictatorship of the proletariat. This might mean a real dictatorship, or it might merely mean some kind of mass democracy (in Marxist thinking capitalist democracy amounts to the dictatorship of the bourgeoisie, the middle class); in any case, the state becomes the instrument of the proletariat, for a change. Once private ownership has been eliminated, however, everyone is proletarian; since classes exist only in relation to other classes, this amounts to a classless society. The early stage of socialism still has some of the marks of the older society, but there is no more exploitation: all contribute according to their abilities and receive according to their work. In the higher stage of socialism, or communism, people will contribute according to their abilities and receive according to their needs. There will be virtually unlimited social wealth and almost all causes of human misery will be gone. For the first time, people will be able to live a truly human life. The state will wither away.

The organization of the world into separate states is itself a product of class society. Nationalism is a bourgeois ideology, a form of what Marx called "false consciousness," a way to trick workers into thinking they have more in common with their bosses than with workers in other lands. Revolutionary strategy may differ from state to state, insofar as states represent societies and societies may be at different stages of development. But the Communist movement is in principle international or, probably a better word here, transnational.

Marx claimed that previous thinkers wanted only to understand the world; he, however, wanted to change it. Our ideas derive from our existence in society, from social practice. The test of a correct idea is its consequences when put into practice (so an idea may be correct in some circumstances but not in another). Correct ideas provide a guide to practice, allowing us consciously to change social reality; ideas are themselves corrected by being tested in practice.

V. I. Ulianov, or Lenin (1870–1924), the Russian revolutionary, was even more of an activist than Marx, but also made contributions to Marxist theory. We have already discussed Lenin's theory of imperialism. Among its other functions this provided a rationale for a communist movement in a poor country, something that might seem out of place in the light of Marx's thinking. While it was certainly not Lenin's intention, his theory also opened the way for a reconciliation of Marxism with nationalism, at least in countries exploited by imperialism.

Lenin had earlier elaborated an equally important concept, that of the Communist party. By 1900 or so most European countries had some kind of parliamentary system and most socialist parties were becoming increasingly respectable participants in that system, hoping to achieve at least the greater part of their programs by democratic means. Lenin believed that in Russia this was not possible, since that country was still a despotism. A tightly disciplined party of professional revolutionaries was needed to seize power from a despotism.

There is another aspect as well. A central Marxist tenet is that existence determines consciousness: how we see ourselves and the world depends upon the circumstances of our material existence in society. Yet this relationship is not a mechanical one. Lenin concluded that workers for the most part, left to themselves, would develop only "trade union consciousness," not a truly revolutionary class consciousness. Workers would become content with better pay, shorter hours, improved working conditions, more respect from the boss, and would not push for the truly basic transformation of the system (Lenin did not explain why this would be such a bad thing). The revolution had to be organized and planned by his party of professional revolutionaries. Party members, who may or may not be of proletarian origin, have true proletarian consciousness (that is, the set of attitudes and beliefs Marxist theory says they should have). The Party is the *vanguard* of the proletariat, its most advanced elements, both conducting the revolution and, it turns out, directing the society after the revolutionary seizure of power.

Marxists, especially those of a Leninist stripe, pride themselves on being tough-minded. They don't whine and moan about the injustices of the present and dream of the wonderful things that would be if only things were the way they want them to be. They recognize the necessity of present reality as well as the necessity of its revolutionary transformation. In spite of this, with Lenin, Marxism took on a *voluntarist* coloration, putting increased importance on the role of human will. Marx did not neglect the role of conscious human action, but seems to have thought the revolution would come basically as a result of certain objective conditions. While far from neglecting the importance of objective conditions, Lenin believed that revolution still had to be planned, organized, led, and controlled by a vanguard elite. Stalin, Lenin's political and intellectual heir, took this voluntarism a step further. In earlier Marxist thinking the socialist organization of society (public ownership and the like) was the resolution of the contradictions inherent in advanced industrial society. For Stalin, socialist organization became a way to rapidly transform a backward, rudimentary industrial system into an advanced, powerful one. Chairman Mao, for his part, sometimes seemed to imply, especially in his later years, that human will itself could transform objective reality.

Leninism also has what I guess should be called an ethical dimension. For Marxism there is no morality autonomous from the particular social order. Those who wish the revolutionary transformation of that order obviously don't accept its morality. The only close-to-objective definition of morality is whatever contributes to social progress, although progress here can only mean the materially determined phases a society goes through. Lenin extrapolated this particular insight to assert that whatever contributes to the success of the revolution—be it murder, hypocrisy, lies, whatever—is moral. More simply, since the Party is the instrument of revolution, morality is whatever serves the interests of the Party. Leninists add, however unconvincingly, that the Party has no interests apart from those of the proletariat, and the proletariat, ultimately, has the same interests as the entire human race. Leninism is not really a matter of good ends justifying bad means. Rather, anything that serves the good of the Party, however mean or cruel it might appear to the ordinary person, is by that fact good.

Early Maoism

The Thought of Mao is the application of Marxism-Leninism to the Chinese revolution. It has sometimes been called the Sinification (or "Chinesification") of Marxism. This does not mean it necessarily bears explicit resemblance to what has commonly been considered Chinese philosophy. There may be some implicit similarities. Thus, Mao's attraction to the Marxist concept of contradiction may owe something to the yin–yang mode of thinking that may be a part of the Chinese cultural subconscious. Some Chinese writers have implied this since Mao's death, although one purpose of doing so seems to be to subtly denigrate Mao's philosophical sophistication, which had been grossly overrated when he was alive. Mao sometimes did say interesting things about contradiction, although his abstract writings on it are pretty pedestrian, not really going beyond his translated Russian sources and serving often to make the obvious (or even the questionable) pretentious. One example of a contradiction is that peace gives way to war and war to peace.

One of Mao's main lieutenants, the Soviet-trained party organizer Liu Shaoqi, did make apt use of Mencius in talking about the training of party members. Liu quotes Mencius: We and the sages share the same nature, and anyone can become a sage. In the same way, anyone who applies himself to it can develop a true proletarian consciousness. The Confucian gentleman was supposed to practice self-cultivation to bring his thoughts, desires, and actions into harmony with the will of Heaven. This self-cultivation was the first step of a process of bringing true order to the world. Liu recommended an adapted version of self-cultivation for party members, so that in thought, word, and deed they consciously and gladly subordinate all personal advantage to the discipline and good of the Party. The historical and political background to this is the aftermath of the Long March, when the CPC was cut off from any possibility of a mass base among real proletarians (factory workers), but the leadership wanted to build a disciplined Leninist party from the heterogeneous mixture of peasants, intellectuals, and adventurers available to it.

Liu Shaoqi was less "creative" in his treatment of Marxism-Leninism than Mao, but his work highlights a central tension in Maoism: does social class refer to a person's position in society, or does it mean a state of mind? Earlier I brought up an inherent amorality of Marxism-Leninism. This does not mean that communists were supposed to be moral degenerates. In fact, all Leninist parties would prefer their members to be real paragons. But they must subordinate their own moral judgment to that of the Party, and by the logic of Marxism they have no rational foundation for their individual judgment anyway. For the Chinese, however, ideological correctness becomes virtually a moral choice, and to be proletarian means not so much to work in a factory but to be a good person (by the Party's lights). This is perhaps an unconscious extrapolation from the Confucian cultural background.[6]

The central tenet in Marxism is practice. The Thought of Mao is the concrete practice of the Chinese revolution. The polemical point here was directed during the Rectification movement of the early 1940s against Wang Ming, the leader of the "Bolshevik" faction. He allegedly knew all about Marxist theory, but had no idea about how to make it work in China. Theory by itself means nothing, Mao said, unless it is properly applied, and proper application requires detailed knowledge of local conditions as well as good political judgment. A mechanical, unthinking approach to theory can lead to disaster: in the official version of party history, it was only when Mao took over that things began to go right for the CPC. Marxism is not a dogma but a guide to action.[7] Theory is necessary in order to give direction to practice, but theory is tested and corrected by practice. We need to study to understand the world, but we learn to make revolution by making revolution, not by reading books about it.

One of these applications was the appeal to peasant grievances to build the Leninist revolutionary movement. In Marxist theory the peasantry is an unreliable, generally backward force. Peasants are individualistic and hard to organize. Their idea of revolution is to get a little land of their own, after which they would prefer no more change at all. Their attitudes and values reflect what Marx called the idiocy of rural life. Some Western scholars have contended that by basing his movement on the peasantry Mao tacitly broke with Marxist tradition, although others have said that the older Leninist and Comintern tradition contains plenty of precedent for organizing among peasants. Mao and the CPC would certainly take umbrage at any implication that they were leading a traditional peasant rebellion (although they consider themselves heirs to that tradition). Their movement was a proletarian one guided by a proletarian worldview, something no peasant is capable of coming up with on his own. The poorer peasants, especially, were a friendly class, allied with the proletariat but accepting proletarian leadership. In this context, however, proletarian means simply the Communist party, nothing more, nothing less. The best resolution of the issue is perhaps that of Richard

---

6. It is relevant to note here as well that Japanese radical nationalists were not given to the "evil-be-thou-my-good," "transvaluation of all values" posturing affected by their Nazi allies.

7. As Mao once put it, "Your dogma is not worth shit. Dog shit can fertilize the field and human shit can feed the dog. Your dogma can't fertilize the field, neither can it feed the dog." Mao's editors chose not to include this perception in his *Selected Works*, and here it's best relegated to the obscurity of a footnote.

Lowenthal. Leninist party organization allows revolutionaries to free them-selves from dependence on any particular social base, so that they may op-portunistically take advantage of whatever social cleavages there may be without becoming the captive of any particular interest.[8]

We should not think that peasants were passively manipulated by the Party. They had problems of their own and the Party could get their active support only by helping them out with their problems. What peasants would tolerate limited the Party's freedom of action prior to gaining national power. But the policy initiative always came from the Party, and the decisive consid-eration was always the interest of the Party, not the peasants. After Libera-tion (as the 1949 Communist victory has come conventionally to be called by almost everyone on the mainland), the Party certainly showed itself willing to disregard peasant preferences, enforcing unpopular (at least with males and with older people generally) marriage reforms and collectivizing land it had previously distributed to individual households. The radical Maoists liked to think they had some kind of affinity with poor peasants, but the peas-antry did not really prosper until the post-Mao period, when policy was set by urban-oriented reformers, some of whom had an irrational fear and loathing of peasants.[9]

Another tenet of Maoism, sometimes respected, sometimes not, is the mass line. The Party must always keep close links with the "masses," a con-descending term that refers usually to ordinary people, persons not members of the Party. Policy comes "from the masses" and goes back "to the masses." Party cadres (persons in leadership or managerial positions) should investi-gate to discover what problems there are. Ways of dealing with the problems are formulated within the Party. The Party then attempts to persuade the masses of the correctness of the chosen solutions and reevaluates the solu-tions if they seem not to work. At the same time, the Party works tirelessly to educate the masses in the correct "worldview," that is, the Party's perception of things. This is not exactly democratic—again, the initiative remains with the Party—but at its best the mass line means that party policy will address problems of real concern to real people and will remain within the confines of what people are willing to tolerate. Radical Maoists sometimes used the mass line to justify attacks on party policy, claiming their own opinions to be the will of the masses. In other contexts, this actually could have democratic implications.

---

8. Richard Lowenthal, *World Communism: The Disintegration of a Secular Faith* (New York, 1964). Benjamin Schwartz made the earliest systematic argument for the significance of the role of the peasantry in Maoism, and his thesis was disputed by Karl Wittfogel.

9. One problem is that many Chinese intellectuals actually accept the identification of Maoism with peasant attitudes, and Maoism has long been unpopular among intellectuals.

Mao gave much attention to military matters. The Chinese Communists came to power on the basis of their army. Mao's guiding strategic insight is that the army should be patient and should not fight battles it is not sure to win. Military tactics must be closely coordinated with political action. The army depends on the conscious and voluntary support of the general population for recruits, supplies, and information (the army are the fish, the people the water). The army is not a warlord organization but is the tool of party policy, subject to absolute political control by the Party. Soldiers, like the Party generally, should cultivate good relations with the masses. They should not slaughter the local population or loot their property or rape women. They should be courteous, pay for what they take, and go out of their way to lend a helping hand. This may be pretty basic, but it is a basic insight not always implemented by Chinese armies, including that of the Nationalists. Officers should share the hardships of ordinary soldiers. Ordinary soldiers should be treated with dignity and courtesy, albeit with strict discipline. They should have some training in Marxism and should understand their role in the scheme of things, whether in the war or revolution as a whole or the particular engagements in which they fight.

The united front with the KMT disintegrated after World War II and had been hardly nominal even before that. But the united front policy remained a part of Maoist practice. The CPC remained willing to form a united front with any parties or forces not hostile to it or hostile to its enemies. The theoretical justification was that China is not ready for socialism, a classless society. The proletariat cannot monopolize all power, but must share with friendly forces during this democratic stage. Sun Yat-sen's attempt at a democratic revolution (the "old democracy") had failed, but the Communists would lead a "new democracy" or what is also called a "people's democratic dictatorship." This is the equivalent of Marx's dictatorship of the proletariat. The difference is that while the proletariat (the Communists) would be the leading force, until conditions were right for the building of socialism they should share power with the entire people and the people's representatives.

People here means persons and social categories not hostile to Communist rule. It is perhaps needless to add that this talk of a united front meant more before the seizure of power than afterward. *People*, in any case, is a flexible term, varying with historical circumstances or, a cynic might say, the convenience of the Party. Thus, when it came to fighting Japan, Chiang Kai-shek was part of the people. Once the Japanese were beaten he became an enemy of the people. Dictatorship is a weapon used to suppress the enemy. Among the people there is democracy. Democracy here means mainly consultation and the soliciting of outside opinion. It does not necessarily mean free speech, and certainly does not mean competitive elections. The Party also decides for itself when an opinion is well-intentioned constructive criticism and when it is counterrevolutionary subversion.

In 1956 and 1957 Mao announced that not only were there antagonistic contradictions between the people and their enemies but also nonantagonistic contradictions among the people themselves. These should be settled by bargaining, compromise, or reasonable discussion. For example, workers want cheap food, while peasants want good prices for their crops—these two friendly classes have a chronic problem that they need constantly to work out. Mao also claimed there could be nonantagonistic contradictions between the Party and the general population, as the Party, grown complacent with victory, became arrogant and bureaucratic. The solution was to encourage free debate and constructive criticism from society: let a hundred flowers bloom, a hundred schools contend. A deeper reason was perhaps Mao's desire to shake up the Party as he sensed his own leadership becoming ever more superfluous. The criticism from intellectuals and students, once they worked up the courage to voice it, turned out to be a lot harsher than Mao had anticipated. Thousands of the more vocal critics were branded "rightists" and shipped off to labor reform camps. The theory of contradictions among the people is probably the last development of the earlier, more moderate version of Maoism.

Radical Maoism

At the CPC's Eighth National Congress in 1956, Liu Shaoqi proclaimed that the storm of revolution had passed. China was now entering the more constructive phase of "building socialism." Deng Xiaoping, the head of the party administrative apparatus, boasted that unlike some other parties, the Chinese had never been cursed with a cult of the individual leader (a few months earlier the new Soviet dictator, Nikita Khrushchev, had denounced the cult of Stalin). References to the Thought of Mao were dropped from the new party charter adopted at that congress.

Up to the middle 1950s Mao might be considered on balance among the moderate and cautious exponents of communist theory, despite some earlier evidence of impatience and a willingness to take risks. In 1950 he was one of the few Chinese leaders to actively favor Chinese intervention in Korea against the United States, and a few years later he was more eager to form agricultural collectives larger than the Party's specialists in rural policy thought prudent. Mao may have felt a little out of place in the new China, where the revolution had been won and the job now was to get on with the business of building the economy.

There were also threats to Mao's position, partly from international communist trends, where some of the criticism of Stalin might rub off on him, and partly from his own colleagues, who may have thought it was now time for Mao to take things a little more easy. The same new party charter that removed references of Mao's Thought also had a provision for the designation of an "honorary chairman" of the Party.

The Chinese response to the Soviet criticism of Stalin was that to blame all errors on a single leader is unscientific and un-Marxist. Stalin, to be sure, made a few mistakes, especially in his China policy, but he was a great

Marxist-Leninist revolutionary. It may be, however, that a ruling party becomes complacent after its successes, and no longer tries to find out what others think or what is really going on. Thus, the Party needs to remain flexible and to remain open to new ideas and information. This was part of the reasoning behind Mao's theory of contradictions among the people and his call for a hundred flowers to bloom. This trend of thought potentially leads to a break with the Leninist notion of the Party's having a monopoly on truth and, therefore, a monopoly on power. In China, however, it served more to rationalize the party leader's assertion of his own power over the party organization.

The vehement, thoroughgoing criticism of the Party by intellectuals in 1957 destroyed the optimism of the previous year. The party line remained that China was building socialism. Socialism, however, classically implied that class struggle was coming to an end, that antagonistic classes no longer had power. The hundred flowers episode showed to the Party's satisfaction that China was still crawling with class enemies. Class struggle became the dominant theme of Mao's thought in his last two decades of life. He came to argue that, whatever earlier Marxists might have thought, class struggle continues under socialism—it even grows more intense as the class enemy becomes more desperate. It is necessary to remain eternally vigilant, to impose harsh dictatorship over the class enemy and continuously educate the people in the proletarian worldview.

Those who had sounded off in the spring of 1957 were sent to reform themselves through labor (that is, put in work camps). Ideological indoctrination intensified. This atmosphere set the background for the Great Leap Forward of 1958, a new initiative closely identified with Mao.

The guiding slogan of the Great Leap was "politics takes command," a break from the more orthodox Marxist focus on economics. During the hundred flowers episode various intellectuals had lectured the Party on how ill-advised some of its policies were. The Maoist interpretation was that this showed how limited those intellectuals were by their bourgeois educations and worldviews. They had no idea of the limitless creativity of the masses, once the masses were properly led and inspired by the Party and leader, their minds liberated from the "superstitious reverence for expertise." Subjective will, spirit, can transform material backwardness—reasoning rather similar to that of the Japanese fascists of the World War II period. The Chinese people, Mao decided, were "poor and blank." Because they are poor, the masses want revolution; because they are blank, they have no mental fetters holding them back and can work miracles unburdened by bourgeois preconceptions of what is possible. Those who doubted the expediency of working miracles were deterred from saying so by the well-based fear of being labeled counterrevolutionaries or right-wing conservatives, in need of a good brainwashing and a stint at forced labor. The cult of Mao grew to unprecedented proportions, as people vied to claim supernatural powers from internalizing the notions of the Red Sun in Our Hearts. The Thought of Mao was said to be effective for everything from growing melons to raising the dead.

In 1958 propaganda detailed how China would enter the stage of communism directly, by means of a great leap, as the name implied. The state was already beginning to wither away, it was asserted. In practice, this meant that jobs previously performed by government agencies were being taken over, not always very competently, by the party organization or by mass organizations under the direction of the Party. In the countryside the Party introduced a "free supply system," an application of the principle of from each according to his ability, to each according to his needs. Peasants were encouraged to eat all they wanted for free in communal dining halls; these dining halls also freed women from the drudgery of housework, allowing them to work in the fields. The dining halls soon ran out of food. In the meantime, household cooking utensils had been melted to scrap in backyard steel furnaces, part of a program to eliminate the differences between rural and urban life.

It was clear by the winter of 1958 that things had gone seriously wrong. The Party made some preliminary efforts at reform. At a meeting in the summer of 1959, however, Mao chose to construe some of the criticism of the Leap as a personal attack on his leadership, and forced the comrades to choose between him and the critics. The critics were purged and the Leap continued another year. Mao may have felt he had no choice. His position depended on the correctness of his thought and (although no one was saying this directly out loud) he had already blundered in the hundred flowers business. Also, in December 1958, when the first cautious retreats were enacted, Mao had resigned in favor of Liu Shaoqi as head of state (although Mao remained chairman of the Party). Counterattacking his critics may have been Mao's way of recovering slipping power. The original premise of the Leap had been that there would be three years of hardship followed by booming prosperity. With the failure of the 1960 harvest China entered this century's worst famine. The weather got the official blame for this, and it had not been ideal, but the real cause was party policy.

After 1960 the Party radically revised the Leap policies. The amount peasants or workers received in income again became linked with how much work they did—encouraging, Mao and his supporters said, a capitalist mentality. The policy took a more tolerant attitude toward traditional customs and attitudes.

In the meantime, China was entering a political dispute with its Soviet ally, the grievances being asserted in ideological terms. The Chinese position was that the Soviets had become "revisionist"—gorged with material success (as it then seemed), the Soviets had lost any enthusiasm for revolution and wanted only to make peace with the imperialist United States. Reflecting back on Chinese politics, this dispute prevented the formulation of an explicit ideological repudiation of the Leap, even though the Leap had been abandoned in practice. Mao's continued primacy in the Party also prevented a systematic reevaluation, since such an exercise could have led to questions about his wisdom.

Trying to explain the failure of the Leap, Mao concluded that the problem was really not with the policies but with the attitudes of the people, whose thinking was not sufficiently advanced to appreciate the policies. China had adopted a socialist economic, political, and social system, but the culture—people's customs and habits—had remained feudal or bourgeois. This backward mentality penetrated the Party itself. There were, Mao eventually concluded, persons in authority inside the Party who were walking the capitalist road. Rather than building socialism, China's cultural conservatism meant the country had not even entered the stage of the dictatorship of the proletariat. In order to prevent a restoration of capitalism—something that seemed to Mao to be happening in the Soviet Union—China needed a Great Proletarian Cultural Revolution (which began in 1966 and lasted, in one form or another, until Mao's death in 1976).

The Cultural Revolution is most usefully understood as a multifaceted power struggle, with the ideological issues presented here not necessarily beside the point but in most ways only a pretext. Still, the ideology influenced the manner in which the struggle was carried out. Since the Party was dominated by capitalist roaders (Mao meant primarily Liu Shaoqi and Deng Xiaoping), one early Maoist tactic was to organize the masses independently of the Party so they could make revolution against the capitalist roaders. This took the form mainly of Red Guard groups formed among high school and university students, although similar groups also formed among factory and office workers. The mass movement was backed by the army, the police, and the propaganda apparatus. It did not take long for the Red Guards to start fighting each other and the army, which, when things got wild, moved in, sometimes brutally, to restore order.

In many ways, Cultural Revolution Maoism was radically antiauthoritarian. The most prominent Red Guard slogan was: To rebel is justified—a phrase Mao coined decades earlier, perhaps without irony, to describe the meaning of Stalin's life. Some Maoists denounced Leninist principles of obedience to the Party as "slavishness." These Maoists, and maybe even, for a time, Mao himself, flirted with the idea that the Party had not only been infiltrated by persons holding bourgeois ideology but had itself become a new oppressive ruling class. Any system of law or rule becomes a way of freezing in place a system of privilege and repressive power. It is necessary through uninterrupted revolution to tear down any system of authority as soon as it starts to congeal. Western observers at the time, influenced by the then fashionable "new left" mentality, fancied that Maoism represented a force for human liberation. The Cultural Revolution was, instead, a time of totalitarian terror, a removal of any legal or moral restraint on the exercise of cruelty and brutality by those who held power. It was, as Mao once put it, a time of "no law and no Heaven."

Still, it is not completely inaccurate to find some liberating elements in Cultural Revolution thinking. As a social movement the Cultural Revolution was a fraud, organized from above; but the groups that made up the movement were composed of persons who knew how to think, and many groups escaped for a while from official control. Some of these groups developed more systematically the idea of the Party as a new ruling class, concluding that the only effective way to check this kind of power was real democracy—competitive elections, limited power, protected freedom of speech. While very few dared say so, millions of Chinese drew the obvious inference that Chairman Mao himself was a big authority, not necessarily to be trusted. The notion of the Party as a new ruling class figured in the early 1980s as part of the critique by the more democratic wing of the reform movement. These persons, however, soon came to emphasize more the alienation resulting from the monopoly of power by a single party without wondering whether this party was itself a social class. The Cultural Revolution had made the subject of class struggle and even class analysis something odious.

Mao was rather out of favor during most of the 1980s, although the Party could not afford to explicitly repudiate him. The official evaluation was that he accrued merit until 1957, and thereafter, having become complacent, made grave mistakes. A more radical appraisal, proposed by some in the Party but not adopted, was that until 1957 Mao's merits outweighed his defects; from 1957 until 1966 he made mistakes; after 1966 he was guilty of crimes. In 1989 and subsequent years, however, there was a "Mao fever." There were several sources for this, aside from historical curiosity. For many of the old guard, on the defensive after the democratic movement of 1989 and the collapse of communism in eastern Europe and the Soviet Union, the Maoist period was an age of faith, a time when party people could have confidence in what they were doing, when they knew that anyone who opposed them must be a counterrevolutionary or some other kind of class enemy. This nostalgia affected even persons who had been victims of Mao's wrath in the Cultural Revolution. Mao also attracted certain young people, especially those with no memory of the Cultural Revolution, much less the Great Leap Forward. For them, Mao, safely in his crystal coffin, was a hero, a glamorous leader, a rebel—someone who had given a very hard time to the same old men whose domination they now found so oppressive.

The Ideology of Reform

In late 1964, Zhou Enlai, then head of China's government, spoke to the National People's Congress (NPC), the country's nominal legislature, about the "four modernizations"—of industry, agriculture, science and technology, and national defense. The general idea was to develop China's economy, to allow China to hold its own against the other countries of the world and to raise the living standard of its people. Any discussion of the four modernizations ended with the Cultural Revolution, but Zhou returned to the theme at the same forum in 1975, in his last public speech before his death.

The Maoists were not opposed in principle to modernization, but in practice they hindered it. They claimed to believe that an open emphasis on economic development would lead to a capitalist mentality, so they stressed the priority of "spirit" and politics. If people had the right kind of thought in their heads, namely the Thought of Mao, prosperity would follow as a matter of course. If China chased after prosperity and disregarded ideology, the country would become revisionist, even capitalist: China would become just like the Soviet Union or the United States.

Mao's death in September 1976, was followed in about a month by the purge of his radical entourage, the "Gang of Four." Radicals of this stripe had dominated the propaganda system all during the Cultural Revolution. The victors of the power struggle returned to the theme of the four modernizations. Ideologically, they emphasized the more orthodox classical Marxism, blaming the radical and subjectivist interpretations that had been so prominent not on Mao but on the Gang of Four. Classical Marxism-Leninism justified a reassertion of the authority of the Party, which had been rudely questioned during the Cultural Revolution. It also justified a reemphasis on economic development rather than on politics.

Those who defeated the Gang of Four repudiated radicalism, but not Mao. The front man for the group, Hua Guofeng, who had succeeded Zhou Enlai as head of government, claimed his right to leadership on the grounds that Mao had personally chosen him. A more impressive figure was Deng Xiaoping, who had been the Party's general secretary, the head of its organization, from 1954 to 1966. Although a hard-liner on matters of party discipline and social control, Deng was not dogmatic about economic policy. During the famine period he had said: It doesn't matter if a cat is black or white, as long as the cat catches the mice. This was a way of saying that it doesn't matter if some people should call the policies used to deal with the famine capitalist; the important thing is whether a policy is effective, not how it is classified. Deng was purged in 1966 as a capitalist roader. He returned to public life in 1973, under the sponsorship of Zhou Enlai. By 1975 Zhou was on his deathbed. Deng attempted a power play to curb the influence of the radicals, but failed and was again in disgrace following Zhou's death in January 1976.

Hua understandably resisted pressure from his allies to bring Deng back again one more time. He developed his own little ideological thesis: the Party must carry out whatever Chairman Mao had decided and was bound by whatever Chairman Mao had said. This not only showed his commitment to Maoism but also reminded the comrades that one of Mao's decisions had been to purge Deng. Nevertheless, during the summer of 1977 Deng was again rehabilitated, and by 1980 had completely routed Hua in a power struggle—although a much gentler power struggle than the earlier ones.

Deng and his allies condemned Hua's "two whatevers," elaborating their own theme to counter it: Practice is the criterion of truth. This slogan had been coined by Mao. In its new context it meant that while certainly much of what Mao, Marx, or others said was in fact true, the test of its truth was not whether someone had said it but whether it worked in practice. The slogan—in practice—opened the door for all kinds of change. If practice is the criterion of truth, some might think, there is no need for some ideology or the Communist party to tell us what truth is.

Deng's answer, in effect, was that the Party can decide just what counts as *correct* practice. Partly to reassure public opinion, partly to reassure high-ranking victims of the Cultural Revolution who were regaining power, Deng and his allies had proclaimed that class struggle, whatever Mao may have thought, was no longer the central issue in Chinese life. On the other hand, they added, class struggle still exists—so those who get too far out of line can again become the "objects of dictatorship." Even before his cronies had fully developed the practice criterion, Deng had declared "four cardinal principles" that would set limits to change: all words and policy must not violate the socialist line; Marxism-Leninism and the Thought of Mao; people's democratic dictatorship; the leadership of the Communist party. The last of these was in practice a little more "cardinal" than the others.

While Deng did not want to repudiate the Thought of Mao, he did want to redefine it. New evaluations of the history of the Party admitted that Mao had made errors in his life, that he was only a human being, not a god. The Thought of Mao, it turns out, is not every thought that ever passed between Chairman Mao's ears: only correct Thought counts as the Thought of Mao. Also, this Thought was the work not just of Mao as an individual, but of other leaders as well and, if it came to that, the entire Party. Thus, it came eventually to be said, Deng Xiaoping had made creative contributions to the Thought of Mao. By the 1990s some ideologues were even discussing the Thought of Deng Xiaoping, although this concept did not generate universal enthusiasm.

In the meantime, Deng's economic reforms—the decollectivization of agriculture, encouragement of some private entrepreneurship, increasing turn toward a market economy—were all going ahead without apparent need for any ideological justification: they were justified by their results. Marxist theorists tried to come up with explanations for the ongoing social and economic development. A major line of thought, attributed to Deng, was that China was only now entering the "initial stage of socialism." This initial stage turns out to be the substitute for the capitalist stage that China never had. It entails a "commodity economy," that is, the production of goods for sale in the market (rather than, in the Maoist-Stalinist pattern, production at the behest of the planning and political leadership). By 1992, "socialism with Chinese characteristics," sometimes said to be a product of the Thought of Deng Xiaoping, was directly identified as a "socialist market economy."

Party theorists of a liberal persuasion increasingly became so bold to say, prior to 1989, that economic reform had to be accompanied by political reform. There had to be greater respect for law and greater allowance for diversity not merely of taste but also of opinion. The Communist party operated as a secret society, exercising real power over society but responsible only to itself; its power should be cut back. Political and economic reform required unfettered policy debate, and policy debate was possible only with full civil liberties. The more creative developments of Marxism in China were turning it into something close to liberal democracy—not necessarily to the pleasure of Deng and other political leaders.

The problem was, farmers, business people, managers, economists, and ordinary people were going ahead indifferent to any ideological justification. The only reason ideology had to be adjusted was to accommodate continued party rule. The Party, however, was actually relinquishing much of its control over the economy, and its monopoly of political power made less and less sense to more and more people. It is probably fair to say that the CPC did not successfully develop an ideology of reform.

Bankruptcy of the Marxist Vision?

The massive student demonstrations of April, May, and June 1989 and their brutal suppression exposed the failure of the Communist regime to legitimize its rule after 40 years and after 10 years of valiant attempt at reform. The 1989 democracy movement was complicated. The protesters did not really have a coherent political position and lacked the kind of organization that would allow them to develop one. The protests began with complaints against corruption inside the Party and with unfocused discontent over a probably necessary slowdown of economic reform. But the reform program was probably by its nature doomed to stall, and by 1989 the regime had done as much as it could to bring about change within the system without changing the system itself. The demonstrations escalated into open-ended demands for democracy, demands probably no government could have satisfied.

In recent decades, among Chinese who care about politics, democracy has had at least as much appeal as Marxism, and many of those who were attracted to Marxism believed that theory provided a way to democracy, or as much democracy as China in its circumstances could reasonably hope for. The 1989 demonstrations were the largest in the history of the People's Republic, but they were far from unprecedented. In 1957, during the hundred flowers period, students and liberal intellectuals criticized the Party for its authoritarianism, its ignorance, its subservience to the Soviet Union. The Cultural Revolution some years later was manipulated from the top, but it also opened the way for a genuinely radical democratic critique of the regime. In April 1976, a massive pro-democracy demonstration took place in Tiananmen Square in Peking, and like the 1989 events at that place, was also brutally put down. In 1978 and 1980 Deng Xiaoping used pro-democratic opinions in society for his own advantage, to consolidate his own position, although he turned against his democratic supporters once their enthusiasm became too easy a target for his critics in the regime who argued that he wanted to return to Cultural Revolution–style chaos.

In modern times democratic theory is probably a natural product of political repression. We might in principle like to get our own way on all things all of the time, but there is not much chance of that. On the other hand, in an autocratic system, those in power are fairly sure to get their own way against us all the time. Under the circumstances, it seems reasonable enough to let the majority decide. In China, however, Marxism also generated a kind of democratic critique of itself.

Actually, there were two critiques, one radical and one that might be called orthodox. The Cultural Revolution called for "the masses" to "rebel" against "capitalist roaders in authority in the Party." This rebellion was styled "Big Democracy." It was, of course, a Maoist technique to bring down their enemies. But disillusioned grass-roots Maoists had little problem in turning the radical demand for democracy against the establishment radical Maoists. The establishment radicals also had their own internal contradictions: their ideology was hostile to any structure of authority, but they themselves wanted to exercise power. In 1973 and 1974 three former Red Guards in Canton, calling themselves by the pseudonym Li Yizhe, came to additional insights: the Maoist radicals were as repressive as the capitalist roaders had ever been; to curb repression we need not only mass control over those in power, but also a rule of law to protect this democratic control. Democratic rule must also be limited rule.

Zhou Enlai died in January 1976, and his then-protégé, Deng Xiaoping, was purged immediately thereafter. On April 4, the date that year of the "bright and clear festival," a day when Chinese families traditionally tidy up the graves of their ancestors, office workers, administrators, scientists, and technicians in Peking placed wreaths on the small monument to Zhou on Tiananmen Square. Passers-by became angry the following morning upon discovering that the wreaths had been removed, and began a spontaneous protest. The crowd eventually grew to 100,000 persons. The gathering mourned the death of Zhou and protested the removal of Deng. People compared Mao to the First Qin Emperor (an identification Mao himself may have been promoting) and his wife, a leader of the radical Gang of Four, with the Empress Dowager. They demanded an end to "feudalism" and the implementation of the four modernizations. This demonstration was crushed by the police, army, and militia, with some loss of life. It was condemned as counterrevolutionary. In 1978, with Deng's return to the top, what we now must call the first Tiananmen incident was discovered to have in fact been democratic and completely revolutionary, a display of the people's devotion to the Party and to proper policies. Deng, however, was too prudent to play up the anniversary of the demonstration very much. If Li Yizhe was a radical democratic critique of radical totalitarianism, the first Tiananmen incident is a modernist criticism of radicalism and a reflection of a common Chinese conviction that democratic government is not only humane but also a necessary condition for material progress.

This modernist approach to democracy was incorporated into an orthodox Marxian criticism of totalitarianism in the 1980s, combining with some of the spirit of the radical critique as well. The basic principles included the idea that history develops in stages and that policy should reflect the objectively valid stage; that historical advance depends upon material progress, and to put in socialist social and political structures leads to "poverty communism" at best and, at worst, to "feudal fascism"; that, to be sure, socialist democracy is superior to bourgeois democracy, but that means it must be more democratic, not less. Democracy requires limitations on power, and these limitations should be expressed in law.

The main impression left by democratic thought in the 1980s, however, is just how irrelevant Marxism had itself become. Party intellectuals labored to find an ideology that would fit the need with reform, but the main accomplishment was to coat liberal democracy with beside-the-point Marxian verbiage. Many of the more famous democratic apologists for Marxism were in jail or exile following the events of 1989.

It is possible that this general sense of the irrelevance of Marxism was shared not only by reformers and democrats, but even by the radical Gang of Four itself. In the early 1970s, they seem to have found the Chinese tradition a more compelling model for understanding the current situation than the Marxist categories could provide. In their interpretation at that time, the struggle in China was a continuation of the aeons-long conflict between Legalism and Confucianism. The capitalist roaders and counterrevolutionary revisionists were heirs of the reactionary Confucian tradition, whereas the radical Maoists were in the line of the progressive, modernizing Legalists.

Most Chinese now consider this discussion to have been juvenile nonsense, pretentiously ignorant discussions of philosophy and history used in a grab for personal power. A puzzling thing, however, is that the reformers of the 1980s shared many of the ideas the radicals attributed to the Legalists and, by implication, to themselves: the rule of law, political appointment based on merit rather than class background, even private control of agriculture.[10] The reformers, of course, do not favor the Legalists' brutality. Yet they do speak as if they consider the older party establishment to be virtually identical with the old Confucian rulers, whom they see in the poor light of the May Fourth movement. In this sense, both radicalism and reform may be in the tradition of modernist discontent with current Chinese reality that dates from the Reform movement of 1898 and earlier. The party establishment, itself the

---

10. It is possible in this campaign that those who did the actual writing were more critical of the system than those who directed that the writing be done, and that those sponsoring the campaign did not fully appreciate its significance.

product of the iconoclasm of the May Fourth movement, has in some ways come to identify with the Great Tradition, to see itself as the guardian of the precious Chinese heritage against the nihilistic forces of both native and Western barbarians.

For most Chinese, even those with an education, this rarefied discussion of ideas may be beside the point. All the talk here of democracy should not lead to an overestimation of the importance of political ideas in the minds of most people in China. The system of "politics takes command," since 1958 but in practice since 1949, has left a legacy of revulsion against the very notion of politics. Politics more than economics is seen by the ordinary Chinese as the major cause of human misery. Many, perhaps most, would prefer to withdraw from political life entirely. At worst this leads to a mindless and shameless chase after fashion, pleasure, and profit. More often it simply means the centering of concern on private life: love, family, work, amusement. These should probably be the central concerns in any healthy society, but this concern must be balanced by a sense that our opinions and desires have some relevance to public life, to the tone of the community in which we live. On an intellectual level the concern for the private has led to fads for old-fashioned Western worthies such as Nietzsche, Freud, and Sartre. The party establishment condemns the generation that came of age during reform for lacking ideals, even while admitting that the heritage of the Cultural Revolution could only encourage cynicism. The younger generation does not lack ideals, but desires that the ideals be their own, and does not passively accept those persons in power telling them what ideals they should have. This is treated as a new phenomenon, but it may also be in part a reversion to the ambience of the 1920s and 1930s.

When the Chinese, especially the educated young, break out of political passivity, their activism takes a democratic form. Democracy for them is as much a moral as a political commitment. The student demonstrations of 1989 showed little concern for democracy as a method of decision making involving clashes of opinion and interest, and no concern at all for democracy as an art of achieving acceptable compromises. Older Chinese democrats (and older here may sometimes simply mean having graduated from school) often have a technocratic orientation, as seen in the pairing, both in the May Fourth movement and the reform period, of Mr. Science with Mr. Democracy. Democratic government almost seems to mean a system that allows the educated to serve society as best they can in conformity with their own consciences without ignorant interference either from party cadres or from the population in general.[11] In 1989, in the weeks before the demonstrations, one well-connected group of intellectuals proposed what they called a "neo-authoritarianism," in which educated "elites" (not necessarily

---

11. This scientism was perhaps also part of the appeal of Marxism, "scientific socialism."

the Leninist vanguard party—here, too Marxism seemed entirely irrelevant) would put in place a free economic system. This would bring economic prosperity, which would provide a foundation for political democracy. The neo-authoritarians took their inspiration from some possibly misunderstood American political science theories and from their interpretations of the experience of areas such as Chile, South Korea, and Taiwan.[12] Although criticized by both democrats and communists, it seems appropriate to classify neo-authoritarianism as one variety of Chinese democratic thought. In fact, it only makes implicit what seems to be implicit in the ideas of self-proclaimed democratic, dissident scientist Fang Lizhi: in a democratic society, it is the educated who call the shots. Chinese democratic thinking, in some of its aspects, anyway, may be a modern transformation of the Confucian mentality. It shares with Confucianism a sense of both the position and the responsibility of the educated, a moralistic concept of public action, and a distaste for the give-and-take, wheeling-and-dealing of politics. Of course, "practice is the criterion of truth," and any ideas about democracy in China will surely be transformed once they need to operate within genuinely democratic institutions.

After 1989 the attempt to bring Marxism into conformity with the needs of reform did not stop entirely, but the dominant official line at first was a reversion to a narrow Marxism, a reemphasis on the "four cardinal principles" and whining that the United States was attempting to bring about a "peaceful evolution" from communism by spreading notions of "bourgeois liberalization." The main principle turned out to be leadership of the Communist party. A favorite slogan was: Only socialism will save China. Sarcastic critics pointed out that a more apt slogan would be: Only China will save socialism—since, aside from oddities like North Korea, Vietnam, and Cuba, almost every other country had abandoned Leninist socialism. It seemed evident that Marxist ideology and Communist rule had not resolved China's chronic cultural crisis.

Institutions of Rule

In Marxist theory, the state is the instrument the ruling class uses to preserve its ruling position. In China the ruling class is alleged to be the proletariat, but in alliance with other friendly classes. The Chinese state formed in 1949 is said to be a "new democracy," or "people's democratic dictatorship." This

---

12. The neo-authoritarians worked out of Peking. In 1991 intellectuals in Shanghai argued for a "neo-conservatism," which, they said, was just about the same thing. This may in fact be becoming the really operational, if unacknowledged, ruling ideology in China.

last strange-sounding term means that among the people there is democracy, but the people exercise dictatorship over their enemies. The people, again, means the proletariat and the classes friendly to it and accepting its leadership. Proletariat, in turn, really refers to its self-appointed vanguard, the Communist party. The formula asserts the Party's leadership of the political system and the entire society.

In 1956 the Party claimed China was building socialism, which implied that China was on the way to becoming a classless society. A few years later, however, Chairman Mao decided that class struggle was fiercer than ever, and one premise of the Cultural Revolution was that China had not yet even had a dictatorship of the proletariat. A constitution adopted in 1982 (the fourth one for the PRC since its founding) described China as a socialist state under the people's democratic dictatorship, which means "in essence" the same thing as the dictatorship of the proletariat.

When the People's Republic was established, in theory the leading institution of state power was the Chinese People's Political Consultative Conference (CPPCC). This was a united front organization, a coalition of various "democratic parties" and "democratic personages" representing intellectual, religious, and ethnic groups, all hostile to Chiang Kai-shek and willing to give the CPC a chance. The CPPCC as a whole and its members individually were supposed to accept the "leadership" of the CPC, which was itself a member of the CPPCC; party members also controlled the organization's full-time administrative staff.

After a regular constitution was adopted in 1954 the National People's Congress (NPC) or legislature became the highest institution of state, but the CPPCC continued to play an advisory role. During the hundred flowers period in 1957 too many of its members were too free with their advice; in the aftermath they had to make humiliating self-criticisms and some were jailed. In the following years the CPPCC faded into obscurity.

Rather surprisingly, it was revived after the Cultural Revolution. The democratic parties still existed and even had some new members, although one might have thought the conditions that had given rise to the parties had long since passed into history. In Marxist theory, parties represent social classes, although the Chinese also say that the democratic parties represent, instead, trends of opinion. In practice, most of the new members of the minor parties seem to be children and other relatives of the older members, and membership may be most useful in dealing with problems of daily life, such as housing or medical care. If the member of a minority party has some trouble, he can go to the local branch of that party, whose staff in turn may talk to the staff of the local CPPCC, who may have access to persons able to take care of the problem.

In 1990, following the student democracy movement and the collapse of the Leninist regimes in eastern Europe, the rulers gave even more prominence to the CPPCC. Official CPC resolutions stressed that China's political system was based on "multi-party cooperation and political consultation." The CPC wanted to show that China was not a one-party dictatorship. However, the various parties all voluntarily accepted CPC leadership and did not compete for power. A competitive system, spokesmen argued, would make China a Western-style parliamentary system, a very inferior political form.

For all practical purposes China has a single-party system, or what might more properly be called a party–state system. This term implies that the Party and government are blended into an all-encompassing structure. The two can be analyzed separately, however, even though there is much overlap of functions and even more of personnel. The army is legally a part of the state, but politically it operates as an instrument of the Party as well, and it also has sometimes had its own institutional weight. Party, state, and army are sometimes called the three pillars of proletarian dictatorship.

The Communist Party of China

The CPC's function is to set policy and lead the society and the state. Its members are supposed to constitute an elite; they comprise about 4 or 5 percent of the population. The type of people recruited into the Party varies from period to period. Prior to Liberation the greater number of entering members were of peasant origin, although not necessarily of poor peasant background; the leaders then were on the whole children of landlords and rich peasants. During most of the time since 1949 the Party has tried to recruit high school and college graduates, although during the Great Leap and Cultural Revolution it aimed to bring in more "proletarian" types.

Party members are expected to conform to party discipline. The organizational principle is the Leninist notion of democratic centralism. This means that lower party organizations elect the membership of the immediately superior organization and in turn accept unquestioningly the policies decided at the higher level. Prior to making a decision, members are free to discuss the issues and propose their own views (as long as they do not disagree openly in front of the "masses"). After a decision is reached, either by a majority vote in the particular group or by an order from above, those who don't like the decision may keep their dissenting views, but are expected to support the decision publicly and work in good faith to implement it properly. Party members are not allowed to form cliques and factions (which may sometimes imply they can get in trouble even for discussing things among themselves outside official channels). They are expected to display selfless devotion to the nation, socialism, and the people, and to always think of others instead of themselves. Party membership has normally been the most reliable road to power and privilege, but for junior members responsibility and pressure may outweigh the privilege.

Until 1982 the head of the Party was called the Chairman. That year the terminology was changed. The top ranking person in the formal hierarchy was then termed General Secretary, following the Soviet and east European practice. Officially, the general secretary heads the Party's internal administration. In most communist countries the general secretary was in effect the boss of the whole regime, a practice that began with Stalin in the Soviet Union. In China the position seems to be less powerful in actuality than that of the premier, the head of government.

The National Party Congress is the most authoritative decision-making institution in the Party. This normally meets every five years (although there was a 13-year gap between the Eighth Congress in 1956 and the Ninth in 1969). The congresses may be occasions for major changes in policy and personnel. The congress itself is too large (about 2,000 delegates) and meets too seldom to make any routine decisions; its main function has been to legitimize decisions already made.

The National Party Congress elects a Central Committee (along with a list of alternates). The Central Committee members and alternate members number around 300 to 400 persons. The Central Committee meets in full (or "plenary") session at least once a year. Like the Party Congress, it mostly ratifies decisions made elsewhere. It may be treated, however, as a name list of China's top elite. Its members usually hold the most important roles in the Party, state, and army at the central and provincial levels.

The Central Committee elects a Political Bureau (or Politburo), normally about 20 members. This probably meets about twice a month, although members not resident in Peking may not always attend. The Politburo in its turn elects a Standing Committee of five to seven members. In 1992, after the Fourteenth National Party Congress, the Politburo Standing Committee consisted of Jiang Zemin, the Party general secretary; Li Peng, the premier, or head of government; Qiao Shi, in charge of the police, supervisory, and espionage systems; Li Ruihuan, in charge of propaganda, including the mass media and much of the educational system; Zhu Rongji, who supervised economic work; Liu Huaqing, a military man; and Hu Jintao, who probably handled party organizational affairs. This composition gives some idea of what the strategic functions in the system are.

Subordinate to the Central Committee are several special commissions or organizations. The most important is the Central Secretariat, the Party's administrative headquarters. The Secretariat, headed by the general secretary, embraces the work of several departments, whose number changes from time to time. The more important include the Organization department, which supervises personnel appointments in both Party and state; the Propaganda department, supervising the mass media; the International Liaison department, coordinating relations with foreign political parties, both communist and noncommunist; and the General Political department, in charge of political work in the armed forces.

The various provincial party committees also report to the Central Secretariat. Although the situation is not as clear since the 1980s as before, the first party secretary of a CPC provincial committee is in fact the boss or chief executive of the province, more important normally than the provincial governor. Similarly, the head of the party committee at the county or city level is for the most part a more important figure than the county magistrate or mayor.

The Party's Central Discipline and Inspection Commission is on the same hierarchical level as the Secretariat. As its name implies, it enforces party discipline and punishes party members who are guilty of violating discipline or of crimes or of other misbehavior. In principle it can act only against party members and the most severe punishment it can give is dismissal from the Party. If a member has violated the law as well as party rules or discipline, that is a matter for the courts. In practice, the scope of the Discipline and Inspection Commission is probably broader than its nominal powers.

In 1982 the Party set up a Central Advisory Commission, with an implied function somewhat like that of the Meiji genro. The idea was Deng Xiaoping's; it was his way of providing an honorable place for the older generation of top leaders to retire to, so allowing younger and more flexible minds to run the country on a day-to-day basis. At the time, the only really important old timer willing to join the commission was Deng himself, and he presumably had no choice because it was his idea. Afterward it became an institutional base for the older generation of leaders, many of whom were unsympathetic to reform. Deng came to think of the commission as a temporary expedient that would vanish (like the genro-in) with the passing of the older generation. His more conservative rivals seemed to want instead to make it permanent, but the institution was abolished at the Fourteenth Party Congress, held in 1992. The power of the older leaders derived more, of course, from their personal prestige and connections than from membership on the Advisory Commission; membership was more a sign of their influence than a cause of it.

The other major central party organization is the Central Military Commission, the apex of the country's defense apparatus. This is discussed in the section on page 200, on the army.

At its most ambitious, the Party tries to control not only political but all other activity in the country. Government offices, factories, firms, and schools all have their party membership and, if large enough, a party committee. Each of these "work units," as they are called, has a full-time party secretary responsible for the routine party work and sometimes even for the work of the unit itself. Outside of work or in addition to work, the population is organized into groups: labor unions, youth organizations, women's organizations, even religious groups. Each of these also has its own party organization.

In principle, the party committee at any level or in any unit sets the general direction (in conformity with more general party policy) and checks to see that the correct direction is followed. In practice, the Party often becomes an inner circle of the true elite, those who have access to power and privilege. There has sometimes been a tendency for the party secretary to become in effect the boss of the organization. Since the 1980s official policy has been to enforce a clearer distinction between Party and government and between politics and economics. This should make the system seem less arbitrary to the ordinary person, and might even enhance party control by making clearer and more efficient divisions of responsibilities and functions.[13]

Prior to the 1980s the Party held a real monopoly on power. Since then agriculture has reverted to family farming and in positions requiring specialized knowledge professional competence counts at least as much as political reliability. The Party still monopolizes political power, but no longer has quite the same control over the life and well-being of the ordinary person. It has also become a little more difficult to recruit qualified people into the Party. In the past people might have wanted to join because they believed in Marxism or the revolution, or were patriotic, or were interested in public affairs, or wanted to help others. It is increasingly assumed, perhaps unfairly, that now one joins the Party only for opportunistic, self-serving reasons.

The State or Government

If the state is, as the ideology claims, the executive committee of the ruling class, it is appropriate that the PRC government be led and controlled by the Communist party, the vanguard of the proletariat. Virtually all high-ranking government officials—probably most low-ranking ones as well—are party members, and the few who are not have less authority than subordinates who do belong to the Party.

According to the constitution, the National People's Congress is the highest organ of state power. It is elected indirectly: people elect local people's congresses, these elect provincial congresses, and the provinces elect the national congress. A rule stipulates that in the lowest-level elections there be more candidates than positions available, but candidates are not allowed to oppose the Communist party, nor are they encouraged to engage in any real debate among themselves on possible issues.

---

13. In 1993 Jiang Zemin became chairman of the state as well as Party general secretary. Qiao Shi took over the chairmanship of the NPC Standing Committee, and Li Ruihuan also became head of the CPPCC. This is something of a deviation from the reform-era policy of separating Party and state functions, although the new positions are mostly honorific.

The NPC meets in full session once a year, and is much too large to have a meaningful impact on policy (although much discussion does take place in committee meetings, and changes in law or policy sometimes result from this discussion). Its main function is to applaud speeches by leaders and approve those laws the regime wants approved. Even the regime leadership admits the NPC tends too much to be a rubber stamp. In 1982 it set up a Standing Committee of the NPC, and this body, which meets several times a year, actually does provide a forum for the discussion of legislation and the conduct of government. The NPC Standing Committee has on the whole been dominated by the more conservative elements in the Party and has probably been more a brake on liberalizing reform than a propeller for it.

The NPC elects a State Chairman, or President, who is China's head of state. This is a ceremonial position with no power attached to it. Holders of the position may be quite influential, but this is because of their personal prestige and connections, not their institutional position as such. The post also has a "symbolic" function. For example, in late 1958, when the initial difficulties of the Great Leap Forward were becoming apparent, Mao Zedong stepped down as state chairman, while remaining chairman of the Party. He was replaced by Liu Shaoqi. The "inner" meaning of the change may have been that Liu became for all practical purposes the party chairman, or head of regime, with Mao becoming effectively, but not officially, the honorary chairman mentioned in the 1956 party charter. In any case, Mao reasserted himself within a few months and Liu was purged and discredited in 1966, the major victim of the Cultural Revolution. Yet Mao seems to have developed an antipathy for the position of state chairman. For the rest of his life he refused to allow the post to be filled; perhaps as far as he was concerned it no longer existed.

The NPC designates a State Council (Cabinet), headed by a premier. The State Council includes the heads of the various government ministries—foreign affairs, finance and trade, agriculture, industry, public security, and the like. These are the political heads of the ministries, although in a country like China the distinction between political and administrative functions is not as clear as in more orthodoxly democratic systems. Because so much of the economy is owned and controlled by the state, many ministries have an economic character, in effect owning complex strings of factories and business firms. State Council commissions, such as those dealing with education or economic planning, try to coordinate the work of related ministries.

The premiership may be the single most powerful institutional position in China. Normally, in communist systems the regime "boss" would be the head of the Party rather than the government: the Soviet leaders from Stalin through Gorbachev were all first secretaries of the Communist party, and by Gorbachev's time it was taken for granted that the party head would be the leader of the country.

The PRC's first premier, Zhou Enlai, served from the founding of the state in 1949 until his death in 1976. He was careful never to antagonize Chairman Mao. His successor, Hua Guofeng, emerged as leader of the regime after Mao's death. The reforming General Secretary (previously, Chairman) Hu Yaobang was purged in 1987 for being too tolerant of dissent from society. He was replaced by the equally reformist premier, Zhao Ziyang. The policy at the time was not to allow the same person to serve as head of both Party and government—that might lead to personal dictatorship—and Zhao pleaded to be allowed to remain as premier, instead, where he would have greater influence on economic policy. General Secretary Zhao was purged for his liberalism during the street demonstrations of 1989; his replacement as premier, Li Peng, survived in fine shape.

Hu and Zhao fell because of their political alliances and opinions, not because they were party heads. Nonetheless, the position of premier would seem to be more secure and even more substantial than that of the general secretary. Of course, to say that the premiership is the single most important institutional position in China may not be saying much, since it need not be vastly more influential than other positions, and power in the Chinese system remains more personal than institutional in any case.

The power of the general secretary in most communist systems comes from the Party's control of promotions and appointments. The Party serves this function in China as well. Perhaps surprisingly, given the country's history and tradition, the PRC has no civil service system, although there has been discussion about developing one. Appointments to office, whether in the Party, state, or state economic enterprises, are made from lists approved by the party committee at the level supervising the relevant unit, on the basis of records kept by the Party's organization department at that level. Yet in China, perhaps more than in other Leninist states, it may be that the Party cannot simply dictate appointments. Rather, appointments seem to be made by the functional "system" (a term embracing a combination of party and government functions) for which the person works.

The functional systems are informal but very real relations among institutions, including both party and government agencies. The systems would include different types of industry, agriculture, education, the police, the military, and many others. Each system operates in relative isolation from the others and includes within itself functions performed by the others (in the past, at any rate, the police system managed several factories, for example). Appointments and promotions are made within the system, and the system also takes care of the welfare needs of its employees. The systems are coordinated with each other perhaps only at the State Council or Secretariat level.

One of the aims of the reform movement since the death of Chairman Mao was a clearer separation of the functions of Party and state. One result would be to clarify lines of accountability. Another consequence would be the enlargement of the civil liberties of the person (who would be subject to punishment only for violation of a law or properly promulgated regulation, not for being out of sympathy with some vague party policy). The reform establishment did not question the leading position of the Party, but argued that party policy should be binding on the entire society only after it had been formally incorporated into the laws of the state. The separation of Party and state would not by itself make China a democracy, but it would help put the country under the rule of law.

The Army

The Chinese People's Liberation Army (PLA), which also includes the navy and air force, is an anomalous institution. It is as much an agency of the CPC as it is of the Chinese state. This is understandable historically: the CPC gained power through a civil war won by its own armed forces. The emphasis on the leading role of the Party over the army continued after Liberation.

The most important command institution, in fact if not formally, is the Party's Central Military Commission (CMC), designated by the Central Committee. The chairman of the Commission is usually the regime's top leader: Mao Zedong, Hua Guofeng, Deng Xiaoping.[14] The actual working head of the CMC is its ranking vice chairman, who is usually China's most prestigious soldier (and often holds the concurrent appointment of Minister of Defense). The CMC's membership consists of high-ranking military officers. It oversees the formulation of defense policy and the internal affairs of the armed forces.

During the reform period, some argued against having the country's armed forces so obviously subordinate to a political party rather than to the legal state, and proposed that the CMC be converted into a state organization. As a kind of compromise, the regime set up another institution, the State CMC, whose composition and leadership are virtually identical with those of the party organization (which shares the same office building). In the wake of the June 4 incident the regime strongly reasserted the army's absolute subordination to the Party.

The military can itself be considered one of the functional systems discussed above. It is divided, however, into three major subsystems of its own. There is a Ministry of Defense under the State Council, and the Minister is usually the ranking vice chairman of the CMC. The ministry, however, unlike the American Defense Department, has administrative rather than operational responsibilities. At the Central level, apart from the CMC, which has

---

14. In 1989 Deng resigned in favor of his new protégé, Jiang Zemin, who had no military background. This was part of a program to bolster Jiang's prestige, and, given the general weakness of institutional position in Chinese politics, did not necessarily guarantee that Jiang would carry any weight in the armed forces.

overall policy responsibilities, the major military institutions include: the General Staff, the General Political Department, and the Rear Services or logistics department.

The General Staff, headed by its chief, is responsible for the professional functioning of the army and for its major task: the fighting of wars and preparation for the fighting of wars. Under the General Staff are the various service branches: infantry, artillery, armor, air force, navy, and the like. The General Staff also coordinates the various regional and district commands.

The General Political Department (GPD), under the Central Secretariat, administers the system of political officers in the armed forces. This system is adapted, ultimately, from the Soviet Union. In that country the Bolsheviks, after their revolution, had to rely on officers who had served under the tsar to fight their civil war, and one job of the political officers was to keep an eye on the regular military commanders to make sure they did not betray or subvert the Communist cause. The CPC had itself a plethora of military expertise, and there is little of the heritage of distrust between the regular and political branches of the army. Officers in each system will occasionally quarrel about how much time should be devoted to their own type of training. The tendency since 1980 has been to give more and more importance to regular professional training. The GPD and its political officers try to make sure that the army understands and adheres to the party line; it gives ideological instruction to officers and troops; it plays a role in the investigation of crime and other misbehavior in the armed forces; it runs entertainment and leisure programs to keep up the soldiers' morale. The GPD system is in principle distinct from the system of party committees in the various military units, but it is likely that most of the time the political officer serves as well as the party branch secretary.

The Rear Services system is in charge of weapons development and procurement and logistics. It is a huge combination, at one time controlling several State Council ministries (which had deliberately vague names—the Fourth Ministry of Machine Building, for example—to conceal their function). In the 1980s these ministries were reorganized as state corporations and became notorious for promiscuous sales of cheap and deadly weapons to Third World countries, including both sides of the Iran–Iraq war. The weapons sales seem to have been motivated more by a desire to make money for the army than to serve any of China's particular foreign policy goals.

China is divided into several military regions, and under the military regions are the military districts (whose boundaries coincide with those of the provinces). These military regions can also be considered "systems," in that officers tend to spend their entire careers inside one regional command. The regional forces originally were composed of the PLA forces that occupied the area at the conclusion of the civil war. The regional commanders remained unchanged from the 1950s into the 1970s, and during the Cultural Revolution most of them became the dominant political figures in their localities, taking over both the top local party and the government positions.

Observers inside and outside the country worried about a revival of warlordism, should central authority break down. Two generations past Liberation and one generation after the Cultural Revolution such a development remained possible, if not necessarily likely. The local systems could be bases for networks of personal connections, and under some circumstances—weak, incompetent, or illegitimate central authority—personal loyalty might override the legal chain of command. The tendency of the provinces and regions toward increased economic autonomy might reinforce the danger of the new warlordism.

The CPC itself might act as a counterbalance to tendencies toward political autonomy, but its influence in turn might be counterbalanced by the demand that the army participate in politics. Since the 1950s there has been a tension between demands for professional competence and political activism (which is not necessarily the same thing as tension between regular and political officers). The Maoists in the 1950s and 1960s argued that too much attention to professional technique and weapons technology would turn the army into a "bourgeois" force, divorced from the people and uncommitted to the socialist enterprise. Instead of trying to emulate the armies of the United States and the Soviet Union, China's main rivals, the PLA should stick to the doctrine of "people's war" as defined by Chairman Mao. As a slogan of the times had it, "man" (meaning politically correct man) was more important than weapons. The Thought of Mao was a "spiritual atomic bomb." The mentality is reminiscent of that of Japan's more ardent military nationalists in the prewar period.

The propaganda for people's war was partly compensation for China's material backwardness, and its advocates were as eager as anyone else for China to get advanced weapons. But people's war had political significance as well. A professional military ethic would not necessarily have affected the soldiers' loyalty to the Party and state, but it would have allowed them a certain autonomy in their own sphere of competence, in the art and science of war and in internal military affairs. This would have reduced the Party's sphere of control.[15]

In 1959 the regime's top soldier, Marshal Peng Dehuai, former commander of the Chinese forces in the Korean War, was removed as minister of defense, condemned for "right opportunism." The immediate occasion of his purge was that he had pointed out the economic suffering caused by the Great Leap Forward. He was also said to have fostered a "bourgeois military line."

Peng's successor, Lin Biao, whose brilliant exploits against the KMT make him contemporary China's most successful soldier, did not make the same mistake. In the early 1960s, while China was in famine, Lin intensified

---

15. This issue is not restricted to the military, but extends to all other issues of professional competence.

political indoctrination inside the PLA, ascribing superhuman abilities to Chairman Mao (whose reputation for acuity was being silently questioned in the Party at large) and supernatural efficacy for his Thought. Mao came to consider the army a more reliable force than the Party. For a time (until his disgrace and death) Lin Biao became Chairman Mao's heir apparent. As public order disintegrated during the Cultural Revolution (itself a consequence of Lin's machinations), local party and government organizations, and even factories and business firms, came under military control.

The process was reversed during the early 1970s, and after Mao's death the military's focus was more and more on professional developments. The student demonstrations of 1989 showed that the army could not avoid political involvement. There was disagreement inside the army about whether the students should be repressed by force and, if so, whether the army were the proper people to do it. The point is controversial (and it may be a while before we have anything close to a full story about what happened that June), but there may have been a danger that army units would actually fight each other. In the end the army acted on behalf not merely of the Party but of a faction within the Party (although it also acted in accord with orders of the government). After the repression, propaganda emphasized the army's political subordination to the Party, but the interest of professional soldiers remained more on their professional development. This tendency was only reinforced by the American war against Iraq in 1991, a demonstration of the damage advanced weapons skillfully used could do against a backward opponent with a politicized army.

The PLA is a conscript army, but traditionally it had little trouble getting people willing to serve. Soldiers enjoyed high social prestige, and army life, for all its rigor, was easier and more interesting than what the peasant kids left behind on the farm. After the reforms, rural life grew more attractive and the PLA itself desired manpower with more education than rural adolescents were apt to have. The PLA had to recruit among groups less attracted to the service. Among the four modernizations, that of the military consistently held lowest priority, and this had a natural effect on morale.

The general trend was for the retreat of the army from politics. Should there be extensive unrest in society or should the civilian leadership prove excessively incompetent, the independent political role of the military will grow. What this might mean is unclear, and with luck will always remain so. The army might provide overall cohesion, but it might instead itself fragment along factional or regional lines.

Informal Structures

It is important to have a general understanding of the legal structure of the Chinese state and the formal organization of the Communist party. The organizational charts and sets of regulations, however, often have only a remote relationship to the way things really work.

Chinese culture must certainly be relevant here, but we should take care not to be too simple or crude in deciding what it is. The importance of personal connections, or guanxi, was outlined earlier, and these have been given much attention in recent years. Confucianism, remember, defines moral obligations in personal terms. On the other hand, the use of public office to do favors for friends and relatives was a distortion of Confucian ethics rather than its fulfillment, and in any case China had a strong Legalist heritage as well as a Confucian one. On the whole, I think, a formal organization chart of traditional Chinese government would more nearly reflect the power relationships and realities of that time than would a formal institutional description of the PRC. The influence of informal power structures in Chinese politics (and, to a lesser degree, in Japanese politics) shows that the formal legal systems fit the actual political culture only to a limited extent.

China today has not only a traditional heritage but also a totalitarian one, one that found resonances in certain aspects of the Chinese tradition. Totalitarianism is no longer a very popular concept among Western academicians (it fell from favor when scholars decided its main use was as an anticommunist ideology in the cold war), although it seems to make sense to most people who have had to live under systems described by that concept. The concept may be often misconstrued. It seems to imply an absolute concentration of power, as well as power that pervades the entire society and has effective domain over everything that happens. Evidence of power struggles, policy debates, inefficient exercise of power, or personal corruption is then taken to indicate that totalitarianism does not apply.

I think this is a shallow reading of what the word implies. Perhaps the most interesting exposition of the concept, that by Hannah Arendt,[16] does not stress effective or efficient control over policy, but rather, the penetration of all aspects of life by arbitrary political power (with terror, often held to be a mark of totalitarianism, a manifestation of this arbitrary power). The totalitarian premise, according to Arendt, is not merely that everything is permitted, but also that everything is possible. There are in principle no moral or even physical restraints on what people—that is, in effect, people with power—can do. It is a condition, as Chairman Mao once put it, citing an old Chinese proverb, of no law and no Heaven. In the totalitarian flux both ruled and rulers are chronically insecure. No group or institution is strong enough to resist penetration from without. This logic leads to the holding of power by a single leader, who keeps power by forming coalitions to smash any coalitions that might compete with him and smashing the coalitions he has formed once they have served their purpose. Hannah Arendt

---

16. Hannah Arendt, *The Origins of Totalitarianism* (Cleveland, 1958).

developed her theory by abstracting and extrapolating from the Nazi and Stalinist examples. That it should apply to China and other countries that were not part of the original examples indicates it may have some scientific basis. This "model," in any case, predicts that in a totalitarian system formal authority need not describe real power, that there need be no stable structure of power, and that we should expect constant struggles for power.

Arendt pessimistically believed that such systems would endure forever, since there was nothing in them to push them into some other form or stage. In fact, it may be that full-blown totalitarianism rarely survives the death of the Great Leader.[17] The Leader's subordinates become weary of their insecurity and are unwilling to defer absolute power to each other; at the same time, they are eager to preserve the system that gives them so comfortable a position. Scholars have taken to describing the Leninist state (or what I have been calling the totalitarian system) as *neotraditional* (although the term may not be well chosen, and what it describes has only a superficial resemblance to tradition as used in this study). Neotraditionalism is sometimes proposed as an alternative theory to totalitarianism. I think it is more appropriate to consider neotraditionalism a "post-totalitarian" phenomenon, although something like it may also be at work at the grass-roots level during the totalitarian phase.[18]

The neotraditional pattern is woven by the pervasiveness of party or political controls throughout society combined with the absence of clear lines of authority or accountability. This means that those with access to political power are able, within limits, of course, to use it for their own good, to reward those who help them and hurt or deprive those who do not. This opens the "back door," the use of personal connections—those who are supposed to perform a function may not do it unless it is made worth their while, or unless requested to do so by someone they share a guanxi base with. There is a paradox here, in that a mild totalitarianism, at least, is compatible with a decentralized, arbitrary, almost anarchic distribution of power. It allows for outrageous misconduct among the more self-indulgent officials. One Chinese report tells about a peasant who accidentally killed a cadre's pet dog. The cadre made the peasant take the dog's place: walk around on his hands and knees and live in the doghouse. In the old society an ill-natured landlord might have been able to force a desperate tenant to do such things, but it is less easy to imagine a government official getting away with this kind of abuse.

The personal nature of power makes corruption easy and makes it difficult to distinguish corrupt from normal behavior. Even during the Maoist totalitarian phase, those with power could use it to get personal comfort and

---

17. In some cases it may be reconstituted, as, perhaps, in Rumania under Ceaucescue.
18. See Andrew G. Walder, *Communist Neo-Traditionalism: Work and Authority in Chinese Industry* (University of California Press, 1986).

privilege. During the reform period, the opportunities for making money proliferated and corruption became more visible. It was the impression of all-pervasive corruption more than lack of democracy as such that fed the popular discontent of 1989.

If power adheres to the person, perhaps it can be passed along to family and friends. This occurred in the old society as well, despite institutional checks put in to prevent it. In the Maoist period the concept of power as a family possession was actually encouraged: the children of cadres were by that fact considered "proletarian" (or "Red"), and so entitled to all kinds of social and political favors.[19] This particular system ended in 1978, but the role of family connections if anything increased. By the mid-1980s numbers of the children of the first generation of leaders were themselves taking prominent positions in the regime. The most notable, of course, was Li Peng, the foster child of Zhou Enlai. Many of these "princes" were in fact capable, dedicated people, but the phenomenon left a bad impression.

Personal relations may also explain political alliances, although Chinese factions are not as cohesive, stable, or well-organized as those in Japan. Factions may organize on policy lines, although even there the members may share a guanxi base in principle irrelevant to the policy position. In the 1980s, for example, there was talk of a "Shanxi gang," a group of older cadres opposed to reform who had either been born in Shanxi province or who had worked there prior to Liberation. It is at least as common for persons who have similar opinions on policy to be personal and political rivals. It is not uncommon for political allies to hold different policy opinions. Deng Xiaoping and the former State Chairman Yang Shangkun, for example, cooperated with each other, even though Yang seems to have been less than enthusiastic about Deng's liberalizing reforms.

Personal leadership often transcends institutional limitations. Mao Zedong did not owe his prestige to his position of Chairman of the Party's Central Committee. His successors in that position, Hua Guofeng and Hu Yaobang, had nowhere near his authority or power. Mao's personal leadership and the cult that developed around it reflect the totalitarian pattern, but may also show certain tendencies in Chinese culture.

Mao's successor—itself an informal position—was Deng Xiaoping, who seems genuinely to have wanted to end the pattern of one-man rule. He did not encourage the development of a cult around himself. He refused to take the top position in either Party or state, on the grounds that his personal prestige would overwhelm the institutional function and upset what should be the proper balance between the two institutions. Rather, he put his supporters in the top positions of the state and Party. This only served, however, to reinforce the pattern of personal rule. Deng's supporters held official positions

---

19. This is an anomaly, in that it is not easily explained by the standard totalitarian model.

but became, by that fact, rivals for Deng's favor. Deng continued to make the final decisions from behind the scenes, and brought about the dismissal of those whose actions displeased him. Formal institutional power in the end counted for little, but the will of the retired emperor counted for a lot.

Deng's prestige slipped especially after the 1989 democracy movement and its suppression. He remained the most influential person in China, but found himself sharing the stage with a small number of other surviving first-generation Communists. These persons had differences among themselves. Most were more conservative than Deng, but all agreed on the need to keep the socialist system and the supremacy of the Party—with the supremacy of the Party meaning really the current structure of power, not necessarily the formal organization and procedures of the Party, which by themselves did not permit this kind of rule from behind the curtain. These elders bickered over who should hold formal office in the Party and state, different ones sponsoring their own protégés. They set general guidelines for policy, or at least determined the limits within which policy must stay. They acted, in fact, very much like the genro of the later part of the Meiji period.

State and Society

According to Marxist theory, class struggle is the motive force in human history, and for much of the Maoist period the leading slogan was "Never forget class struggle." China, however, was probably not a class society in Marx's sense of the term. There was plenty of class struggle in Mao's day and something like class struggle may continue today. The classes, however, were not spontaneous expressions of social or economic interest, but were, rather, artifacts of state policy. There is an element of continuity here with the older Chinese tradition, since in imperial China the major social division was that between the gentry and everyone else, a division created by the state examination system.

The Political Construction of Society

In the early days of the People's Republic, the officials divided the population into various "classes" or categories, according them different treatment. Some enjoyed special favor while others were regarded as hostile. The good or "Red" categories included workers and poor peasants. They also included Communist cadres and their families. There were also "Black" categories, subject to special restrictions: landlords, rich peasants, counterrevolutionaries, rightists,[20] "bad elements" (usually common criminals). Among the disfavored,

---

20. This category was created in 1957, in the wake of the hundred flowers movement.

only landlords and rich peasants were anything like classes in the usual Marxist sense; the other categories were based on political opinion or personal behavior. Most of the population belonged to categories neither specially favored nor especially burdened: intellectuals, bourgeoisie, middle peasants, and so forth. These social statuses were inherited along family lines, in reality if not clearly in theory: sons and daughters of landlords were landlords, even if they had never owned land, even if their land had been redistributed before they were born.

Although artificial, the categories had real meaning. The Black categories served as permanent pariahs, ready-made scapegoats for anything that went wrong. Every political movement would begin with the "digging out of class enemies," with the Black categories in the work unit or locality being subject to public criticism or more serious abuse. This inhuman system was ended in 1978, with the legal abolition of the categories.

The story of the Red elements is more complex. Their position in the social structure had probably its greatest significance during the period around the Cultural Revolution. Probably the greatest impact of class distinctions was in schools, where there was intense competition among pupils for admittance to the limited number of advanced educational institutions (not just colleges but even senior high schools) and for good jobs after graduation (by the early 1960s, graduates or those who failed to get admitted to higher education were being sent to remote rural areas). Students were evaluated on both academic ability and political attitude. Generally speaking, students of Red background were assumed to have good political attitudes; they were not, on the whole, as good with the books as students from "bourgeois" (mostly professional or other educated) family background. This led to chronic tension, especially in elite urban high schools, between the children of cadres and the children of intellectuals.[21]

During the Great Leap, Redness counted for almost everything. In the famine that followed, grades ruled supreme. In the early 1960s the policy of those functionaries most influential in educational policy was to encourage good political attitudes but to stress how someone from a nonfavored class background could, by effort and dedication, become utterly politically correct. Students from intellectual background were moved to hyperbolic demonstrations of political enthusiasm. The Red students, disadvantaged academically and too proud for hypocritical pandering to the authorities, felt increasingly insecure and aggrieved.

---

21. These schools had few children of really "proletarian" background. Those who were enrolled were pulled in two directions. They tended to be smart, which inclined them to the intellectuals. On the other hand, their class background meant that they, like the cadre kids, did not always have to work that hard. Whatever the official ideology said, their social status was low, and many felt especially alienated.

The Cultural Revolution was an artificial mass movement, a product of intrigues among the political elite. But it also drew on real social discontents. The first Red Guards were organized among the Red students in high schools and, to a lesser degree, in colleges. They were encouraged to vent their unhappiness with their teachers and classmates as well as "bourgeois" elements in society, sometimes quite violently. Chairman Mao's idea was to eliminate "persons in power inside the Party" who did not agree with his particular line. The Red Guards, for all their devotion to the Chairman, were not eager to make revolution against their own parents. Within a few months the high-ranking Cultural Revolution radicals themselves attacked the notion that some people were "naturally Red" and encouraged youths from less-favored backgrounds to form Red Guard groups themselves. The Red Guards from good class backgrounds tended to become, in the jargon of the time, "conservatives" or "royalists." The more radical Red Guards were, on the whole, those from categories not specially favored by the regime. The Red Guard groups were soon at each other's throats.

Eventually Mao and his allies suppressed the movement. The Red Guards were sent off to the countryside or to state farms, there humbly to learn from the masses (a continuation, on a much wider scale, of a policy begun in the early 1960s to rid the cities of economically superfluous people). Because of their family connections, children of cadre background could often find factory jobs in the city, a more desirable station than assignment to a rural village. Factory workers who had previously been Red Guards in conservative factions played a relatively large role in the early democracy movement in the years immediately following Mao's death.

Empirical Social Structure

As noted above, the official class distinctions were abolished at the end of 1978. Redness, at least for relatives of cadres if not for workers and peasants, continued to confer advantage. I mentioned earlier how the children of old cadres were moving into political office by the late 1980s. An even more common pattern was for the children of officials to go into business, using their family connections to gain advantage over their rivals.

Even before its abolition, the division into Red and Black and in between classes only imperfectly described society. A more realistic picture identifies four general classes or statuses: peasant, worker, intellectual, and cadre. This system is as much a product of state policy as the old good class–bad class division, but has more daily relevance.

Peasants are persons who farm the land and depend upon the land for their living. Now many rural people only farm part-time, and earn the greater part of their living from working in privately or collectively owned small factories and workshops. Formerly the main indicator of peasant status was an administrative one: peasants were not eligible to receive state grain coupons;

they were expected to grow their own grain, not buy it in a store.[22] Unlike city people, they did not eat the "state's rice" (rice, it goes without saying, they, not the state, grew).

Western scholars used to think that Maoist policy was especially favorable to peasants since, it was generally assumed, the Communist revolution had mobilized a peasant mass base. In fact, rural people in Maoist days had low incomes and low social position. It is common to find denunciations in China of the Cultural Revolution, which subjected intellectuals to unspeakable abuse, since intellectuals are articulate and voluble. The even greater post-1949 trauma, however, was the Great Leap Forward and the subsequent famine, whose impact fell mainly on the peasantry. In the early 1950s land reform eliminated landlordism and gave land to individual peasant households. Within a few years (in some places, a few months) this land was collectivized. The peasant then had to work at the direction of the leadership of the collective and received his pay according to a complex system of work points rather than according to how much he directly produced. This was supposed to instill socialist consciousness into the peasant, and it no doubt contributed to political control, but it stifled initiative and kept agricultural productivity and rural incomes artificially low.

Deng Xiaoping's most successful reform was the dismantling of the system of collective agriculture, in effect returning to the system right after land reform. Technically the household did not own the land, but rented it from the collective. Yet the lease could be as long as for 30 years and could be passed on to heirs or, in some cases, even sold to third parties. During the 1980s rural living standards grew faster than for centuries, and peasants were freer than they had been since 1949 from the control of local political elites.

The reforms did have some bad results. The collapse of the collectives meant that the useful things they had done were done no longer. Ditches and embankments were neglected. Medical help became less available than it had previously been, and rural education declined as peasants, realizing that their own children had little chance of getting into higher education in any case, refused to finance schools beyond the most elementary level and withdrew their own children as soon as they could write and figure so that they could stay home and earn money. Peasants were faulted for not reinvesting their new found wealth, preferring to spend it on fancy weddings and funerals and building comfortable houses. Perhaps people who have been deprived for so long might be permitted a little indulgence.

The reform program was also in tension with the regime's population policy, the one-child family. Since the 1980s the policy was enforced rigorously, but not always consistently, in the countryside. The agricultural reform put a

---

22. Grain rationing was supposedly eliminated in 1993.

premium on large families and ample labor power, and many families preferred to pay the various fines and penalties rather than to forego the bearing
of children. Where the policy was enforced, it sometimes led to increases in
female infanticide, with the midwife quietly drowning the baby in a bucket of
water if she proved to be a girl, an old and sad practice known as "washing
the infant." Both the forced abortions and the infanticide took their moral
and emotional toll, especially on women. In many areas sex ratios became
increasingly disparate, with males greatly outnumbering females. This may
have been typical enough in traditional China as well, and today, as then,
the poorer males may be destined to remain bachelors all their lives, "bare
sticks." By the late 1980s the tacit policy was to allow peasants a second birth
if the firstborn were a girl, and in many localities the party and state cadres
more or less gave up on enforcing the policy, as it was hardly the road to
popularity and they did not necessarily have that much stomach for it themselves anyway.

Workers have probably been over the long run the most favored social
category. Except, possibly, for housing they continue to live better than peasants (on the whole), and they are not subject to the political tensions imposed
on cadres and intellectuals. Regular workers in the past enjoyed virtually absolute job and income security, regardless of their personal performance or
that of the firm that employed them—the policy of the "iron (that is, un-
breakable) rice bowl." Their tenure was even more secure than that of Western college professors, since they could often pass their jobs on to their
children upon retirement.[23] Workers had low social status and life was not
always comfortable. Urban housing was owned by the state or by work units,
and rents were astonishingly low (the equivalent of two or three U.S. dollars
a month). The state, like any capitalist landlord who is not turning a profit
on his investment, was not inclined to waste money on repairs, so housing
was crowded, dirty, run-down. Yet these conditions were not restricted to
workers, and housing for cadres and intellectuals, unless of very high rank,
was only marginally if at all better.

Not all workers had the same degree of job security. Regular workers had
regular jobs; another category, contract workers—school leavers who had
not yet managed to get a permanent job, apprentices, or migrants from the
countryside—might live from day to day. They might be hired for specific
tasks or to fill in during temporary labor shortages. During the Cultural Revolution there were fights in the factories as well as among the student Red
Guards (the countryside was spared much of this). The contract laborers supported the radical Maoists, while the regular workers were staunch supporters of the status quo.

---

23. This was most useful for women, who tended to retire early, in their 40s, and so could
leave their jobs to their daughters in their late teens.

The reforms had a mixed effect on workers. Chinese wages are low and the reforms opened the possibility for higher pay and also for engaging in private enterprise. The reforms also threatened the iron rice bowl. In fact, job security seems to have remained high, but the reforms introduced a sense of threat not previously present. In the mid-1980s the reform policies led to high rates of inflation, much higher than the increase in workers' incomes. In 1989 there was about as much unrest among urban workers as among students. Both groups were unhappy with what they perceived to be high levels of official corruption, but while the students were concerned with democracy, the workers worried more about inflation.

The term *intellectual* in China has connotations somewhat different from those in the West. It is a general term for anyone with a certain degree of education (until recently it could even be someone who had graduated from junior high school) who performs mental rather than physical labor, and who is not in a managerial, command, or leadership position. It includes people such as teachers, journalists, scientists, engineers, actors, even certain types of clerical workers.

China does not have quite the same tradition of alienated intellectuals as the West. Educated Chinese, except, perhaps, for a few Daoists, did not see their role to criticize the values and ways of their societies from an independent, personal perspective. Intellectuals in traditional China certainly saw themselves as the conscience of society, but rather than being critics of the established order, they virtually constituted it. They felt a duty to serve the community and the state, but not necessarily always to belabor how far short the real fell of the ideal. Western observers, and even some Chinese, sometimes berate even dissident Chinese intellectuals for an unwillingness to break completely with the ruling regime and for a willingness to cooperate with authority when authority is sufficiently hospitable to them. Chinese intellectuals no doubt define their duty differently from the way their Western critics think they should.

The older tension was that between Red and Expert. Actually, the official demand was for Red Experts, for specialists who had completely internalized the dominant ideology and were completely subservient to political direction. In practice, Expert on the whole meant intellectual and Red meant cadre, and the demand was that the cadres have control over intellectual activity. The fear was not really that experts would somehow subvert the government. Rather, even after Liberation, intellectuals enjoyed independent social prestige. Also, experts and various specialists were sometimes given to pointing out that certain projects favored by the politicians (for example, the Great Leap Forward taken as a whole) were not feasible, given either existing resources or the laws of nature.

Intellectuals (and students) have always been at the forefront of protest against the regime. Again, this has usually not been an expression of alienation, but an assertion of both responsibility and independent judgment. The main examples of intellectual protest include the hundred flowers episode and the various democracy movements of the 1980s (although the first post-Mao protest, the 1978 democracy wall movement, was dominated by workers who had previously been Red Guards). Intellectuals have also protested more quietly, often in alliance with the more liberal or enlightened factions within the regime. The rest of society seemed willing to concede protest leadership to intellectuals, although this in itself may have weakened the impact of the protest.

Anticommunist protest in eastern Europe from the 1950s on was usually organized around an alliance of workers and intellectuals. Such combinations have formed in China, but have not been stable. Workers seem generally unwilling to risk their security for what they consider futile posturing, and as a group may even be quite uneasy with the direction of many of the reforms. The active working class support for the 1989 protest came mainly from younger workers and irregular workers and from private entrepreneurs (who tend to be scruffy youths in their 20s, not cigar-smoking, top-hat-wearing capitalists). Intellectuals tend to keep the protest at a moralistic and abstract level and may not give sufficient attention to the workers' economic complaints. On a daily level, there is often palpable hostility between students and younger workers.

Intellectual relations with peasants may be even worse. Intellectuals do in fact respect the economic rights of peasants, but tend to see peasants as a class as ignorant and shortsighted. They also equate the attitudes of the political leadership with those of peasants, as if to say that the politicians are ignorant boors lacking proper respect for the abilities of their intellectual betters. Many intellectuals from the Cultural Revolution generation have bad memories of their time in the countryside, when they suffered physical and emotional (and, the women, sexual) abuse from the rural leadership.

In spite of tensions, other social groupings have usually been willing to concede moral leadership to intellectuals. Mao Zedong perceived this to be a real threat to the kind of regime he intended, and responded with what can only be called hatred. During Mao's time, the intellectuals were the "stinking number nine," the lowest of all social categories, even more depraved than prostitutes and secret foreign agents. This may not have damaged intellectuals' overall prestige. The post-Mao regime stressed the four modernizations and hailed the use of education and skill; intellectuals became overnight the "sweet number one." Yet a consequence of reform was a newer, less vicious but possibly more pernicious anti-intellectualism. Opportunities to make money multiplied, but those jobs traditionally held by intellectuals (teaching, medical practice in state clinics or hospitals, or work in large state-owned firms) remained poorly paid. As the saying had it, the barber's scissors are worth more than the surgeon's knife. Even in school, sometimes those who took their studies seriously were regarded as simpletons: if they were smart they would be wheeling and dealing, making money. This disdain for academic achievement is an anomaly in Chinese history and is not shared by the materially dynamic East Asian societies of Japan, South Korea, and Taiwan.

Cadres are persons in positions of leadership, whether in the Party, state, a business firm, or other organization.[24] Most may be party members, although a cadre need not be (the important ones almost all are, of course). They are not all at high levels of leadership. Most cadres perform routine administrative chores in factories, schools, or government or party offices.

Cadres and intellectuals share a common lifestyle. The older generation of cadres, those who had been with the Party prior to 1949, were in many cases of limited education and rural background, which helps explain why intellectuals sometimes regard cadres as ignorant peasants. Many persons of low economic status ("workers, peasants, soldiers") were recruited as cadres in the waning years of the Cultural Revolution, but later seem to have blended in with the others. In more recent times it is likely that urban cadres at least come from about the same background as the normal run of intellectuals, with roughly the same levels of education.

Cadres are supposed to be moral paragons, and many fall short of the standard. In fact, the general reputation of cadres may be lower than is justified. Since the reforms the opportunities for corruption multiplied, and cadres are placed to take advantage of those opportunities.

Rural cadres opposed agricultural reform at first, since dismantling the collective took away their major powers. They soon discovered, however, that they still had political office, and this allowed them to make the decisions about who would get what land and for what price. They sometimes allocated the best land to themselves or their families, or to persons who had done them favors or whose goodwill they courted. Rural government offices, resuming a practice of lower officialdom prevalent in periods of dynastic decline, also collect various fees and fines from peasants, and given the rudimentary legal system there is not always a clear basis for what should be collected and how much it should be. In many cases these fees amounted to rake-offs and kickbacks.

There were analogous opportunities in the urban sector. Part of the reform program entailed a "double track" pricing system for certain "strategic" goods (grain, steel, capital goods generally). The prices would be allowed to fluctuate with market supply and demand, except large state firms were guaranteed the ability to buy what they needed at the low set price. The obvious ploy was for those firms to buy up everything they could and then resell it at what the market would bear, making a nice profit for the firm and for the cadres working in it.

---

24. The French word *cadre* originally meant a group of persons organized for a task—a cadre of soldiers, for example. Soviet usage applied the term to individuals and pluralized the word when it referred to more than one person. The Chinese translation, *ganbu*, is chosen partly for its sound, but also has a relevant meaning—it means, roughly, backbone element.

The division between cadres and everyone else is not quite that between rulers and ruled. Most cadres are as "ruled" as everyone else, and many are quite enlightened in their opinions. Low-ranking cadres supported the protests of 1989, as, indeed, did not a few high-ranking cadres. The failure of the Soviet coup in 1991 and the collapse of communism there led to a hardening of opinion among ordinary cadres. It seemed to indicate that a genuine political reform was not possible in a Leninist system, that a basic change would wipe out the system itself and deprive them and their families of their livelihood.

In addition to these distinctions, Chinese society is also divided on generational lines. Thus, those who came of age in the 1950s were supposedly full of hope and ideals, and while they have certainly been through many disillusioning experiences, still retain something of the original flavor. Those who grew up during the Cultural Revolution learned not only to doubt everything but also saw the brutality that normally remained under the surface of society. Yet this generation provided most of the ideas and energy for the programs of liberal and democratic reform. The younger generation is said to lack not only all political conviction but even the most basic moral sense. It is probably more fair to say that they have their own moral sense, not the one the political leadership thinks they ought to have. The events of 1989 show they are capable of true heroism. But when there is no opportunity for heroism, they may retreat into themselves, at best concentrating on love, family, and work; at worst seeking only money and pleasure without any concern for the means of attaining them.

Social Control

Social control—the keeping of public order, the prevention, detection, and punishment of crime, the regulation of personal behavior—in China as in other countries is partly the job of the police and courts. But in China the mechanisms of control grow out of the general structure of political power and the society shaped by that power.

China has police, including secret police, as well as laws, courts, jails, labor reform camps, and execution grounds. It also has had terror, and after especially intense periods of terror, especially the Cultural Revolution and perhaps the 1989 repression as well, the police system has gained influence relative to other institutions. Mao Zedong's immediate successor, Hua Guofeng, came from the public security system, and the head of that system often holds a place on the Politburo Standing Committee. If it comes to that, the regime probably thinks of the army as as much an instrument of social control as a defender of the state from outside enemies. But China has probably had less purely police or armed terror than other totalitarian systems. The Chinese police have never been as powerful as the secret police of Stalin and Hitler, and the Communist police system has probably been less relatively influential than that of the KMT. Rather, the communist system in China has worked by mobilizing social pressure to serve the purposes of the regime.

One method for doing this, of course, is through propaganda, especially control of the mass media. Censorship in China often dictates not merely what must not be said, but has a positive role, specifying what must be said. In principle, all information is under official control and reflects the interpretations approved by those dominating the political system. In practice, it seems the general population often has a fairly good idea about what is really going on, whether in China or the world at large. The nature of media control also produces a mentality that automatically doubts anything published under official sanction. Technology—fax machines, e-mail, and the like—may make anything like complete control over information impossible.

The face-to-face methods of control are possibly more effective. These techniques were based upon Chinese cultural traits, particularly the importance of small personalized groups. The techniques were used, however, to undermine the authority of the more traditional groups, such as family, clan, or friendship clique, substituting for them groups defined and organized by the authorities.[25] The most important group is the work unit. The population is encouraged to enroll in other organizations as well. Thus, there are "mass organizations" for women and for youth, and even for religious believers. Neighborhoods are organized for the purpose of mutual aid but also mutual surveillance. The system is structured so that it is not only Big Brother who is watching you: simultaneously everyone watches everyone else.

The most famous use of social pressure to enforce compliance is probably the thought reform or "brainwashing" programs of the early 1950s. These were designed mainly for intellectuals and others of relatively high social status, and the purpose was to produce converts, persons who not only accepted the regime's authority but enthusiastically internalized the regime's aims. Both the KMT and the Japanese used similar techniques, and the CPC had used analogous techniques in the training of party members during the Rectification movement. They have at least a remote connection with the Confucian practice of self-examination. Participants in the thought reform sessions compiled detailed autobiographies, criticizing their class origins, the behavior of their families, and their own deeds, words, and thoughts that did not somehow conform to the interests of the Party, proletariat, and people. Participants were expected to reveal to the group their own weaknesses and failings and to criticize the failings of others, such failings including lack of sincerity in self-criticism and lack of heat in criticizing others. The mechanism, apparently, was that while people may have doubts, there is no way to

---

25. This manner of social control was used in Japan prior to World War II and to a certain extent continues there in an informal manner. Because of the different nature of group identification, it is probably less oppressive in its operation in Japan.

express them, so each doubter feels utterly alone and is eventually inclined to think that the doubts indicate something is wrong with him, a wrong that will be made right as soon as he gives up his obstinate resistance. At that time there were hopes or fears that a totalitarian system would be able to control not only people's actions but also their minds and wills. The pressures of thought reform were responsible for numerous suicides. There is no evidence that it was very effective in producing more than outer compliance, and as often as not it may have led to inner resentment against the Party where previously there had been basic goodwill.

A less intense but more protracted version of thought reform used to go on in work units as well, with regular political study sessions held weekly. These would usually center on current party policy or on current affairs. If the sessions were properly conducted, those attending could not sit back and listen (or fail to listen), nor could they simply parrot what they figured those running the session wanted to hear. Rather, they were supposed to defend the correctness of party policy in their own words and with their own reasons. Especially in times of political tension, the meetings involved criticism and self-criticism. It was virtually impossible to avoid attacking your workmates, since if someone had done or said something wrong and you tried to ignore it, then you yourself would be exposed to criticism. The same was true, of course, if you tried to cover up your own faults. After the meeting you might whisper to someone you had attacked that certainly the other person could understand that you had no choice but to do what you had done. That person, naturally, would understand, but still could not but be hurt and resentful: the whole system worked to create mutual mistrust and individual isolation.

The structure of work units reinforced the more explicit techniques of social control. This term, *unit* (in Chinese, *danwei*), is a little like the American military term "outfit." The unit would generally mean your place of work, particularly the place that paid you. But if you worked in a factory, within the factory you might refer to a particular workshop as your unit, while outside you would call the factory itself your unit.

The work unit not only provided pay but was also responsible for most other aspects of your life. Thus, a unit might control housing, and different units would have different kinds of welfare benefits. Your boss and the party organization of the unit were expected to take an interest in every aspect of your life, including monitoring your menstrual periods to be sure you were not pregnant in violation of the birth control policy. If your child were a student not behaving properly in school—playing around too much, or in unwholesome contact with foreigners, or hanging out with questionable companions, or involved in illicit sexual relations—the comrades at the school would get in touch with the comrades in your unit, and these would drop around your home after work and offer to help you keep better control of your children. The ideal was for everybody to mind everybody else's business.

Because the work units (and above them the functional systems of which they were a part) were so self-contained, encompassing all aspects of your life (and dividing families if husband and wife did not work in the same unit), Chinese society had a "cellular" structure, with a certain autonomy for grassroots organizations that might seem incompatible with totalitarian politics. There was often poor if any coordination among units, and orders from above involving more than one unit might not be carried out. As the saying went, "The superiors have their policy, but we have our response."

The system's efficiency lay in social and political control. The Party linked the different units, while within units individuals were isolated, cut off from support against pressures to conform and usually unable to communicate easily with people in different units. Everyone was a comrade, no one was a friend.

Over time, political pressures moderated and people could enjoy relatively normal human relationships. The units then became the bases for neotraditionalism, vesting power in millions of petty emperors. One aim of the reform program was to break down this cellular structure, fostering, for the sake of economic efficiency, horizontal links across society rather than a multiplicity of vertical links with the Center. A cost was less efficient political control.

Stirrings of Civil Society

Fashions in political science move in cycles, and recently a rather old concept, that of civil society, has come back into favor. Students of democratization once again realize that it was not sufficient simply for "the people" to rule if the democracy were to be both meaningful and enduring, but also that rule itself had to be limited. Limited rule is furthered by constitutional arrangements but especially by a strong society, one able both to assert interests within the framework of the state and to defend its interests against the state.

The concept of civil society centers on the *public*, a word that refers both to the governmental or state sphere and to the area of our lives that is not official, but that is beyond the purely private—our open participation in society. The public mediates between our private lives and the state, allowing us to protect our privacy and also to participate actively in the life of the politically organized community. The Chinese word *gong* has about the same meaning and connotation as the English word *public*, and also the same ambiguities. Legalists and Confucians both asserted the priority of the gong over private desires and personal interests. For the Legalists, gong implied the power of the state, while for the Confucians it referred to the good of the community and the community's moral consensus.

Chinese traditional government, remember, was not aggressively interventionist, but generally allowed families and local communities to go their own way. The local government was obliged to consult with the local gentry, and the local gentry often undertook public projects with little or any reference to the state. In big cities, especially new cities growing beyond the legal and administrative structures of the state, the government might lack the capacity to enforce the law with any degree of thoroughness, and would delegate its functions and authority to merchant guilds and other organizations, who would police their own membership and bargain among themselves over what rules should be established.

Yet this was not a civil society in the early modern or modern European sense. Social status—gentry rank—still depended upon a certain state structure, and was not something that could be held autonomously from the state. There were no institutions allowing routinely for the representation of particular social interests in the state or allowing any routine influence from society to the state.

The totalitarian system, including its cellular structure, was designed to keep society weak and, in the post-1949 period, the goal was to have Chinese society shaped entirely by politics. While conducive to a certain kind of political control, this system kept the people impoverished and deprived the political leadership of economic resources.

The reform movement meant a "depoliticization" of much of Chinese society and economy, a retrenchment of the scope of politics in the hope this would make strategic political control more effective while allowing room for whatever spontaneous activity might be required for economic growth. In restricting the sphere of politics, the reforms opened the way for a potentially stronger society.

A key phrase during the reform period was a "socialist commodity economy," later changed, more bluntly, to a socialist market economy. A commodity economy is one in which goods are produced for sale in the market. The contrast is with a "production economy," in which central planners decide what needs to be produced and at what price. In the commodity economy the producer has to satisfy customers, not the state. The state should not dictate to producers, but exercises "macroscopic" control, regulating economic activity indirectly by economic means such as taxation or adjusting access to credit, not by issuing direct orders. The plan is supposed to set the parameters for the economy, but firms and consumers operate as they think best within those parameters. The conservative reformer Chen Yun called this a birdcage economy: the bird can't leave the cage, but the cage itself can be larger or smaller, and the bird can fly as he wants inside the cage.

In agriculture it was not merely that the communes were dismantled and land returned to the household. Previously the communes were expected to be "large and complete." That is, in accord with the cellular model, the commune should have the capacity to take care of almost all the needs of the "members," as the peasants were then called. The new fashion was for "small and specialized." The households were encouraged to concentrate on one kind of activity: to grow grain, or to raise vegetables, or to breed chickens, or to cultivate flowers. The household would produce for sale on the market and would use the money it earned there to take care of its other needs and desires.

One goal of the Great Leap Forward had been to end the urban-rural distinction through such means as the backyard furnaces. The idea in itself was not bad, only its manner of implementation: there had been neither reward nor rationale for the encouraged activity, and rural industry implied hard work to no purpose. The reforms did much to achieve the goal of the Leap, as peasants, either collectively in small groups or as individuals, were able to set up their own businesses—small shops or manufacturing plants—sometimes in partnership with local government units. This new rural industry is perhaps at least as responsible as the purely agricultural reforms for the increase in rural incomes in the 1980s.

The commodity economy spread into the cities as well. Private business, albeit on a small scale, has become a common way of earning a living, even, if you are lucky, a fortune. Great numbers of people, both in the city and in the countryside, no longer depend directly on the state or the goodwill of the Party to survive. There may be developing a "bourgeoisie" or middle class that will demand increased public influence to match its new social and economic status.

There is still reason to doubt, however, that this amounts to a true civil society. The Communist party has retreated from direct control over large parts of the economy, but it has not given up its monopoly of political power. It is unwilling to tolerate any combination able to threaten its hold. The "state" (that is, the party-state) remains hegemonic over society.

In China since 1949, and maybe perennially, politics rather than economic exploitation has been seen as the source of human misery. Rural people, and perhaps most others as well, prefer in general to *avoid* politics rather than to influence it. As long as the agricultural reforms remain in place, the peasantry may show little enthusiasm for political activity, not because peasants think the government is wonderful or that they have no problems, but because they know that things could easily be much worse than they are.

There is a similar pattern in the cities, with additional complications. For one thing, the economy has hardly been completely depoliticized. Material incentives—money and profit—have replaced what foreigners in Maoist times called moral incentives—work for the sake of the people, socialism, and Chairman Mao. But there is still enough political involvement in the economy that political connections remain helpful in making money, and the possibility of getting rich becomes one more incentive to seek political power.

At the same time, the half-depoliticized economy is neither well regulated nor well protected by law, as the reforms were not always carried out in a very systematic manner. Workers in state firms may be well protected— some would say overly well protected—by regulations governing hours, wages, and job security. Private factories, especially in the countryside, may operate as virtual sweatshops. Private entrepreneurs may not always have the best of reputations among their neighbors, and may not have the moral weight for political leadership.

At the other end, the vague laws governing private enterprise mean that the entrepreneur has to operate on the fringes of the law. The category of entrepreneurs has come to overlap with the *liumang*, the gangsters and grafters. One way around legal restrictions is to bribe those in authority, so there even develops a corrupt system of relations among gangsters, business, and party or state cadres. Businessmen are subject to extortion and violence, and business itself is somewhat associated with sharp practice. Despite a flourishing commodity economy, China has not yet evolved a sturdy, self-confident, respectable bourgeoisie.

Students in recent years have been the most active politically dissident force. Students support reform, but have been disinclined to couch their arguments in terms of the interests of specific social categories. They prefer to argue for democracy as a moral more than a political principle. They have no sympathy for democratic compromise and tend unconsciously to equate democracy with respect and deference accorded to themselves. Those who make the economy run tend to be apolitical, while those who interest themselves in democracy tend to the antipolitical. The combination inhibits the development of a strong civil society.

8
◆
Politics and Policy in Contemporary China

There have been several general themes in Chinese politics since 1949. At the beginning it seemed the new regime was consolidating itself. The Party was establishing a routine and institutionalized control over the country and was carrying on "socialist transformation," a program that in those days could plausibly seem to be a way to justice, national strength, and personal prosperity. The institutional strength of the Party came into contradiction with the personal position of the Party's Chairman. Mao's reassertion of his influence was accompanied by a radical turn in economic policy. The poorly thought-out and implemented policies led to a major famine. Political problems in the aftermath of the famine set the background for the Cultural Revolution, a brutal purge of the Party and a major upheaval in society. With Mao's death came a return to moderation and, eventually, a liberalization of both politics and economy. This relaxation encouraged escalating demands for ever more democracy and freedom, a movement climaxing in major protests in 1989. These were brutally suppressed. China entered the 1990s with a political system of questionable stability and legitimacy, dominated by an aging cohort of first-generation revolutionaries no longer in positions of official authority.

Socialist Transformation, 1949–1957

A united, highly motivated Communist party took power in 1949. The top party leadership were men in their 40s and 50s; some were in their 30s. The general membership was much younger, most having joined the Party during the last years of the War of Resistance or during the civil war.

Almost immediately after the establishment of the People's Republic, China entered into alliance with the Soviet Union. The Soviets acquired certain military privileges in China, so this might be considered the last of the unequal treaties.[1] But China received generous aid in return, both in money and in technical advice. China wholeheartedly adopted the Soviet Union as its "big brother," modeling its political, economic, and social systems on those of the Soviet Union.

One fruit of this alliance was China's participation in the Korean War. After defeating the North Korean attack on the south in September 1950, U.S. and South Korean forces moved north. In October Chinese soldiers entered Korea to protect the northern regime, in late November winning a major victory over the United States, perhaps the first Chinese military victory over a Western power. Eventually the war resolved itself into a stalemate. The Chinese leadership as a whole had not been eager to go to war, only Mao and one or two other Politburo members showing any enthusiasm. China was motivated in part by self-defense and also by a desire to show that the United States could not intimidate it. A further consideration seems to have been to do Stalin a favor, to save his face after his miscalculation in permitting the North Korean attack in the first place. The Soviet Union promised China large amounts of additional military aid and also air cover for Chinese troops; it did not deliver on this last promise. The war did, however, establish China as a world power, a force to be taken seriously (and, in fact, the American reaction may have been for the next several decades to take China much too seriously).

The war was also an opportunity to tighten social and political control over the population. Intellectuals and others who had any connections, however tenuous, with the United States were dragooned into thought reform. In 1949 the Communists had promised to respect private business for some indefinite period. During the war businesspeople faced confiscatory fines on often trumped-up charges of graft and were also expected to make large "voluntary" contributions to the war effort. Christians were harassed and persecuted on the grounds that foreign missionaries and, for that matter, foreign religion were agents of "cultural imperialism."

In the early 1950s, private businesses underwent "socialist transformation." The state took ownership of private firms, the owners having been

---

1. The old unequal treaties had been ended by Chiang Kai-shek in 1943.

induced "voluntarily" to sell out to the state. The owners received periodic payments in compensation. These ceased during the Cultural Revolution but, surprisingly, resumed in the early 1980s. In many cases the former owners were retained to manage the new state firms, since at that time there were not many comrades qualified to do the job. In this case, of course, the former owner received a salary in addition to dividends.

In the first years the regime redistributed land in the countryside, eliminating landlordism. This process had actually begun in the civil war years prior to Liberation. In some areas the land reform was quite violent, with the summary execution of landlords who were either sufficiently wicked to be made examples of or sufficiently powerful or popular to constitute threats to the new order. In the early 1950s the regime began to move to the next stage, the collectivization of agriculture, establishing rural cooperatives. Collective agriculture suited the ideological needs of the regime and also made it easier for the state to expropriate what it needed to support industrial development in the cities; it also tended to damage general agricultural productivity. Mao Zedong became a strong proponent of collective agriculture, although those officials most directly concerned with implementing the Party's agricultural policy tended to be more cautious.

The regime enforced a marriage reform law more radical than the earlier one promulgated by the KMT, making it easier for women to divorce their husbands and disobey their mothers-in-law. One purpose was to break the power of the patriarchal family, although the long-term effects have been less dramatic than expected at the time. The rural changes eliminated the power base of the local elites who had dominated the countryside since the collapse of the Qing state. The communist cadres became the new rural elite, and at that time there was no other force able to check their influence.

The regime tried to establish ideological control over the population. In the early 1950s there were several minor harassments of various intellectuals, artists, writers, and moviemakers. The major purge was that against Hu Feng, a left-wing writer who had protested the regime's censorship and intimidation policies. The persecution of Hu Feng served as the pretext to root out a "Hu Feng counterrevolutionary clique." It became a witch hunt against anyone who might harbor independent thought.[2]

In the first decade of Liberation there was only one major internal party conflict. Gao Gang, the boss of the Manchurian region, is said to have collaborated with Rao Shushi, the party boss of Shanghai, to take power from

---

2. Although Hu Feng defended free speech, it is also relevant to know that he had for years been involved in personal and professional squabbles with those in control of the Party's propaganda system. Hu Feng survived to see everyone involved in his persecution accorded the same treatment he had received. He was rehabilitated shortly before his death, some 30 years after his imprisonment.

Mao's then right-hand man, Liu Shaoqi. Even after all this time, the details remain murky. Gao is said to have argued that the CPC actually consisted of two separate groups, a "Red areas or military party," typified by himself, and a "White areas or civilian party," exemplified by Liu Shaoqi. Gao seems to have had a certain amount of support in the military, but Liu won the fight. Gao committed suicide during the investigation, while Rao simply disappeared. The incident might be taken to symbolize the restoration of civilian control over the political system for the first time since 1911, removing for the time being any threat of a revived warlordism. A Red areas man who had refused to collaborate with Gao Gang, Deng Xiaoping, was brought in to take charge of the reorganized central party machinery.

Things had calmed down by 1956. Premier Zhou Enlai discussed the government's determination to make better use of the talents of intellectuals, while the head of the Party's propaganda department revealed Chairman Mao's wish that a hundred flowers should bloom, a hundred schools of thought contend. Mao made a speech implicitly critical of the shortcomings of the Soviet model of economic development and proposed a commonsense approach more attuned to the conditions in China. Mao soon repudiated this moderation, and this speech was not officially published until some months after his death.

In the early fall of 1956 the Party held its Eighth National Congress, the first full meeting since 1945. At the congress Liu Shaoqi announced that the "storm of revolution has passed." Now was the time for peaceful construction. Deng Xiaoping explained that China, unlike the Soviet Union, had never been cursed with any irrational cult of the individual, and that explicit references to the Thought of Mao would be removed from the revised party charter. Life was returning to normal.

Some, including radical young intellectuals, worried that things might be too normal, that the Party had lost any drive to lead social change and was ready to settle down as a ruling group dominating a stable society. Mao made a short speech at the Party Congress, opining that the Party had become too bureaucratic and turned in on itself, that it needed to be rectified by exposure to critical public opinion.

Mao had been wanting a blooming and contending for many months, but he had few takers, possibly because most of the rest of the party leadership were sending out signals that they would not welcome overly frank criticism. After the turn of the year, Mao made his speech on contradictions among the people, and as the weather began to warm up, the complaints became louder and more extreme. They were, in fact, more extreme than Mao is likely to have anticipated. Criticism came from the Party's united front allies, from intellectuals, and from students. The Party was accused of being even more dictatorial than the KMT, of being servile to the Soviet Union, and of ignorant interference in scientific and cultural matters best left to those who know something about them.

The regime allowed this to continue for a few weeks before cracking down. The Party then turned its attention from rectifying itself to rectifying the general population. The more visible of the dissidents were induced to make humiliating self-examinations expatiating on their ingratitude to the Party for its many blessings. The dissidents were branded "rightists," a new category of "Black elements." It appears even that each work unit was told to come up with a certain quota of rightists to be treated as examples. Many of these rightists were sent to forced labor, not by order of a court but by administrative action of the police or the leading cadres in the work unit.

The general moral Mao drew from the hundred flowers episode was that class struggle continued and the class enemy had to be hit even harder. There had been some tension between the Party and the Chairman prior to the hundred flowers, and that episode could easily be construed to show that Mao lacked good judgment. The upshot, however, was to bring about a reconciliation, as the hunt for rightists and the trashing of improper thought served to increase the scope of the Party's competence. Mao also concluded that more-radical economic policies were necessary. The Soviet-style economic development plans had been under the jurisdiction of the government bureaucracy, which relied on experts and specialists and whose head, Zhou Enlai, had been sympathetic to the liberalization. The new radical policies enhanced the role of the Party at the expense of the state.

The Great Leap Forward

In the last part of 1957 the regime rectified rightists and planned radical developments in the economy. In the spring of 1958 the regime announced a Great Leap Forward. In a matter of years or even months, China, in the "era of Mao Zedong," would leap to the forefront of the developed countries of the world. There was even talk of making a leap directly into communism. According to one theme, the state was already beginning to wither away. This was true in a prosaic sense, in that the Party was performing more and more of the state's functions.

The most dramatic artifact of the Great Leap must be the people's commune system. This took shape first in the summer and fall of 1958, spurred on by a casual comment of Mao's: "The people's communes are good." The communes were supercollectivized farms. Their boundaries originally coincided with those of the township (*xiang*), a subdivision of a county, the lowest unit of local government. The townships were themselves abolished, making the commune's party committee the main grass-roots governing unit—a concrete example of the withering away of the state. All land, trees, and livestock became the property of the commune, and all commune members (as peasants came to be called) shared equally in the harvest. Villages set up public dining halls, freeing women from the drudgery of housework and allowing them to contribute to social development by working in the fields along with the men. The members supposedly were allowed to eat their fill in these dining halls without paying any money.

The communes were alleged to be a manifestation of the communist spirit, encouraging peasants to think of the common good rather than of themselves. They were also supposed to eliminate the difference between city and countryside, as peasants came to consider themselves a rural proletariat. Small-scale rural industry, such as the "backyard steel furnaces," was encouraged. The general idea, again, was not necessarily a bad one, but it was not implemented in a rational manner.

The Leap meant cutting back on the role of state planning. The central planning system was reduced and functions of the central economic ministries transferred to local government and party organizations. Once again, decentralization was not necessarily a bad idea, but it was not accompanied by the necessary movement to a market system, to the use of the principles of supply and demand. The guiding slogan of the Leap was: Politics takes command. Central planning stifled the masses' initiative, but a market system was bourgeois in its essence. The economy was left without regulation and without a rational price structure.

The year 1958 was full of good news. The weather had been exceptionally fine, leading to good harvests. An even bigger element in the good outlook, however, was lies. Local cadres, either carried away by enthusiasm or fearful of showing insufficient enthusiasm and so demonstrating themselves to be rightists, exaggerated output figures, and those they reported to added some more of their own. In 1959 there was a radical downward revision of production figures, and for almost two decades after that the regime ceased to publish economic data.

Even in 1958 there were hints of trouble. A high official from the economic and finance system, a set of roles that had been brushed aside in the Leap, noted that just because the communal dining halls claim to serve "free food," this does not mean that all of a sudden there is indeed a free lunch: the food still has a cost, and there must be a proper accounting for this cost in the allocation of resources. He also observed that since chickens had become the property of the commune, no one bothered to take care of them any more, and they were running wild or starving from neglect.

The Great Leap emphasized mass campaigns, not all of them well-advised. One campaign was to "sweep away all pests." On the first go-round, swallows were included as one of the pests, on the theory that they ate a lot of grain. People were organized to shout and bang gongs, keeping those graceful and useful birds in the air until they fell from exhaustion, after which they would have their necks wrung. It turned out, of course, that the swallows ate a lot more insects than they did grain, and their near extermination was one of many ecological disasters at the time. Bedbugs quietly substituted for them among the pests, but the damage had been done. Agricultural techniques, such as "deep plowing," which worked well in some regions, were imposed universally. In some places fields were illuminated at night to keep the photosynthesis working around the clock, although the cost in energy exceeded any gain in agricultural productivity. Large areas in northern China were exposed to poorly thought-out irrigation schemes, rendering the soil alkaline for decades thereafter.

Lunacy was not a necessary feature of the Leap. The chronic, "structural" problem was incentives: the scale of the communes was so large and the compensation for work so evenly distributed that there was no connection between effort or personal achievement and income. Many people, of course, had consciences, but output declined as more people perceived the futility of effort. As a popular rhyme had it, *Gan bugan, sanliang-ban*: Work or not, three and a half ounces.

First intimations of major problems with the Leap probably contributed to Mao's decision in December to step down as State Chairman, a move, as explained in Chapter 7, that could be interpreted as moving into retirement.

In the spring of 1959 the regime began to give more attention to the ideas of the Politburo member Chen Yun, a relatively conservative economic planner who had argued unsuccessfully a few years earlier that decentralization had to rely on a market mechanism. There were some adjustments of the commune system. The number of communes was increased, so lowering their average size. The main level of collectivization became a subunit of the commune, the "production brigade," consisting maybe of 500 families, rather than the commune itself. Peasants were allowed to keep small private plots for growing vegetables, which they could then sell on the market to get extra money. Households were also encouraged to raise income through handicraft production, such as making brushes from pig bristles. Chickens and some other livestock returned to household ownership.

During the summer of 1959 party leaders convened for a series of meetings at the southeastern vacation resort of Lushan, to discuss further reform of the Leap policies. The top leaders had been making their own grass-roots inspections, often in their old hometowns. Mao had gone back home to pay his respects at his parents' graves, but was given a sanitized version of local conditions. His colleague, Peng Dehuai, a Politburo member, Minister of Defense, and China's top soldier, enjoyed a more eye-opening visit. He learned that the food in the community dining halls was inadequate but people had no means to prepare food at home, having given all their cooking utensils to be melted to scrap in the backyard furnace campaign. Peng also disagreed with China's drift away from the Soviet Union, which he considered to be China's only protection against a hostile United States. He worried that the Leap was damaging China's ability to build a modern military force.

At Lushan, Peng Dehuai addressed a "letter of opinion" to Mao, criticizing the Leap. The criticism was itself fairly moderate, although Peng may have phrased some of his criticisms tactlessly (talking about the Leap's "failures and successes" instead of "successes and failures" and intimating the Party had fallen into "petty-bourgeois fanaticism"). Mao chose to take the letter as a personal affront.

Some interpret Mao's behavior to show that he had grown so self-important that he could no longer take any criticism. It is tempting to think, however, that his rage was calculated. Mao may have been in partial retirement in 1959 (even as early as 1956 he had talked about retreating to the "second line"), but he probably was not happy about it. He had already been personally identified with two questionable policies, the hundred flowers and the Leap; but his own leadership and the prestige of his Thought were based upon the idea that he had been right when everyone else had been wrong. The political consequence of admitting that the Leap was simply a mistake could have been his permanent removal from active leadership. The challenge at Lushan may, then, have represented to Mao a chance to reassert his primacy.

Mao began a series of tirades against Peng Dehuai, in which he did include a few by-the-way self-criticisms,[3] but treated Peng's objections as if they had challenged the rule of the Party. Mao in effect forced the other leaders to choose between him and Peng. In practice, of course, the other leaders had no choice. In choosing Mao, the Party also reaffirmed the Great Leap Forward. The Leap and Mao's leadership were bound together, so that thereafter to question one had to mean to question the other. Peng Dehuai and those who supported him were purged, labeled "right opportunists." A general purge in the army and society rooted out Peng's sympathizers and others who shared his reservations. Serious reform of the Leap was delayed for a year, allowing massive harvest failures that forced reform.

The Great Proletarian Cultural Revolution

The economic crisis forced a change in policy. In agriculture the whole country adopted the "three tier" system for the communes. This meant that beneath the commune proper there was not only the brigade but a further subdivision, the "production team." The team consisted of about 30 to 50 families and coincided with the natural rural village. Each level had its own functions, but the main "accounting unit" was the team. In general, the lower the level of collectivization, the greater the agricultural productivity.

Policy broke with the Leap's egalitarianism. Greater work was rewarded with greater income. Rural compensation was based on a complicated system

---

3. They are more like self-justifications. He said, as should not be controversial, that no one is perfect. Lenin made mistakes: Mao knew, because he had seen some of Lenin's manuscripts, and all sorts of words and lines had been crossed out. Also, he said, Confucius made mistakes. So, therefore, Mao should not be blamed too much.

of "workpoints." Workpoints were a rough measure of the quality of the work each person was capable of. An experienced farmer in the prime of life might be awarded, say, 15 workpoints a day; his wife might be valued at 10, and their oldest child at 8. The teams would hold a meeting about once a year to decide, usually by consensus, what the workpoint value of each member should be. Compensation would be determined by a formula awarding an individual income in proportion to the value of the individual's workpoints times the number of days actually worked.

Families were allowed private plots, as well as ownership of most livestock—now including pigs, a notoriously capitalist species that never thrived on collective management. Household industry was also encouraged, and teams were allowed to rent their labor to other teams or to urban construction projects. Critics charged the whole system encouraged capitalism, since people were now working for money instead of for socialism. The need to keep records and accounts for the teams and other organizations reinforced the political control of the Party, however, in that peasants' incomes depended to a great extent on how local leaders allowed the evaluations to go. The workpoint system by itself should also have undermined the authority of the family, since the points were assigned to individuals, not to households. In practice, however, it seems that most families continued to pool their income, with the head of the household deciding how it would be used.

Some of this reform may have been inspired by Chen Yun. Chen had made an inspection of a commune near Shanghai and had reported the peasants saying: In the bad old days of Chiang Kai-shek we had rice to eat; in the blessed era of Chairman Mao we eat only gruel. Chen may have been too outspoken and, while not disgraced, he remained in eclipse until well after Mao's death. He was one of the very few CPC leaders who refused to recant his views in the face of political pressure. Chen was supported (quietly) and protected by Premier Zhou Enlai. Zhou certainly favored the reforms, but was too prudent to commit himself too unambiguously and unequivocally to any position. The highest-ranking major supporter of reform seems to have been Liu Shaoqi, who, to all appearances, had remained a sponsor of the Leap until well past the Lushan meetings.

Since productivity went up every time the level of collectivization went down, some local and provincial authorities went all the way, setting quotas at the household level. As long as the family was able to meet the state quotas, it could keep anything else it produced, either to consume or to sell. This system in effect meant a return to conditions after land reform. The more radical comrades said this was capitalism, not socialism. Deng Xiaoping's famous comment (not, of course, reported at the time) was that it doesn't matter if a cat is black or white; all that matters is that he catches mice. That is to say, it doesn't matter whether you call policies capitalist or socialist, as long as they work.

Mao was much less casual about the color of the cat. Given the desperate situation, he could not but go along with the reforms, but he insisted that they were temporary expedients. He refused to allow any attempt to institutionalize the reforms, nor did he allow household quotas. While these reforms were going on Mao sponsored the ideological dispute with the Soviet Union, accusing the Soviets of revising Marxism in the direction of capitalism.

On domestic matters the party leadership could try to ignore Mao. Mao later complained that Liu Shaoqi and Deng Xiaoping treated him as if they were holding a funeral for their father (you show honor to your dead father, but don't consult him on things). The Central Propaganda department, along with Peng Zhen, the party boss of Peking and an old subordinate of Liu Shaoqi's, supported party intellectuals who published indirect satires on the Leap and oblique hints that it was time for Mao to retire. Peng Zhen organized a semisecret committee to conduct a thorough examination of the Leap to determine how things could have gone so wrong. Peng Dehuai wrote a long essay arguing that events since his purge had vindicated the position he had taken at Lushan. Liu Shaoqi argued behind the scenes for Peng Dehuai's rehabilitation. At party meetings in the summer of 1962 Mao and Lin Biao (Peng's replacement as head of the army) blocked Peng Dehuai's rehabilitation, reversed any tendency toward household quotas, and silenced criticism of the Maoist position. There was no reversal of the reforms of 1961–62 (a period the Maoists came to call the time of the "capitalist road"), but neither was there any expanding of them. Fortunately, the reforms had already been sufficiently successful. The famine was over and the economy was recovering.

Prelude to the Cultural Revolution

Lin Biao, who replaced Peng Dehuai at Lushan, did not go along with the derogation of Mao during the capitalist road period. Lin had been a brilliant military leader during the civil war period, sweeping the KMT forces before him from Manchuria to Canton. But he also had political ambitions. Upon taking over the PLA he increased the importance of political indoctrination, something Peng Dehuai had come to take less seriously than it had been before. Propaganda among the troops exalted Chairman Mao and Mao's Thought, while Lin's subordinates gave the Party and the world to understand that Lin Biao was Chairman Mao's best pupil. In 1963 China began a campaign to learn from the PLA. The army tacitly replaced the Party as the best embodiment of the correct political line. Demobilized soldiers took positions in local party and government organizations and as guidance counselors in schools.

Mao initiated what he called a socialist education campaign in the countryside. The premise was that the policies of the Leap had not really been incorrect, but that the people still did not have the right kind of consciousness to appreciate them. Rural people should, therefore, be indoctrinated with the proper socialist consciousness. Hints that there might be a return to Leap policies tended to demoralize the peasants, and Liu Shaoqi diverted the campaign into a crackdown on corruption. The campaign also became a vehicle for various local factions to purge their rivals.

The campaign to emulate Dazhai was related to the socialist education movement. Dazhai was a town in Shanxi province; the commune at Dazhai had managed to overcome famine and increase agricultural productivity by dint of its own efforts, without asking for state subsidies. It was a good example of the socialist spirit of self-reliance. Also at Dazhai, the level of collectivization was the brigade, not the team, although this was not as openly publicized as its spirit of self-reliance. Another feature was the allocation of workpoints. Rather than being based upon skill and effort, workpoints at Dazhai were awarded for political attitude. That is, someone who had an enthusiastic attitude and always talked about how wonderful Chairman Mao was would be awarded more workpoints than a grumpy malcontent, even if the grouch was a more-knowledgeable and harder-working farmer. After the Cultural Revolution Dazhai was exposed as a fraud, although there might well be almost as much exaggeration in its debunking as there was in its glorification.

The Maoists had their best success with another initiative, the reform of the Peking opera (a form of entertainment popular since Qing times). Here the story must introduce a new character, Jiang Qing (the pseudonym by which she is best known to history), Mao's wife.

Jiang Qing was born to an impoverished family in Shandong province. As a young woman she made her way to Shanghai where she found roles in several movies. She had the kind of social and love life the popular imagination attributes to movie stars, and also dabbled in leftist politics. After the outbreak of the War of Resistance she and some of her radical chic friends made their way to Yan'an. There she caught the eye of Chairman Mao. They began to live together, and decided to get married.

This was a problem. Mao was already married. His wife[4] was one of the handful of women who had completed the Long March. These women were high party leaders in their own right, as were their husbands, and had, naturally, a strong sense of solidarity. They were scandalized by the Chairman's treatment of their sister-in-arms.

The other party leaders approached Mao, telling him, in effect: His private life was his own and he could do as he thought best. But he must assure them that Jiang Qing, this starlet, would remain a housewife and never

---

4. She was his second, not counting a marriage arranged by his parents that was never consummated; his first wife was shot by the KMT in 1931, but by that time he was already living with his next wife.

meddle in politics. That suited Mao well enough, and his wife was sent off for a rest cure in the Soviet Union.

As this adventure suggests, Mao was not always a scrupulously faithful husband. He soon sought other diversions, and Jiang Qing perhaps did not find the satisfaction she had hoped for in her marriage. She had a behind-the-scenes role in some of the literary purges of the 1950s, but remained in obscurity, nursing bitterness against the party hierarchy.

Around 1960, she later said, she had not been feeling well. The doctor advised her to get interested in outside activities: she had been an actress; maybe she ought to take a hand in arts and drama. She was horrified by what she found: plays and movies all promoted bourgeois and feudal ideas and lifestyles; she found very little revolutionary, proletarian art. Here was something obviously in need of correction.

Specifically, Jiang Qing found a plethora of essays, stories, and plays written in the early 1960s that seemed to mock the Great Leap Forward and Chairman Mao. The most famous was a new play written in the style of the Peking opera, "Hai Rui Is Dismissed from Office." The author was the historian Wu Han, who was also a vice mayor of Peking under Peng Zhen, the party boss and mayor of the capital city. The story concerned an upright official in the Ming dynasty (Hai Rui), who tried to prevent evil local gentry from stealing the land of the peasants. The local leaders had influence at court, and arranged to have Hai Rui removed from office. The Maoists later claimed all this was allegory: the gentry were the local cadres, the land theft was the Great Leap, and Hai Rui was Peng Dehuai.

Jiang Qing wanted to put an end to this kind of reactionary, subversive trash. Instead there should be modern revolutionary operas reflecting the themes of socialist society and the Chairman's Thought. She was thwarted in Peking, where Peng Zhen had tight control—in fact, at one point Peng Zhen himself even tried to take over the work of reforming the Peking opera. Jiang Qing moved her operation to Shanghai, where the party establishment was more sympathetic. Around the beginning of 1965 she formed an alliance with Lin Biao, when Lin asked her to take direction of all the entertainment in the army.

In the meantime, Lin Biao had strengthened his control over the army. His chief of staff was Luo Ruiqing, who prior to Lushan had been head of Public Security. He was appointed, one assumes, in order to help purge the army. Luo, however, apparently disagreed with Lin's political emphasis, and pushed instead for more professional military training. He may have also argued for more active involvement by China against the Americans in Vietnam, a course that would have required both better weapons for the army and a reconciliation with the Soviet Union. Luo was purged in the fall of 1965 and put under arrest. The word was spread within the Party that he advocated a "bourgeois military line." Luo's purge may be considered the first move in the Cultural Revolution.

Around the same time, one of Jiang Qing's friends in the Shanghai party apparatus wrote an essay attacking Wu Han's play about Hai Rui, claiming Wu Han opposed collectivized agriculture and socialism. Peng Zhen (who had successfully prevented the publication of this article in Peking—it was first carried instead by a Shanghai paper and by the army's own newspaper) arranged to have himself appointed head of a special group to investigate Wu Han. In February 1966, Peng's group issued a report saying that Wu Han might have misinterpreted history, but that the question was an academic one, a hundred flowers should bloom, and it was a contradiction among the people.

There was a minority opinion, however. One member of the group was Kang Sheng, head of China's secret police and espionage system. Kang came from the same town as Jiang Qing, and her mother may even once have been a servant in the house of Kang's parents. He had sponsored her entry into the Party when she was an actress in Shanghai and had probably covered up a confession she made around that time to the KMT.

Kang was able to prevent the closing of the case on Wu Han. In May a party conference repudiated Peng Zhen's report; Lin Biao made a colorful speech accusing Peng of plotting a coup d'état. Peng Zhen and the leadership of the propaganda department were purged. The country learned it was in the midst of a "socialist cultural revolution."

The Maoists did not yet completely dominate the movement. Rather, Liu Shaoqi and Deng Xiaoping took charge, cruelly diverting it from a party purge toward the elimination of "bourgeois" influences in society. Students from Red backgrounds were encouraged to humiliate, beat up, even lynch their teachers and fellow students. Organized into new Red Guard groups, they ransacked private homes, confiscating old books and works of art—in fact, anything they wanted—that might smack of "bourgeois" or "feudal" influence. They beat or killed persons they came across whose dress or makeup might show too much individual flair.

Mao may have been ill around this time; at least he was lying low. Toward the end of July he reappeared, taking a swim in the Yangtze River at Wuhan. He was reported to have swum for several miles, backstroke, at speeds that would have set a world record at every hundred-meter split. After this exhibition he returned to Peking and announced that the Great Proletarian Cultural Revolution, as it would now be called, was not yet on the mark. Meritorious as all these attacks on bourgeois things might be, the real target of revolution was persons in power inside the Party walking the capitalist road.

Jiang Qing and other radical Maoists formed a Central Cultural Revolution group, with Kang Sheng as their advisor, to take over the detailed direction of the movement. This soon came to function as the equivalent of the Party Secretariat, which itself soon ceased to function at all. The Cultural

Revolution group and Lin Biao together formed the radical core of the Maoist alliance.

The other major component of the Maoist coalition, Premier Zhou Enlai, was not radical at all. In 1964 he had broached the subject of four modernizations (of industry, agriculture, science, and defense) that would become the slogan of the repudiation of Maoism after the Chairman's death. While he certainly agreed with the policies of the capitalist road period, he may have considered Liu Shaoqi a political rival. Ever since 1935, whether from conviction, lack of moral courage, or other reasons, Zhou had refused to oppose Mao. Perhaps he considered his role to be to go along and pick up the pieces afterward.

In gross political terms the Cultural Revolution lineup, at its beginning, might be considered to consist, on the one side, of the Leader (Mao), the army (Lin Biao), the government (Zhou Enlai), and the leader's entourage, perhaps the contemporary equivalent of the old inner court (Jiang Qing), arrayed against the party machinery (Liu Shaoqi, Deng Xiaoping, Peng Zhen). In a system such as China's, the Leader and the Party may be rivals, alternative focuses of legitimacy. The Party is the institution most apt to dominate the others, causing other forces to line up, where possible, on the side of the Leader against the Party.

The Red Guards and the Cultural Revolution

This kind of blow directed by a Leader against the party machinery has taken place in other totalitarian regimes. Early in his rule Hitler carried out the "Night of the Long Knives," murdering many of those prominent in the early organization of the Nazi party. Stalin consolidated his power through the Great Purge. Hitler's tool was the secret police and the paramilitary SS; Stalin also relied on the secret police. Mao's coalition certainly included the secret police and was backed by the military. In the early stage, however, the purges were conducted by "the masses," mobilized students forming Red Guard groups. The idea was to present the Cultural Revolution as a genuinely revolutionary movement.

Chairman Mao occasionally professed concern about the moral fiber of the younger generation, who had grown up in peace and prosperity (he apparently did not take the troubles of 1960–62 very seriously), ignorant of the rigors of war and revolution. These sentiments served as a rationale for mobilizing the Red Guards.

The first Red Guard groups formed in high schools throughout the country in the late spring of 1966 with the assistance of the schools' political instructors (who served the role of what in other countries would be guidance counselors). When Liu Shaoqi was in charge of the movement he sent "work teams" (outside party groups) into the schools to guide Red Guard activists.

When Mao took control in August he withdrew the work teams, "unleashing the masses." The schools did not open that fall for class, as students were too busy making revolution.

Originally only students from good class background could be Red Guards. The Maoists were not slow to realize that students of ordinary background were more likely to attack the establishment figures who were the objects of the purge, so they denounced the theory that some people were "naturally Red." The new Red Guards were more enthusiastic about attacking those the Maoists considered to be capitalist roaders inside the Party. Red Guards were given access to the dossiers of party members in disgrace, and published all the inside gossip on wall posters or in their own mimeographed newsletters. The Red Guard material remains a major source of information on the history of the PRC, although it must be used with caution. Under the onslaught of Red Guard attacks, Liu Shaoqi, Deng Xiaoping, and countless others fell from power and were put under arrest. Lin Biao rose to the number two position in the regime.

Red Guards were brought to Peking from all over the country to attend giant rallies held throughout the fall of 1966. They could gaze on Chairman Mao atop the Gate of Heavenly Peace, a very emotional experience for them. The Red Guards were also encouraged to roam the country, linking up with groups from different regions. They received free train transportation, so snarling up the rail network.

The Red Guard movement, working more or less in conjunction with the radical Maoists around Jiang Qing, continued to develop through the last quarter of 1966. In January 1967, one of Jiang Qing's allies put together a coalition of radical Red Guard groups and seized power in Shanghai. They proclaimed a "Shanghai commune" in which the "revolutionary masses" took direct control of all party and state authority. This was too much even for Chairman Mao. The "rebels" did in fact keep power in Shanghai, but had to give up any idea of turning that city into a "commune."

What happened is that by the time of the "January storm," as far as a party purge was concerned the Cultural Revolution had achieved its goals. The energies released by the movement, however, could not be brought back under control. The Maoist coalition began to turn against itself.

In February 1967, a group of very high-ranking and famous leaders of the State Council deplored the course the movement had taken. It looked to them as if the rule of the Communist party were about to disappear into anarchic chaos. They bewailed their wasted lives, some of them wondering why they had ever bothered to join the revolution in the first place. The Jiang Qing group, of course, immediately denounced them as capitalist roaders. Zhou Enlai tried to defend his subordinates and old comrades. A sometimes open, sometimes submerged struggle between Zhou and the radicals became a principal motif of Chinese politics over the following years.

At the grass roots, the Red Guard groups began to fight each other on the pretext of deficiencies in each other's understanding of Mao, but more realistically over who would have the greater access to local power. Probably the major source of cleavage between Red Guard groups was the "class composition" of the members of the various groupings. Groups of youths from ordinary background tended to be more radical and looked for inspiration and guidance ultimately from Jiang Qing and the Cultural Revolution group, while Red Guard groups composed of kids of Red background were "conservative" or "royalist" and allied with what was left of the local authorities. Too much weight should not be given to these general ideological or policy divisions, however, since the fight soon took on its own logic, with groups (or gangs, as by now they amounted to) taking whatever positions and making whatever alliances would best help them against their rivals.

With the collapse of local authority in the face of Red Guard attacks, responsibility for keeping public order fell upon the military. If the local soldiers were too rough in attempting to control Red Guard depredations against the general public, each other, or themselves, the soldiers were blamed for "suppressing the revolutionary masses." If they were not forceful enough, they were scolded for allowing anarchy. Lin Biao was not as much help to his subordinates as he might have liked to have been: because of his alliance with Jiang Qing he could not afford to let the local soldiers quell Red Guard insubordination. Zhou Enlai was much more sympathetic to soldiers seeking his advice. He told the local commanders that he understood their problem and urged them to be patient.

In July 1967, the military commander of the Wuhan military region allowed the more conservative Red Guards (groups made up of factory workers) to crush the radicals. Representatives from the Cultural Revolution group came to Wuhan to investigate and were put under arrest. Lin Biao sent in special forces units, and Zhou Enlai used his famous negotiating skills to resolve the question. Shortly after this, radical Red Guards in Peking temporarily took control of China's Ministry of Foreign Affairs, while some of their friends burned down the British embassy. Mao, Lin, and Zhou apparently agreed that enough was enough.

In the ensuing weeks it was the soldiers rather than the masses who were unleashed. The Red Guards were told they had served their historical function and now it was time for them to learn from the workers, peasants, and soldiers. They were sent to farm villages or to military-run state farms in the border regions. The focus of the party purge turned against the left. Jiang Qing, Kang Sheng, and their closer associates sacrificed some of their allies to save themselves. Prominent leftists were said to have formed a "May 16 corps," a secret group that pretended to be ultraradical as a way to bring about the overthrow of the socialist system. For years after that a brutal but unpublicized campaign was carried on against "May 16" elements in society.

The story of these remains hidden, and the purge of the May 16 corps remains the only part of the Cultural Revolution that has not been officially condemned. Indeed, it is not mentioned at all. The anti–May 16 campaign was probably intended to root out radicalism, but most of its victims do not seem to have been all that radical; rather, they were ordinary people who dared question or object to the existing structure of power.

The Ninth Party Congress, held in April 1969, ended the more tumultuous period of the Cultural Revolution. The new party charter named Chairman Mao as the Party's leader for life, with Vice Chairman Lin his best pupil and successor.

The Red Guards cannot be considered entirely as part of a spontaneous social movement. They were mobilized from above, used as tools in a power struggle, and shut down when they had served their purpose. Yet they did have ideas of their own. The 1966 Red Guards were infatuated with Chairman Mao, and they perceived the Chairman as the spokesman for the masses against the party oligarchy. By 1968 or so, most had become disenchanted with Mao but kept the idea that the masses—the people—ought to have more control over the state. Their perception of their own mistreatment intensified their new commitment to democracy. Some of them came to define democracy in more orthodox ways, in terms of majority rule determined by competitive election. A few even sensed that democracy itself had to be both defined and limited by law, that a decent government must be not only democratic but also limited. The Red Guard movement of the 1960s generated the seeds of the democracy movement of the late 1970s and the 1980s.

The Succession to Mao

The dominant theme of Chinese politics in the early 1970s was a morbid one: everyone waiting for the old man to die. The Cultural Revolution left China's political institutions in a shambles. During the movement personal alliances provided what little security there had been, and in the wake of the movement Chinese politics became even more a matter of personal relations and factional alliances. There was also an ideological division defining the content of politics. The radicals had limited influence on actual economic policy, since everyone tacitly realized that their ideas would have disastrous consequences; but they dominated the mass media and other instruments of propaganda, so the policies actually followed received no official legitimation.

Mao remained at the center of things, although his health was deteriorating. Around him circled an amorphous, shifting congeries of factions. The institutional bases for these factions, such as they were, included the police system, the government bureaucracy, and the army. Probably the most important was the "inner court," Jiang Qing and her friends, a kind of personal entourage of the emperor (although by the later biased accounts, it seems that most of the time Mao and Jiang Qing were no longer on comfortable personal terms).

Among the institutions, the army was the healthiest. But even the army was divided. Headquarters in Peking was dominated by Lin Biao's personal following, including his wife and son. The local soldiers were deeply entrenched in their own areas, dominating the local party and government organs. The regional commanders shared a common interest in protecting themselves from arbitrary interference from the center, combining this with a distrust of each other. Politics had been reduced to palace intrigue, and although the People's Republic was barely 20 years old, the atmosphere was that of a dynasty in decline.

The Lin Biao Affair

In reaching the pinnacle, Lin Biao had antagonized most of his former allies. By 1970 or so, he had also begun to antagonize Mao.

Late that summer another Central Committee meeting was convened at Lushan, the first to be held there since 1959. The meeting discussed a draft of a new state constitution. Lin Biao apparently urged that the position of state chairman, the office held most recently by the disgraced Liu Shaoqi, be restored. Chen Boda, a former personal secretary to Mao Zedong, the advisor of the Central Cultural Revolution group and editor of the Party's major theoretical magazine, supported Lin's proposal: Chairman Mao should be state chairman, and Lin should be vice chairman. During the Cultural Revolution, Chen had worked closely with Jiang Qing, but the purge of the May 16 group had damaged his clients more than it did hers.

Mao somehow interpreted Lin's proposal as evidence of his deputy's overweening ambition. He made some sarcastic comments about Lin, but was most scathing about the more defenseless Chen. Chen had been wont to hail Mao as a genius, and Mao pedantically pointed out that Marxism teaches that history is made not by geniuses but by the masses, the true heroes of history. It seemed that Mao himself was now turning against Cultural Revolution Maoism, perhaps because it had come to be more than anything else the ideological basis for Lin Biao's claims to power. The new atmosphere allowed Zhou Enlai to restore some semblance of normality in China's diplomacy and domestic administration.

Lin suffered no visible loss of prestige after the second Lushan plenum. Poor Chen Boda was purged, denounced as a phony Marxist political swindler. Mao worked behind the scenes to undermine Lin's status in the army and to make sure that Lin's people did not monopolize all the major military posts.

This led Lin to begin to plot against Mao. Actually (assuming, as we probably should, that the whole incident was more than simply a fabrication by

Lin's enemies), it is not clear that Lin was himself actively involved in the plot. Its main instigator was his son, Lin Liguo, a young man known to his family and friends as Tiger. Tiger, like Mao a genius, had been made chief of staff of the air force, over the heads of numberless more experienced officers. Tiger collaborated with and accepted direction from his stepmother, Ye Qun, a rather elegant lady Lin Biao had married around the time of Liberation. During the Cultural Revolution Ye Qun got a cushy job at PLA headquarters and in 1969 was elevated to the Politburo.

In order to explain his coup, Tiger (perhaps) prepared something he called "Outline of Project 571" (in Chinese, 571 is pronounced almost like the phrase *armed righteous rebellion*). This document denounced Mao (code named B-52) as a capricious, arbitrary tyrant, and criticized the Cultural Revolution for impoverishing the country and persecuting the educated. It also implied that China should seek a reconciliation with the Soviet Union (around this time Mao and Zhou were instead pursuing rapprochement with the United States). Project 571 sounds like a repudiation of all the policies and attitudes Lin had worked so long to make dominant. This must be evidence of how unpopular the Cultural Revolution actually was and also of how irrelevant specific policy and ideological issues had become in the power struggle. It is tempting to speculate that Zhou Enlai forged the document after the fact as a way to air the sentiments everyone felt, but played it safe by putting them into the mouth of a villain. The affair came to a head in September 1971. Part of the plan, allegedly, was for someone to blow up a train Chairman Mao was riding in. The officer entrusted with the job chickened out. He confessed to his wife, who urged him to go to the police. According to one story, that same night Lin Biao's daughter, who, unlike Tiger, did not get along with her stepmother, revealed the whole plot to Zhou Enlai. Lin Biao and Ye Qun were then at their seaside summer cottage at a resort area on the northeast coast. When they found out the plot had failed, they allegedly tried to escape by air to the Soviet Union. The airplane crashed in Outer Mongolia, killing all aboard.

At about this same time Lin Biao's clients at military headquarters were arrested. All told, roughly half the Politburo were dead or in jail as a consequence of the affair. Tiger thought the regional commanders might support the coup once it seemed to be under way, because of their hatred for Jiang Qing and the radicals. The coup was never given a chance, and in any case the regional soldiers did nothing to help Lin.

Accounts vary on whether the bodies of Lin and his wife were really found after the crash. Lin may have been killed before he could get on the plane. Some have wondered why, if Lin were trying to get to the Soviet Union, he took the long route over Mongolia rather than the short, quick dash to Vladivostok. We still do not know what happened in September 1971. At any rate, Lin Biao ceased to be a factor in Chinese politics, except as a symbolic figure, replacing Liu Shaoqi as the most wicked man who ever lived.

Palace Politics and Popular Malaise

Lin Biao's death temporarily tilted the balance of power in favor of Zhou Enlai and the moderates. To strengthen this tendency Zhou caused the rehabilitation, in early 1973, of Deng Xiaoping. Deng had been attacked under the code name "another person in power walking the capitalist road," but unlike Liu Shaoqi had not been mentioned by name in the public media. Before returning to work, Deng assured Mao he deeply regretted his former lapse into capitalism.

The radicals recovered the initiative in propaganda, if not necessarily in policy. By this time the radical tendency at the Center had congealed into what was later known as the Gang of Four.[5] These included Jiang Qing and three party officials from Shanghai who had worked with her throughout the Cultural Revolution: Zhang Chunqiao, the first secretary of the Shanghai party committee and in the early 1970s de facto head of the Party's central administrative machinery; Yao Wenyuan, a seasoned literary inquisitor who was in charge of the propaganda system; Wang Hongwen, a young man who had formerly been a security guard at a Shanghai textile factory and was now presented as a model of the kind of stalwart proletarian the radicals hoped would control the Party. In 1973 Wang was unexpectedly elevated to the third position in the party hierarchy, ranking only beneath Mao himself and the aged veteran Zhu De. Zhou Enlai praised Wang to the skies when speaking with foreign visitors, either to protect himself or in the hope that he could induce Wang to imprudent actions by feeding his conceit.

The police system was also generally allied with the left. Its dominant personality was probably still Kang Sheng, although he was sick and he died toward the end of 1975. The head of public security at that time was Hua Guofeng, who had spent most of his career as a party functionary in Mao's native province of Hunan and had been brought to Peking in 1972 to head the investigation of the crimes of Lin Biao.

In 1973 and 1974 the radicals seem to have sponsored a series of articles attacking Confucius or, later, engaging in a "criticism of Lin Biao and Confucius." The idea was that Lin Biao had been a great admirer of Confucius, news, probably, to most of those who had known him. Confucius was depicted as a great reactionary who had opposed the forces of progress in his own day (supposedly the transition of the slave society to a feudal one) and the patron saint of all that was dark and regressive in Chinese culture and history.

Confucius was a fairly transparent symbol for Zhou Enlai. There is a problem, however. As noted in Chapter 7, the Legalists figured as the great

---

5. Mao is said to have cautioned Jiang Qing and her friends: "Do not become a gang of four." This was later quoted to indicate Mao did not approve of them. It seems more likely from the context, however, that Mao was worried that the radicals would become too isolated from the other centers of power.

progressive antagonists of the Confucians, and were identified with positions anathema to the radicals. Perhaps the radicals at the top did not fully appreciate the import of the material they sponsored. The essays were produced by various "writing groups" and even by freelancers who submitted their own ideas, and these persons may not have had opinions identical with those of their high-ranking sponsors. Zhou Enlai was widely admired as a person, at least by those of good class background; but he was also associated with the pre–Cultural Revolution party dictatorship (a radical Red Guard group once dubbed him the "representative of China's Red bourgeoisie") and with the repression symbolized by the continuing hounding of the May 16 elements. The Gang of Four were universally despised, but may have been considered to hold out hope for radical change in the system. Leftist propaganda in the 1970s may be evidence of a profound discontent in society.

Discontent is certainly shown in a long wall poster, written in 1973 and revised in 1974, put up in the southern city of Canton. Its authors were three former Red Guards who signed themselves "Li Yizhe" (a pseudonym made up from components of each of their real names). They attacked what they called the "Lin Biao system," a code phrase for radical Maoism. In its place they recommended democracy and legality. Their concept of democracy was not quite that of the Maoist "great democracy." It was a democracy limited by and embodied in law. They even had kind words for persons associated with the moderate, antiradical tendency, such as Zhao Ziyang, who was then governor of Guangdong province. The moderates at that time, if only for reasons of self-preservation, did not reciprocate, but we see here the germs of the tacit, unstable coalition of democratic forces in society first mobilized by the radical aspects of the Cultural Revolution with the moderate tendency of the Communist party, the coalition that more or less shaped the reform decade of the 1980s.

The Li Yizhe dissidents were put in jail and the power struggle at the top continued without regard for people like them. By 1975 Zhou Enlai was on his deathbed and his work was taken over by Deng Xiaoping. Hoping, perhaps, to consolidate his position while Zhou was still alive, Deng attempted to discredit the radical faction, accusing them of unrealistic economic thinking and of factionalism disruptive of party unity. Deng did not control the propaganda system and, given Mao's continued influence and his apparent backing of the radicals, he could not organize a strong enough coalition. His attacks were easily parried and by the end of the year he himself was in trouble.

Zhou died in January 1976. Deng delivered the funeral speech and then vanished. The newspapers began to drop hints about an "unrepentant capitalist roader," someone who used to talk about the "color of the cat." Hua Guofeng, then in close alliance with the radicals, became acting premier, replacing Zhou. This was a compromise. Deng had been eliminated, but the radicals' own candidate, Zhang Chunqiao, the most competent of the Gang of Four, was too controversial and had insufficiently broad support in the Party. During the Cultural Revolution Deng had been in house arrest under constant supervision. In 1976, however, he escaped south and was given sanctuary by the commander of the Canton military region—an indication in itself that things were falling apart.

On Qingming in April 1976 factory and office workers in Peking put flowers and wreaths on the small monument to Zhou Enlai in Tiananmen Square, in the heart of the city. There was some dissatisfaction among the people at the neglect shown by the radicals to Zhou's memory and also disturbance at the new purge of Deng, although at that time Deng had yet to show any ability to please a crowd. During the night the decorations were removed. The next day, April 5, a crowd gathered at the square; this gathering, which eventually grew to about 100,000 persons, became rowdy. Speeches denounced the radicals, and poems denounced the "First Qin Emperor" and the "Empress Dowager"—Chairman Mao and Jiang Qing. Some people praised Deng Xiaoping as the man to save the country from misgovernment. Police, militia, and army attacked the crowd, which fought back. There was some loss of life on both sides, and arrests continued for many days afterward. This April 5 incident (which takes its place with May 4, and now June 4), what we now have to call the first Tiananmen incident, was the use of Cultural Revolution methods against the radical Maoists themselves and evidence of how bankrupt the radical program had become.

Hua Guofeng had organized the repression and for this merit he was elevated officially to the premiership—no longer simply acting premier. Chairman Mao said to him: "If you take charge, my heart's at ease"—words Hua was subsequently to put to good use. Deng previously had been denounced obliquely, but now the media attacked him openly, accusing him of having plotted the disturbance. Many senior figures disaffected by Deng's treatment and unhappy with the radical ascendency were now frightened by this evidence of popular hostility to the regime, and rallied temporarily to the side of the radicals in a show of solidarity—the rulers against the people.

In July Zhu De, with Mao the founder of the first Communist guerrilla forces and commander of the Communist armies until Liberation, died. Later that month northern China from Peking to the ocean was wracked by a horrendous earthquake that killed hundreds of thousands of people. The newspapers printed stories demonstrating there was no such thing as a Mandate of Heaven. They also told of people who had remained buried for days but who kept up their spirits by thinking about how much they loved Chairman Mao and how much they hated Deng Xiaoping. The people were reminded that an earthquake only lasts a few minutes, while capitalist roaders in the Party go on forever. The radicals had lost all sense of proportion.

On September 9 Chairman Mao finally died, a lonely old man relatively sound in mind but no longer in control of his body. His companions in his last months were his servants and his last girlfriend, an uncomplicated young woman who had been an attendant on a railway train.[6]

The Era of Hua Guofeng

Intrigue among the elite continued after Mao's death. Within less than a month Jiang Qing and her friends—the Gang of Four—lost the power struggle and were put under arrest. The winning coalition consisted of State Council bureaucrats who earlier had been associated with Zhou Enlai; the military, both central and regional; and nonradical leftists, primarily from the security system, who previously had seemed to have been allied with the Gang. The front man for the victors was Hua Guofeng, whose claim to legitimacy was that he set Chairman Mao's heart at ease. The new order was wildly popular among the general public, who were happy to be rid of the Gang. Over the next few months the media tried to fan a cult of Hua, making him to be the worthy successor to Mao. Hua even began to style his hair in the fashion of the late Chairman.

The new rulers, to distance themselves from the radicals, emphasized the "four modernizations" (of industry, agriculture, science and technology, and national defense). Zhou Enlai had urged this program in his last public speech in early 1975, and the four modernizations had been one of the demands of the April 5 demonstrators. According to the new line, the Gang (who, it was claimed, in no way represented the will of Chairman Mao) had deliberately and maliciously kept China backward and poor. The Hua regime had no intention to foster liberalism in the economy, much less the political system. Its economic program was similar to Soviet-style central planning, the kind of policies China had followed in the early 1950s. Policy would seek economic rationality, however, as well as political correctness, and would no longer consider anything that made life a little more comfortable to be "capitalism." The new rulers lacked the Gang's distrust of education and intellectuals and realized that China's development would require people with technical skills.

Deng Xiaoping had fought the Gang when the new rulers were still kowtowing to them. Many soldiers and bureaucrats were eager for Deng's good name to be restored. Deng also had support among the still numerous first-generation leaders (Hua was about 20 years younger than Deng, and was very much a newcomer to the top). By January 1977, Deng's rehabilitation seemed

---

6. Mao and Jiang Qing no longer lived together in the early 1970s. There is indirect evidence that they may have reconciled during his last months, or at least that she had easy access to him. If this is so, given her rapid fall from grace and continued bad favor, the propaganda media would not say so.

assured. Hua, understandably, was reluctant to see Deng back, and in February counterattacked, causing the official party newspaper, the *People's Daily*, to publish an editorial asserting that the Party would always be bound by whatever Mao had said and whatever Mao had decided. One of the things Mao had decided, of course, was that Deng Xiaoping should be fired (although the editorial left this implicit). The best Hua could do was to delay Deng's rehabilitation, which took place in the summer of that year.

At that stage, Deng could count not only on the military and the bureaucracy but also on the general public to support him against Hua—for whatever the support of the public was worth. Deng worked quietly to consolidate his own position, achieving a decisive victory at the famous third plenum of the Eleventh Central Committee, a meeting held in December 1978. There were many dramatic and unexpected changes at this time. The April 5 movement was suddenly discovered to have been an expression of the patriotic and revolutionary fervor of the masses, not at all counterrevolutionary. The policy of categorizing people by class origin was abolished. Those who had been labeled rightists in the 1957 hundred flowers purge were rehabilitated, although it was also said that their earlier treatment had been appropriate at the time. High-ranking leaders who had been purged in the Cultural Revolution reappeared in increasing numbers. Hua Guofeng made a self-criticism at the meeting, although it was not published. His power had not been completely broken, and he was to keep his official titles until 1980; but he had lost his primacy inside the regime. He was later publicly criticized for failing to break sufficiently with the policies of the Cultural Revolution, but was not otherwise denounced or humiliated. He remained popular among the Party's rank-and-file, not because they necessarily approved of his policies but because they considered him an honest person, someone who never sought special advantages for himself and his family, who did the best he could according to his no doubt limited lights.

The third plenum coincided with the "democracy movement." The Peking citizenry, especially young workers who had previously been Red Guards, put up wall posters in the fashion of the Cultural Revolution, but this time the posters demanded freedom and democracy. They attacked Deng Xiaoping's enemies, and Deng himself at first took a very relaxed view of the movement. He quoted Mao from 1957: "Let the people speak—the sky won't fall in." As the weeks went by and it became clear that Deng had no intention to break the Communist party's monopoly of power, the democrats on the street began to turn against him, calling him a tyrant. What probably bothered Deng more was that the demonstrations were becoming an embarrassment to him. The defeated Hua Guofeng and his allies began to intimate that Deng and his friends were fostering disorder, that they wanted another Cultural Revolution to throw China into chaos. To shore up his position Deng called off his campaign against the leftists, turning instead on the democrats.

In the spring of 1979 Deng announced that free speech was fine, but that it had to meet four conditions: it could not depart from Marxism-Leninism, the Thought of Mao; from the socialist road; from "people's democratic dictatorship"; and (most importantly) from the leadership of the Communist party. The posting of wall posters (a freedom explicitly granted by the Maoist constitution of 1973) was outlawed. The most outspoken of the dissidents, a former Red Guard named Wei Jingshen, had argued that the four modernizations would mean nothing unless there was also a fifth modernization, democracy. Wei was arrested on partly specious charges and later sentenced to a long prison term.[7] The democracy movement exposed the contradictions inherent in Deng's reform program even before the reforms had properly begun.

The Reform Experiment

The defeat of Hua Guofeng at the end of 1978 was only partial, and Hua was saved in part by the perception inside the Party that the drive against him threatened public order. Hua and his allies in the military and security system kept their titles into 1980; by that time their reformist enemies had fallen into disagreement on the scope and direction of change.

In 1979 and 1980 Deng Xiaoping was able to associate Hua and the leftists with various Cultural Revolution atrocities. His allies in the propaganda system mounted an attack on Hua's "whatever" line, proposing instead that practice (not the words of Mao or Marx) is the criterion of truth.

The new order contained its own contradictions. Deng wanted a rather more radical reform than that favored by many of his allies against Hua. Deng's major collaborator in 1978 and 1979 was probably Chen Yun: Chen may in fact have been the more creative thinker at that time. In the early 1950s Chen had been in charge of the planning system, and by 1957 he had concluded that state plans would be successful only if they incorporated a healthy use of the market mechanism. With the Great Leap he fell into obscurity and semidisgrace, and this eclipse probably saved him from deeper disgrace during the Cultural Revolution. The reforms of 1978 and 1979 were based on Chen's 1957 program: planning supplemented by the market. It turned out that Chen meant exactly what he said: the market should only *supplement* the plan. Deng's program advocated expanding the role of the market, whereas Chen became increasingly outspoken in favor of central planning, of what he called the birdcage economy: the bird is free to fly as he wishes, but only inside the confines of the cage.

---

7. He was released in 1993, a few months short of his full term, as part of China's attempt to win goodwill so Peking could become the site of the Year 2000 Olympics.

The tendencies represented by the two men disagreed in their interpretation of history. In 1979 the CPC made a momentous announcement for a Leninist party, that it had been guilty of basic errors in line (previously such parties had been willing to admit only errors in the implementation of a uniformly correct policy). There was a behind-the-scenes dispute, however, on when the errors began. The Chen Yun tendency dated the errors only to 1957, to the hundred flowers policy and the disruption of the planning system in the Leap. The more radical reformers wanted to say that mistakes began with the "founding of the state," that is, in 1949. Chen's tendency was sometimes called "restorationist," *fubi pai*: the word refers to those who want to bring back the rule of a dynasty that has been overthrown. Here it means that they thought everything would be fine if China would simply go back to the way things had been in the early 1950s. This tendency was also called the conservatives and, after the overthrow of Hua Guofeng, the leftists. Their interpretation of party history remained the orthodox one, and the reform program was a compromise between the restorationists and the reformists, a compromise in which the good points of each sometimes cancel each other out while the shortcomings of each reinforce each other.

At first it seemed that the restorationists would be senior cadres who, unlike Deng, had not been purged in the Cultural Revolution, while the reformers would be those who, since they had been purged, had no incentive to keep up the reputation of Mao's last years. It turned out, however, that most of the older cadres restored to favor also eventually gravitated to the conservative side. Some of the first-generation leaders who continued to side with Deng did so more on the basis of personal connections than political conviction. The main reformers included second-generation cadres purged in the Cultural Revolution and younger party intellectuals. The restorationists included old cadres, some second-generation technocrats, especially, perhaps, those who had studied in the Soviet Union in the early 1950s, and some hard-line ideologists who previously had supported Deng against the Gang of Four.

The terms *reformer* and *restorationist* refer to general tendencies, not to hard-and-fast factions. Both sides agree on much: they maintain the primacy of the Party; they think policy should be judged more by its economic effectiveness than its ideological purity. At different times the same person may take positions on one side and then on the other—Deng Xiaoping is a good example. Actual reform policies, again, represent compromises between the tendencies. As reforms progressed, however, the differences between the tendencies grew and bitterness between them increased.

At least since 1980 Deng Xiaoping knew that economic reform would not fully take root unless it were coupled with political reform. That year, partly out of conviction about the right thing to do, partly as a power play against the restorationists, Deng proposed a bold plan for political decentralization and greater democratization, as well as for more limits on the scope of political power generally. After a flurry of discussion the plans were dropped—perhaps because the leftists were too strong, perhaps because Deng himself lost his nerve.

At the end of the year Deng did something else: he put the Gang of Four on public trial, along with remnants of Lin Biao's clique and other assorted Maoists. The unrepentant Jiang Qing was allowed to scream in open court that Chairman Mao knew, approved, and even directed everything she did. The judges called her a liar, a hag, a witch, all the ugly names they chose, but she had given voice to the truth that everyone believed but no one could safely utter. The gutsier of the Gang of Four—Jiang Qing and Zhang Chunqiao—were sentenced to death, but the sentences were later changed to life imprisonment.[8] The other defendants were given long prison terms. The trial was a kind of political reform on the cheap: it signified the official discrediting of radical Maoism, but did not raise the difficult question that there might be something wrong with the system itself.

Political and Social Tension in the Reform Program

The Maoist period can perhaps be summarized by one of its famous slogans, "Politics takes command." Deng's reforms, and even those of Hua Guofeng, meant allowing the economy to function according to its own logic, with relatively less direct political control. Given what had been the omnipresence of the Party in society, the reforms meant a shrinking of the function of the Party. As opportunities opened up to earn a living by private farming or private business, or as objectively measured competence in some skill or other came to be rewarded more highly than political correctness, the Party enjoyed less direct control over daily life, and ordinary people became less concerned with keeping the goodwill of the Party. If the economy was to operate by objective economic laws, with "practice as the criterion of truth," there seemed to be no clear role for the official ideology. Yet the leadership, whether reform or conservative, wanted continued party rule, even when the Party and its doctrines were losing their functions.

Party officials could, of course, adapt. Local rural cadres at first opposed the dismantling of the communes, because the communes gave them position and power. They soon learned, however, that in the new system they remained the local political leadership, and the connection between politics and the economy was still sufficiently solid to allow them to allocate the best lands to themselves, their families, and their friends, and to sell the necessary licenses and permits for business to those who were willing to pay. Corruption had been a feature of Chinese politics since the Cultural Revolution, but reform multiplied the opportunities for it. The commitment to keeping the Party the unchallenged ruler of society meant that the separation of politics

---

8. Jiang Qing committed suicide in 1991.

and economy had to be incomplete. The guiding value now was material gain rather than ideology, but in the half-reformed economy those with power could make sure the material gain was directed toward themselves.

At the same time, there was no longer a clear line between what was corrupt and what was not. In one famous case, officials on Hainan island, an area that enjoyed special access to foreign currency, bought cars from abroad and resold them to units on the mainland for a profit, using navy ships for transport. The officials claimed they were making money for the good of their organization, not lining their own pockets. In 1985, when the conservatives were fairly strong, the Hainan officials were disciplined; some months later, when the reformers regained influence, they were promoted. There were no longer any clear rules about what was proper and what was not.

In addition to corruption, the reforms bred inflation. If the market mechanism were to work, prices had to reflect the real costs of the resources used, but prices had been fixed administratively and frozen for decades: they no longer had much relationship with costs. The move to a market economy meant price increases. Other things were at work as well. Managers had more freedom on how they could spend money and, to keep workers happy, issued pay raises and bonuses in excess of any increases in productivity. China's monetary system was rather rudimentary, and the shortage was made up by expanding credit and printing new bills. As inflation set in, the government authorized additional bonuses to workers to compensate for the rising cost of living. Peasants and temporary workers did not share in this largess, and a result was social unrest by 1985. Local governments, wanting to make more money themselves, used their ability to get capital and credit to invest in projects that would not show returns for a long time, if ever, such as luxury hotels for which there were no customers. The effect was to bid up the price of scarce capital resources. Both rulers and people could not help but think of the massive inflation of the late 1940s, an inflation both rulers and people thought was a prime cause of the collapse of the Chiang Kai-shek regime.

Corruption and inflation led to social demoralization—in that there was both a general sense of discouragement and a confusion of moral standards. The Party elders complained of a crisis of faith: no one believed in Marxism or in communist ideals, but chased only after money and pleasure. Reformers blamed everything on the Gang of Four, whose actions had allegedly discredited Marxism. The reformers asserted that the people would come around if the regime started once more to stand for real Marxism. In fact, many had long been cynical about politics and resentful of any attempts at ideological control. The conservative critique was unfair: the people had their own notions of right and wrong and were no longer as receptive of the politicized morality, which was often no more than a disguise for the self-serving desires of those in authority. But there was enough objective foundation to the conservative complaint to cause a sense of unease.

The social and moral consequences of the reforms gave leverage to the leftists, especially since these consequences caused ambivalence among just about everyone else. In late 1983 the leftists were able to convince Deng Xiaoping to endorse a campaign against "spiritual pollution," giving rise to fears of a return to Cultural Revolution–type repression and terror. Deng called off this campaign after a few weeks, when it became apparent it was scaring away foreign investment. Deng and the reformers were strengthened in their conviction that the reforms would be safe only if there were a fairly thorough makeover of the political system as well. But this was difficult not only because of conservative opposition but also because some attempts at political reform misfired. Deng had always opposed the cult of Mao and genuinely wanted to institutionalize the structure of authority. He believed that no single person should hold simultaneously the top position in both party and government, as this was asking for personal dictatorship. He refused to take either top position himself, since his personal prestige would overshadow the authority of whichever institution he headed. Each was headed instead by one of Deng's clients: the Party by Hu Yaobang, the government by Zhao Ziyang. But this meant that Hu and Zhao, the two most enthusiastic reformers among the regime leadership, were as much rivals as allies, while disagreements between the Party and the government would be resolved by Deng, who no longer held an official position. Power became even more personalized, and policy was subject to personal whims and the shifting balances of influences.

The Politics of Reform

The defeat of the movement against spiritual pollution in 1984 led to renewed vigor for reform. Previously the rural reforms had remained largely a matter of local option and had been routinely sabotaged by local cadres. Now the reforms became virtually nationwide. The euphoria led to a greater push toward urban reform, applying the reforms to state-owned industrial firms, giving the managers greater discretion in planning, the use of funds, in hiring and firing. Firms were allowed more leeway in making deals with each other, rather than having to go through the various ministries and the central planning mechanism. If problems could not be solved by discussion, they would be adjudicated in the courts. In principle, firms would no longer feed their profits back into the central ministries; they would keep their profits and pay a tax on them.

The first consequence was inflation, a result of freeing previously frozen prices. By 1985 there was a certain amount of unrest in the cities. Problems also spread to the countryside. Peasants contracted in the spring to sell grain to the state at a certain price after the fall harvest. Inflation meant higher prices of fertilizer and other agricultural inputs, so that by the time harvest came around the peasants were taking a loss. The state was unwilling to pay enough for grain to make its cultivation profitable, and peasants used their new freedoms to move into more remunerative crops, such as vegetables or even flowers. Grain output began to fall. Previously the conservative argument against reform had been that it was bad for public morals and undermined the control and prestige of the Party. Now the leftist case began to make sense to a wider range of ordinary people.

In 1986 Deng again sponsored a wide-ranging discussion of political reform, with the idea that this would allow economic reform to be on a firmer and more rational basis. Some of the public debate became quite bold, questioning the universal validity of Marxism and the role of the Party as a self-perpetuating elite responsible only to itself. The discussion had been confined to circles of intellectuals, some of them affiliated with "think tanks" associated with various reform politicians, some in spontaneously organized groups of persons interested in particular topics (called "salons," after the somewhat similar groupings in pre-Revolutionary France).

By the end of the year the ferment had spread to college campuses—the famous Science and Technology University in Anhui, and educational institutions in Shanghai, Peking, and other cities. The protests began over local student gripes—the quality of food in the dining halls, especially—but soon moved on to a general demand for democracy (although it was not always clear what the demonstrators meant by the term). The students were encouraged by the astrophysicist Fang Lizhi and by some other famous intellectuals. The authorities allowed the demonstrations to continue relatively unmolested, a dramatic indication of how much had changed since 1979, not to speak of 1976.

The regime waited until the winter vacation, when the students had gone home. A meeting of party elders and the Politburo removed Hu Yaobang as Party general secretary on the grounds that his attitude had encouraged the demonstrations. He remained, however, a member of the Politburo. When the students returned for the new semester they found themselves placed under stricter supervision and exposed to more political indoctrination.

Deng Xiaoping's anger toward his protégé was the major reason for Hu's fall. Although he was a reformer, Deng did not tolerate argument either from the public or, unless he had to, from colleagues. Hu was replaced by Zhao Ziyang, who, contrary to the new policy on tenure of office, remained for the time being as head of government as well. Hu's purge marks a shift in the status of Deng Xiaoping relative to the other Party elders, especially Chen Yun. Deng could no longer be sure of staffing the important positions with people to his liking. The Thirteenth Party Congress, held in November 1987, reaffirmed the general reform line, but also saw the elevation of a group of technocrats not necessarily in sympathy with market reforms and not at all in favor of political loosening. The most prominent was Li Peng, foster son of Zhou Enlai and the darling of the emerging gerontocracy.

In the spring of 1988 Li Peng replaced Zhao Ziyang as premier. Zhao remained general secretary, although he publicly said he would really much prefer to keep the government post instead. Zhao was more interested in economic issues, normally handled by the state, than in the ideological matters the Party is supposed to take care of. Even after ceasing to be premier Zhao kept control of economic policy. In 1988 he sponsored a major price reform, hoping to make the market mechanism more effective. The consequence was the most frightening inflation yet and growing social unrest. Zhao's prestige suffered and Li Peng took over the economy, adopting a program of "readjustment." He did not really reverse the reforms, but neither did he introduce new ones, and he renewed the stress on centralized planning and coordination. By early 1989 Zhao was probably on the way to political oblivion, and the reform program was stagnant.

Rebellion

The events of 1989 are evidence that reform had gone as far as it could without a change in the system itself. By the beginning of that year society was in general unease, brought on by inflation and fear of the retrenchment that might be necessary to contain the inflation, as well as disgust with the pervasive corruption among the political elite. Workers especially were troubled by inflation, peasants by inflation and by the failure of the state to pay for the grain it had contracted for. Intellectuals were also discontented but no longer intimidated, and many famous intellectuals expelled from the Party on grounds of "bourgeois liberalism" after the 1986 unrest agitated in the spring for the release of political prisoners. One of these intellectuals, the scientist Fang Lizhi, had been invited to a reception for U.S. President George Bush, and he generated a lot of publicity when the police prevented him from entering the building where the party was being held.

Discontent was endemic among students. They perceived the outer society as one that rewarded education with neither esteem nor money, where someone who set up a bicycle repair stand on the street could make a better living than a doctor, a college professor, or an engineer. In 1988 there had been some reforms in the system of assigning jobs to college graduates: graduates were increasingly expected to find their own jobs. This might have been seen as increasing freedom, but in the context students interpreted the new policy to mean that now no one without political connections would ever get a decent job.

In April Hu Yaobang suffered a heart attack at a Politburo meeting; he died a week later, on April 15. By that time Deng Xiaoping had come to regret the purge of Hu and the way that purge had exposed the reform's vulnerabilities. The party leadership decided to act as if Hu had not been in disgrace, and put on a great show of official mourning.

The mourning for Hu Yaobang became the occasion for the student demonstrations. Peking students showed their sorrow for the martyr's death by marching from their campuses to the huge Tiananmen square in the middle of the city. There they remained, camping out, demanding (at least at that point) that the Party show itself worthy of Hu by ridding itself of corruption.

Hu had not in fact been wildly popular during his lifetime. Yet he had always had good relations with intellectuals (even though at various times he had strongly supported party control over the expression of ideas). He had been a decent person and an honest official. In the election of delegates to the Thirteenth Party Congress in 1987, he and Hua Guofeng had received more votes than anyone else. But whatever sorrow the students may have felt at Hu's passing, they also used the occasion to express their deep if unfocused discontent with the regime in general and Deng Xiaoping in particular. The largest demonstration was in Peking, but similar ones developed in Shanghai, Nanking, Sian, Chengdu, and other cities.

After a week or so the students and especially the general public were losing interest in the protest, whereas the regime had behaved with exemplary restraint. On April 26 the *People's Daily* published a commentary allowing that most of the students were acting in good faith, but that they had been misled by a malicious handful who wanted to destroy the socialist system and throw the country into turmoil. The effect was to regalvanize the demonstrations. Student representatives demanded that the leadership conduct a "dialogue" with them; they eventually tried to exert moral pressure on the rulers by embarking on a hunger strike.

The student movement became the obvious focus of the power struggle inside the regime. Zhao Ziyang hoped to use the movement to show that reform and, therefore, he himself, had the support of the people. Zhao had been out of the country when the *People's Daily* comment appeared, although he had supposedly approved it over the telephone. When he got back home he appealed for stability but also praised the students' patriotism and good faith. This increased the hostility Li Peng and the party elders felt toward the demonstrations. Already by the end of April they had goaded Deng Xiaoping into making intemperate comments to the effect that if the protest continued there would be bloodshed. Deng now began to lose faith in Zhao.

Soviet President Mikhail Gorbachev visited China in May. This was supposed to mark the formal end of the long Sino-Soviet conflict; it should have been, for the Chinese leadership, one of the major events of the decade. Gorbachev was completely upstaged by the student demonstrations, which received unprecedented publicity from the world's news media, which had gathered in Peking to cover the visit. In a televised meeting with Gorbachev, Zhao Ziyang told the Soviet leader that even though Deng Xiaoping had formally retired from public life, the Party continued to seek his guidance on all important issues. For this Zhao was later accused of giving away state secrets to a foreigner. His real offense was to hint publicly, albeit in the subtle Chinese way, that Deng continued improperly to meddle in politics, interfering with the duties of those who should be doing the job.

The students began their hunger strike on May 13, the strikers demanding to talk with the leadership. Li Peng actually did hold a meeting with some of the more-celebrated student leaders on May 18. The students wanted Li Peng to say the demonstrations were entirely proper and justified. Some even imprudently suggested that while the demonstration had so far been peaceful, they could not guarantee that it would remain so. The only thing Li Peng wanted to talk about was ending the hunger strike before someone really got sick and so damaged the prestige of the regime.

Early the next morning Zhao Ziyang, tears in his eyes, visited Tiananmen Square. "No matter how you have criticized us," he said, "I think you have the right to do so." Later that day a party meeting removed him from all his posts, and Li Peng announced the imposition of martial law. Troops were deployed in Peking suburbs and in the railway yards near Tiananmen Square. Still nothing happened. The students took to proclaiming that the "people's army supports the people." The soldiers, well-indoctrinated, bright, but otherwise ignorant peasant kids who remained day after day in cramped, hot quarters, thought of the students as the spoiled brats of the privileged class, and took the students' attempt to appeal to their sense of shame as taunting.

The crackdown came in the early morning hours of June 4, with violence between the citizenry and the army continuing for about a week. The number of fatalities can only be estimated. The regime admits that a few dozen people were killed, mostly gallant soldiers and a few innocent bystanders.[9] Some outside observers say about 10,000 were killed. The true number is probably in the low thousands—more than 1,000, less than 5,000. The massacre shocked both China and the world. The brutality itself was not so surprising, perhaps; rather, it was unexpected that the regime would react so viciously after having shown so much restraint for so long.

The outcome of the demonstrations could certainly have been different, although there was a political dynamic building toward tragedy. Forces in the regime feared the consequences of a peaceful resolution. The State Chairman, Yang Shangkun, is alleged to have said that if we give in now, it's just as if we had been overthrown. It would hardly have been the regime's last gasp, but it would have meant that the regime would have been faced down by militant public opinion, and it would have had a hard time afterward reasserting its authority.

The play of palace politics generated a bias toward violence. The hardliners used the demonstrations and later the massive use of force against them as a way to crush the political standing of the reformist tendency. It certainly seems that every time the public appeared to be tiring of the confrontation, the regime did something (the *People's Daily* editorial; the declaration of martial law) to further antagonize the students and reanimate the crowd.

---

9. The regime claimed that not a single person died on Tiananmen Square. It is possible that this is actually true, although not highly likely. The statement is probably intended as a sophistry: most of the killing took place on the crowded approaches to the square.

This process was reinforced by the dynamics of the protest itself. The students showed great self-discipline in preserving general order, preventing violence against persons or destruction of property. But the demonstration was truly spontaneous, with no leadership able to control its political tactics or direction. The very large number of would-be leaders had the normal share of ambition and competitiveness as well as minds of their own. If any set of leaders attempted to match possibly conciliatory moves by the regime, they would lose influence to more militantly outspoken rivals. In early June, the very radical collection of student spokesmen who had sassed Li Peng a couple of weeks earlier had forebodings of tragedy if the protest continued, but were accused of selling out by the next set of leaders when they urged the square be cleared.

It is possible that the events of 1989 show the slow formation of a "civil society" in China, able to keep in check an arbitrary and despotic state. Yet the protests may exhibit a more traditional cultural syndrome, the articulation by the educated of the general grievances of society. It may not be useful to try to analyze the 1989 movement in terms of particular social classes or interests. The protesters did not necessarily have common opinions or interests. Many workers, for example, resented what they considered to be the privileged status students held in society; many more were thoroughly disenchanted with the reform policies, while students on the whole favored reform. But students and workers shared a general discontent with what they saw as a corrupt, unresponsive, and irrational structure of rule. Workers, who had jobs to lose and families to support, were willing to concede leadership to the students. The general social discontent, it is safe to say, was not assuaged by the massacre, although the massacre will certainly influence the ways in which the discontent shows itself.

The Continuing Revolution

Having given up on both Zhao Ziyang and, earlier, Hu Yaobang, Deng turned in June 1989 to Jiang Zemin, party boss of Shanghai, making him general secretary of the CPC. Jiang, like Li Peng, was a Soviet-trained technocrat, but he had a more urbane personality and more of a reformist reputation. He had cracked down very early on liberal reformists in Shanghai, without spilling blood. The propaganda apparatus tried to depict Jiang as a great leader, but in action and appearance he was not very impressive, and most people seem to have seen him as at best another Hua Guofeng. Following the massacre Deng strongly defended the economic reforms, asserting they had nothing to do with the political turmoil. Although Deng was more responsible than anyone else for the slaughter, a political consequence of it was even more of a drop in his influence; he had to share power even more with other behind-the-scenes elders.

In the months following the crackdown there was a reassertion of political control of the economy, mostly in the name of fighting inflation. These controls were aimed mainly at the booming small-scale rural firms and at the southern provinces that were growing rich from exports. Denunciations of "bourgeois liberalization" continued, with attacks on decadent lifestyles and propaganda for socialist and collectivist ideals. The collapse of communism in eastern Europe was an ambiguous vindication of the rulers' behavior. Particularly relevant was the Rumanian drama where, at the end of the year, the army of that country, unlike the Chinese army, refused to turn on the people. The Chinese leadership no doubt pondered deeply the fate of their good friend Ceaucescue, the Rumanian tyrant, who was shot down without mercy or dignity. They probably reflected that the same might have happened to them—and also worried that the only thing keeping them in power was military force.

The 1991 collapse of the coup against Gorbachev (a coup the Chinese leadership discreetly but actively welcomed) and the subsequent collapse of the Soviet Union reinforced political conservatism. Many party cadres had vocally or silently supported the students in 1989, hoping that China would move toward democracy. After August 1991, many rethought their position, concluding that democracy in China would not be compatible with the Communist party, that democratization would not only eliminate the system that had nourished them but would also destroy their livelihood.

In the official Chinese view, the collapse of European communism had nothing to do with resistance to political tyranny. Rather, it was a consequence of economic deprivation. They claimed, perhaps not without reason, that Gorbachev's mistake was to push for radical political reform without introducing effective economic reforms.[10] While China certainly had economic problems in the late 1980s, its economy was healthier than that of the Soviet Union and eastern Europe. The rulers seem tacitly to have concluded that the regime would survive as long as the people could be kept economically content. As Laozi might have put it: fill the bellies and empty the minds. Propaganda for greater austerity and more socialist spirit faded in 1990. It was as if the regime had come to a silent understanding with the people: the people could make money and live pretty much as they chose, and in return they would keep their mouths shut about politics and not challenge the power of the regime. Without admitting it, the regime was moving toward a "neo-authoritarian" policy.

In early 1992 Deng Xiaoping made a dramatic tour of the boom areas in southern China. He redefined "Chinese-style socialism." Previously it meant the priority of public over private ownership and the priority of centralized

---

10. Soviet specialists argue that Gorbachev had no choice; given the entrenched nature of the Soviet ruling elite, there would not have been effective economic reforms without political reform. In China the Cultural Revolution had shaken things up, giving the Chinese system greater flexibility.

planning over the market. Now, Deng said, it was a "socialist market economy." He spoke of the need to learn from the good points of capitalism. Deng was no doubt worried about the economic sluggishness the Li Peng retrenchment policies brought on, and by 1992 these policies had in fact successfully controlled inflation. Deng was also concerned, perhaps, with reasserting his own primacy as leader of the regime.

The new emphasis on liberal economic reform seemed to pay off. The economy grew 12 percent in real terms in 1992 and in the closing months was growing at close to 20 percent a year. These high rates, however, brought back fears of renewed inflation.

The Fourteenth Party Congress, held in October 1992, endorsed both liberal economic reform and continued political repression. There was no reason to think this combination would be any more viable in the 1990s than it had been in the 1980s. Presumably, given June 4, society would be more diffident about expressing whatever discontent it might feel. The failure to address political reform left economic reform dependent upon power maneuvers among the elite, although some speculated that economic change had gone so far that it could no longer be reversed by the leadership.[11] The Congress did nothing to clarify what might happen after Deng Xiaoping's death.[12] It did not make much sense to speak of a successor, since Deng held no position, but ruled by his prestige. His prestige, and that of the other elders, hindered the Party and the state from developing their own institutional autonomy and authority.

This lack of clarity in the nature of authority probably means that politics will remain important—even if the leadership cannot reverse the economic reforms, it will still have to handle them correctly. By 1993 the high growth of the previous year was breeding a new round of inflation. The curbing of the inflation became the responsibility of Zhu Rongji, a very tough and competent party reformer (who in 1957 had been branded a rightist). Zhu was probably Deng's candidate to take over from the unpopular Li Peng. Li Peng fell ill, however, at about the time that signs of economic overheating were becoming clear, and may have taken his time recovering, so that Zhu would bear the blame for the painful if necessary retrenchment. One reason for the overheating was the inability of the central authorities to control spending by local officials, who were doing their best to make use of the economic

---

11. David Bachman, "The Limits on Leadership in China," *Asian Survey*, 32, 11 (November, 1992), pp. 1046–1062.

12. The leadership appointments give a few hints, however. The speculation was that Deng was disappointed with the unimpressive Jiang Zemin, and that the reformist Li Ruihuan had proved unable to challenge Li Peng's control of the government. Among the new appointees to the Politburo Standing Committee, it was likely that (as far as Deng was concerned) Hu Jintao would eventually take over from Jiang, and Zhu Rongji from Li Peng.

boom. Some worried that this increased autonomy for the localities would lead eventually to the disintegration of central authority entirely, with the rise of a new economic equivalent of warlordism. This new local autonomy was also recreating, or reinforcing, the post–Opium War disparity between coast and interior, as well as the gap between rich and poor. Peasants, who prospered in the early 1980s, were somewhat left out of the 1990s growth, and were becoming increasingly restive. Although by the early 1990s much of the international opprobrium resulting from June 4 had worn off, China was more exposed to international influences than it had been for decades. This might lead to greater liberalization: the fact that the entire world could see what was going on is certainly one element in making the repression following 1989 milder than some earlier examples. China took to publishing long official pronouncements on why its socialist version of human rights was vastly superior to bourgeois Western notions of rights: at least China was taking the question of human rights explicitly into consideration. But the international exposure could also have other results. In 1993, China, in an attempt to win world favor so it could host the Olympics for the year 2000, engaged in an orgy of prisoner releases. Sydney, not Peking, won that contest. The prisoner releases had, of course, been transparent exercises in hypocrisy, and no city has an inherent right to host the Olympic games. Still, the Chinese rulers might be tempted to reflect that whether they are good or whether they are not, the powers in the world are still going to treat them like dirt. In the meantime, fearing what it saw as a meddlesome, moralizing, and trigger-happy United States and disturbed by the disorder in the post–cold war world, China was engaging in a large-scale military buildup, emphasizing the use of advanced technology.

According to Sun Yat-sen's last testament, the Revolution is not completed. Chairman Mao used to talk about continuous revolution. In some ways, China in the 1990s seems considerably less affected by the revolution than in the 1960s, and, mostly for the better, sometimes for the worse, traits of traditional China were reasserting themselves. For the better is the return of vitality, popular culture, and common sense. For the worse is closed and obscure palace politics, increasing crime and vice, economic and social polarization, and a cynical materialism among many of the young.

Mao was probably correct to think in terms of a cultural revolution, however perverse his understanding of what it should mean. The 1989 democracy movement recapitulated criticism of the established system voiced by the student movement of 1919; the reform themes of the 1980s echo those of the 1890s.

However much continuity, China has certainly changed. The institutions that embodied the old moral and political order are gone, but an alternative order has not formed. China in the 1990s seems depressingly reminiscent, politically, of China in the 1900s. The existing political structure lacked legitimacy, but was strong enough to overwhelm any alternative force that might challenge it, much less replace it.

9
✦
The Republic of China on Taiwan

Taiwan (called Formosa by some Westerners) is a large island off the southeastern coast of China, somewhat south of Shanghai. Settlers from the mainland began populating Taiwan during the 1500s. For a few decades after 1644 the island was held by forces loyal to the old Ming dynasty and hostile to the new Qing. After it was incorporated into the Qing empire it remained something of a wild frontier area. It enjoyed a flourishing commercial agricultural economy, producing rice, tea, camphor, and fruit. By the late 1800s the Qing government realized that if it did not exercise greater control over Taiwan, the island would be seized by one of the imperialist powers. In 1885 it became a province of China. The Qing government sponsored a successful drive for the economic development of the island. In 1895, however, China ceded Taiwan to Japan as part of the treaty ending the war between those two countries.

Taiwan reverted to China in 1945. From 1948 to 1950 Chiang Kai-shek transferred what he could save of his regime and army to Taiwan, there to continue the civil war. He regarded his regime, the Republic of China (ROC), as the sole legitimate government of all China, with Taiwan figuring as a province of China. He wanted to recover the mainland. The Communists, for their part, considered the PRC to be the sole legitimate government, agreeing wholeheartedly that Taiwan was a province of China. They were determined, they said, to liberate Taiwan.

With the continuing civil war as their pretext, Chiang and the KMT ruled Taiwan as a harshly authoritarian albeit progressive police state. By the late 1960s or early 1970s, however, the regime had begun slowly to democratize. By the early 1990s the regime should probably be considered a genuine democracy. Democratization on Taiwan, unlike in many other places, came about without the massive discrediting of the established authoritarian regime.

By the 1990s few could take the Taiwan regime seriously as the government of all China (and, in fact, the regime had tacitly abandoned that claim). It did have to be taken seriously as a Chinese government, a clue to the alternatives possible in a modernized Chinese political culture.

The ROC on Taiwan

In September 1945, Chiang Kai-shek sent forces under Chen Yi, a KMT warlord from Fujian province across from Taiwan, to take the surrender of the Japanese troops on the island. The beginning was not happy. Chen Yi's soldiers came mostly from northern Fujian, which is culturally distinct from and rivalrous with southern Fujian, the ancestral home of most Taiwanese. The troops were mainly country boys, unused to the relatively sophisticated atmosphere of Taiwan. They treated the Taiwanese as if they had been collaborators with the Japanese, not victims of colonialism. They acted as an occupying force, a not very well disciplined one. They were much given to plunder. Government and KMT officials took the places of the Japanese bureaucrats and businessmen. The local population was no more involved than before, except that now the public services no longer worked and public order was no longer maintained.

A riot broke out in Taipei, the island's capital, on February 28, 1947, after the military police somehow managed to kill an old woman they were hassling for illegally selling cigarettes on the street. The riot led to an island-wide rebellion. Chen Yi negotiated a cease-fire and promised reforms. When the rebels put down their weapons he had Chiang Kai-shek send in reinforcements, who systematically massacred those who had participated in the rebellion, who might have participated in the rebellion, or who looked as if they might cause trouble, whether they had been in the rebellion or not. The killing struck most heavily against those younger Taiwanese who had received a higher education. For years the February 28 incident, as this series of events was called, was a taboo topic on the island. The government finally published a report on it in 1992, estimating the death toll at from 18,000 to 40,000 persons.

By late March the extent of the debacle became known. Chiang removed Chen Yi, replacing him with a more competent and conscientious governor.[1] As the civil war turned against him, Chiang moved men, weapons, and treasure to Taiwan, building up the island as the fortress either where he would go down fighting or that he would use as a base from which to recover the mainland. Thousands of officials, soldiers, and ordinary people either attached to the Chiang regime or fearful of life under communism moved to Taiwan in 1948 and 1949. These mainlanders, as they and their descendants are called, came to constitute a little less than 15 percent of the island's population. Because of the February 28 incident there was inevitable tension between them and the natives of the province.

Chiang had formally resigned as ROC president in January 1949. He remained head of the KMT, and his personal connections allowed him to dominate the military. In early 1950, settled on Taiwan, he "resumed the Presidency." His son, Chiang Ching-kuo, conducted a party purge, ridding the KMT and state officialdom of their more corrupt and less competent members, as well as those who might show too much independence. As far as both Chiang Kai-shek and the Communists were concerned, the move to Taiwan was simply one more tactic in the civil war. Active fighting between the two sides continued until the outbreak of the war in Korea at the end of June, when the United States interposed its Seventh Fleet in the Taiwan strait, ostensibly to prevent Chiang from launching an attack on the mainland but also effectively preventing any Communist attack on him. The civil war was frozen in place.

Martial law or emergency rule had been imposed on Taiwan after the 1947 business, and Chiang kept it in force. The claim that the ROC remained the sole legitimate government of all China served to rationalize the continued exclusion in the early years of Taiwanese from most positions of real political influence, as, supposedly, it would not do to have the government of all of China dominated by natives of a single province. The rational fear of Communist subversion helped justify the emergency, but it was in fact directed at least as much toward repressing Taiwanese demands that the island become an independent country with no claims on China and allowing China no claims on it. Could this have come about, there would, of course, be no further justification for KMT dictatorship, and this gave the KMT a vested interest in the continuing civil war and also a need to insist that its regime was the legal one for all of China.

The Chiang regime was interested in state power, not in enriching itself. Although the regime remained politically repressive, it sponsored a series of

---

1. Chiang executed Chen Yi in 1950 after he had been caught trying to defect to the Communists.

progressive reforms on Taiwan. A peaceful land reform, carried out with U.S. aid, was particularly successful. It broke the power of the Taiwanese landlords, compensating them with bonds on state-owned industries, and allowed the KMT to establish grass-roots party organizations in the countryside. Relatively honest and extremely competent government contributed to Taiwan's astounding economic success throughout the entire period of KMT domination. The economic performance compares favorably not merely with that of the mainland but with any other country or region with similar characteristics. In 1950 Taiwan's per capita income was perhaps U.S. $100; by 1990 it was about U.S. $8,000. In many countries rapid growth rates are accompanied by increasing inequality. Until the late 1980s, however, not only did Taiwan's population grow richer but the wealth came to be more evenly divided.

The KMT professes Sun Yat-sen's Three Principles of the People: nationalism, democracy, welfare. The nationalism is Chinese nationalism, supplemented by a healthy dose of anticommunism. Taiwan had been a Japanese colony during the traumatic events that had shaped contemporary China and the consciousness of the KMT—the Boxer Rebellion, the Revolution of 1911, the May Fourth movement, the Northern Expedition, the War of Resistance, the civil war with the Communists—and did not always fit comfortably into the KMT's paradigm of Chinese nationalism. By the 1970s, with the passing of the older generation of mainland rulers and a new pro-Peking U.S. foreign policy, the regime felt a need to sink deeper roots into the soil of the island itself. This was probably the long-run driving motive behind the island's democratization.

Institutions of Rule

The Chiang regime's claim to be the legitimate government of China was perhaps unrealistic, but it was not absurd. It was not based on some divine right of the KMT to rule China no matter what anyone thought. The basis lay in the ROC constitution adopted in 1947. This constitution supposedly represented the decision of the sovereign people, and it established the institutions of the regime. The Communists and their allies, of course, did not accept the validity of the procedures used to establish the constitution.

The constitution set up a somewhat complicated structure of authority. It was based on the theories of Sun Yat-sen, who admired the American system of separation of powers and checks and balances. But in addition to the usual division of executive, legislative, and judicial functions, Sun added two more, adapted from traditional China: there is a separate Control branch, charged with investigating official corruption and bringing impeachments against government personnel suspected of malfeasance; and an Examination branch, which conducts civil service examinations to recruit the government bureaucracy. The institutions that embody these five functions are called *yuan*, a word that has no particularly natural English equivalent and is often left untranslated; it might be rendered as *council*.

One complication is that the executive function is not confined to the Executive council. There is also a President of the Republic, who is the head of state and stands outside the five councils. The president is elected by a National Assembly, which is not to be confused with the Legislative council, even though it, like the Legislative council, is chosen by direct popular vote of the citizenry. Apart from electing the president, the only other function of the National Assembly is to amend the constitution. The president appoints the premier, who is the head of the Executive council, and the premier appoints his cabinet. The cabinet presides over a career civil service staffed by persons appointed on the basis of eligibility certified by the Examination council. Although the premier is appointed by the president, he and his cabinet cannot rule without the active support of the Legislative council, which is elected by the people. The premier and the Executive council are responsible for the routine work of governing and also for routine policy making. The president is the commander in chief of the armed forces and also has general powers in foreign affairs. The ROC in effect has a dual executive system, and it is not clear from the constitutional structure itself whether the president or the premier is the more significant figure. In the past, the president clearly had the key role, but this was because of personality, not law. In recent years there has been a debate over whether the ROC is at heart a presidential or a cabinet system. This debate is also connected with the play of political interests within the regime, and its resolution may require major constitutional and institutional changes.

The Legislative council deliberates upon and enacts legislation. Most of the proposals for legislation originate from within the Executive council or from the president; major items are also debated within the leading organs of the KMT. The Legislative council also enjoys the right of interpellation: it may demand that the premier or the ministers appear before it to answer questions about their policies and the performance of their duties. Should the legislature refuse to pass legislation demanded by the Executive council, the minister responsible for the particular piece of legislation must resign; in some cases failure to pass legislation might bring about the resignation of the whole cabinet. As in the American-style presidential system, and unlike the typical cabinet system, ministers of state may not simultaneously serve as legislators.

The people elect both the National Assembly and the legislature. Here was a major anomaly of the ROC regime on Taiwan: the people, of course, meant the people of China. This meant that the National Assembly elected in 1947 and the legislature elected in 1948 seemed destined to remain in session forever. As the regime explained, the government of China could not be responsible to the people of a single province only, and, given the control of the mainland by the communist bandits, it was inconvenient to hold new elections there. The effect was to disenfranchise the only part of China the regime did control, Taiwan province. The members of the Assembly and legislature who retreated to Taiwan were those most committed to the Chiang regime, so the regime had no reason to expect any trouble from them. For years these institutions lingered with extremely truncated powers, playing little real role in the process of governing.

With the passing of the years came increasing impatience with the "old thieves," as the mainland-elected cohort came to be generally, if not entirely fairly, called. They themselves were reluctant to resign their positions, since it was their positions that gave them prestige and gave their families social and political connections. The regime did not want to change the situation either, both for reasons of not creating problems for itself and also for the sake of constitutional continuity, the desire to keep a living connection with the ROC's mainland roots.

For all the attention to constitutional continuity, the constitution could sometimes be treated in a very casual manner. Emergency provisions (obligingly enacted by the National Assembly) allowed the constitution's protections for civil liberties and political rights to be ignored. The constitution limited the president to two six-year terms, but Chiang Kai-shek, under the emergency conditions, continued to be reelected for as long as he lived.

For most of the regime's history the political structure did not closely correspond with that spelled out in the constitution. Rather, actual power was spread through a congeries of the executive bureaucracy, the KMT, the military, and the secret police. Coordination came from the head of the regime, first Chiang Kai-shek and later Chiang Ching-kuo.[2]

Since the early 1950s the bureaucracy has been a highly educated technocracy. Appointments to the bureaucracy come through competitive civil service examinations. The heads of ministries and other political appointments may be recruited from academic or party circles, occasionally from business circles, as well as promoted from the permanent bureaucracy. After the president, the premier is the most important regime figure.

---

2. Note that this chapter, alas, uses a different system of romanization for personal and place names than the other chapters in this book. The mainland has its own preferred system; in recent years this has come into general use abroad, and it is used for the most part in this work. Taiwan, however, adheres to the older, once more familiar system, and if the spelling were kept consistent, readers current in world affairs but not overly familiar with China might be confused. In the spelling approved on Taiwan, Deng Xiaoping would be Teng Hsiao-p'ing. In the mainland spelling, the two gentlemen in the text above would be Jiang Jieshi and Jiang Jingguo. Mandarin Chinese is the official language both on the mainland and on Taiwan. Most natives of Taiwan province speak as their mother tongue "Taiwanese," a variant of the language of southern Fujian. About 20 percent of the natives of the province speak Hakka, another southern Chinese language.

The structure of the KMT is similar to that of the CPC prior to the 1980s. It is headed by a Chairman, who is almost always president of the Republic.[3] In some ways it functions like the CPC, but has nowhere near the scope of control over society. KMT ideology is rather loose and excludes little beyond support for communism and Taiwan independence—and by the 1990s it might even have incorporated versions of those. The KMT does not dominate the economy (although the Party owns various businesses), and it does not have direct control over routine bureaucratic appointments. Civil servants who wish to advance their careers, however, are well advised to take out party membership. The Party nominates candidates for elective office and approves political appointments by the executive branch. If the Party passes a resolution concerning a matter of policy, it is supposedly the duty of party members in the state bureaucracy or the legislature to see that the policy is implemented; it is not clear, however, how much control over policy the Party as such has.

Taiwan's military, like the PLA, is politicized, and has been as much the instrument of the Party as of the state. The KMT maintains a system of political commissars within the army, justifying this practice to skeptical American allies in the 1950s as the equivalent of the corps of chaplains. In recent years the military on Taiwan as on the mainland has developed a stronger professional ethos. Under the Chiangs the army mostly stayed out of direct political involvement, supporting the regime and its policies. This has remained the general practice in the post-Chiang period. In 1989 the minister of defense, a powerful career soldier, did tell the legislature that the army would not defend Taiwan from Communist attack should Taiwan declare independence from China. This is perhaps the closest the army has come to an open attempt to dictate state policy—although there were complexities to this situation[4] and state policy is officially strongly opposed to independence in any case. The real test of the army's political role will come should the KMT ever be voted out of power by a free election.

The police and espionage systems are complicated and rather amorphous. Under Chiang Ching-kuo a National Security Council, responsible to the president, provided overall coordination (supposedly). Components of the system include an Investigation bureau, which on the mainland had been

---

3. When his father died in 1975, Chiang Ching-kuo was premier. He then became chairman of the KMT, but remained head of the Executive council until the presidential election of 1978. Chiang Kai-shek's party title had been Director General, but that title was retired upon his death as a mark of respect.

4. In elections that year the opposition, campaigning on a Taiwan independence platform, had had unprecedented success. This caused the Communists to threaten war. Part of the minister's intention was to show Peking that there was no possibility for independence, hoping thereby to forestall the threat of war.

under the KMT's organization department but on Taiwan was transferred to the Ministry of Justice. Most of its work concerns regular crime, but it has also been used against political opposition. The Intelligence bureau, technically under the military, has spying against the Communists as its main work, but has also undertaken operations against non-Communists obnoxious to the regime—including at least one proven case of political assassination. The Taiwan Garrison command, a military organization technically under the provincial government, was responsible for the administration of martial law. The KMT has its own "special work" organs, which allegedly spy on students from Taiwan in foreign countries, allegations that are widely accepted despite a dearth of hard evidence. Like the army, the police system has been largely an instrument of the regime, not a major setter of policy.

The regime's structure of power was certainly not democratic, but in a way it was pluralistic: there were various competing centers with overlapping competencies. Coordination and general direction came from the Leader. Both Chiang Kai-shek and Chiang Ching-kuo enjoyed unchallenged preeminence; they had a personal following in each of the four systems. Taiwan was not exactly a personal dictatorship, but the regime was held together by "strongman rule."

From the beginning, even in its mainland days, the regime contained democratic seeds. KMT ideology was in principle democratic, and deviations from democracy were justified only by the state of emergency. Sun Yat-sen's thought also affirmed local self-government, and from the beginning of the regime's transfer to Taiwan there had been elections to a whole set of local and provincial-level offices. There were county and city councils, city mayors and county magistrates, and a provincial assembly, as well as numerous local peasants' associations and water-control associations.[5] Real power was at the national level, which for a long time was insulated from electoral concerns, and the regime, under the emergency provisions, did not allow parties to organize to oppose the KMT. The regime did permit individuals to run against KMT candidates, however. The need to win these local elections compelled the KMT to organize at the grass roots, to co-opt local elites, and to do favors for and foster the goodwill of ordinary people. Although it thought of itself as a Leninist vanguard "revolutionary" party, the KMT became as well an electoral party.

---

5. According to the constitution, provincial governors should have been elected as well, but under the emergency provisions the governors of Taiwan were appointed by the president. Later, Taipei and the large southern city of Kaohsiung were given the status of special municipalities equivalent to provinces, and under the emergency their mayors were appointed as well. The change of status was not unrelated to the propensity of their residents to elect critics of the KMT. As part of the post-Chiang reforms, popular elections for provincial governor and mayor of Taipei and of Kaohsiung were scheduled for 1994.

Taiwanese were never totally excluded from political office. Most elected officials were Taiwanese, as were increasing numbers of the civil service. By the 1970s Taiwanese were getting positions both on the Executive council and on the KMT's Central Standing Committee, its equivalent of the CPC's Politburo. By 1990 about 70 percent of the KMT membership was Taiwanese. On the other hand, the higher ranks of the military remained predominantly mainlander.

Chiang Ching-kuo's death in 1988 spelled the end of strongman rule. Chiang was succeeded by his vice president, Li Teng-hui, a Taiwanese. A few days later Li was elected chairman of the KMT by the Party's Central Committee. Neither Li nor anyone else had the kind of prestige that would allow him to dominate the system the way the Chiangs had. Chiang Ching-kuo had sponsored a radical series of reforms prior to his death, and his passing allowed for even more rapid change. The end of strongman rule opened the way for greater use of the formal constitutional institutions and procedures and meant greater significance for elections. It also forced open the basic issue: whether Taiwan is legitimately as well as in fact an independent country, or ultimately a province of China.

Democratic Evolution

By the early 1970s, a period of generational, political, and diplomatic change, there was a confluence of trends on Taiwan. Chiang Kai-shek regarded his stay on Taiwan as a sojourn: he wanted to recover the mainland. He certainly emphasized the economic and social development of Taiwan, as a way to create a strong base from which to launch the mainland recovery. By 1970, however, mainland recovery seemed pretty remote.

By that time, the actual direction of the country was under Chiang Ching-kuo, the President's son. Ching-kuo had an unusual background. In 1925, during the first KMT–CPC united front, as a boy of 15 he had gone to study in the Soviet Union. He remained there after his father's break with the Communists in 1927. He joined the Communist Party of the Soviet Union, married a Russian wife, and took a job as an engineer in a Soviet factory. In 1937, with the outbreak of war with Japan, he returned to China, serving in the KMT's youth corps and in various local government and party positions. He cultivated connections with the KMT's police and military-political systems. On Taiwan he became the major designer of the structures of social control and repression in the 1950s. This background does little to prepare us for his later actions.

The changing international situation complicated things. The United States had continued to recognize the ROC as the government of China, and with U.S. support the ROC kept China's seat in the United Nations. In 1971, however, the United States moved toward rapprochement with the PRC.

Formally the United States kept relations with the ROC until 1979, but for all practical purposes the main relationship was with Peking. The ROC was expelled from the United Nations in favor of the PRC in 1971. Chiang Ching-kuo understood that if the regime were to survive, it would have to sink deeper roots in Taiwan society.

Ching-kuo gained control of the bureaucracy, retiring old cronies of his father who were unsympathetic to reform as well as older civil servants who favored reform but had been affiliated with his rivals within the KMT. He replaced them with younger technocrats, most of them Taiwanese. Chiang's policy of rejuvenation complemented his policy of "localization" or, more bluntly, Taiwanization.

Ching-kuo also encouraged more national-level elections. The first of these was held in 1969, actually a little before Ching-kuo had acquired top power. These were elections to replace some of the National Assembly and Legislative council members who had died since 1949. In 1972 additional elections were held under an emergency provision passed by the National Assembly allowing "supplementary elections" in the "free areas of China" during the time pending recovery of the mainland. Thereafter, with a major break in the late 1970s, there were legislative elections every three years. By 1989 about 100 seats were open to contestation.

Elections gave the opposition a way to make its influence felt. Previously there had been a certain amount of intellectual dissent, always under considerable police pressure. Now, however, opponents of the KMT could run for national office, although, given the preponderance of the old thieves, there was no way they could get a legislative majority, even if they did get a majority of the vote (which they did not).

Chiang Kai-shek died in 1975, about a year and a half before his great rival, Mao Zedong (although Chiang lived to a greater age). Ching-kuo continued for the time being as premier of the Executive council. In 1978 the National Assembly elected him president of the ROC.

"Outside the Party": Elections and the Rise of Opposition

The national elections, like the local ones, were truly competitive, despite the KMT's advantages in money, organization, and control of the state. The opposition could not organize a political party: the KMT slogan during the emergency period was *Dang wai wu dang*, outside the Party there is no party. Dissident politicians, therefore, styled themselves the *Dangwai*, "outside the Party." The regime did not greatly interfere with their efforts to informally coordinate programs and policies. The inability to set up a formal organization in itself did quite enough to make coordination difficult.

The electoral system blatantly favored the KMT. Each legislative district sent several delegates to the legislature, but each voter could vote only for a single candidate. If there is a 10-member district, the top 10 vote-getters are the winners.[6] This, as we shall see, is the same system traditionally used in Japan (until 1994), except the Taiwan districts are larger. Since citizens vote for individuals rather than parties as such, the KMT and opposition candidates compete against their allies as well as each other.

As in Japan, this requires that the candidates have a personal appeal as well as a party appeal. In both places, this personal touch often means doing favors for constituents rather than taking particular policy positions or being exceptionally personable (although personality helps more on Taiwan than it does in Japan). One way of doing this is, bluntly, by buying votes. This is of course a corrupt practice, but it must be understood in context. Hard information is hard to come by; it seems, however, that the typical payment is fairly small, about a third of a day's wage: no one will get rich by vote selling. The principle is a variation of the old Chicago politics maxim: an honest politician is one who, once bought, stays bought. The candidate expects the citizen to do him the favor of voting for him, so the least the candidate can do is to make it worth the citizen's while. The citizen, having accepted payment for his vote, incurs a moral obligation to follow through at the polls.

The electoral system in Japan contributed to factionalism in the ruling party, since the faction was the main source of candidates' financial support. On Taiwan, at least until the 1990s, the KMT central organization still controlled the allocation of most campaign funds. Its vast resources allowed its candidates in the multimember districts the means to establish (or reinforce) personal relations with their constituents. The opposition did not have the same kind of pelf, so the multimember district system forced the opposition to either spread itself thin or engage in a suicidal competition for the limited number of citizens inclined to vote for them in each district.

The multimember districts also allowed the KMT to moderate the effects of indigenous factionalism. Although the phenomenon has not received the systematic study it merits, local politics on Taiwan has long revolved around factional rivalries, these factions antedating KMT rule, probably in some cases going back to Qing times. The KMT tries to incorporate all the factions into itself. Rivalries continue, however, even after the factions have nominally been absorbed into the KMT. The multimember districts allow the KMT to balance the factions, permitting each of them an equitable chance for some of the seats available.[7]

The electoral system, again, encourages the opposition to split its votes. Since the opposition appeal is different from that of the KMT, the system

---

6. There is a rule that at least 10 percent of those elected to office be women, so the top female vote-getter is assured election even over a male who might have received more votes.

7. Some offices, such as county magistrates, can only be winner-take-all. In that case, the KMT tries to see that the local factions alternate in office.

fosters factionalism among the opposition. Especially before the opposition could organize as a political party, the system forced it into a kind of "prisoner's dilemma"; that is, a strategic game in which the overall interest is served by cooperation but each "player" has an incentive to strike out on his own in hopes of getting an even bigger payoff, so courting both collective and individual defeat. It was in the opposition's interest for the various factions or trends in it not to run against each other; but absent a formal nominating mechanism, it was tempting for popular politicians to run where they thought they might win, or for a faction to try to spoil things for a rival by running against that faction's candidates.

The opposition appealed to those alienated from the KMT. The KMT was not attached to any particular social base but contained a wide diversity of opinion within itself; in fact, there was much overlap in opinion between segments of the KMT and segments of the opposition, and even where there were differences these were more symbolic than pragmatic.[8] Opposition focused on two major principles: democracy and Taiwan independence. The KMT had no objection in theory to democracy, while prior to the late 1980s advocacy of independence was a criminal offense, so the opposition had to muddy its stand.

Different members of the opposition put different weights and slants on the opposition principles. For some, Taiwan independence meant merely that the regime should become democratic, that is, responsible to majorities of inhabitants of Taiwan. Many in this tendency had no objection in the abstract to reunification with the mainland, as long as the way it was done protected Taiwan's interests. Another tendency valued democracy for its own sake but at the same time conceived democracy as a means to achieve independence. This "line struggle" within the opposition (as it was called by some commentators, borrowing terminology from the mainland) was reinforced by personal rivalries and differences of temperament and opinion concerning appropriate tactics.

The political dynamic encouraged opposition extremism. The overlap of opinion between the moderate KMT and the moderate opposition gave rise to a perception that the opposition could be co-opted, that opposition members might be willing to abandon their dissident stance for the sake of influence or power. It also encouraged speculation that the moderate opposition were being co-opted. The moderates were then compelled to exaggerate their differences with the KMT and the radicals their differences from the moderates. This helped the regime, since extremism left the opposition isolated and

---

8. For example, if the KMT believed in the unity of China while the opposition desired Taiwan independence, this did not necessarily imply any difference of policy toward either the mainland or the world at large.

vulnerable to repression. In terms of popular support, in those days the regime could get about 70 percent of the vote and the opposition about 20 percent, with the balance going to various independents.

Some trace the decisive point in Taiwan's democratization to 1977. Hsu Hsin-liang, a young politician who had been groomed by the KMT as part of its Taiwanization program, was denied the Party's endorsement for a second term as magistrate of Taoyuan county after he had begun to diverge from the party line.[9] He ran as an independent, but his KMT opponent was declared the winner. This provoked a public riot in the town of Chungli, protesting vote stealing. It was the largest public demonstration of its kind since 1947. In the face of this public display the regime backed down and admitted that there had indeed been fraud. Hsu was reelected. The Chungli incident marked a change of atmosphere, a toleration for active and outspoken political dissent.

The new atmosphere contributed to factional conflict among the opposition. The mainstream group at that time was generally silent on the question of unification and advocated achieving democracy by parliamentary, electoral means (although, given the continued occupation of seats by the old thieves, it was impossible for the opposition to hope for a majority in the organs of opinion). A rival group, organized around a political magazine, *Formosa (Meili Dao)*, was more inclined to independence and advocated direct confrontation with the regime through mass rallies. The Chungli incident and, later, the overthrow of the Shah of Iran seemed to show the effectiveness of this tactic.

Legislative elections were scheduled for December 1978. That month the United States announced it was breaking relations with the ROC, transferring them to the PRC. The Taiwan regime used this setback to justify postponing the elections for a year. The opposition mainstream accepted this with good enough grace, angering the Formosa group. The year 1979 was an extended, increasingly heated election campaign, with the Formosa group attacking both the regime and the opposition mainstream. The Formosa group sponsored a series of public rallies during the fall. The last and largest of these, held a few days before the election, was in Kaohsiung, Taiwan's second largest city and a stronghold of independence sentiment. The organizers lost control of the rally and the crowd, possibly abetted by police provocation, rioted. The Kaohsiung riot, unlike the earlier, milder incident at Chungli, brought on regime repression. The authorities put the elections off for yet another year and court-martialed the main leaders of the Formosa faction, sending them to prison.

---

9. This, however, is not the whole story. KMT policy required, for reasons of factional equity, that Hsu make way for a Hakka candidate. See footnote 7, page 269.

The moderate opposition contested the 1980 elections, which went fairly well: for the first time no one was arrested after the elections were over for having had the audacity to criticize the KMT. The Formosa faction's work was carried on by the wives and defense lawyers of the Kaohsiung defendants, so for a while the group became known as the wives' and lawyers' faction. During the 1980s the old opposition mainstream, which had done so much to pioneer Taiwan's democratization, gradually lost electoral strength. The Formosa faction emerged as the new opposition mainstream, challenged by a more radical group, the young intellectuals of the New Tide faction.

Hsu Hsin-liang moved to the United States where he joined the restless, formless Taiwan independence movement in exile. In 1986 he organized in America a political party advocating independence, and threatened to "bring the party back to Taiwan." He wanted to challenge the regime to either allow him to openly campaign for independence or put him in prison (but since he had not officially been charged with a crime, the inevitable result would have been to embarrass the regime). The opposition leaders on Taiwan complained among themselves that Hsu was trying to horn in, to "eat from their plate." Hsu's behavior challenged the opposition, which had been threatening for years to form a party, but had been dissuaded by fear of the regime's reaction.

As it happened, Hsu's return attempt was a major anticlimax. He had to transfer airplanes at Tokyo; airline officials, figuring he would not be allowed to enter Taiwan, refused to allow him on the flight to Taipei. Nonetheless, the opposition decided to go ahead and form their own party, even though it was still illegal to do so. They formed the Democratic Progressive Party (DPP). The name was chosen to avoid the issue of whether the party was Chinese or Taiwanese or whether its ideology should be leftist or conservative. Its flag, an outline of Taiwan inside a white cross on a green background, symbolized ecological concerns, worries about the degradation of the island's natural environment. The founders included politicians from the old mainstream, the Formosa,[10] and New Tide factions. The party became in fact a Taiwan independence party. The New Tide (whose strength in the party organization was greater than its popular appeal) favored independence outright. The now more moderate Formosans urged instead "self-determination" for the residents of Taiwan. The DPP founders included two mainlanders, but they were forced out of the party after a few years. Taiwanese politicians sympathetic to the idea of reunification also soon felt compelled to leave the DPP.[11]

---

10. By the late 1980s almost all of those imprisoned had been released.

11. In 1989 Hsu Hsin-liang did return, sneaking ashore from a mainland fishing boat he had commissioned to bring him over. He was arrested and imprisoned for illegal entry, but was soon released in a general amnesty. He then became the DPP chairman. He had a certain amount of visibility, but his main advantage was probably that he had not been involved in the bitter factional disputes of the dangwai.

Chiang Ching-kuo's Reform Program

The regime turned more repressive after the Kaohsiung incident. It seemed to sink into a period of doldrums, of drift. The island remained connected to the world through its booming economy, but after the break with the United States, Taiwan was virtually isolated politically.[12] Taiwan was in a passive position in the face of the mainland. The regime remained nominally committed to reunification, but now had less hope than ever of achieving it on its own terms. After the recognition by the United States, the mainland took a milder line toward Taiwan. Eventually the Deng regime came to propose "one country, two systems": Taiwan could keep its own political, economic, and social systems, even its own military forces, but would accept the overall sovereignty of the PRC. Deng also urged that the CPC and KMT join in a united front for a third time, now to achieve the patriotic goal of a unified China. The new line was more credible and, therefore, more insidiously dangerous than the old Peking bluster of its determination to liberate Taiwan. Peking also made it plain, in a quieter voice, that if the KMT continued to refuse to negotiate or if Taiwan should somehow declare itself independent, there would be war. Taiwan's response was the "three nos": there would be no contact, negotiation, or compromise with the Communists. The regime seemed timid, its attitude unconstructive.

Domestically there was drift as well. After 1979 there was a series of political murders, at least one of which was conclusively linked to members of the regime. Less serious but also demoralizing was a major financial scandal involving theretofore respected KMT big shots. Rumors asserted that Chiang Ching-kuo was plotting to transfer power to his own son, the way Chiang Kai-shek had passed power to him (but Chiang Ching-kuo had at least as much experience as any other KMT politician of his generation, while his own son had no visible qualifications). It is likely that Chiang Ching-kuo was in poor health at the time, and not fully in control of the system.

He was not completely inactive. In 1983 he broke the power of one of his own major bases of support, the military-political system, transferring most of its functions to the regular armed forces. Chiang was reelected president in 1984, and the unspoken assumption was that he would probably not live out his term. His new vice president was Li Teng-hui, a U.S.–educated Taiwanese technocrat who had never seen the mainland.

By the mid-1980s Chiang was indeed giving serious thought to what would happen after he was gone. He concluded there would have to be radical change and that it had better get under way while he was still around to oversee it. Even before the DPP formed, Chiang began to hint that organized opposition would eventually be tolerated. In 1986 street demonstrations, with a

---

12. Taiwan kept diplomatic relations with 20-some highly anticommunist countries. The United States and other countries maintained informal relations with Taiwan.

few exceptions unheard of since 1947, became tediously commonplace, the regime for the most part refraining from political arrests. The still illegal DPP ran candidates in the local and national elections.[13]

In 1987 Chiang ended the state of emergency in place since 1947, removing almost all the sanctions against free speech and political activity. He also addressed mainland policy. The "three nos" remained in force at the official level, but now unofficial contacts were permitted. At first this meant that persons who had come to Taiwan in 1949 could go home to see their families on the mainland, a boon especially to the many conscript soldiers who had been brought over as young kids almost 40 years earlier. Within a few weeks, however, anyone, whether mainlander or Taiwanese, was for all practical purposes able to go to the mainland for tourism, cultural or academic activity, or business.[14]

Chiang addressed the question of Taiwan's identity: "I am Chinese," he said. "I am also Taiwanese." This was a little ambiguous, but could be taken as an embryonic legitimation of a Taiwan culturally attached to China but politically distinct from it. A few weeks before his death he also said that any change at all is possible, as long as the change comes about through the proper constitutional procedures.

Chiang Ching-kuo died in January 1988. Li Teng-hui took over as president, and after a couple of weeks and a great deal of behind-the-scenes bickering he was designated chairman of the KMT by that party's Central Committee.

Taiwan After Strongman Rule

Chiang Ching-kuo was respected and even liked, but also feared. The atmosphere after his death was a little like that of an elementary school on the last day before summer vacation. As the saying went, no one was afraid of anyone; no one obeyed anyone. Despite the smooth transition, there was uneasiness in the KMT about President Li. He was not unpopular, but those who had previously been his hierarchical superiors or equals were not happy suddenly to be his subordinates; some of the conservative mainlanders worried Li wanted to make Taiwan independent, while the DPP criticized him for

---

13. A possibly valid conservative criticism was that even if the law banning opposition was a bad one, to fail to enforce it (rather than changing it) tended to discredit all lawful authority.

14. Taiwan remained very cautious about allowing persons from the mainland onto the island, however. By the end of the 1980s, despite this, there were numerous illegal mainland workers who had come to the island hoping to participate in its prosperity.

adhering to the old KMT line. Li's personal style—scholarly and bureaucratic, lacking the politician's instinctive affability[15]—irritated his associates.

The DPP continued to gain legitimacy as an opposition party, even though it refused to grant the regime's own basic legitimacy. The problem of national identity remained unresolved. The DPP could not even accept the existence of a national community, as the flag, the anthem, and the official heroes were all replete with symbols of the KMT. Since the DPP constituted such a small proportion of the legislature—their candidates were a minority of those elected on Taiwan, and their numbers were minuscule when lumped in with the old thieves—they could not hope for much routine influence over policy. Their delegates indulged in disruption, sometimes to the point of vulgar invective and physical brawls.

The legislative elections in 1989 coincided with races for city mayors and county magistrates. Previously the DPP had concentrated on the legislature where, if their candidates won, their main job would be to carp and criticize. In 1989 the Party focused more on positions carrying real authority, the local executives, adapting, they said, the policy of the Communist soldier Lin Biao, who captured the localities to surround the capital. The DPP won top office in six counties. A number of DPP New Tide radicals organized themselves into a New Nation faction, openly proclaiming their goal of independence. Most of them won their races. Regime spokesmen had threatened to jail them for sedition, but after the election the authorities took no action. To the consternation of both the Communists and the KMT conservatives, the island's national identity had implicitly become a matter for open political contestation. The DPP won 26 percent of the popular vote for the legislature in 1989 and 38 percent of the total vote for local executives.

President Li was elected to a full term by the National Assembly in April 1990, although the process was not entirely without incident. Many of the Assembly's old thieves doubted Li's commitment to Chinese unity and hoped to use their new leverage to expand both their pay and their powers. Li Huan, the premier and a major architect of Chiang Ching-kuo's reforms, joined with the conservative soldier Hao Po-ts'un to encourage Chiang's half brother, Chiang Wei-kuo, to run for president himself against Li Teng-hui. The proposed running mate was Lin Yang-kang, a popular and able Taiwanese politician who had risen by means of local politics, in contrast to Li Teng-hui's bureaucratic career. In the end the rest of the party establishment persuaded this "Gang of Four" to back off. The election exposed some possible lines of fissure inside the KMT, fault lines not visible during the period of strongman rule.

---

15. This kind of personality was one of Chiang Ching-kuo's strong points. His personal style contrasted with the aloof, autocratic air of his father.

The National Assembly's antics provoked a large student demonstration in Taipei, in conscious imitation of the Peking demonstrations a year earlier. The Taipei protesters remained in an enclosed park and did not disrupt public order, and there was never any serious concern that they would be suppressed violently. Li Teng-hui met with the students and promised to convene a national affairs conference, representing all trends of opinion, to discuss the country's future.

Following Li's election the KMT decided that the entire National Assembly would finally be reelected, in December 1991; a year later would come the reelection of the entire legislature. Everyone had known that these changes were inevitable, but most observers had not thought them possible before the mid-1990s. These elections perhaps mark the regime's attainment of full democracy. They also ended any rationale for the Taipei regime to claim that it represented the whole of China.

The French novelist Anatole France has one of his characters remark that loyalty must be rewarded. Yes, says the other; and so must treason. After the election Li Teng-hui removed Li Huan as premier, replacing him with the more conservative Hao Po-ts'un, perhaps hoping to punish Li Huan while domesticating Hao. The DPP loathed Hao, but he was popular with the public for his strong stand against crime and social disorder.

Li Teng-hui's national affairs conference concluded without a consensus on the major constitutional questions. The biggest argument concerned the role of the presidency. KMT conservatives wanted the president to become a ceremonial figure, perhaps symbolizing the unity of China, while the Executive council, responsible to the legislature, would become the real locus of power. The alternative was to vest power unambiguously in the president. This would require the abolition of the system of indirect election: the president would have to be elected directly by the people. Conservatives feared this would forever eliminate the possibility of any organic connection with the mainland—for all practical purposes, the constitutional connection would be completely broken. They also worried, of course, that some appealing and popular proponent of independence might gain supreme power in the state. Even some who were not in fact eager for unification feared this sort of thing would provoke an attack from the mainland. A conservative fallback position would be to keep the indirect election through the National Assembly, but to have candidates for the National Assembly pledge beforehand that they would support a particular candidate for president, in that respect duplicating the American electoral college. The KMT was deeply divided on this issue (which, in addition to its wider implications, was also connected with opinions on the style and personality of Li Teng-hui) and decided to defer the decision to later years.

Li's foreign policy both before and after his election can be construed as a variation on Taiwan independence without using the name. Li moved toward a "flexible foreign policy," with a willingness to deal with foreign countries and international organizations regardless of their position on or relations with the mainland. The mainland, for its part, continued to refuse to have diplomatic relations with any country that recognized Taiwan. Taiwan's great wealth enabled it to buy (or, according to even deeper cynics, rent) diplomatic relations with some poorer Third World countries. The disenchantment with China in the West following the June 4 incident and China's loss of strategic leverage after the collapse of the Soviet Union gave scope for greater informal relations between Taiwan and the United States and other Western countries.

After his 1991 election Li tried to argue that China was "one country with two governments," keeping the door open for ultimate unification while allowing Taiwan full diplomatic freedom. This formula was unacceptable both to the Communists and to KMT conservatives. In 1991 Li boldly declared that the civil war with the CPC was over. The KMT drew up its own plan for national reunification: this could come about gradually, as the mainland abandoned single-party dictatorship and adopted a free economy. In the meantime, Taiwan would pursue economic and cultural relations with the mainland. The mainland, for its part, should cease to threaten Taiwan with military force and stop interfering with Taiwan's attempt to establish an international presence. Again, there remained the theoretical possibility of unification, but prior to unification Taiwan and the mainland should interact as any pair of friendly neighboring independent states might. The mainland, again, denounced these proposals.

The DPP campaigned in the 1991 National Assembly elections on an open Taiwan independent platform. Its candidates captured only 24 percent of the vote (winning 20 percent of the seats). The reason for the poor showing was less the unpopularity of independence in the abstract than fear that trumpeting independence would antagonize Peking. In the 1992 legislative elections the DPP called instead for "one China, one Taiwan." Compared with independence, this seemed a distinction without a difference; the formulation, however, is considered to be less provocative.[16] The electoral system had been modified that year. In addition to the district races, each party drew up a separate list of candidates, ranking these candidates any way that it pleased; candidates from these party lists were elected in proportion to the party's total vote in the electorate as a whole. For the KMT, this proportional representation list was a way to assure that at least some mainlanders won legislative seats; it may also have been intended to encourage a proliferation of opposition parties. The DPP that year won 36 percent of this party vote.

---

16. One KMT candidate also endorsed that slogan, causing the Party to withdraw his nomination.

By that time probably the more interesting politics were those within the KMT, not between the KMT and the DPP. There had developed all but open acrimony between President Li and Premier Hao, revolving certainly around personalities but also institutional interests and, ultimately, the relationship between Taiwanese and mainlanders. The fight was not simply one between reformers and hard-liners, however. One generalization about Taiwan had been that not only had incomes increased dramatically, but the distribution of income had become more equal. In the 1980s, however, incomes were becoming increasingly unequal. One reason was the soaring price of land and the opportunities this gave for speculation. By 1992 some in the KMT close to President Li hoped to be able to find candidates for office able to finance their own campaigns, and so cultivated good relations with the newly rich, the "golden cows," as they were called. Right before the election a group of KMT legislators supporting Li foiled an attempt by Premier Hao to tax land at its market value rather than at its assessed value, a move that would have cut into the wealth of the golden cows. They forced the resignation of the minister responsible for drafting the new legislation. In the meantime another group of young mainland and Taiwanese reform legislators, calling themselves the New KMT, strongly endorsed Hao's commitment to China's reunification.

The KMT won the 1992 elections, but with a disappointing performance. The big winner was the DPP. After that, the New KMT should be considered the major winner. The pro-Li legislators and the golden cow candidates did most poorly. In the wake of the elections Li was able to force Hao's resignation as premier, replacing him with someone more likely to cooperate with him, Lien Chan, who became the first Taiwanese to head the government. Lien was hardly a radical or antiestablishment figure. He had long been close to the KMT center; as it happened, he had himself been born on the mainland, and his father was one of Chiang Kai-shek's close cronies. With the appointment of another Li ally as KMT general secretary, the three top positions in the regime were held by Taiwanese. All three gentlemen were from bureaucratic rather than political backgrounds, and persons with skills in local-level electoral politics remained underrepresented in the centers of power.

The KMT represents neither a distinct social coalition nor a distinct shade of opinion. A major reason for its cohesion has no doubt been nothing other than its control of the state. The more closely that control is threatened, the more closely the DPP approaches a majority, the more likely the KMT is to fragment.[17] One possible line of division is between mainlanders

---

17. Thus, in 1992 the New KMT members bolted the KMT entirely, forming a new party, called, conveniently, the New Party. They may have been influenced by the example of the Japanese organization of the same name.

and Taiwanese in the Party.[18] Another may be between bureaucrats and politicians. Yet another may be between those supporting the wealthy and those continuing the KMT's populist traditions. Should the DPP ever gain control of the legislature[19] or the presidency, that would be a major test of Taiwan's democratization; it could well precipitate a crisis of regime and confrontation with the mainland. Should Taiwan survive the challenges apt to face it, we may see a ruling DPP that closely resembles the ruling KMT in organization, methods, style, and policy.

---

18. This cleavage attracted the most comment at the time of the 1992 elections, but it was hardly an absolute one. President Li counted many mainlanders among his supporters and also supported in office mainlanders not necessarily sympathetic to him. When Hao Po-ts'un figured out that he could no longer keep the premiership himself, he and Li Huan threw their support to Li Teng-hui's Taiwanese rival, Lin Yang-kang.

19. At this level a coalition between the DPP and a breakaway faction or coalition of factions of the KMT is perhaps more likely than an outright DPP majority. It is interesting in this respect that in the 1992 elections some DPP candidates tried to capitalize on the popularity of President Li, intimating that he was closer to them than to the rest of the KMT.

SAKHALIN (USSR)

La Perouse Strait

Nemuru Strait

KURIL
ISLAND
(USSR)

COMMONWEALTH
OF
DEPENDENT STATES

Okinawa-
Shoto
Naha

32

Sakishima-
Shoto
Ryukyu Islands

12

HOKKAIDO

Bonin Islands

Sea of Japan

Tsugaru-kaikyo

North Pacific Ocean

3

2

16

45 24

Volcano Islands

Iwo
Jima

Sado

29 8

SOUTH
KOREA

HONSHU

Oki Gunto

10
39

15
43
6
9
26
47
41
14
19
4

TSUSHIMA

Korea Strait

37
11
31
42
13
22
36
38

33
23
28
44

46
17
40
5
20

34
27
7
30
21
25
18
25

SHIKOKU

KYUSHU

East China Sea

Osumi Shoto

Philippine Sea

18

Amami O Shima

Okinawa Gunto

32

Japan

⊕ National Capital
International Boundary
Prefecture Boundary

Prefectures

1 Aichi	17 Kagawa	33 Osaka
2 Akita	18 Kagoshima	34 Saga
3 Aomori	19 Kanagawa	35 Saitama
4 Chiba	20 Kochi	36 Shiga
5 Ehime	21 Kumamoto	37 Shimane
6 Fukui	22 Kyoto	38 Shizouka
7 Fukuoka	23 Mie	39 Tochigi
8 Fukushima	24 Miyagi	40 Tokushima
9 Gifu	25 Miyazaki	41 Tokyo
10 Gumma	26 Nagano	42 Tottori
11 Hiroshima	27 Nagasaki	43 Toyama
12 Hokkaido	28 Nara	44 Wakayama
13 Hyogo	29 Niigata	45 Yamagata
14 Ibaraki	30 Oita	46 Yamaguchi
15 Ishikawa	31 Okayama	47 Yamanashi
16 Iwate	32 Okinawa	

0   miles   200

10

✦

Japan's Political and Social Structure

Japan was under American military occupation from 1945 until 1952. Since the end of the occupation it has been a democracy. Since Japan is a democracy, we know much more about its political process than we do about that of China; given the freedom of groups and individuals to try to influence policy, and given the open competition both among and within parties for public office, the process is itself no doubt much more complex than that of China.

Japan's constitutional structure is very much like that of Great Britain, and some might argue that it might be more usefully compared with other parliamentary democracies than with a communist dictatorship like China. By the same token, China might be compared with the former Soviet Union. Both kinds of comparison are interesting and useful. Chinese communism shows many of the traits of traditional Chinese culture and cannot be understood apart from that culture; the longer Chinese communism endures, the more familiarly Chinese it becomes. The same is true even more obviously for Japanese democracy. Both countries, along with Taiwan, show the modern face of the general East Asian culture.

The Japanese example refutes the sensible argument that democracy cannot be imposed from the outside. By the 1920s, of course, Japan was developing its own indigenous democratic tradition, and the political style of those years has much in common with the politics of the postwar period. But most directly, Japan's political system is a legacy of the American period. The initial assumption of the occupying power was that Japanese culture was responsible both for the Japanese aggression that led to the war and for the atrocious manner in which Japan fought that war. World peace would be served only by a democratic, disarmed Japan; democracy required a complete recasting of Japanese culture. The notion that democracy requires the eradication of traditional culture may remain part of the commonplaces of academic political science.

Japanese culture gained a little respite after 1947 or 1948. It had become clear that the wartime friendship of the United States and the Soviet Union would not last and that China, America's main ally in the Pacific, would be bogged down in civil war, a war the Communists were increasingly likely to win. Americans now wanted a strong, prosperous, friendly Japan. The Occupation took a so-called reverse course. In the first years the main task had been the democratization of Japan. This gave way to relatively greater emphasis on rebuilding Japan's economy, which to a large extent meant letting Japanese elites do things much the way they had been used to doing them. With the end of the Occupation, the American-imposed reforms least to the taste of the ruling elite or with the least resonance in ordinary Japanese life were removed. The basic liberal structure of political institutions and the political liberties necessary to make them work survived, transforming Japanese political culture as well as being transformed by it.

Constitutional Structure

In 1945 Japan was still governed according to the 1889 Meiji constitution. From the American point of view, and probably in reality as well, its main weakness was the concentration of authority in the emperor. Some Americans thought this made the emperor a kind of absolute fascist dictator. In fact, the emperor was a constitutional monarch, unable to exercise direct power. But the constitution left vague just who should exercise real power.

Japan came under the control of U.S. General Douglas MacArthur, the Supreme Commander, Allied Pacific (SCAP—the acronym also refers to the institutions of the Occupation as well as to MacArthur personally), who ruled Japan as a kind of foreign shogun under loose, almost nominal supervision from Washington.[1] From the beginning MacArthur made the political

---

1. In principle, the Occupation was international, by all the powers allied against Japan. MacArthur did not permit non-American forces to set up on the islands, however, so possibly preventing a division of Japan comparable to the division of Germany.

decision to protect the emperor, both because he believed that under the unspoken terms of the surrender he was honor-bound to do so and for the sake of facilitating public order. He did have the emperor publicly renounce his divinity, a move perhaps more meaningful for the Americans than for most Japanese. The loss of the war and the Occupation's humanization of the emperor, however, certainly helped demystify the institution. Although the emperor took personal responsibility for everything Japan had done during and before the war, MacArthur refused to try him as a war criminal, now taking the line that not only was the emperor powerless but that he had also been without authority or influence. Twenty-five "major war criminals" were convicted after a trial replete with procedural and moral irregularities, and seven of these were hanged. Numberless minor war criminals were imprisoned, and SCAP purged bureaucrats and businessmen who had been too enthusiastic in the support of their country's policies.[2] Especially in the early days the United States sought help and cooperation from socialists and even communists, as these had not only been excluded from power in the old days but actively persecuted. SCAP could also rely on numerous conservative bureaucrats and politicians who had been out of sympathy and out of favor with the old regime.

MacArthur had the Diet draft a new constitution to replace that of 1889. The drafting committee produced several versions, all of which the Americans deemed unacceptable because they gave the emperor too great a role. Finally, MacArthur had his own staff write out a document that was then sent to the Diet for confirmation. Some say the new constitution, adopted in 1947, reads as if badly translated from the English. In order to preserve the legalities, in form the new constitution is an extended amendment to the Meiji constitution.

The Meiji constitution was a gift from the emperor to his people, bestowed out of his infinite grace. The emperor retained supreme sovereign authority. The MacArthur constitution, however, is issued in the name of "We, the Japanese people." The emperor is the "symbol of the state," and seems to lack all residual powers. The Queen of England in very unusual conditions may still have a role in the selection of a prime minister or in deciding when to dismiss Parliament. This would not only be unlikely in Japan but impossible. In other ways, however, the emperor acts as a head of state, not merely a symbol. For example, he receives the credentials of foreign ambassadors.

The constitution mandates a separation of church and state, meaning there is no more official support for Shinto. As explained in Chapter 3, this makes for problems. The funeral of an old emperor must involve Shinto ritual, as must the enthronement of a new one. In practice, the government

---

2. The purge was undone and the war criminals released very soon after the end of the Occupation.

uses various subterfuges, distinguishing arbitrarily between public and private aspects of ceremonies and relegating the religious aspects to the private. There are also difficulties in public officials' honoring the war dead, as the souls of the dead are enshrined in a Shinto temple and the entire way of conceiving them resonates with the old state Shinto. Attitudes toward the emperor and toward official expressions of Shinto mark a major cleavage in Japanese society and politics, between a conservative, nationalistic mentality and a liberal, secular one.

The constitution provides the full range of civil and political liberties (freedom of speech and assembly and the like; academic freedom is mentioned separately among the freedoms) along with various welfare provisions ("minimum standards of wholesome and cultural living"; "the right and obligation to work"). In one line of interpretation, the constitution embodies both the U.S. Bill of Rights and the New Deal (a set of policies General MacArthur did not particularly admire in their native habitat). In fact, Japan has not become much of a welfare state, and its relatively low spending on both defense and social programs is probably one reason for its economic success. The welfare functions continued to be taken care of by families and, increasingly, by employers; with an aging population—a low birthrate and a low death rate—there may be pressures for the state to take a greater role. The Japanese constitution, unlike the American, mandates equality between men and women, a provision that has done little to prevent overt discrimination against women in social, professional, and economic life.

The most noted aspect of the 1947 constitution is its Article 9, the renunciation of war. Japan renounces war as a "sovereign right of the state." To give this stance meaning, Japan prohibits itself from maintaining land, sea, or air forces. General MacArthur was in an idealistic phase in 1947. He did not think there would be eternal peace, and, indeed, part of the motive for American support for this clause was to make sure Japan could not repeat its earlier behavior. Also, Japan and Germany had been defeated by the United Nations (as the alliance had come to be called), and after the war the United Nations became institutionalized in the organization now called by that name. It was hoped that thereafter nations would increasingly entrust their security to the United Nations, counting on collective action by the world community to defend them from aggression. Japan was to be a pioneer toward this vision. Both the socialists and MacArthur were abetted, and possibly even manipulated, by conservative politicians who wanted to spare their country high military budgets and themselves challenges to their control of the state by a revived soldiery.

By the end of the 1940s MacArthur had changed his mind about the utility of the United Nations, and part of the reverse course was an attempt to push a reluctant Japan toward rearmament. The eventual solution was to decide that while Japan still renounced war, any state has an inherent right to self-defense. Instead of armed forces, Japan should have Self-Defense Forces (SDF): land, sea, and air self-defense forces, to be exact. This tough, highly professional military has been kept at the political margin and does not enjoy much public visibility (in the postwar period the samurai mystique has been carried more by the riot police than by the military). Its head does not have cabinet status (there is no Ministry of Defense), but answers directly to the prime minister. Its doctrine and to a large extent its capabilities are restricted to a purely defensive role—maybe unrealistically so, since policy can be interpreted to mean that the enemy must actually step on the beach before the Japanese soldiers may shoot at him. In practice, to the extent that Japan has needed an armed defense at all, it has been provided through a controversial defensive alliance with the United States, interpreted by the left wing as an instrument of U.S. imperialism, which in turn, the left says, is heir to the Japanese imperialism of the 1930s. In 1977 a policy decision restricted defense spending to 1 percent of GNP (in the 1950s it was considerably higher), although under U.S. pressure and the influence of a changing world this was symbolically breached in the late 1980s. Given the size of Japan's GNP, however, this makes the SDF one of the world's largest armies: its budget is larger than that of any other U.S. ally.

Despite the American sponsorship of the constitution, the Japanese political system remains much more similar in form to the British. There are a few American touches. The Japanese Supreme Court is explicitly given the power to determine the constitutionality of laws—a power the U.S. Supreme Court at a very early period found implicit in the U.S. Constitution, and although not officially mentioned in that doctrine has for all practical purposes become its heart. But the Japanese court has consistently refused to declare laws unconstitutional—which is what we would expect from the Japanese tradition and probably also from a parliamentary regime, where powers are fused rather than separated.

The legislature, still called the Diet in English, is the "highest organ of the state." It consists of two houses: the upper house, the House of Councillors (which replaced the Meiji House of Peers) and the lower house, the House of Representatives. The lower house is the more important. Both houses are elected by the people. Before the war suffrage was limited to males 25 and over. In the new order, the voting age was reduced to 20 and women were enfranchised.

Members of the House of Councillors serve a six-year term, with half the house up for election every three years. The major power of the upper house is to delay or block legislation. If a bill passed by the lower house is not passed as well by the upper house in 60 days, it cannot become law unless it is passed again by the lower house, this time by two-thirds of the members present. The House of Councillors cannot block a budget bill, however: such bills take effect 30 days after passage by the lower house, whether the upper house approves or not.

Both houses designate the Prime Minister, although, if they cannot agree, the decision of the lower house prevails. The prime minister in his turn appoints the ministers of state to form the Cabinet. The cabinet consists of the prime minister and the political heads of the government agencies staffed by the career civil service. According to the constitution, at least half of the ministers must be members of the Diet. In practice, they almost always are all members of the lower house. If the House of Representatives should vote it has no confidence in the government (the term in a parliamentary system referring to the prime minister and cabinet), the government must resign. Alternatively, the prime minister may dissolve the lower house and call for new elections, putting the decision in the hands of the people. Unless it is dissolved earlier by the prime minister, the entire House of Representatives is up for election at least once every four years.

The Structure of Society

The constitutional system is a liberal democratic one, operating on the basis of majority rule. The Japanese tradition does not fully legitimate this, seeing something arbitrary in allowing a majority to be able simply to impose its will on everyone else. Both outside observers and Japanese commentators stress the role of consensus in Japanese business, political, and private organizations. This implies that if there is disagreement, decisions are postponed until the problem is fully talked out, with the decision somehow emerging from all the talk.

The culture certainly does value consensus, but does not produce consensus automatically. Certain segments of society, perhaps those most apt to dislike the existing distribution of power, are largely excluded from consultation. The search for consensus is not merely letting everyone having a say. It is also a way to discourage open conflict, to intimidate or shame those who might not agree with elite opinion, and so reinforce conformity to the existing order (while allowing considerable flexibility at the margins). Consensus turns out to be compatible with pervasive factionalism and factional conflict.

We may examine culture as it operates through two rather abstract "structures." One, at the "macro" level, is "Japan, Inc.," the interrelationship between bureaucracy, business, and (at least until 1993) the ruling party, the Liberal Democratic Party (LDP). The other, on the "micro" level, is the particular Japanese type of patron–client relationship, the *oyabun–kobun* pattern.

In gross terms, postwar Japan was shaped by a kind of "establishment" consisting of big business, the professional civil service or bureaucracy, and the LDP. This structure should be familiar from the earlier discussion of Japanese society and politics in the 1920s. A difference is that after 1955 and until 1993 there was only one conservative party rather than two—the LDP is, in effect, a merger of the two prewar parties. Additional significant differences include the elimination of the military as an institutional rival to this triangular structure, and the elimination of the imperial institution as a possible alternative focus of legitimacy in opposition to the Diet. Japan is both a formal democracy and a genuine one; the Japan, Inc. structure, however, may allow the elite to act pretty much as it wishes, without worrying about effective opposition from public opinion.

The conventional opinion has been that the bureaucracy dominated the coalition. A bureaucratic career has higher prestige than one in business, and the civil service on the whole attracts the cream of college graduates, with business getting those left over. The dominance of the state over business was established in Meiji times, and its origins can even be sought in the relationship between samurai and merchants in the Tokugawa era. This relationship was strengthened after the "China incident," when the economy was geared to the conduct of total war. The wartime structures and institutions were retained by the Occupation and by the new Japanese governments, directed now toward rebuilding an economy destroyed by war. The bureaucracy (here MITI, the Ministry of International Trade and Industry, the descendant of the wartime Ministry of Munitions, is the most famous) sets economic policy by "administrative guidance" (suggestions rather than direct orders to businesses, but suggestions that businesses are well advised to take very, very seriously), reinforced by controls over access to credit, to licenses, and the like. The LDP controlled the Diet, so allowing that body to enact into law policies deemed appropriate for business. Business financed the LDP.

As far as the Japan, Inc. concept is concerned, business refers to big business. This is not the entire Japanese economy: there are still very many small businesses, small shops and firms, many of them family-run. These small businesses, however, in some cases have direct or indirect connections with the major business combinations. The most important business organization is the Federation of Economic Organizations. Others include the Japan Federation of Employers' Organizations, the Japan Chamber of Commerce and Industry (the oldest, which dates from Meiji times), and the Japan Committee for Economic Development. All of them speak basically for the larger firms, and all have about the same membership. The more politically important connections are probably those between individual firms and individual departments or ministries, and between individual businesspeople and individual bureaucrats.

The older view of the third corner of this triangle, the LDP, was that it carried out the will of bureaucracy and business. The Japan, Inc. system seemed to depend, however, on the LDP keeping control of the Diet. This means that both bureaucracy and business had to take at least such notice of public opinion as to avoid costing the LDP too many votes. In the 1970s large numbers of voters became concerned over pollution, and the LDP lost several local elections to parties promising to do something about it. The LDP and the bureaucracy moved swiftly to impose strong clean air and water standards on big business (and, encouraged Japanese capitalists to set up their fouler factories abroad, in the poorer countries of Asia and the rest of the world). The need to keep the LDP in power also meant the establishment lived with economic inefficiency (pushing the costs of this inefficiency off onto the consumer). Thus, much of the LDP's vote has come from the countryside, so the government supported the price of rice and protected it from foreign competition, keeping alive family farms that would otherwise go bankrupt and making everyone pay severalfold the world price for rice. Political necessities also produce dilemmas. Segments of the bureaucracy and business would like to liberalize policy on imports, for example, to appease the United States and forestall American moves to close its markets to Japan, and also to help Japan's own multinational firms. Liberalization, however, goes against the interests of other businesses and the government agencies shepherding them; it would cost the LDP votes without producing any in compensation.

The bureaucracy probably remains the main initiator and formulator of policy, or at least of routine policy. Especially since the 1980s business has become less satisfied with its subordinate status, and in 1993, sensing the LDP's electoral weakness, began financing that party's conservative rivals as well. The role of political parties and the Diet had been growing since the 1970s relative to that of the bureaucracy. As we shall see in more detail in Chapter 11, the political leadership—who is prime minister and what constraints the prime minister has to face—has always had something to do with Japan's policy orientation. In 1993 the LDP lost its control of government, although it remained the single largest party in the Diet. The new governing coalition, however, was led by politicians who had recently defected from the LDP and who, while purporting to despise the LDP's corruption and timidity, had few if any differences in substantive policy opinion with the bulk of their former party. The conservative breakaway parties together with the LDP constituted a majority of the Diet, even though they were, at least temporarily, rivals for power. This probably implies that the conservative establishment consensus continued to dominate the political institutions, if not public opinion generally. If Japan is entering into a period of unstable coalition governments, even more decisions may go by default to the professional civil service, and the Japan, Inc. pattern may be reinforced.

Consensus functions to keep things more or less as they are. The style discourages bold innovation or radical changes of direction. Japan, Inc. and its component parts share the overall vision of how things should be and have a common interest in maintaining the consensus style of decision making. As long as the basic structures are not threatened, however, relations within the establishment involve constant competition. Ministries compete over policy and resources, and bureaus, departments, and factions within ministries also compete. Firms and business combines compete with each other. In the visible spectrum of Japanese politics, factional politics within the LDP was even more important than competition between the LDP and the opposition—and led eventually to the split in the party that cost it its control of the government.

Japanese factionalism is epitomized by the oyabun–kobun pattern, explained in Chapter 4. The term means "parent–child," but the real meaning is more patron–client, boss–follower, big shot–little shot. The term is colloquial, taken, I think, from the work gangs of longshoremen during the

Occupation, and it also seems to have some underworld connotations. It refers to a tie between a superior and several inferiors, with the link between the boss and followers being the principle of group formation. It is a form of what the Chinese call *guanxi*, "connections." In China, however, guanxi can form between equals as well as between superiors and inferiors, and a group can share a common guanxi. In the oyabun–kobun relationship the only connection between equals is their link to a common boss. It therefore reinforces the Japanese cultural sense of hierarchy and makes persons of equal or near-equal status into rivals. This type of formation means groups will be cohesive against the outside but contentious within. The oyabun–kobun model patterns working relations outside the family.[3]

This group structure helps explain the generally high morale of Japanese workers, their willingness to identify with the company and its goals. The group structure is reinforced by paternalistic practices by the older big companies—lifetime employment and generous fringe benefits. Such practices are not "traditional" in the narrow sense, but date from the postwar period. They are rooted, however, in general Japanese cultural patterns. Paradoxically, the ingrained sense of hierarchy allows a relatively democratic style of management. The boss may defer to subordinates in making decisions and eschew putting on airs without fear that subordinates will become overly familiar or affront his dignity. The function of the boss, in fact, is not so much to be a strong decision-maker as to serve as a benevolent, supportive father figure, stroking the fragile egos of the group members, while decisions emerge from the members' consultations and rivalries. The Japanese style demands loyalty to the group and organization, a faith that you will prosper as the group or organization prospers. The other side of this loyalty is downward. The Chairman of General Motors is said to have bragged that during the Great Depression, no matter how many workers were laid off, GM never missed a dividend payment. A Japanese executive would be ashamed to make a similar admission: it is assumed that stock owners will sacrifice their dividends long before any workers will be expected to sacrifice their jobs.

Morale is upheld by a constant "bonding" within the work group. Most people know the Japanese work long hours. Japanese may not always work particularly hard, however, and spend much on-the-job time chatting, reading newspapers, drinking tea, daydreaming. But intense socializing within the group keeps its cohesion and effectiveness, allowing it to accomplish its tasks. The pattern may be more common among white-collar workers (*sarariman*—that is, salary men) than among those on the factory floor. Quitting

---

3. These generalizations probably apply only to male society, which is often arbitrarily taken as normative for the entire culture. As it happens, one of the best descriptions of the workings of oyabun–kobun is by a woman. Chie Nakane, *Japanese Society* (University of California Press, 1971).

time may be, say, five o'clock, but no one will leave before the supervisor; if the supervisor stays, everyone else will loiter around. When the supervisor is ready to leave, around 6:30, say, he may suggest that they all go out for a bite to eat. This is likely to be followed by a round of the drinking places, accompanied, if spirits really soar, by obnoxious karaoke singing. Toward the end of the evening the poor salaryman may treat a sympathetic bar hostess to a self-pitying discourse on the magnitude of his merits and the blindness of an indifferent world.[4] Eventually the salaryman will stagger off to the train station for the long trip to the suburbs (the only place he and his family have been able to find decent affordable housing) and a bike ride to his home, arriving after midnight, to be up at dawn to begin the whole thing again. The cohesion of the work unit may be bought at the price of the quality of family relations, a cost most Chinese or American women—and, possibly, increasing numbers of Japanese women—might not willingly tolerate.

Big business organization is itself a variation on the oyabun–kobun pattern. Before the war the big Japanese companies were colloquially called *zaibatsu*, "finance cliques." These were not monopolies controlling production of one type of goods, such as cars; rather, they were combinations of complementary industries, linked by overlapping boards of directors. The Occupation tried to dismantle the zaibatsu, but they were quick to form again after the Occupation was over. Before the war they were controlled by rich families; after the war the relationship to particular families became looser and ownership more bureaucratized, with the term *zaibatsu* giving way to *keiretsu* (roughly, "economic linkages"). A keiretsu might include an automobile firm, electronics firms, machine-tool manufacturers, insurance companies, trading companies, and so on. The central firm is likely to be a bank. The keiretsu are sometimes compared to the box lunches you can buy at Japanese railway stations. Each polystyrene or metal lunch box has a generous portion of rice along with, say, a boiled egg, some pickles, and a piece of chicken or fish. Each box lunch contains a good, balanced meal, and each is exactly like every other. The keiretsu form self-contained business systems, the various parts buying from and selling to each other.

The keiretsu system helps maintain lifetime employment. If one sector of the economy is in trouble, workers can be transferred from the affected firms into other firms within the group where things are better. It gives the Japanese economy a certain flexibility. Around 1970, Japan and the United States bickered over textile imports, the Japanese goods threatening the American industry. Some years later, Japanese textiles were being undersold on the world market by goods from Taiwan, Hong Kong, Korea, and mainland China. MITI in effect decided that the Japanese textile industry would

---

4. As Chie Nakane disdainfully notes, the conversation can become incredibly stupid.

be allowed to shrink. The capital could be exported, while the labor could be transferred to other firms inside the relevant keiretsu.

The keiretsu deal with firms within the group as if they were family, while the keiretsu as a whole compete vigorously against each other. A car manufacturer will borrow from banks within the group and buy components from electronics firms within the group, without worrying about competitive bidding. There are similar relations with smaller firms satellite to the larger combinations. The group membership is itself usually reinforced by personal connections, ties of trust and a sense of mutual obligation, among managers of the various firms within the group. This helps explain why foreign businesses often find it difficult to break into the Japanese market, quite apart from any obstructions set up by the government.

Japan, Inc.'s elite is recruited through the educational system (although among conservative politicians family ties may be becoming increasingly important). Here the wealthier retain some advantages: education is free and compulsory and of high quality, but (it is usually thought) must be supplemented by outside study in expensive cram schools if children are to do well in the examinations determining their fate at each level of education. Like much else in Japanese society, schools are ranked hierarchically. Some universities are elite, and some are not; the same is true for high schools in a locality, junior high schools, and even elementary schools and preschools. Good performance on the exams is required to get into the better schools, and getting into the better schools is (it is thought) necessary to a satisfying career in the civil service or big business. The caricature would have the child's life as an endless "examination hell," with homework lasting late into the night, no time for play, and frustrations released in bullying fellow students who are in any way weak or different. The university is the aim of all this activity, and once you are admitted there is little chance of flunking out; university life, therefore, tends to be relatively relaxed.

The bureaucracy and the big companies recruit from the colleges by means of their own examinations, although graduates of the more prestigious schools (particularly Tokyo University and Waseda University) still seem to have an edge. Within the ministry or firm the recruits are treated in a way designed to counteract the inherent tendencies toward rivalry among equals. Everyone in the incoming cohort will be treated in exactly the same way, regardless of differences in individual ability or achievement, over a long period, perhaps 10 years. Everyone will be given experience in a wide range of jobs. After about 20 years on the job, one member of the cohort will be given a major promotion. Since it would not do to keep his peers around to work under him, in the private sector those not selected may be transferred to other (generally less prestigious) firms within the keiretsu. In the bureaucracy the remainder face retirement in their early 40s. They may look forward, however, to lucrative second careers in the private sector, in the firms they had previously been in charge of regulating, a move known as the descent from heaven. This helps keep the government–business relationship on a personal as well as a pragmatic level.

The organization of Japanese business and business life—emphasis on group over individual achievement, guaranteed employment, and the like—looks much like the kind of thing a Western liberal economist would predict would lead to economic stagnation: there is little incentive either for individual initiative or for innovation. Similar practices in China (the iron rice bowl) are condemned by reformers precisely because they do discourage economic growth. The Japanese work group, for its part, has a strong superficial resemblance to the "work unit" in communist China.

These similarities highlight an important difference between Chinese and Japanese culture. Chinese are also group oriented; but the groups are not the same type, and the structures are different. Chinese tend to have many kinds of social connections, some hierarchical, some among equals. The connections are rarely "dyadic," but every member of the group is considered to have a direct relationship with every other member. The major connection a person has remains the family. For Japanese working males, however, the hierarchical work group becomes the most important set of relations his life—with the possibly pernicious effects on family life indicated earlier. The work group possibly provides psychological satisfaction, but whether it does or not, it is the context for personal advancement. The CPC, in its quest for social control, tried to impose an organizational system possibly appropriate to Japan. The system was felt by the participants as stultifying and repressive, and it did in fact contribute to economic stagnation.

Japan, Inc. is not all of Japanese society. Some of society is virtually excluded from it. Other social categories play a subordinate role. Thus, small business, taken as a whole, is as important for the economy as big business, and in recent years probably considerably more dynamic. Small businesses may have informal ties with the larger firms. Certain types of small business are established and run by women, who largely remain excluded from big business. Owners of small businesses have been one of the traditional sources of LDP votes, and a generalized middle class may be becoming increasingly important there as well, and probably, over the long run, increasingly demanding that politicians meet certain standards in terms of personal and political honesty.

Japanese agriculture enjoys a political influence disproportionate to its role in the economy and the number of farmers. The Occupation put in a land reform similar to the one later adopted on Taiwan, and rural Japan became a land of small family farms. Farming is heavily subsidized by the government, and much of the rural way of life would collapse without the subsidies or with the need to compete with world agriculture in general through an opening of the Japanese economy. Few families depend solely on farming for a living, and for many it is becoming either a part-time occupation, performed after work, or something left to the women and children as a way of supplementing the main income from work in the local factory. Rural electoral districts traditionally contained far fewer persons than urban ones, so that a farmer's vote "counted" severalfold more than an urbanite's. Malapportionment reflected the LDP's desire to assure its permanent hold on power (although some of it may also be a consequence of a declining rural population). Since the 1980s the LDP had become somewhat less rural than before. Also, farmers became more willing to vote against the LDP when they saw it going against their economic interests, as, for example, when the government yielded to U.S. pressures for liberalizing imports.

Another prop of Japan, Inc. is, probably, the underworld. Japanese organized crime, the *Yakusa*, sorts itself into rather open gangs that even publish their own house magazines. The gangs maintained moderately cordial relations with the police, at least until the 1990s, when the gangs' excessive greed and increasing propensity for violence against ordinary citizens as well as each other generated a public reaction against them. The Yakusa likes to think of itself as the embodiment of Japan's traditional virtues of loyalty, self-sacrifice, and courage, a mainstay of the traditional social order. It became harder to project this image to the general public in the booming 1980s, when there was simply too much easy money to be made. Yakusa members dress like the movie versions of American gangsters of the 1930s. They cover their bodies with elaborate tattoos. They are generally missing several finger joints, chopped off in shows of loyal contrition for some failure that let the boss down.

The Yakusa has intimate ties with nationalistic right-wing groups, the genealogy of some of those ties reaching back to the 1920s or earlier. Through these groups it also has links with various conservative politicians. In some areas it also has links with Socialist politicians, often through the owners of pachinko parlors (pachinko is a kind of pinball game many young Japanese workers become addicted to). It also has connections with big business. I indicated earlier that Japanese companies often do not have to worry about what the shareholders think. One way of achieving this result is to have the Yakusa send some burly thugs to a shareholders' meeting to scowl at anyone who might be inclined to raise embarrassing questions. If a company prefers not to avail itself of this service, the Yakusa might take it on itself to disrupt the meeting. The role of organized crime in Japanese political economy should not be sensationalized, but neither should it be ignored. It is part of what Chalmers Johnson calls the "structural corruption" of Japanese politics.[5]

The focus on consensus in tracing the relations among the Japanese establishment should not make us forget that certain segments of society are

---

5. Chalmers Johnson, "Tanaka Kakuei, Structural Corruption, and the Advent of Machine Politics in Japan," *Journal of Japanese Studies*, 12 (1986), pp. 1–28.

excluded from consultation. The more important include labor, women, and consumers.

Despite the danger of oversimplification, the term *Japan, Inc.* can be justified as pointing to a significant aspect of Japan's social and political system. Like most of the contemporary European states and, to a lesser extent, the United States, Japan functions along *corporatist* lines.[6] That is, public policy is decided through consultation among the bureaucracy and representatives of various social interests, with these interest groups sometimes even delegated the power to make policy within their specific areas. In Europe, one of those interests is organized labor. In Japan, organized labor was excluded.

Prior to the war, labor unions were weak and at best of questionable legality, under constant police harassment. The Occupation encouraged the growth of organized labor, considering it a force for democracy. The Japanese labor movement has tended, like much else in Japanese society, toward factionalism. In the late 1980s the unions came together to form a new general federation, *Rengo*. Organized labor is the main base of support for the Japan Social Democratic Party (JSDP) and of the more moderate Democratic Socialist Party (DSP). Rengo also puts up candidates of its own in upper house elections, and there is even talk of its supporting the conservative New Party.

The Japanese labor movement has been more militant in voicing political opinions than in furthering the material interests of workers. The oyabun–kobun pattern and the paternalistic practices of big business encourage workers to identify with the company and discourage "class" solidarity. In the early days after the Occupation, labor leaders, as patriotic as anyone else, accepted the need to rebuild the economy and the consequent long hours and low pay. At the same time, they engaged in anticapitalist political agitation. In recent decades workers (along with everyone else) have become more impatient with a system that keeps living standards so low relative to the country's strength. The problems are more related to the structure of society, however, than to pay, working conditions, and hours, which are now in fact not that bad. There may not be very many who think the labor movement holds the answers.

The government, unlike big business, is not very paternalistic, and the more militant unions are those of government employees, such as railway workers. The teachers union fights a running battle with the Ministry of Education, one of the heirs to the prewar thought control system and often refuge to the LDP's more retrogressive nationalists. The quarrels turn on symbolic and political issues: should kids sing the national anthem and salute the flag? how much detail should history texts devote to Japan's wartime

---

6. A better term might be "neo-corporatist," to distinguish the democratic variety from the corporatism in traditional Catholic thought and practice and the expropriation of the term by the Fascists.

atrocities? how much justification can be found for Japan's actions prior to the war?

The constitution guarantees women equal rights, and women enjoy the full range of political and civil liberties. Things, as always, are changing, but social expectations remain fairly traditional. It is common for married women to remain housewives, at least until the children are well into their school years. Women typically work for a few years after graduation from high school or college but leave work once they marry (perhaps to go back to work in later years). In family-owned stores (still the norm in Japan) women participate fully, and much of the vibrant small-business sector is apparently female owned and operated. In larger firms, women by and large remain temporary workers, with those in white-collar jobs serving as "flower vases," there to look pretty and make themselves useful.

The female temporary work force provides something that Karl Marx would call a reserve army of labor, whose existence helps maintain the employment of the regular work force. As temporary workers they are not part of the lifetime employment system. The assumption or rationalization is that they are working either to help out their parents or to save up for their wedding. If they lose their job, their dad will still feed them: loss of work will certainly be a misfortune, but hardly a disaster.

Women are not necessarily politically inactive, and they seem to provide the brains and muscle of the "residents" or "citizens" movements that grow up in the wake of various social problems. Women are highly influential in the grass-roots politics of the Komeito, or Clean Government Party. At least once women seem to have been mobilized politically along lines of sex. In 1989 Prime Minister Takeshita Noboru had become implicated in a financial scandal after having pushed through an unpopular consumption tax, unpopular among women to begin with since they control the spending of virtually all the family's money. It turned out that his successor, Uno Sosuke, had some years earlier enjoyed a liaison with what the newspapers called a "geisha." At the same time, the Socialist leader was a well-spoken female professor, Doi Takako, the first woman to head a major political party in Japan. The combination—an overwhelming sense of the general shabbiness of the LDP system and the presence of a possible attractive alternative to it— brought on a women's rebellion, and that year the LDP for the first time lost control of the House of Councillors. This Madonna effect,[7] as it was called, seems to have dissipated rapidly, because a few months later the LDP did quite well in the more important House of Representatives elections, without showing evidence of a newfound consciousness of higher moral standards, either sexual or financial.

---

7. The reference is to the Italian word for *lady*, not to the Flint, Michigan singer.

Japan, clearly, is no feminist paradise. Even so, it may show the issue itself has complexities. Great numbers of Japanese women work, but are mostly relegated to particular "women's" roles. Foreigners are sometimes tempted to speculate about the waste in human resources resulting from this exclusion. On the other hand, the fact that children continue to be raised by their mothers (however much, in principle, the fathers should also participate) does not seem to hurt Japan relative to other advanced industrial democracies. The other side of women's seeming subordination is their domination of the household, both morally and in terms of control over spending. Japanese women would certainly prefer to be treated with more dignity than they often are, but it is not obvious that large numbers of them crave to join the corporate rat race. Nor do they necessarily want to play the political game under the existing rules.

Consumer interests as a whole are not routinely represented in the Japanese system, although they were acted on when problems accumulated sufficiently to cut into the LDP vote. Consumer activism is one political arena where women are quite active. Particularly in the 1970s there developed large-scale (although mostly local in scope) citizens' movements and residents' movements directed against environmental degradation. These would often be organized by housewives, although the activists might ask a respectable retired gentleman in the neighborhood to serve as figurehead, so that the group would be taken more seriously by the authorities. These movements were sometimes able to ally themselves with the opposition parties to elect Socialists or Communists to local office. The movements were not able to insert themselves permanently into the parties, however, and in Japan protest politics, now as in the 1920s, remains something largely apart from the routine business of parties and elections. This is one more element insulating the normal political process from popular pressure.

Some segments of Japanese society are no doubt thoroughly alienated from the system, although this seems less prominent than before. Student protest used to be a regular feature of Japanese political life. The cliché was that freshmen and sophomores, making full use their newfound leisure, would give themselves over to street demonstrations and the other excitements of student activism. Juniors and seniors, however, cut their hair and put on a sober demeanor, making themselves presentable to potential bureaucratic or corporate employers. Student protest took on a ritualized character, almost a choreography of student advances and riot police counteradvances, each side holding itself to tacit limitations on the level of violence. At the extreme, there was a rather vicious new left movement in Japan in the 1960s and 1970s, similar in style if not ideology to the radical rightists of the 1930s. The most famous such group, the Japan Red Army, tore itself apart in the early 1970s in a sadistic orgy of suspicion and infighting. The longest-lasting radical protest is that against the Narita airport. Student radicals joined with local farmers in the 1960s to resist the confiscation of land for a new, larger airport for the Tokyo region. Some of the farmers were war veterans and instructed the students in the art of siege warfare. The protests continued long after the airport had been built, into the 1990s.[8] The heavy security adds to much else to make Narita one of the world's most unpleasant airports. Leftist radicalism fell from fashion during the 1970s. From time to time, however, extremist groups will lob homemade rockets toward the imperial palace and other public places on the occasion of visits by foreign dignitaries or actions by the emperor they do not approve of.

The social system is maintained as a structure: to a degree, Japanese act as they do because they respond to the social environment. Workers are loyal to the company because the company shapes their lives. The system also depends on attitudes. Many of these attitudes would be appropriate for any country: a sense of duty to others, a willingness to defer gratification for the sake of the general good or the long-term good of your family, respect for education and for older people, an active search for harmony. There is also a certain intolerance for differences and tremendous pressure to conform. However much harmony may be valued, it is not always evident in the individual soul.

Attitudes and structure mutually shape each other, and it is often arbitrary to say which is more important. It is often said that the postwar system was the product of the generation of the Taisho regency, of persons born in the early 1920s. This generation came to maturity during the world depression, fought and lost history's bloodiest war, and rebuilt their country from scratch. Some of the temperament and drive of Japan, Inc. must reflect this historical experience.

The grandchildren of the wartime generation have been called the *shinjinrui*, the "new human race." Their ideas and ideals are supposedly alien to the minds of their elders. They have grown up in affluence and have never known a day of deprivation in their lives; they are grasshoppers living for the pleasures of the moment. To the extent that this characterization is accurate, however, it is not obvious what it really means.[9] The phenomenon may be more a matter of age than of generation: in a few years the shinjinrui may become more like their elders, and the notion of the degeneracy of the younger generation has been a staple of Japanese social comment since the Meiji era. The parents of the shinjinrui used to be accused of "my-home-ism," a yearning for the private joys of family life and respite from the excessive demands of

---

8. For a case study, see David E. Apter and Nagayo Sawa, *Against the State: Politics and Social Protest in Japan* (Harvard University Press, 1984).

9. This is how Chairman Mao in China thought of the younger generation of the 1960s, at the beginning of the Cultural Revolution, and it is how the older Chinese generations regard the younger since the 1980s. The phenomenon is hardly unknown in the West as well. This sort of thing may be a universal constant.

work—things they probably did yearn for, but not always to great effect. The parents of the wartime generation were the mobos and mogas of the 1920s. In short, it is at least possible that the *structure* of Japanese society could endure even with widespread attitudes incompatible with it.

Nature may challenge the system more effectively than attitudes. Japan has a low birthrate and the world's longest average life span. The aged proportion of the population will continue to grow. This alone will put pressures on some of Japan's characteristic strengths, such as low levels of welfare spending and lifetime employment.[10]

The Conservative Tendency

There is a certain paradox in Japanese voting behavior. The main determinant of the vote, it seems, is party identification, but the electoral system, at least prior to 1994, encouraged voting for specific persons rather than a given party, and for many voters there seemed to be little evidence of a link between the vote and any opinion on programs or policy. There is probably a fuzzy division along traditional-modern lines within the Japanese electorate, which is reflected in support for conservative and "progressive" parties. On the progressive side, voters may well identify with certain parties, thinking of themselves as Socialists, or Communists, or Clean Government people. Prior to 1993, however, the LDP monopolized the conservative end of the spectrum. A vote for the LDP, then, meant generalized support for the way things were, either from conviction or from a sense that the alternatives were even worse. In 1993 splits within the LDP cost that party its control of the government, and the new splinter parties joined with the progressive parties to form the successor government. The new parties, however, consist of people who used to belong to the LDP, and despite their early political alliance should probably be considered to belong to the same general tendency as the LDP. They may think of themselves as more vigorous, principled, or honest than the average Liberal Democratic politician, but they share roughly the same opinions and vision of the world.

The Liberal Democratic Party

According to the common joke, the LDP is neither liberal, democratic, nor a party. To the extent that the LDP has an ideology or set of principles beyond the perpetuation of its rule, it is conservative. It can be argued as well that it does not particularly represent the interests of the people, nor does it particularly care to. Rather than a cohesive, well-articulated political party,

---

10. Even as it stands, the lifetime employment system requires relatively early retirement.

LDP Factions Following the 1990 Elections

Faction Leader	Number of Followers
Takeshita*	103
Nakaido	5
Miyazawa	82
Abe[†]	86
Watanabe[‡]	82
Komoto	35
Unaffiliated[§]	19

*In 1992 the Takeshita faction split, with about 46 members forming a new faction (and, some months later, a new party) under Ozawa Ichiro and Hata Tsutomo. Prior to 1986 the Takeshita and Nakaido groups had been part of the Tanaka faction.

[†]Mr. Abe died in 1991 with no obvious successor to leadership, and his faction was in disarray.

[‡]Watanabe was the nominal leader of a faction whose backstage boss was Nakasone; Watanabe fell ill in 1993, and the future of the faction was unclear.

[§]Some of the unaffiliated were newly elected members who had not yet decided what faction to join.

the LDP is more like a confederation of factions. With its fall from power, there are questions about how long it can endure, at least without major reforms it proved unable to adopt while in office.

The LDP formed in 1955 in reaction to the combination of several left-wing parties into the Japan Social Democratic Party (JSDP).[11] It was (to oversimplify only a little bit) a combination of the two main prewar conservative parties. One called itself the Liberal party in 1955, while the other termed itself the Democratic party—whence the name of the combined organization. Unification was expedient because a united left posed a possible threat to conservative dominance of the government and because there was no issue of principle dividing the Liberals and the Democrats to stand in the way of union. The LDP factions can trace their heritage back to the two older parties, but this heritage is not always relevant to subsequent factional alliances.

The LDP has a formal party organization, outwardly similar to that of the CPC under Mao or to the KMT. It is headed by a President (or Chairman, as the same term is usually translated in discussions of Chinese politics). The LDP president serves as Japan's prime minister, at least as long as the LDP controls the lower house of the Diet. There is also a General Secretary, usually a factional subordinate or ally of the president, who takes care

---

11. This is how the party chose to render its name in English after 1991. Previously it was known simply as the Japan Socialist Party (JSP), which is, as it happens, the proper translation of its official Japanese name.

of the party's general business, such as it is. Party membership is in practice confined largely to the party's Diet representatives and to politicians holding elected office at local levels. There is a mass membership of sorts, members of the personal staffs of the various elected politicians. But these staff members identify with (and are paid by) the politician, not the party. In the early years Diet representatives tended to be retired bureaucrats (most bureaucrats retire in their early 40s) and persons who had made a career of electoral politics, along with a sprinkling of businessmen. With the passing years the number and importance of career politicians has grown. There is a tendency for the sons of LDP politicians to go into politics themselves, inheriting their fathers' constituencies.

One of the earliest systematic studies of contemporary Japanese political parties concluded that for LDP politicians the faction rather than the party as such is the major focus of loyalty and that politicians will act against the good of the party for the sake of factional advantage.[12] This generalization remains valid. Over the years the LDP factions have become fewer in number and, on the average, larger in size. In the early 1990s the system may have been undergoing a major readjustment, and while previously the tendency had been toward larger factions, by that time some of the larger ones were splitting. Following the lower house elections of 1990, there were six LDP factions in the Diet. After the 1993 elections the situation was less clear.

The factions form on the basis of loyalty to a leader. The different factions have mildly different flavors. Thus, the Miyazawa faction (previous leaders: Ikeda, Ohira, Suzuki) liked to think of itself as having better-qualified people than the others. The Komoto faction (previous leader: Miki) was considered perhaps the most nearly honest. Members of the Watanabe faction (previous leader: Nakasone) may be more militantly nationalistic than the LDP average. The Takeshita faction (previous leader: Tanaka) was, as it were, the LDP's LDP, devoted to gaining and holding power. But the factions are in no sense opinion groups. Every faction would like to include within itself the widest range of policy preferences, to maximize its possibilities of influence. In earlier years some factions tended to have a relative preponderance of former bureaucrats, while others were more hospitable to professional politicians. These differences, however, seem to have washed out over the years.[13]

The factions are another manifestation of the oyabun–kobun pattern. The faction head is not necessarily an inspiring leader. Rather, he is someone able

---

12. Robert Scalapino and Junnosuke Masumi, *Parties and Politics in Contemporary Japan* (University of California Press, 1967).

13. Some rivalry may remain, however. There is speculation that some of the drive behind the exposure of corruption in the 1980s and 1990s was a desire by the ex-bureaucrats to limit the influence of the professional politicians, who were, perhaps, the marginally more venal category.

to provide rewards—campaign money, cabinet positions—for his followers. As the oyabun–kobun model would predict, the factions hold together against the outside, but may quarrel internally, especially as the leader's political life span draws to its end. As a politician gains seniority he will seek to cultivate his own following in the faction. The "pure" oyabun–kobun model would predict that the factions would dissolve upon the death or retirement of the leader. From the 1960s into the 1990s, however, there was a fairly clear line of continuity in most of the factions. Sometimes reasons for this are apparent. Thus, Abe took over the faction previously headed by Fukuda, but Abe was the son-in-law of Fukuda's former boss, Kishi. In other cases, by the time a leader became inactive one of his closer lieutenants had managed to rise above his rivals, and ordinary members found it expedient to transfer their loyalty to him.

While factionalism reflects a more general Japanese cultural pattern, it is also maintained by the structure of the system. The electoral system, detailed in the next section, encouraged the prevailing form of factionalism. Factions were crucial to the functioning of Japanese politics under the LDP. Normally only a faction leader had a chance to become party president and, hence, prime minister. The LDP president's term of office is two years. Some (Sato, Nakasone) have held the office through several terms. For the most part, the LDP bosses not currently president preferred to keep the tenure in office short, so that everyone would have a turn. The party president is selected in practice by bargaining among the faction bosses, with the heads of the bigger factions carrying the greater weight. The winner must put together a "mainstream" coalition controlling more than half of the LDP membership in the lower house. In the 1970s, as part of an effort to make the LDP more responsive, the party decided to let its "mass membership" vote for president. The vote was still structured by factional loyalty: the "mass members" were the Diet members' support staffs, and they voted as their employers told them. The new procedure gave the factions incentives to expand the number of staff persons in the employ of the faction members and helped set off an apparently unending escalation of campaign costs. The process was not only expensive but also divisive, and it was quietly dropped.

The years 1989–1992 saw an exception to the rule that only a faction head could be prime minister. In 1989 the prime minister, Takeshita Noboru, was deeply implicated in a stock market scandal and could no longer continue in office. The problem was that every other LDP faction boss was also implicated in the same scandal. The LDP was forced to find an untainted leader of the country, and chose first Uno Sosuke (a retainer of the Nakasone faction). He fell after a few weeks in a "sex scandal," to be succeeded by Kaifu Toshiki (Miki/Komoto faction), who was both honest and chaste. In historical perspective the Uno–Kaifu interlude may prove to be not an anomaly, but a sign of the disintegration and transformation of the old system.

Factions also serve to allocate cabinet positions. These are valuable for enhancing a politician's prestige, clout, and access to funds. The more prestigious portfolios, such as the Ministries of Finance or of Foreign Affairs, are often held by faction heads. The others are distributed to LDP Diet members who have a certain degree of seniority. A prime minister must perform a balancing act in building the cabinet. He must reward his own followers and also those of his fudai, the bosses allied with him. But he couldn't afford to neglect rival factions, since otherwise they will obstruct the work of government at every turn and seek to undermine him by making deals with his allies. In order to give everyone a turn in office, there is rapid turnover in cabinet seats. This helps keep policy control in the hands of the professional bureaucrats, since a politician is unlikely to head a ministry long enough to establish effective command of it. The coming of coalition governments will probably intensify the kinds of political calculations necessary.

Factions were also a major source of political financing. Both the law and practical difficulties limit the degree to which the party can help its candidates, so that job falls to the factions.

Factional competition normally followed a pattern similar to what some scholars of international politics identify with the classical balance of power.[14] Factions attempted, not always successfully, to prevent any single faction from becoming too strong. Every faction is willing to ally with any other faction against any other. Factions will maneuver for advantage, but will not try to destroy each other utterly. Sometimes elements of sentiment intruded into the calculations of power. The Tanaka–Takeshita faction and the Ohira–Suzuki–Miyazawa faction both stemmed from a single faction headed by Yoshida Shigeru, the grand old man of postwar politics, and the two factions seemed to be allied with each other more frequently than might be expected from random maneuvering. If the tacit rules of self-restraint were violated, the rivalry became bitter. One rule is that no faction will provide two prime ministers in a row. In 1972, a weakened Prime Minister Sato was expected to step aside in favor of Fukuda Takeo. But Sato's consigliere, Tanaka Kakuei, wrested control of the faction from Sato and built an alliance to give himself the prime ministership. The resulting "Kaku–Fuku war" raged for more than a decade and almost tore the LDP apart. In 1993 the LDP actually did split, with two different factions or fragments of factions each establishing itself as an independent party.

The larger the faction the more intense the conflict within it is likely to be. Tanaka had more or less been Sato's choice for successor, however much Sato deplored Tanaka's eager haste. In 1985 Tanaka found himself physically stricken and his legal appeals on a graft conviction exhausted. While not really willing even then to give up control over his faction, if worse came to worse he favored his lieutenant, Nakaido Susumu. Nakaido's rival,

---

14. See Morton Kaplan, *System and Process in International Politics* (New York, 1962).

Takeshita Noboru, proved to be more aggressive in courting the faction's membership, however, and won the leadership against Tanaka's wishes. Takeshita became prime minister in 1987 and fell in the midst of scandal a couple of years later. From behind the scenes Takeshita continued to intrigue for a comeback, but actual control over the faction came into the hands of his consigliere, Kanemaru Shin. In 1992 Kanemaru fell in a scandal of his own and the faction began to disintegrate.

For reasons discussed in Chapter 11 Tanaka built his faction to tremendous size. This meant that every prime minister needed Tanaka's support, even though Tanaka himself could never become prime minister again. Over the long run, however, it was hard to maintain a very large faction. A faction leader had to reward his followers, and if there were too many of them they couldn't all be rewarded adequately. Even if skilled operators like Tanaka, Takeshita, and Kanemaru were able to come up with enough money, there was still only a limited number of cabinet seats, and many of these must go to allies or enemies. The faction can grow because the boss is able to get money for his followers, but beyond a certain point the ordinary Diet member may see better chances for himself in a smaller faction.

A common criticism of the LDP is that it has no principles and no program. It stands for nothing except its hold on office. Sophisticated political scientists, however, may question whether the programmatic, supposedly "modern" political party is appropriate either to Japan or to postindustrial democracies generally. The LDP evolved from a combination of politicians with a predominantly rural electoral base into a "catch-all party" able to garner votes from a wide spectrum of social interests.[15] Under LDP rule Japan rose from devastating military defeat to become the world's second economic power. While it is possible to wonder just how much the LDP had to do with it, Japan is also arguably one of the world's best-governed countries.

Still, it doesn't take a stuffy idealist to question whether the constant pointless factional infighting and a political discourse centering on one grotesque scandal after another are entirely healthy for democracy. The LDP's low public reputation and its continued ability to get votes suggest a disparity between public opinion and the political process. On the other hand, that party's continued success must also be understood in terms of the alternatives to it.

---

15. Gerald Curtis, *The Japanese Way of Politics* (Columbia University Press, 1988). Otto Kirchheimer, who coined the phrase "catch-all party" to analyze the loss of distinct ideological identity among German parties especially, deplored the development as effectively depriving the public of a choice in the substance of public policy. "The Transformation of Western European Party Systems," in *Political Parties and Political Development*, edited by Joseph LaPalombara and Myron Weiner (Princeton University Press, 1966), pp.177–200.

The New Parties

In 1976 some younger LDP politicians broke away to form the New Liberal Club (NLC), hoping to create a principled, honest conservative alternative to the ruling party. It peaked in the first election it ran in, and in 1986 was reabsorbed into the LDP. Somewhat ironically, the former NLC leader, Kono Yohei, became president of the LDP after that party's loss of the July 1993 election. The hope was to give the party a new image, although it seemed that Kono, without a faction of his own, still had to respond to the powerful faction bosses.

The LDP lost in 1993 not because its traditional opposition did so well (in fact, it did rather poorly) but because the party itself did not hold together. In 1992 Hosokawa Morihiro, scion of an important southern daimyo family and one-time LDP representative in the House of Councillors, broke from the LDP to form a group reminiscent of the NLC, called the Japan New Party (JNP). That winter a subleader of the Takeshita faction, Ozawa Ichiro, broke with about 40 followers to form his own faction. The occasion was probably mainly ambitions and personal rivalries, but Ozawa was something of a sport in the notoriously corrupt Takeshita group: he seemed to be personally honest (if also obnoxiously pushy) and genuinely committed to major reforms in style and policy. In early summer, 1993, Ozawa voted against the LDP government, causing it to lose a vote of confidence and so precipitating a new election. Another LDP group of parliamentarians, led by Takemura Masayoshi, joined the defection. Takemura and Ozawa shared common opinions, but otherwise despised each other.

After the fall of the LDP government, Ozawa organized Shinseito, or Renewal party (it may also be translated as New Life, or Renaissance party). Takemura's followers joined in the Sakigake, or Harbinger party. Although the new parties contained differences of opinion (greater within each party than between the parties) and sometimes seemed actively desirous of keeping their positions vague, on the whole they favored a more active international role for Japan and a more open Japanese economy. After the new elections these three new conservative parties joined with the noncommunist traditional progressive opposition to set up a new government. The conservatives, although still a minority in the dominant coalition, dominated the major cabinet seats.

The NLC failed because the LDP continued to control the government (and since it was a conservative party, there was little incentive for the voters identified with the progressive tendency to vote for it). With the LDP out of power (however temporarily) the newer "new" parties may have brighter prospects, although it is questionable whether Japan can support a plurality of conservative parties. There was a possibility that the New and Harbinger parties might merge, and Ozawa wanted a merger of the Renewal party with the Clean Government Party. If the LDP should continue to cohere to some

Some Recent Japanese Election Results
House of Representatives
Percent Popular Vote Per Party

	1972	1976	1979	1980	1983	1986	1990
LDP	47	42	45	48	46	50	46
JSDP	22	21	20	20	20	18	24
CGP	9	11	10	9	9	9	8
CPJ	11	10	10	10	9	9	8
DSP	7	6	7	7	7	6	5
NLC	-	4	3	3	3	2	-
USDP	-	-	1	1	1	1	1

minimal degree, it could well continue to form the core for future governments. If the LDP fragments, rule may be thrust upon the progressive opposition, which so far has demonstrated little capacity or taste for national responsibility.

The Progressive Tendency

Before the war the conservatives had a monopoly on power. Perhaps they still hold that monopoly, but at least now they have to compete for it. The Japanese left was persecuted by virtually all prewar regimes. It was a natural ally of the Occupation, at least until the "reverse course."

In 1955 various socialist factions joined to form the JSDP, and the conservatives merged to form the LDP. For a time in the 1950s Japan seemed to be evolving a two-party system. This term, however, should probably be reserved for a system where the two parties alternate in power, or at least where each has a realistic chance of sometime holding power.[16] By the 1960s the LDP seemed to be permanently in power, the Socialists doomed to perpetual opposition. Observers called Japan a "one-and-a-half party system."[17] Virtually from its founding the LDP's share of the popular vote fell with each election, but the Socialists' share fell even faster, with a variety of smaller parties growing up at the Socialists' expense.

16. Giovani Sartori, *Parties and Party Systems* (Cambridge University Press, 1977), p. 185.

17. Scalapino and Masumi, *Parties and Politics.*

The Socialists are about as factionalized as the LDP, and the factions are also probably as much a matter of personal relationships. In the Socialist party, however, factionalism requires the coloration of ideology. The ideological range of the party is very broad. Some factions would make Chairman Mao and the Gang of Four seem timidly conservative; others are at the center of the political spectrum. The JSDP mainstream, in addition to its ambiguous opposition to capitalism, is strongly pacifistic and supports Article 9 of the constitution. During the cold war it was anti-American, opposed especially to Japan's security connection with the United States. The major organizational support for the JSDP comes from labor unions. The party normally receives about 20 percent of the popular vote.

The Democratic Socialist Party (DSP) came into being as a result of a schism among the Socialists. It advocates a moderate socialism; it is anticommunist and has no animus against the United States. It supports a more active role for Japan in the world, and to this end favors (sometimes in a hedged fashion) rearmament. Despite support from some labor unions, the party has not caught on, and normally gets a little more than 5 percent of the popular vote. The United Social Democratic Federation (USDF) is another conservative socialist party that, like the DSP, also broke from the JSDP. In practice it seems to be little more than the personal faction of its founder, and during its first five elections received less than 1 percent of the vote.

The Communist Party of Japan (CPJ) was formed in 1921 but remained illegal prior to 1945. It had been the group most consistently hostile to the war and to the prewar order. At the beginning it enjoyed warm support from the Occupation. With the freezing over of the cold war the CPJ tried to obstruct both the Americans and the government and came under police pressure. Japan was hardly ripe for revolution, and in the 1950s the party stagnated. After 1949 the Japanese Communists had come under the general supervision of the CPC, and they took the Chinese side at the outset of the Sino-Soviet split.

In 1966 some CPJ leaders visited China and had an audience with Chairman Mao, who lectured them to the effect that if they were true revolutionaries they would forget about trying to win Diet seats and take to the hills to fight a people's war. The Japanese bowed politely and concluded to themselves: That old man is crazy. The CPJ broke its connections with China as well as with the Soviet Union and resolved to make itself "lovable" to the Japanese people.[18] Its support among voters rose, to level off at about 10 percent of the

---

18. In the 1970s there was a brief fad for "Eurocommunism." Certain European communist parties purported to eschew attempts to establish a dictatorship and asserted their desire to work for progressive policies by democratic means. By this measure the CPJ would be the pioneer of Eurocommunism.

electorate, much of this doubtlessly a protest vote, a way of showing disgust with the LDP. It lacks the Socialists' support from organized labor.

In the 1970s, Socialist-Communist alliances were able to capture various local offices, including the governorship of Tokyo. The two parties, however, have been less successful in cooperating at the national level. On specific matters of practical policy, Communist politicians and activists often give an impression of greater moderation and wisdom than the Socialists. Nonetheless, Communists are not well regarded by the rest of the opposition. They have a reputation for entering into deals concerning alliances with other parties during elections, and then breaking the alliances whenever they think they may gain by doing so. The Communists were excluded virtually as a matter of course from the 1993 anti-LDP coalition government.

The Clean Government Party (CGP), or Komeito, began as the political arm of the Soka Gakkai ("Value Creation Society"), a "new religion" founded in the 1930s that gained many adherents after the war. The Soka Gakkai is based on a version of Buddhism preached by the twelfth-century Japanese monk Nicherin, who was more nationalistic and less tolerant of differences of religious opinion than the typical Buddhist. The Society appealed to persons who felt out of place in the modern world, who were worried about the collapse of traditional morals and virtues. Japanese not members of the Society regard it as an intolerant, aggressive cult that exercises too much power over adherents and desires too much power over everyone else. In the 1970s the official connection between the CGP and the Society was severed, although the Society remains the party's main electoral base. In some ways the Society and CGP may be analogous to the American religious right, although the Japanese ideology is more pacifistic and softly leftish. Many of its voters and grass-roots activists are women, although men predominate among its Diet representatives. The socio-economic status of CGP voters is about the same as that of the Communists, with the main difference perhaps that of opinion: CGP voters are more traditionally inclined, the Communists more modern. Like the Communists, the CGP usually gets about 10 percent of the vote.

Like the opposition on Taiwan, the Japanese opposition faces a dilemma. If it is too critical of the government, it is not taken seriously; if it is too cooperative, there is even less reason to choose it over the LDP. The opposition also has problems cooperating among itself. The JSDP dreamed of leading a grand coalition combining all the opposition. In 1993, although it was the largest party in the governing coalition, it may well have been the least influential. In fact, the DSP and CGP are probably closer in temperament and opinion to the LDP than to the mainstream of the socialists. A revivified LDP might well court their favor, hoping to induce them into a coalition, probably at the expense of the renegade "new parties." Ozawa Ichiro and his Renewal party seemed to hope for a merger with these smaller

Lower House Elections
Party Strength in House of Representatives

	1972	1976	1979	1980	1983	1986	1990
LDP	271	249	248	284	259	300	275
JSDP	118	123	107	107	113	85	136
CGP	29	55	57	33	59	56	45
CPJ	38	17	39	29	27	-	16
DSP	19	29	35	32	39	26	14
NLC	-	17	4	12	8	6	-
USDF	-	-	2	3	3	4	4
Other	16	21	19	11	3	9	22

opposition groups, although it is not clear their leadership would want to give up their organizational integrity. The strategic calculations in Japanese politics, both in election behavior and in government building, will certainly become more complex than they have been. The complexity will be compounded by changes in the electoral system, which has been a major cause of the LDP's hold on the electorate.

Political Parties and Political Structures

Culture may predispose certain outcomes in Japanese politics, but the effects work through specific institutional causes. There must be many different reasons Japanese politics works as it does. This section concentrates on the electoral system, as this gives leverage to understanding how the LDP kept its dominance, how factionalism came to play such a large role in the LDP, and how corruption became a structural feature of the system.

Simple malapportionment helped the LDP keep its majority in the lower house. Farmers tend to vote for the LDP, and rural districts contain fewer people—in some cases, several times fewer—than do urban districts. Farmers, however, are not slavishly attached to the LDP, and the LDP has become increasingly able to attract urban voters. Malapportionment was only one reason, and probably not the main one, for LDP dominance.

In 1990 Japan's lower house consisted of 512 representatives, chosen from 130 electoral districts, most districts sending three to five deputies to the Diet. The most important skill for any politician is the ability to divide by two and add one: exercising this skill, we find that the LDP needed to elect a minimum of 257 representatives, or an average of two per district. In many countries with multimember districts each voter gets to vote for as many candidates as there are positions to be filled: if your hometown sends three people to the parliament, you vote for three candidates. In Japan, however, each voter voted for only a single candidate.[19]

Japan used this kind of electoral system since the 1920s. Electoral systems are put in place through law, and those who make the laws have particular goals in mind. The major reason for the Japanese system was probably that it worked against the smaller parties. Parties lacking the LDP's resources and geographic scope were hard put to capture the necessary two seats per district average. The smaller parties tried to maximize their seats by concentrating on those districts where they had the greatest strength; otherwise, they were forced to spread themselves too thin. Chances are that the typical Socialist voter would favor some other opposition party over the LDP for a second choice—meaning that the opposition parties typically took votes from each other rather than from the LDP. The electoral system forced the opposition to compete against itself. Alternatively, the opposition parties may strike deals, agreeing not to run candidates in the same district; but this limited the number of seats any particular opposition party could even hope to win. A major complaint about the Communists was that they acted as spoilers, running candidates in most districts whether they had a chance to win or not, and so hurting the chances of other progressive parties.

The system also, obviously, forced LDP candidates to compete with each other as well. As a party, the LDP even had a positive incentive to discourage dynamically appealing candidates, as there was a danger that some charismatic personality might take all the available LDP vote in a district, leaving the other conservative candidates with nothing. Since two or more LDP candidates ran in each district, and since each had to win his own share of the votes, each had to find some way to distinguish himself from the other. As implied above, chances are this was not going to be a matter of personality. Chances are also that it wasn't a matter of policy, either. The LDP as a party had little interest in encouraging open policy conflicts among its candidates. While the LDP is much given to factional infighting, in the Diet it normally behaves as a typical party in a parliamentary system, with all representatives voting the party line, whatever their private opinions on the issue at hand

---

19. This description applies to lower house elections. The upper house is selected differently. It has 152 Councillors, with half elected every three years. Fifty-two are elected from Japan's 52 prefectures; the remainder are elected in a nationwide proportional representation vote. Each party prepares a list of candidates, and voters vote for the whole list. The proportion of representatives sent to the house by each party is roughly proportional to the party's overall vote: if the LDP gets 40 percent of the vote, 40 percent of its candidates will be deemed elected. The candidates are chosen according to the order in which they appear on the party list. This system encourages a proliferation of many small parties in elections, although most fail to win any seats.

may be. This means that the policy views of any particular candidate are of negligible importance.

The candidates must, in effect, establish some kind of personal bond with the voters.[20] This is done by bestowing favors, that is, doing "constituency service." The relationship is a variation on the patron–client one, except the politician has become more a beggar for the voters' favor than a local big shot who graciously distributes his largess and offers his protection.

The candidate must try to identify and build his *jiban*. The word may be translated as constituency; it does not refer to everyone in his district, however, but, rather, to those persons the candidate thinks will vote for him. It may be concentrated in a few villages or neighborhoods, or it may consist of various families scattered throughout the district.

In order to cultivate his jiban, the politician has a *koenkai*, a support organization. The koenkai are perhaps the closest thing the LDP has to grassroots membership. The members of the koenkai are not really directly affiliated with the party as such, but are in the employ of the particular politician. The koenkai organizes campaigns. It keeps track of births, weddings, and funerals in the jiban, providing voters appropriate gifts for the occasion. It helps constituents who are having trouble with government agencies or who have a special need for government services. It hires luxury tour buses to take constituents to Tokyo for "seminars"—a half-hour speech by the politician; maybe, if it can be arranged, a meeting with a few of the higher-ups in the politician's faction; and lots and lots of eating, drinking, and sight-seeing.

The cost of all this is not small. Democratic politics have become increasingly expensive everywhere. In the United States most campaign spending goes for television and radio advertising. In Japan, given the electoral system and the compact geography of the country, that has not been as important. Rather, the money goes to pay the koenkai and to buy favors for the jiban.

This insatiable need for money reinforced the LDP's factional structure, as the factions were the candidates' major source of funding. While the LDP must run multiple candidates in each district, it would be extremely unusual for two politicians from the same faction to be among those candidates.

Reform of the electoral system was long on the political agenda, more as a statement of what would be desirable in the abstract than as an indication of what anyone really intended to do. The smaller parties would prefer a system of proportional representation (PR), which assigns votes in the Diet in rough proportion to a party's votes in the electorate. The LDP failed in 1993 in a vote over the issue of electoral reform. A reluctant government had been maneuvered into proposing reform, favoring a return, in effect, to the pre-1925 system of single-member districts, the U.S.–British electoral pattern. This would give an even greater advantage to the LDP as the country's largest party, and its proposal seemed, to the opposition and to the defectors

---

20. This sort of thing remains relatively more important in rural than in urban areas.

in its own ranks, to be blatantly insincere. Given the LDP's lack of a majority in the upper house, where it needed the support of the DSP and CGP to get its bills through, there was little chance that this proposal would carry no matter what the vote in the House of Representatives. The Socialists, as the second largest party, favor the single-member system over any of the alternatives liked by its allies, but were more than willing to let this go in order to help topple the LDP.

Since the LDP had been brought down on the issue of electoral reform, the victorious coalition had to take up that cause. After a long, debilitating political fight, in early 1994 the Diet passed a reform, reducing the size of the lower house to 500 members, 300 of whom would be elected in single districts and 200 by PR. The original proposals had wanted to have half the house elected by PR. The outcome, which required some LDP votes to pass, reflected more the interests of the opposition LDP than it did those of the smaller parties in the ruling coalition. The new system would go into effect in early 1995, a year after its being passed into law. The LDP should do well in the single-member district elections if its candidates are able to keep the financial support that allows them to build their organization and conduct their campaigns. With the LDP out of power and with the system not necessarily guaranteeing an easy return, however, donors may have less incentive to lavish money on LDP candidates. The new system may help undermine factionalism in the LDP, especially if older factions are in fact on the way to decay, and in other parties as well. The PR aspect, however, may allow factional wheeling and dealing in the construction of the party lists. A result of the use of PR in the upper house elections is to encourage the formation of very small, sometimes frivolous parties. If the new system has the same consequence in the lower house, or even means that the governments will be composed of coalitions embracing wide policy differences, the middle-range result of reform may well be to strengthen some of the more pathological aspects of the policy-making process.

Policy Making

"Who governs" (or, more bluntly, who rules) is one of the questions a student of politics would want to ask about any country. Some political scientists who adopt a pluralist theory of power rather than an elitist view claim the question is misconstrued: it takes for granted that there is some identifiable set of groups, persons, or institutions that does in fact rule.[21] Pluralism is usually associated with democracy. Karel van Wolferen, a Japan basher,

---

21. For the classical pluralist position, see Robert Dahl, *Who Governs: Democracy and Power in an American City* (Yale University Press, 1961); Nelson W. Polsby, *Community Power and Political Theory* (Yale University Press, 1963).

albeit a very well-informed and astute one, finds that Japan has no clear locus of decision making—in effect, no one rules—but that does not make Japan democratic. His picture of Japan has been compared to a headless monster—actions or decisions are somehow produced by the whole organism, but not by any particular part of it, and not necessarily with any coherent direction. "There is no supreme institution with ultimate policy-making jurisdiction. Hence there is no place where, as Harry Truman would have said, the buck stops. In Japan, the buck keeps circulating."[22] Kent Calder describes Japan as a "reactive state." Especially in foreign policy but in domestic policy as well the government refrains from initiatives, but responds incrementally to pressures as they come.[23]

Van Wolferen stresses the weakness of the Japanese state, referring to its inability to make authoritative decisions breaking with current practice. Most analysis, including that in this book, stresses the relative strength of the state. Van Wolferen does not mean, however, that the state is an ineffectual and pliant tool of strong, autonomous interest groups in civil society. Rather, he asserts that state and society are virtually fused into a single system, rather similar to the Japan, Inc. model used earlier in this chapter. Within this system, the bureaucracy probably remains the major locus of influence.

A classical conception of democratic government has the political leadership, held responsible to the people through elections, formulate policy that is then carried out by a professional bureaucracy. In all advanced industrial democracies, the bureaucracy has a major role in actually formulating policy. In Japan, however, it may have more of a role than in most. The bureaucracy also operates through consultation and consensus. In one format—*nemawashi* or root-binding—a junior bureaucrat will come across a problem and will consult with all his relevant counterparts in his own ministry and in other ministries. As consensus emerges and opposition is forestalled, policy percolates up through the civil service hierarchy, ultimately (if the issue is important enough) to the cabinet and (if new legislation is needed) to the Diet. There may be conflict in the process, but rarely confrontation, so disagreements may be ignored or papered over. The disagreements tend to be more over interests and jurisdictions than over the content of policy for its own sake.

The need for consensus means that no particular person or institution can make a definitive decision. This is true even of the prime minister. American presidents complain that when the Japanese say yes they really mean no; they are irked when they explain their troubles to visiting Japanese prime

---

22. Karel van Wolferen, *The Enigma of Japanese Politics* (New York, 1990), p. 5.

23. Kent E. Calder, "Japanese Foreign Economic Policy Formation: Explaining the Reactive State," *World Politics*, 40, 4 (July 1988), pp. 517–541. Calder explains this pattern in part by reference to Japanese culture. Prior to the war, however, Japan had the same kind of decision-making system, but the consequence in foreign policy was, if anything, a state that was *too* "proactive."

ministers and foreign ministers, and the Japanese statesmen say: "I understand; I will do my best"—and then nothing happens. For one thing, "I will do my best" may be a polite way of saying no—as any Japanese in that circumstance would understand.[24] But also, the prime minister is not a dictator; he can't make commitments without consulting with the cabinet, the bureaucracy, certain Diet members. The process of generating consensus also means that radical and sudden departures from standard routines are rare.

The bureaucracy is itself no monolith. Bureaucratic agencies tend to act as advocates of the social institutions they deal with. The Ministry of Agriculture, for example, looks out for farmers. This means there will be policy disagreements within the bureaucracy. The most prestigious agency, the Ministry of Finance, may be the closest thing to the central decision-maker van Wolferen says does not exist, since any proposal requiring the raising and spending of money must go through the Finance Ministry. That Ministry's predisposition is to say no to everything, in the hope that there will be enough funds for the projects that actually manage to get through; it also has a bias in favor of higher taxes and against budget deficits. The Ministry of Foreign Affairs is often accused of being docilely subservient to the United States. More accurately, it has an unsentimental appreciation of Japan's vulnerabilities and an active desire to avoid trouble with a potentially dangerous friend. It might urge going along with U.S. pleas to limit the amount of Japanese goods sold in America, so coming into conflict with MITI's mission of aggressively promoting Japanese exports. MITI, however, may favor a more liberal policy on imports, if only to help Japanese businesses set up in foreign countries. The Ministry of Agriculture, however, is adamantly opposed to import liberalization.

The bureaucrats may prefer that all these conflicts be worked out before the issue is brought to the political leadership. Some observers, however, detect an increasing role for open politics in the setting of policy. There is, of course, a strong political constraint on policy built into the political system: no matter what is done, it must not threaten the LDP's electoral chances. While the bureaucracy as a whole may be more weighty than the Diet, the individual civil servant cannot afford gratuitously to offend Diet members, and bureaucrats are well advised to be as accommodating as they can to politicians' requests. If the deadlock within the bureaucracy on a policy proposal cannot be resolved, then the decision must be made by the political leadership, however uncomfortable the politicians may be making that decision.[25]

---

24. In the West, sincerity usually means to show your true feelings and give your true opinion. In Japan, and to a lesser degree in China, to be sincere means to show goodwill toward the other, to refrain from hurting the other's feelings (while expecting the other to be bright and alert enough to pick up the true significance of what you say).

25. For a general discussion, see Leon Hollerman, *Japan Disincorporated: The Economic Liberalization Process* (Hoover Institution Press, 1988).

Chalmers Johnson has shown how during the 1970s and 1980s, as politicians' need for money increased, LDP factions began to function more like political machines, helping Diet members channel government benefits to their constituents.[26] Nakasone Yasuhiro, prime minister during much of the 1980s, liked to think of himself as a dynamic leader, and tried to open up the process of formulating policy, setting up forums of academics and businesspeople outside the regular bureaucratic channels. This resulted in some interestingly radical suggestions, but they did not always have the political and bureaucratic support required to bring them to reality. Although bureaucrats are bound always to be better informed about specific matters within their competence than are legislators, Diet members have redressed the balance somewhat, forming policy "*zoku*," "tribes," monitoring and offering suggestions on policy matters. These zoku, which cut across factions and parties, concentrate mainly on policies that translate into benefits for constituents and help secure reelection, not on the grander matters of state.

Much of this political influence implies redistributing the benefits of existing policy rather than exercising responsible democratic control over the country's direction. Legislators in all countries probably think a lot about the next election and how they can influence policy so as to further their chances for it. Given the situation, however, this may make for special problems in Japan. Japan is a resource-poor archipelago, and its security and well-being depend on access to the rest of the world. An attempt to gain this by military force failed. Since the war Japan has sought access by economic means, sometimes in a ruthless fashion, sometimes without much sensitivity to the interests of others. In the 1990s, however, whether from justice or envy other countries became more inclined to limit Japan's access, giving Japan a strong motive to change its orientation. But the increasingly political—democratic, if you will—approach to policy making, with the politics focused narrowly on gains for specific constituencies, threatened only to reinforce Japan's increasingly disfunctional self-absorption.

The leadership of the coalition government, Prime Minister Hosokawa and his backstage supporter Ozawa Ichiro, were determined to exercise greater political direction over policy and to break from the reactive pattern. But they were probably even more subject to the constraints of consensus than the LDP regimes, as their hold on the government depended on the support of a Socialist party whose center of gravity favored not only a pacifist but a passive foreign policy and protection from foreign competition of Japan's most inefficient producers. LDP control of the Diet was one of the three legs of Japan, Inc., but some of that particular pattern may survive the passing of automatic LDP control.

---

26. Johnson, "Tanaka Kakuei."

11

✦

Politics and Policy in Contemporary Japan

Contemporary Japanese politics has not shared the drama and the cataclysmic shifts of politics in China. The formative events for modern Japan have been the Meiji Restoration and the American Occupation. Lesser junctures perhaps include the 1912 Taisho change, which introduced the possibility of responsible parliamentary democracy, and the 1936 Young Officers' rebellion, which ended that possibility. The critical changes in the postwar period are the formation of the LDP in 1955, which set the tone of Japanese politics for a generation, and, probably, that party's loss of the government in 1993. These are more on the order of the Taisho change than the Restoration or the Occupation, and are pretty tame compared to China's upheavals. Japan is a democracy with, outwardly, few widely divisive issues, with policy shaped by extremely competent bureaucrats and enacted by relatively faceless political figures. Episodes of truly spectacular financial scandal give splashes of color to an otherwise gray tableau. Japan has moved from broken poverty to flourishing prosperity, and the political system, like the economy and society, has evolved and changed. But it has gone ahead along a fairly consistent road.

Japanese politics, much more than Chinese, is conditioned by the international environment—despite the inward-looking nature of the Japanese political process. To prosper, certainly, but even to survive Japan requires the broadest possible access to the outside world. The country has grown rich by exporting to other countries, and has protected its own businesses by keeping its own economy relatively closed to foreign goods and investments. Japan's most accessible market was the United States. Because Japan was relatively demilitarized, to the extent it needed protection from foreign enemies its security also depended on the United States.

In the early cold war, when the United States was the world's dominant military power and the world's only economic power, America was happy to bolster Japan by providing it with a market. At the same time, Japan grew rich from America's Asian wars and enjoyed access to those Asian countries within America's sphere. As time went by, some Americans began to grow impatient with what they called Japan's "free ride" on the American security system. Japan had no easy way to defend against American wrath, but also found it difficult to satisfy American demands on defense. There was, of course, the American-imposed constitution, which on its face forbade any kind of military power.[1] Apart from America, none of Japan's former enemies (and current trading partners) wanted Japan rearmed. By the 1970s, U.S. economic strength had declined in relative terms against the rest of the world (because Europe and Japan were recovering from the devastation of war, not because the United States was declining absolutely) and lost its earlier easy tolerance of Japanese imports.[2] By the 1990s it was questionable how open the American economy would remain, and even more questionable how involved the United States would remain in Asia. The Japanese political system was comfortably adapted to a world that was slipping away.

Shaping the Postwar Order

The Occupation was not really a military government of Japan, with Americans and other foreigners taking over most official positions. Rather, SCAP worked mainly through existing institutions, purging them of persons who had been too deeply involved in the prewar and early war policies. It worked somewhat through left-wing politicians, but more through conservatives who had not been closely associated with the military.

---

1. Even at the time of the constitution's formulation, some of the Japanese founders speculated that it would be legitimate to keep war potential if it were not used as a means for the "settlement of international disputes." See Richard B. Finn, *Winners in Peace: MacArthur, Yoshida, and Postwar Japan* (University of California Press, 1992), p. 116.

2. I am speaking figuratively here. When it comes down to it, the only reason any country "tolerates" Japanese imports is that they are better or cheaper than the alternative.

The most important of these was a dignified former diplomat, Yoshida Shigeru, who served as prime minister for a time in 1946 and then from 1948 until 1954. Yoshida, in the opinion of an interesting revisionist study of the postwar settlement, was motivated to accept the U.S.–imposed constitution as a way of saving the emperor (although it also turned the emperor into an irrelevancy), and later defended it on the grounds that, given the way of the world, the constitution provided the surest way to safeguard Japan's national interests.[3]

Yoshida's calculation was rather complex. First of all, he figured the only countries that could really hurt Japan were the United States and the Soviet Union. The United States had already conquered Japan, and there was no way Japan could defend itself against Russia by itself. Japan, then, would have to rely on the United States for security. By coming into the American system, Japan would hasten the end of the Occupation. Refusal to rearm would prevent the reemergence of the military as an institutional interest group to threaten the bureaucratic-business order.

An attempt to rearm would also arouse a public opinion thoroughly disenchanted with war and understandably fearful of nuclear weapons. Socialist opposition had taken pacifism as its central core, along, increasingly, with anti-Americanism. Yoshida could more or less ignore their anti-Americanism, since the United States had a good image among the Japanese public at large and Japan was receiving tangible economic benefits from its association with the United States. Yoshida may even have encouraged the Socialists' pacifism as a counterweight to the pressure from other conservatives to rearm. Meanwhile, a focus on economic growth would rob socialism and communism of the only other appeals they might have.

The Yoshida doctrine allowed Japan to get rich, not least by avoiding big military expenditures, while the alliance with the United States gave Japan access to the American market. Japan's real postwar recovery did not begin with the reverse course but, rather, with the Korean War. The Yoshida doctrine kept Japan out of both the Korean and the Vietnam wars while allowing Japan to prosper by feeding the war machine's voracious appetite. By the 1970s the high level of military and welfare spending were undermining the strength of the U.S. economy while Japan, which had avoided both, had become a major economic rival to the United States.

Yoshida's main antagonist was Hatoyama Ichiro. While Yoshida had been a bureaucrat prior to the war, Hatoyama had been in party politics. Hatoyama did not oppose the American alliance, but he wanted Japan to become more self-reliant. Yoshida was no less patriotic or even nationalistic than Hatoyama, and he certainly was not a sentimental pacifist. He simply had a colder appreciation of what was good for the country.

---

3. Tetsuya Kataoka, *The Price of a Constitution: The Origins of Japan's Post-War Politics* (New York, 1991).

Hatoyama became prime minister in 1954. During his tenure he and Yoshida's followers joined with other conservative politicians to form the LDP. The LDP's program neatly combined the two foreign policy viewpoints: during the 1950s the party platform called for "repatriating" the constitution—that is, getting rid of the antiwar clause—but the party refrained from doing anything serious to achieve it.

Partly to free Japan from an overly close dependence on the United States, Hatoyama tried to negotiate a peace treaty with the Soviet Union. The Soviets had declared war on Japan at the last minute, shortly after the Hiroshima bomb (certainly for their own purposes, but also in response to a request from the United States, made when it thought the war would last two or three years longer than it actually did). The Russians had captured thousands of Japanese prisoners when they invaded Japanese-held Manchuria, and most of these had not been returned 10 years later. The symbolic focus of differences was the northern islands issue. The allies against Japan had demanded, as part of the settlement, that Japan give up all its fruits of aggression. The Russians seized the southern part of Sakhalin island and several smaller islands to the north of Hokkaido. These, however, were not fruits of aggression, and in fact had been ceded to Japan in a friendly border treaty between Russia and Japan in the nineteenth century. The Soviet Union indicated ambiguously that it might give up some of the islands once a treaty was signed, but would not make any firm commitment. Japanese public opinion (and the unenthusiastic attitude of the United States) caused Hatoyama's initiative to fail. There was still no official peace treaty between the two countries by the early 1990s. Hatoyama's failure tied Japan even more closely to the United States.

This dependence on the United States and the lack of a strong military meant Japan's political clout could not match its growing economic strength. Japan had to practice "merchant politics." Japan was like the merchant in Tokugawa times, who, for all his wealth, energy, and brains, had to grovel in front of the arrogant, dull-witted, posturing samurai, all the while extracting material benefit from his association with the samurai. The United States was the main samurai, but there were others, particularly China. Japan's dependence on the United States meant it could not get close to communist China, its major potential area for economic expansion. Until 1972 Japan kept official relations with the ROC on Taiwan (where, of course, Japan already had strong historical and economic ties), partly in gratitude to Chiang Kai-shek for his generous attitude after the war, but much, much more to please the United States. By the late 1950s Japanese companies were able to do limited business in China. To gain this privilege Japanese business people had to go through humiliating public rituals abjectly denouncing U.S. imperialism and Japanese militarism: an example of merchant politics in an almost literal sense.

In 1950 Japan and the United States signed a security treaty formally tying Japan to the U.S. security system. This helped prepare the way for the peace treaty the next year and the end of the Occupation the year after that. The treaty was set to expire after 10 years. Kishi Nobusuke, prime minister from 1957 to 1960, had opinions that more or less corresponded with Hatoyama's (although he had not been part of Hatoyama's faction, and had himself been of bureaucratic background, like Yoshida). He hoped to renegotiate the treaty, putting relations on a more nearly equal basis. The process of treaty renewal became the focus for radical leftist opposition to the government. The Socialists, who at that time only partly accepted the legitimacy of the LDP-dominated system, obstructed the passage of the revised treaty in the Diet. Diet members vote by going up to the front of the chamber to record their position. The Socialists put into play the "cow walk." Stout left-wing deputies would stand blocking the aisles, moving toward the front of the chamber at a glacial pace, a few feet, if that, per hour. The Diet antics were accompanied by massive student demonstrations in the streets, previewing a new decade of leftist student activism. The scope of the demonstrations prompted a humiliated Japanese government to call off a proposed visit to the country by U.S. President Eisenhower.

Kishi eventually got the treaty through by having the police clear the Diet of the Socialist deputies, leaving only the LDP to vote. The other LDP leaders went along and then sanctimoniously criticized Kishi for his high-handed, undemocratic ways. Kishi was succeeded by Ikeda Hayato. Ikeda left Japan's international position as it was and focused the government's policy on doubling the national income within the decade.

Economic Animals

Ikeda died suddenly in 1964 and was succeeded by Sato Eisaku. Sato was close to Kishi: in fact, they were brothers.[4] Even though they headed different LDP factions, they thought alike. Nevertheless, Sato continued Ikeda's economic emphasis. He served as prime minister until 1972, the longest tenure as head of government since the Restoration. The political pattern set in the Ikeda–Sato period held until at least into the 1990s. At each election, the LDP's share of the vote fell, but the Socialists' fell even faster, with the benefit going to the smaller parties: the CPJ, CGP, DSP. This helped free the LDP from whatever worries it might have had about losing control of the government. The Vietnam War fueled an economic boom while feeding

---

4. Kishi was born a Sato, but was adopted into his wife's family upon marriage. This is a common enough practice in Japan when there are no sons in the wife's family.

leftist sentiment against the government for going along with the United States. By the early 1960s the world had gradually come to realize that "Made in Japan" was no longer synonymous with junk, but was a guarantee of high-quality, extremely reliable, reasonably priced goods. Symbols of Japan's new status included the 1964 Tokyo Olympics (perhaps until 1988 the last genuinely decent Olympic games) and the 1970 Osaka World's Fair.

This was also a time of chronic cultural crisis. The 1960 fiasco over the security treaty raised serious questions about how genuine and legitimate the new democratic order really was. Increasing prosperity might cover up problems of political legitimacy, but the chasing after wealth also gave a sense that materialism was corroding Japan's soul. A best-seller complained the Japanese had become "economic animals," and people masochistically told each other how Charles DeGaulle, the haughty French president, had allegedly called a visiting Japanese prime minister (probably Ikeda; maybe Sato) a "little transistor salesman."

There was some revival of nationalist sentiment. In 1970 the novelist Mishima Yukio, who idealized the Young Officers of the 1930s and had his room fixed up neater than any kid on the block's with flags and samurai swords and other warrior paraphernalia, invaded the headquarters of the SDF with his "private army." He stood on the commander's balcony and harangued the soldiers below on their lack of spirit, and then cut open his belly. This produced no long-range change, but even Japanese unsympathetic with Mishima's opinions felt stirred, despite themselves, by his act. In the early 1970s a group of younger LDP Diet members formed the Seirankai, "Green Hills Association," to lobby for a more active foreign and military policy. There was no mass movement for rearmament, but neither was there much evidence of the former sense of shame in Japan's culture and tradition.

Left-wing groups were probably more visibly active at that time, if also more distant from the centers of power. The 1960 demonstrations provided a start and an inspiration for alienated student movements. At their most benign, the students staged colorful street demonstrations, a process that helped build the very competent riot control police into national heroes. At their worst they formed tight little terrorist organizations whose members shared much of the mental attitude of the 1930s-era fascist groups, who were as willing to die for what they believed as they were to kill for it.

There was also a proliferation of more sober protest in the late 1960s and early 1970s, by ordinary citizens who ordinarily do not figure much in the policy process. These turned on issues of air pollution, poisoned water, urban sprawl, all the social costs of economic growth. These citizens' movements were able to help elect opposition candidates to local offices. But the organizers seem to have identified the electoral process in general with corruption. The opposition parties, jealous of their own spheres, were reluctant to really try to incorporate the mass movements.

Like much of the industrialized world, the Japanese economy slowed down in the early 1970s, mostly because of the sudden rise of oil prices in

1973. Japan's handling of the problem shows the flexibility of the "reactive state." Japan did go into a recession, suffering a surging inflation at the same time. MITI and other agencies moved, however, to impose strict measures economizing energy (and also encouraged the development of nuclear energy), at the same time directing the economy as a whole away from industries that used energy inefficiently. The drive to conserve energy also helped promote general environmental conservation, taking over the concerns of the mass movements and reinforcing the LDP's inclination to appease any discontent that cost it votes. Tanaka Kakuei, Sato's successor, even had a program to disperse industry throughout the archipelago, breaking up its concentration in Tokyo and other large cities. Had this been acted on, it might have benefited not only Japan as a whole but also Tanaka personally, as he was big in the construction business. The relative autonomy of the bureaucracy and the party from its support in business (and the general confidence by business that the state would continue to look after its interests) allowed Japan to move more quickly and effectively than countries where the political leadership was more in need of courting the goodwill of economic elites, or where the relationship between state and the economy was less intimate.

Japan's dependence on the United States and its helplessness in the face of conflicting international pressures remained a central fact. Sato's major foreign policy achievement was to get the United States to agree to the return of Okinawa (taken in the last months of World War II) to Japanese control. As part of the bargain, Sato had to agree publicly that Japan had a continued interest in the security of Taiwan. China, of course, considered the Taiwan question its own internal affair, and let it be understood that it would never normalize relations with Japan as long as poor Sato remained in charge.

A couple of years later, in 1971, the United States suddenly shifted its own China policy, with President Nixon announcing his forthcoming pilgrimage to Peking. The change affected Japan more directly than it did any other American ally except Taiwan, but was made without notifying Japan, much less consulting it. That summer Japan suffered yet more "Nixon shocks." The U.S. economy was weakening as a result of heavy welfare spending combined with spending on the Vietnam War. All during the postwar period the United States had kept the dollar a stable international currency by fixing its price against gold. With inflation in the United States, this caused U.S. goods to be at a disadvantage in international competition. President Nixon reacted by taking the United States off the gold standard, sending the price of the yen soaring overnight, increasing the price of Japanese goods abroad, and making clear the dark side of Japan's dependence on the American market.

Sato's government could not survive in the face of these humiliations, and other faction leaders thought it was high time they had their turn. Sato was kept in office long enough to save his face, but resigned as prime minister in 1972.

Civil War

Sato was succeeded by Tanaka Kakuei. Tanaka was able to rapidly establish relations with China, but his tenure was marred by the economic problems brought on by the oil crisis of 1973. It was also marred by the consequences of certain of Tanaka's habits that had helped him advance his political career but were unbecoming to the dignity of a prime minister.

Tanaka, like Hatoyama, was a professional politician (whereas Yoshida, Kishi, Ikeda, and Sato had all been bureaucrats prior to going into politics). He was a self-made millionaire without a university education. After the war, as a young man out of the army Tanaka had gone into the construction business, a field of unlimited opportunities in a flattened country. In Japan, as in most other countries, there are numerous interconnections between the building trades and politics. Tanaka's business acumen helped him in his political career, and his political connections helped advance his business. By the 1960s he had become the LDP's main fixer.

Tanaka was second-in-command in Sato's faction, Sato's consigliere, as it were. As Sato's political position weakened, Tanaka assumed factional leadership himself. He put together a coalition with other factions to assume the premiership. This broke a major guiding norm of factional politics in the LDP, which stipulated that the same faction should not hold the premiership twice in a row. Tanaka frustrated the ambitions of Fukuda Takeo, the new head of the Kishi faction, who had expected to replace Sato. The play of LDP politics required that any faction be able to ally with any other. After 1972, however, Fukuda became Tanaka's eternal enemy.

In 1974 Tanaka's government was enveloped in the "black mist" of numerous minor scandals, and Tanaka stepped aside in favor of another vocal critic, Miki Takeo. Miki, leader of the smallest of the LDP's factions, had been a professional party politician since before the war. He had a reputation for scrupulous honesty. In 1976 officials of the Lockheed corporation revealed to a Senate investigating committee in the United States that they had paid huge bribes to an unsavory array of Japanese gangsters and politicians to get Japan Airlines to buy their aircraft (as part of a postwar arrangement with the United States, Japan had not redeveloped its own aircraft industry). One of the recipients had been Tanaka Kakuei at a time when he was serving as Japan's prime minister. The Japanese police arrested Tanaka, and he was arraigned before an examining magistrate. Another rule of LDP politics was that leaders may humiliate each other, but not destroy each other. Miki's conscience, however, would not allow him to interfere with the investigation, and he ordered that justice run its course. In the 1976 elections the LDP's share of the vote fell to about 42 percent, indicating that the voters do become concerned if the party's malfeasance becomes gross enough. Miki had to resign, not because he himself was involved in corruption but because the other party leaders thought his unwillingness to cover up corruption made the party look bad. Fukuda Takeo, Tanaka's less scrupulous archenemy, finally had his turn as head of government.

The only thing that could slow Tanaka's progress toward prison was political power. Given his circumstances, there was no longer any real possibility that he could become prime minister again. Although he was sufficiently popular in his hometown that he did not have to worry about winning reelection, technically he was no longer even a member of the LDP: that party, it seems, was too pure to tolerate the likes of him. Tanaka kept control of the party's largest faction, however, by virtue of a combination of personal loyalties, his wide range of connections, and his unsurpassed fund-raising abilities. In fact, Tanaka was driven toward seeking ever more factional followers in order to assure that even though he could no longer directly head the LDP himself, anyone who was party head would require his support and blessing. Tanaka's strategy made more plain than it had been the connection between money and politics and exerted upward pressure on political costs.

Rather ironically, a Miki-era reform only enhanced Tanaka's influence. Miki hoped to break the power of the factions by opening up the selection of the party president to the membership at large, rather than having the leader selected by backstage maneuvering of the faction bosses. The problem was that there was no general party membership, aside from the koenkai of the various elected politicians. This meant that faction leaders had an interest not only in the size of their following in the Diet, but also in increasing the size of the koenkai of all their Diet followers. To buy not only Diet supporters but also supporters for those supporters required massive amounts of money. Garnering massive amounts of money was, of course, one of Tanaka's best-developed skills.

In 1978 there was a kind of primary election among the mass membership in the selection of the party president. Tanaka gave his support to Ohira Maseo, the boss of what had been the Ikeda faction, defeating Prime Minister Fukuda's attempt at a second term as party leader. Fukuda resigned in favor of Ohira. Thereafter the LDP gave up its experiments in internal democracy, although the cost of politics kept increasing anyway.

The LDP did better in the lower house elections of 1979 than in the "Lockheed election," but only marginally better. Fukuda demanded that Ohira take responsibility for the "loss" (as Fukuda saw it) and resign. According to the constitution, the prime minister is elected by the Diet, and in practice this meant, during the period of LDP majorities, that the president of that party was automatically the head of government. After the 1979 election, however, the Fukuda and Miki factions refused to accept Ohira's continuation as LDP president, and refused to vote for him in the Diet, supporting Fukuda instead. Tanaka and the LDP "mainstream" backed Ohira, who won only by attracting the votes of the four New Liberal Club deputies. The progressive opposition sat on its hands—abstained. It remains a question whether the opposition should not have actively sought to make a deal with Fukuda. This episode showed the fragility of the LDP, and may come to be considered a dress rehearsal for 1993.

Another crisis followed within a few months. The LDP majority was relatively thin, and during a vote on a minor issue the Fukuda and Miki factions deliberately absented themselves from the Diet chamber, causing a government bill to fail. The Diet no longer had confidence in the government, a circumstance requiring either the prime minister's resignation or the dismissal of the Diet and the calling of new elections. Ohira dismissed the lower house, and in the course of the ensuing campaign suffered a heart attack and died.

Ohira's death temporarily touched Fukuda's and Miki's sense of shame. The LDP rallied behind Ohira's lieutenant, Suzuki Zenko, and the party as a whole did well in the 1980 election, riding partly on a wave of popular sympathy for Ohira. That election marked a halt in the long-term decline of the LDP's share of the popular vote.

In 1982 the ultracolorless Suzuki resigned in favor of Nakasone Yasuhiro. Nakasone headed a small LDP faction and had consistently backed the Tanaka mainstream. Nakasone had strongly nationalistic opinions and, unlike most Japanese politicians, a desire to be a real leader. The small size of his faction limited his ability to do things. He depended on an alliance with Tanaka to gain power. In Nakasone's first cabinet the justice minister, the person in overall charge of criminal investigations and prosecutions, was chosen from the Tanaka faction. People joked that the prime minister's real name should be Tanakasone.

Yet by the mid-1980s the civil war inside the LDP was fading away. Fukuda and Miki had become old and tired. The wheels of justice, however hampered by the political process, continued to grind, and in 1986 Tanaka was convicted and had exhausted all his appeals. At the same time his health collapsed. Tanaka's faction had grown so large that its members could no longer be adequately rewarded with cabinet positions, while the higher-ranking members brooded that as long as Tanaka remained active they were excluded from the premiership (since it would not do to have an underling in that office when the boss was still around).

In 1987 the faction split. Tanaka wanted to remain boss himself, but if he could not, his choice was Nakaido Susumu. Takeshita Noboru, however, with the help of Kanemaru Shin, perhaps an even more skilled fixer than Godfather Tanaka himself, won the overwhelming majority of the factional membership over to himself.

All during the "Kaku–Fuku war" Japan continued to prosper. Although scholars were writing about the increasing importance of the LDP in the policy process, the episode may show instead the general irrelevance of politics to government in Japan. During this period the opposition was unusually responsible and constructive. The LDP's slim majorities meant that it (and the bureaucracy) had to be sensitive to opposition opinion; Diet rules also gave the opposition great weight in the committees where the details of legislation are discussed and where bills take their general shape.

There was no certainty that responsibility would be rewarded, however. In 1986 Nakasone, more or less free from the shadow of Tanaka, led the LDP to a tremendous electoral victory. The Socialists ran on a moderate platform and performed miserably.

Politics in the Bubble

In the 1980s Japan emerged as a major world economic power. A little discussion of political economy and of the Japan–United States relationship may give some context for the politics of the period.

In 1945 the United States was the world's sole economic power. As Europe and Japan recovered from the war's devastation, the relative position of the United States declined. The Vietnam War, fought without any cutback in personal consumption and with increases in welfare spending, fueled an inflation that cut into America's economic advantages. The U.S. manner of conducting the war also led to or exposed a political weakness that may have allowed the oil price increases of 1973, and these increases created further inflationary pressures.

By the late 1970s the United States was experiencing "stagflation." Previously, the conventional wisdom had been that inflation was the price for a growing, full-employment economy, and that measures to hold back inflation would lead to an economic slowdown. Similarly, if inflation became too great, the measures adopted to fight it would inevitably cause some unemployment. By the late 1970s, however, there was both high inflation and high unemployment in a stalled economy.

The "Reaganomics" program called for tax cuts. The extra money, allegedly, would be spent on investment, which would increase the economic base, providing both more jobs and more tax revenue. Although some skeptics called this "voodoo economics," the program may not necessarily be theoretically unsound—and, in fact, U.S. productivity did go up in the 1980s. But much of the extra money was spent on consumption rather than on material investment, and much of what investment there was, was wheeling and dealing in paper rather than increasing the amount of goods and services. Tax revenues did not increase sufficiently to cover growing government spending: social spending fell little, if at all, and military spending increased greatly, to counter what President Reagan and his supporters feared was the military superiority of the Soviet Union.

The overall results may point to a *structural* problem not accounted for in the Reaganomics model. That is, the American economy may have been at a point where it did not really foster much additional real investment, where

much of what had once been produced in the United States could more effi-
ciently be produced elsewhere. The revenue shortfall by the U.S. government
built up a huge peacetime debt (in absolute terms—it had been relatively
higher at other periods, and other countries have a debt larger in proportion
to their GNP). The combination in the 1980s of high consumption, high government spending, and heavy public and private debt should have led to continued and higher inflation, an excess of money in pursuit of goods that were
not being produced. Yet prices in the 1980s were generally stable.

Here, of course, is where Japan (and Germany and a few other countries)
comes in. In effect, prices were held down because much of the spending was
on imports, which competed with American goods and with each other.[5] The
money earned by Japanese manufacturers selling goods to the United States
was not in general spent on U.S. goods. One reason was the still relatively
closed nature of the Japanese economy: the bureaucracy made it difficult to
import things. At least as important was a sense by Japanese businesses and
consumers that America made nothing they really wanted to buy. The dollars earned from imports went into U.S. banks and U.S. government securi-
ties. In effect, the U.S. trade deficit financed the government's fiscal deficit.

As the decade wore on and the double deficit continued to swell, Japanese
investors naturally wondered whether they might not try to get something
more tangible for their goods than pieces of paper. This led to moves to acquire actual American assets. The Japanese purchases of Rockefeller Center
and Twentieth Century Fox are among the more widely publicized examples.

As the two countries became economically more interdependent, bitterness between them grew. Americans voiced fears that the Japanese were destroying American jobs and taking over the country. Japan was politically too
weak to resist forthrightly U.S. pressures against its economy, but the United
States was too weak to induce real change to the baroque and nebulous Japanese economic system. U.S. pressures against Japan stirred resentments in that
country: Americans were lazy, self-indulgent, ignorant; they had lost all the
qualities that made their country great, and resented anyone else—especially,
some Japanese thought, anyone nonwhite—who showed similar qualities
themselves. The Americans still wanted to rule the world but had squandered
the capacity to pull it off.

If looked at in one way, the trade balance was not entirely unequal. In a
sense, Japanese loans could be said to have financed the U.S. military, and U.S.
power arguably provided a secure world order for Japan to do business in. This,
however, brings up the problem of Japan's alleged "free ride" on the U.S. security system. Americans demanded that Japan assume its proper share of
world responsibility and leadership. Should Japan ever do so, it would not be a

---

5. Thus, in the 1980s U.S. prices soared for commodities not really subject to foreign
   competition: medical care, college tuition, movie tickets are a few examples.

total surprise if Americans found that to be something else to complain about. In some ways the U.S. desire for Japan to become a world leader may in the end be little more than a ploy to undermine Japan's competitive advantages.

Conservative Japanese scholars, for their part, elaborated a kind of theory or ideology to explain their country's behavior: *nihonjinron*, or "Japanese-ness." At its core is the very valid insight that Japanese values must be understood in terms of Japanese culture, and that Japanese culture is a legitimate influence on Japanese policy. At its extremes, however, it can assert that this Japaneseness is something foreigners are incapable of grasping, and even if they could understand it they could not possibly appreciate it for the wonderful thing it is.[6]

Prime Minister Nakasone Yasuhiro was a nationalist who genuinely wanted Japan to reassert its role in the world, and for reasons of his own advocated the things desired by the Americans. At least half-sincerely he promoted a greater opening and internationalization of the economy. The weakness of his position within the LDP and the position of the LDP as a whole with respect to the rest of the establishment limited how much he could accomplish. Nakasone had more success in fostering rearmament. He was helped by the objective situation, a massive Soviet naval buildup in the North Pacific. He could also point to American nagging as a way to make rearmament palatable to others in the party: look, whether we like it or not, we have to do what the United States wants.

With the end of the decade and the collapse of world communism, U.S. interest in Japanese rearmament diminished somewhat, and what remained was a sense of economic rivalry. The United States and Japan were certainly not enemy countries, but in many ways each may have come to regard the other as one of the closest things it still had to an enemy.

Yet during this same period there were signs that the Japanese economy was not itself entirely healthy. Japanese accused Americans of wanting to get rich by manipulating paper rather than providing goods and services, but they were not themselves totally immune from that temptation. Liberalized banking practices in the mid-1980s allowed freer speculation in land and on the stock market, and the price of both land and stocks soared. Bank loans to purchase either could be secured on the premise that prices would continue to rise, and the increased value of the assets served as collateral for further loans. By 1990 or so the air was rushing out of this bubble, and Japan fell into a stubborn recession, the deepest and longest since the war. The high prices of land had made it difficult to impossible for the average family to

---

6. A forerunner of the nihonjinron school is perhaps the Tokugawa-era scholar Motoori Norinaga, discussed in Chapter 3. Motoori, remember, had appropriated without acknowledgment Mencius's theory of human nature, but attributed exclusively to the Japanese people those traits Mencius held were common to humanity as a whole.

328 ◆ Chapter 11 Politics and Policy in Contemporary Japan

buy a home.[7] The bubble economy also fostered income inequalities, something that had not been a major problem in postwar Japan. The bubble also reinforced the already strong pressures toward political corruption.

Prime Minister Nakasone led the LDP to triumph in July 1986. The Japanese government debt had been growing, and the Finance Ministry was eager to impose a value-added tax to generate additional revenue. During the campaign Nakasone promised there would be no such tax; after the election, with a huge, safe majority, he introduced into the Diet a bill to impose it.

Not surprisingly there was a public outcry. Given its now secure majority the LDP no longer had to concern itself with opposition opinion, and the opposition had no incentive for responsible cooperation. The cow walks began once again, in opposition to the tax bill. The other LDP bosses gloated over Nakasone's vulnerability and were lukewarm in their support. In the end, Nakasone decided to withdraw the bill. He remained premier in this weakened condition until the fall of 1987, when he was replaced by Takeshita Noboru. Takeshita's winning coalition was, in effect, the greater part of the old Tanaka faction (which he now controlled), along with the old antimainstream factions: Abe (formerly Fukuda) and Komoto (formerly Miki).

Takeshita was actually able to get the tax bill through, despite the cow walks. In the meantime, a new scandal many times the scope of the Lockheed business was taking shape. The Recruit Cosmos conglomeration was an exemplary product of the bubble economy. It was a new company without the wide set of connections enjoyed by the established keiretsu. It threw its money around with the vulgar abandon of the newly rich, boldly buying itself friends among the financially insatiable politicians. Beginning in the fall of 1988 came an endless stream of revelations about politicians on the take from Recruit. The bribes, if that is what they should be called, were issued mostly in shares of stock, and the market value in those days was constantly increasing. The original publicity had been directed mainly against Nakasone, but it soon developed that all important LDP leaders had benefited from Recruit's largess. Also on the payroll were leaders of the DSP and CGP, and even some Socialists. The scandal spilled over into the bureaucracy, which, unlike the political parties, had a reputation for honesty.

Takeshita himself eventually admitted to receiving $150,000 from Recruit, and he resigned in April 1989. The problem was, there was no leader available to replace him: all viable candidates for the premiership were up to

---

7. High land prices also made it difficult for Japan to move away from the small retail economy, a move the United States thought would help open up Japanese markets. Japanese, like most people anywhere, would probably prefer to have numerous small, convenient stores in the neighborhoods, but supermarkets and the like can sell things more cheaply and might possibly be open to a greater variety in their sources of supply. However, with land so overpriced, in the 1980s it was impossible to find enough space to build larger stores.

their necks in the scandal. Takeshita finally gave the nod to Uno Sosuke, an uninspiring but nonavaricious underling in the Nakasone faction. For the first time Japan had a prime minister who was not a faction head. A few weeks later came the revelation that some years earlier Uno had kept a mistress, and that he had broken off the relationship in a rather shabby manner, or at least on terms that she did not think financially fair.

Uno was hardly the first adulterer to hold office in Japan. The news came at a bad time, however. The general public was disgusted by the Recruit scandal, and consumers were still indignant about the value-added tax. The combination meant that women were particularly hostile to the government, as they see politics more moralistically than men, have, in general, less tolerant attitudes toward extramarital sex, and do most of the household spending. Uno's sexual adventure served as a kind of symbol for the general shabbiness of LDP rule. The Socialist party, meanwhile, was headed by a woman, Doi Takako, an articulate economics professor eloquent on the moral failings of the ruling establishment. Half of the upper house was due for election in July 1989, and for the first time the LDP lost its majority in the House of Councillors.

Uno took the blame and resigned. The new premier was Kaifu Toshiki, a retainer of the relatively honest Komoto (that is, Miki) faction. In the vote for prime minister the House of Councillors selected Doi Takako; but if the two houses disagree, it is the decision of the lower house that prevails. After that the LDP was for the most part able, albeit with difficulty, to get its way in the upper house, by making alliances with the DSP and the CGP. Kaifu showed his sensitivity to the issues of the day by appointing two women to his cabinet.

Perhaps the most surprising thing about the July 1989 election was that it did not really prove to be a portent of things to come. The lower house was up for election in January 1990. By then, apparently, the fevered indignation had burned out and politics as usual reasserted itself. The LDP lost seats from its 1986 high point, but kept a comfortable majority. The Socialists did better than in any election since the 1960s, but still got less than a quarter of the vote. Kaifu took advantage of the respite and unceremoniously dumped the women from his cabinet.

Kaifu Toshiki was a decent man and a competent prime minister. Since he depended on the support of the Takeshita faction, however, there was not much he could do to put through genuine political reforms. In 1991, when the party leaders judged the public had probably forgotten about Recruit, Kaifu was removed, and replaced as LDP president and premier by Miyazawa Kiichi, the new leader of the Ohira–Suzuki faction.

The Heisei Political Change

The Showa emperor died in January 1989. Even though the emperor had been less than central to political life since 1945, it is natural for Japanese to identify the passing of an emperor with the passing of an age. If nothing else, the years of the calendar are dated according to the imperial reign. Showa had reigned longer than almost any monarch in the history of the world, and his times had seen numerous radical shifts in the daily life of the Japanese people and the fortunes of their country. A new emperor would symbolize a new page: one without militaristic fascism, the war, and the recovery from the war. The new emperor took as the title of his reign *Heisei*, "accomplished peace."

The new imperial reign more or less coincided with changes in Japan's domestic and international environment. The recession of the early 1990s raised questions about the keiretsu system, lifetime employment, state agricultural subsidies, and other institutions that made the Japanese system what it was. The "Yoshida system" (broadly construed) had defined Japan's place in the world, but the world was not what it had been. There were fears that the political system was so well adapted to a passing world that it could not easily make the decisions so necessary to cope with the changes.

The end of the cold war intensified the popular American perception of a Japan that benefited from the established world order without doing anything to maintain it. Behind this was a fear that the United States, with its economic problems and without a Soviet threat, no longer had the long-range will and capacity to maintain order alone: the collapse of the Soviet empire did not mean that predictions of the end of U.S. "hegemony" were necessarily wrong, at least over the longer period. There was outside (mainly American) pressure on Japan to take a more active political role.

The Persian Gulf crisis of 1990–91 brought some of the problems to a head. In the fall of 1990 the government, with American prodding, bruited a plan to send troops to the Middle East on the grounds that if they were part of a United Nations peacekeeping effort, this would not contravene the constitution. Socialists and Communists immediately denounced the idea and were able to mobilize a certain amount of pacifist sentiment. Hard-line nationalists in society and the LDP also demurred, complaining that the United States was trying to drag Japan into a war it did not need[8] and that the United States could not afford to fight. An additional complication was that Japan's neighbors perceived the desire to participate in peacekeeping as a way to legitimate a full rearmament and a more active military policy.

The government wanted to go to the Middle East not because they thought it was the right thing to do but because they wanted to humor the United States. But in the longer view, the government may in fact have been

---

8. Japan was much more dependent on Middle Eastern oil than was the United States. Japan reasoned, however, that even if Iraq should control all the oil from that region, the only thing Iraq could do with it would be to sell it, and probably at fairly close to what the world price would have been. Japan knew it had the money to buy the oil; it was not sure it could prudently intervene to defend Kuwait, however much it might deplore Iraq's conquest of that small country.

thinking that a more active policy would be necessary anyway, and that Japan needed to acquire more political—and, to that end, more military—weight. In some ways Kaifu and his colleagues sympathized with the nationalist resentment of American bullying. The irony for them was that the way to reduce the country's vulnerability to America meant giving in to American pressure, at least at first.

Kaifu could not get authorization to send peacekeeping forces to the Gulf.[9] In the upper house he needed support from the CGP and DSP. The DSP was generally favorable to rearmament, but also not reluctant to use its leverage for whatever advantages it could get. The CGP, with its religious and heavily female social base, was less enthusiastic about military force, and backed away from a bill authorizing the sending of soldiers. In February 1991, Kaifu was able to work a deal with the CGP allowing Japan to send money (eventually about 13 billion dollars) to help pay for the allied effort in the Gulf. This was received with rather bad grace by the American government and public.

In 1992 the Miyazawa government was able to pass a bill sending Japanese soldiers to help the UN peacekeeping effort in Cambodia. The soldiers were unarmed and their use was hedged with all kinds of restrictions. The Socialists stridently opposed this bill as well. In the House of Councillors elections held in July 1992, the JSDP did poorly while the LDP did fairly well—although it did not recover the majority it lost in 1989. The government took this as a vindication of its more active foreign policy.

The context for all this high politics was an unending stream of squalid, grotesquely undignified financial scandals. By 1992 the LDP's most powerful faction had overreached itself. Kanemaru Shin, Takeshita's main lieutenant, had by mysterious good fortune escaped being implicated in the Recruit scandal. In 1992, however, he was convicted of having received some four million dollars from shady business and gangster interests. The appearance of impropriety was intensified when the punishment given by the court turned out to be a fine equivalent to about $1,600. It also came out that some years earlier a Yakusa group, offended by Takeshita Noboru's lack of respect for boss Tanaka Kakuei, had induced a right-wing nationalist group to keep up loud heckling against Takeshita, and Kanemaru had tried to buy the gangsters off.

At any rate, Kanemaru's effectiveness had been destroyed. This brought on an insurgency in the Takeshita faction, led by Ozawa Ichiro, a relatively young protégé of Kanemaru's. Although he was a member of the LDP's most militantly unprincipled faction, Ozawa was a consistent proponent of political reform. He was also a strong nationalist, somewhat in the Nakasone mold.

---

9. Eventually Japan did send a couple of minesweepers, calculated to arrive after most of the work should have been done.

He claimed he wanted to revitalize the LDP, get it cleaned up, and identify it with a workable, rational program. Ozawa's brash, aggressive manner hindered his political effectiveness. It is said that while Kanemaru admired Ozawa, Takeshita himself disliked him.

In 1991 Ozawa was LDP general secretary, in charge of the party organization. He wanted to run a dynamic reform candidate, who also had the support of the CGP and DSP, for the governor of Tokyo, and so denied renomination to the LDP incumbent. That incumbent was highly popular and close to the party establishment, but also quite up in years. The incumbent ran anyway, defeating the LDP's official candidate. Ozawa resigned from his party post.

In 1992 he tried to take over the Takeshita faction. Many members were offended by his readiness to distance himself from the fallen Kanemaru, and this attempt failed. Ozawa broke from the faction, taking about 46 of its members with him. The nominal head of the new Ozawa faction was Hata Tsutomu, an older, less abrasive man. The new group claimed to stand for radical political reform. Hata, however, was a strong proponent of agricultural protection, an integral part of politics as usual.[10]

In May 1993, Prime Minister Miyazawa made an offhand comment in a television interview supporting the principle of reform of the electoral system, perhaps the most strategically important issue in Japanese politics. His rivals seized on this statement, and he was forced to take action. The government proposed a change to the Anglo-American "first past the post" single-member system, with the seat going to the candidate winning more votes (not necessarily a majority) than anyone else. This reform was not offered entirely in good faith: it would give an overwhelming advantage to the LDP and would probably annihilate the smaller parties. The bill was doomed to fail in the upper house, since there the LDP depended on the votes of the DSP and CGP, who had no reason to choose suicide. As it happened, the bill also failed in the lower house: Ozawa and his faction voted against the government, as did another group of LDP Diet members led by Takemura Masayoshi. Miyazawa, therefore, no longer had the confidence of the Diet. He dissolved the Diet and called for a new election. Ozawa and Takemura each formed a new political party: Ozawa's took the name Renewal party, and Takemura's called itself the Harbinger party. The election was also contested by the Japan New Party, a product of another schism from the LDP, led by an aristocratic local politician, Hosokawa Morihiro.

For the first time since its founding, the LDP lost majority control of the House of Representatives. The election was not clearly a repudiation of

---

10. Hata was perhaps most famous for his assertion, while serving as Minister of Agriculture, that Japan should not be expected to import American beef, since Japanese intestines were too long to digest it. Hata became foreign minister in 1993 and prime minister in 1994.

Lower House Elections, July 1993

Party	Seats Won	1990 Seats	% Vote	% Candidates Elected
LDP	223	285	36.6	78
JSDP	70	136	15.4	49
Renewal	55	–	10.1	79
CGP	51	45	8.1	94
JNP	35	–	6.8	64
CPJ	15	16	2.9	34
DSP	15	13	3.5	53
Harbinger	13	–	2.6	81
USDF	4	4	7	100
Independents	30	21	6.9	27

everything the LDP stood for, however: the conservative tendency as a whole had an overwhelming majority of both the seats and the votes. The New Party candidates had not been as well integrated into the LDP system as those of the other schismatic new parties, so votes for the JNP might be construed, where citizens had a chance to support it, as votes for conservative reform. The JNP, however, was able to elect only 64 percent of its candidates. The LDP, Renewal, and Harbinger parties had similar rates of electoral success, each electing roughly 80 percent of its candidates. This may suggest that there had been no great change in either candidate or voter behavior, that the use of koenkai, cultivation of the jiban, and personal relationships remained important.

Aside, of course, from the LDP the Socialists were the party most disappointed with the outcome. In 1990 that party had won about 24 percent of the popular vote, more than they had enjoyed for decades. Their increased share of the vote had come at the expense of the smaller parties, who had been taking votes from the Socialists since the 1960s. There were even grounds for speculating that if they could only settle their internal problems, the Socialists were on the way to becoming what they had once promised to be, Japan's second party, with a chance of actually taking charge of the government. In 1993, however, the Socialists won only 15 percent of the vote, lost more than 50 seats in the House of Representatives, and were able to elect fewer than half of the candidates they nominated.

Hosokawa Morihiro was the most likely prospect for prime minister, as he was the major leader least associated with the old system. For a few weeks Hosokawa played coy, hinting he might be persuaded to unite his forces with the LDP. In the end, however, he took over the government at the head of a coalition of seven parties, with the LDP and the Communists left in the cold as the opposition. The main engineer in forming the ruling coalition was Ozawa Kichiro, although for the time being he was content to work from behind the scenes.

Miyazawa Kiichi, taking blame for the party's loss, resigned as head of the LDP. That party was eager to show itself as reformist, and elected as head Kono Yohei, who had led the New Liberal Club during its decade of existence. After rejoining the LDP Kono had thrown in with the Miyazawa faction, but could not necessarily command its support on his own. Without a firm factional base of his own, he was not guaranteed the long-term support of the other faction bosses, either. By 1993 the LDP may itself have been undergoing structural change. The factional structure had been fairly stable for a quarter of a century, but personal relations remained the basis for factional cohesion, and many of the persons were in trouble. The Takeshita faction had fragmented. Abe Shintaro, heir to the Kishi–Fukuda faction, died unexpectedly in 1991, and the faction fell into disarray. The Miki–Komoto faction had trouble getting its people elected in 1990. Watanabe Michio, heir to the Nakasone faction, fought Kono for the party presidency, and may have also been negotiating with Ozawa on the possibility of forming yet another party. But the Nakasone faction was small and Watanabe's health questionable. The LDP could well remain the same party with a different set of factions, but the changes might also presage a major structural transformation. An extended period in opposition would also change the logic of factionalism, as it would affect the faction leaders' abilities to reward their followers.

The universal expectation was that the Hosokawa government would be fragile and transitory. Hosokawa himself had only a small group of direct followers, and the impression was that they were of a relatively "modern" cast of mind, more interested in principles than in persons. He and Ozawa seemed committed both by conviction and by circumstance to continuing the Nakasone–Kaifu–Miyazawa policies toward a more positive, assertive foreign policy and greater openness in the domestic economy. The coalition was able to do some impressive things. It passed the electoral reform, eliminating the multimember district system and replacing it with a combination of single-member districts and proportional representation. To achieve this, however, it had to compromise with the LDP, and it antagonized Socialist coalition members and members from the smaller traditional opposition parties. The coalition began to open Japan to imported rice (another policy opposed by the Socialists as well as by most of the LDP), and openly defied unreasonable American demands on trade policy. It attempted, although at first with at best limited success, to curb the power of the bureaucracy. In April 1994, Hosokawa resigned. The occasion was the discovery of old financial irregularities. The real reason was deadlock over the budget, a product of personal, factional, and partisan rivalries within the coalition. Hosokawa was replaced by the Renewal's Hata Tsutomu.

The Socialists, the largest party in the coalition, withdrew, refusing to support the new Hata government. They were out of sympathy with the thrust of the Hosokawa–Ozawa policy. They also were dubious about the effects of electoral reform. Since Miyazawa had been beaten on electoral reform, the credibility of the coalition required action on this issue. The Socialists, as the country's second largest party, preferred, if truth were told, to keep the old multimember district system, and, like the LDP, probably liked the single-member plurality system best among the alternatives. Some possible effects of the new system might be to reduce the role of personal relationships in election strategy while enhancing the functions of the party at the expense of party factions. The PR aspect, however, might counter this somewhat by allowing factional bargaining in drawing up the lists of party candidates. PR would also virtually guarantee the perpetuation of the smaller parties, and conceivably lead to further fragmenting of the LDP and the Socialists and the formation of yet more new parties.

If Japan is entering into a period in which no single party is able to control the government, the short- and medium-term consequence will probably be to reinforce the patterns that have become familiar since 1945, namely bureaucratic dominance in the reactive state. There may be contradictions between the reformist aspirations of the politicians and the immobilist system they preside over.

Over the longer term, Japan may be evolving a new pattern, undergoing changes hardly comparable to those of Meiji or the Occupation, but perhaps to the Taisho change or those of 1955. There would seem to be a good abstract case to be made for the evolution of a principled, honest conservative party. In 1994 Japan had four conservative parties indistinguishable in philosophy and with leaderships holding each other in mutual contempt. In 1955 Socialist unity forced the conservative parties to unite. In the 1990s, however, the Socialists did not seem to pose an impressive threat.

To be a threat the Socialists would have to become a credible alternative governing party. Much classical party theory assumes that a party's goal is to win votes. Some parties, however, may be more sensitive to internal forces contending over the party's scope and direction than to victory at the polls. The LDP was shaped as much by factional maneuvering as by a desire for electoral popularity, but since the factions were indifferent to policy, the infighting did not greatly influence the party's platform. The JSDP factions, however, sort themselves out ideologically, so the party's program reflects the ideological balance within the party.

In 1991 Doi Takako resigned as JSDP head. The party had done well at the polls under her leadership, but she had no base of her own within the party and was too dependent upon the left wing.[11] Her successors were unable to unite the party either. In 1993 a new leadership brought the weakened party

---

11. In 1993 she was elected Speaker of the House of Representatives.

into the ruling coalition, but at the expense of most of what the more convinced Socialists held dear. There was speculation that the leftists might bolt to form their own party. The problem for conservative Socialists is that they can't even make the "classical" argument: A moderate program does not necessarily pay off in additional votes.

Japan's politics in the 1990s was not at quite the same impasse as China's, although the condition of both countries might seem familiar to some observers. Japan in the 1990s looked a little like the 1920s. It was not exactly the same of course, and by 1990 there was no reason to fear that Japanese democracy itself was fragile. Any talk of a militarist revival was unconvincingly anachronistic, and there was no institutional threat from the military to the democratic system.[12] If there was a threat to democracy in the 1990s, it was, as in the earlier period, from the nationalist right[13] rather than from the left. In the 1920s the left was repressed; in the 1990s it was irrelevant. In neither period was there any strong, popular antidemocratic movement, but in the 1990s the democratic institutions were considerably stronger than they had been before the war.

In both periods, however, it was too easy for the ordinary person to identify the democratic process with corruption and privilege, as a game played among politicians having no relationship to ordinary life. The danger, as before, was less overt hostility to democracy than an indifference to the institutions that embodied it.

---

12. Even here, though, there were things to think about. The SDF command had quietly expressed its lack of enthusiasm about having the soldiers sent unarmed to Saudi Arabia, and this was perhaps the first time the professional military had voiced a policy opinion since 1945. More alarmingly, in 1992 an SDF major published an article speculating that a military coup might be the only thing that would rid the country of corruption. He was quickly disciplined.

13. Around the time of the emperor's death, a right-wing group tried to murder the Socialist mayor of Nagasaki (the second city to be destroyed by an atomic bomb): the mayor had intimated that the emperor might bear some responsibility for the war.

12

✦

Tradition and Modernization

China and Japan share a common "higher" culture. The popular tradition in each country has its own origins, but the popular cultures have also become more alike under the influence of the common "great tradition." The way the higher culture was expressed in each country differs in details, and some of these differences help us understand the different ways each reacted to the challenge from the modernized West. Today the political, social, and economic systems of each country are radically different from each other, but there are underlying similarities in the way people interact and also political similarities in that area of politics not covered by the official constitutional provisions and formal institutions. The politics of neither country can be understood without reference to the formal institutions, but neither can that politics be understood by referring only to the formal institutions.

If political culture is our approach to the two countries, both may be interpreted as "post-Confucian" societies. This is an ambiguous term, but maybe we can give it some content. It implies, first of all, that there have been some basic changes in the two societies: one possible meaning of post-Confucianism is that the society it refers to is not Confucian anymore. On the other hand, a second implication is that the change should be understood in terms of the earlier culture—just as Europe and America should be understood in terms of a transformation of an earlier Christian culture. It is also worth pointing out that to say a society is post-Christian or post-Confucian does not necessarily imply that Christianity or Confucianism no longer have any influence, much less that they no longer have any validity or lack relevance to contemporary thought or action[1].

The end of the cold war brought about revived interest in cultural differences. Samuel P. Huntington, an always provocative American political scientist, has asserted that culture has become the main line of cleavage in international affairs, and (referring mainly to Chinese sales of weapons to some of the less salubrious Middle Eastern regimes) speculates that the "west" may have to guard itself against an alliance of Confucian and Islamic states.[2] The beginning of the twentieth century saw a certain hysteria in the West against a "Yellow Peril," and it is disturbing to think that the century may go out embracing another version of that fallacy. But it is certainly valid to point to the continuing importance of culture in human affairs. Culture may be more important in understanding how different societies operate, not necessarily in predicting international alliances. China and Japan have not shared many interests this century and, apart, perhaps, from a common resentment of increasing American economic protectionism, would be at best uneasy allies. In East Asia those political systems closest culturally to each other—China and Taiwan; North and South Korea; until 1975, North and South Vietnam—have also been the bitterest enemies. At the risk of fatuous banality, it is also worth pointing out that a proper appreciation of cultural differences should, all else being equal, contribute to understanding rather than to hostility. Cultural analysis allows insight certainly into differences but also into our common humanity. It makes sense of and gives the context for the actions of those who otherwise would remain mysterious, exotic, alien, and possibly threatening.

In this discussion, *Confucianism*, whether current or past, should not be taken too literally when it is used to characterize an entire society. We have learned that Chinese and Japanese Confucianism were not entirely alike, and also that both societies contained philosophical or religious currents different from, sometimes contradictory to, Confucianism. Confucianism should in this context be interpreted as a kind of "marker." It refers to an entire

---

1. Generalizations about culture are not, of course, substitutes for specific political, social, or economic analysis, and no one can seriously argue that we have all the answers to the questions of modernization of East Asia (or, probably, anywhere else). Compare Robert Wade, "East Asia's Economic Success: Conflicting Perspectives, Partial Insights, Shaky Evidence," *World Politics*, 44, 2 (January 1992), pp. 270–320.

2. Samuel P. Huntington, "The Clash of Civilizations," *Foreign Affairs* (Summer, 1993), pp. 22–49.

cultural pattern or congeries, this pattern having its own internal logic, and containing Confucianism properly understood as one of its components.[3]

To focus on the issue of modernization, some relevant traits of post-Confucian society[4] include "growth with equity"[5] in economic development and authoritarian politics. These are tendencies rather than absolutes: the socialist regimes at certain points stagnate economically, and there is overwhelming evidence that the post-Confucian pattern is compatible with at least a type of democracy. A further trait, as it happens, is widespread acceptance of democracy as the political form most suited to human nature in the current age. The gap between democratic aspirations and nondemocratic practices raises questions of political legitimacy in the post-Confucian systems.

There are background traits relevant to both Confucianism and post-Confucianism. In these systems the state is strong relative to the society. There is no sense that the state should be omnipotent, but there is a tendency to think of state limitations and, for that matter, all political controversy in moral rather than instrumental terms. There is a continuing emphasis on the importance of personal relations, in practice if not always in principle.

The Western tradition usually conceives the state as a component of society, the state expressing the interests of society as a whole or of some groups or categories within society. Aristotle divided his regimes into those ruled by the one, the few, or the many. For him, the few really meant the rich and the many the poor. A democracy thus reflected the interests of the poor, an

---

3. Not every possible common trait is as effective a marker. The Confucian societies, as it happens, are also the only societies that use chopsticks, and so, presumably, could be referred to as the "chopstick societies." But the use of chopsticks by itself does not lead as effectively as Confucianism to a comparison and contrast of other social institutions or cultural artifacts within the societies. The Japanese began playing baseball not long after the Americans, but I would be surprised if it turns out to be useful to group, say, the United States, Japan, and Cuba together as "baseball societies." Baseball has certainly become integral to contemporary Japanese culture, but, once we move beyond an interest in the sport for its own sake, I think Japanese baseball is best understood within its Japanese cultural context, and not as something linking it with a cultural pattern shared with other countries.

4. I would include Korea and Vietnam under this rubric; Singapore is another possibility. The inclusion of Hong Kong (considered as an entity separate from China generally) would be a more controversial addition.

5. I think I would argue that this generalization is not entirely invalid even for Maoist China. The growth rates were much lower there than they should have been, but China did fairly well economically when compared with other countries at its level and, disregarding political repression and the consequences of blunders such as the Great Leap (disregarding, some may say, an awful lot), the standard of living was rather higher in China than figures on per capita income would suggest.

aristocracy or an oligarchy the interests of the noble or rich. Liberalism explicitly holds that the political system should be directed and limited by society, and modern democracy attempts to build institutions to assure that state policy more or less accurately reflects the will of shifting majorities of society's members. Karl Marx was a critic of liberalism, but his own view of the state is a variation on the liberal model and is also strikingly close to Aristotle: the state carries out the will and acts in the interests of the dominant class or set of classes in society.

Confucianism proper may be interpreted to hold that the state ought to reflect the order of society.[6] The more nearly relevant East Asian tradition here is Legalism, which attempted to structure political power in such a way that, precisely, it would not respond to the interests and opinions of society. The Chinese examination system was Confucian in content but Legalist in form: it was a way of selecting state personnel on the basis of objectively measured merit rather than from a hereditary privileged social group that would use the state for its own ends. The examination gentry did, of course, become a privileged elite, and members of this elite did sometimes oppose state goals, whether from selfish or altruistic motives. But the elite did not have an autonomous social standing; its position depended entirely on a particular political form.

Japan did have a hereditary nobility in a society less open than China's. But Japan's social structure seems, if anything, more a product of state policy than China's. India had a caste system, with a person's status fixed at birth for life. Western Europe had a similar, if considerably more flexible, system. The Tokugawa regime imposed a rigid, closed status system on Japan. This was removed almost overnight with the Meiji restoration, with only an insignificant fraction of the time, turmoil, and bloodshed that accompanied, say, the French Revolution. The Meiji regime peacefully imposed a thorough reformation of Japanese society. The American Occupation was able even to impose a democratic system from outside. I don't think this has ever happened anywhere else, and most serious political thought should probably consider it impossible. Paradoxically, this is another demonstration of the strength of the state against society.

Modernization, where it was successful, helped reinforce state power. Since the social order depended on the political order, the weakened political order in China, resulting from the combination of dynastic decline and Western imperialism, led to social chaos. The imperialist challenge led Chinese elites who wanted to end chaos and Japanese elites who wanted to avoid it to try to strengthen the state; there was little if any concern for developing a strong and free society.

---

6. More profoundly, it holds that both state and society must represent an objectively valid moral order, the Way of Heaven.

Recent years have seen the return to fashion of an old term, *civil society*. This refers to the "public" sphere, groups and institutions that are not necessarily explicitly political but that are more than purely private. In a healthy civil society, these groups are autonomous from the state, having a life and existence independent of the state. They may be bases from which to influence state policy, and they also help protect the individual from undue interference from the state. Much theory holds that a strong civil society is a requirement for democracy. East Asia does not have strong civil societies. There were and are many private and public groups in China and Japan, and the governments would sometimes even delegate state functions to these groups. These groups were not always creatures of the state and, where they were (the examination gentry in China, the samurai class in Japan), might even protest against the state. But they were not protected from the state and were always vulnerable to state pressure.

Confucian and post-Confucian society "expresses" itself through relatively small groups based on personal relationships. There is a tendency for China to have a wider variety of relevant groups—some hierarchically organized, some organized on the basis of equality—than Japan. Individual Chinese may participate in a wide variety of groups. Japanese groups tend to be hierarchical and exclusive. Guanxi, "connections," is one manifestation of this personalism, as is the oyabun–kobun pattern in Japan, a special type of guanxi. This personalism helps explain the relative importance of informal politics in China and Japan. It is an expression of the importance put on specific, concrete human relationships in Confucian ethics, although the more publicized examples of guanxi are usually perversions of that ethic rather than manifestations of it. Factionalism is one consequence of this personalism. An interesting consequence is "genroism," control of the system by its founding elders. This late Meiji era pattern[7] turned up in China in the late 1980s and early 1990s. Corruption is also in part a product of personalism, of personal relationships that have escaped all public control.

Confucianism treated political issues in moral terms, and this trait carries over into post-Confucian society. Politics often does in fact involve grave moral issues. Liberal politics, however, assumes conflicts over differences of opinion, and this means it necessarily includes conflicts over interest. Confucianism has no problem with differences of opinion. It does not accept, however, political struggle for private interests against those of other people: this is the epitome of selfishness and an abuse of the public good. But, of course, much political conflict in whatever society, non-Confucian, Confucian, or post-Confucian,

---

7. The Meiji genro were a faction of equals not in the typical oyabun–kobun pattern. The genro, however, were as much rivals as allies, as might be expected in a Japanese coalition of equals. A contemporary analogy would be the LDP faction bosses, considered as a group.

does turn on differences of interest. The Confucian or post-Confucian pattern is not well suited to handling such conflicts—just as, perhaps, liberal politics does not always do a good job in treating moral issues.

The cultural background has consequences for the relationship between tradition and modernity. Among the non-Western cultures, East Asia has clearly been the most successful in implementing modernization. The traditional culture, unlike that of the West, did not spontaneously lead to modernization, but once it was induced, it took hold relatively successfully; it is even possible that the East Asian societies will adapt themselves better to the conditions of modernity than has the West.

If we take a broadly Marxist view of modernization, one reason revolution is supposedly necessary is that the old political system—the existing structure of power and privilege—hinders the economic and technical forces that are transforming society. Thus, the French Revolution supposedly came about because economic power was passing to the bourgeoisie, but the absolute monarchy and the residues of the feudal nobility, threatened by that bourgeoisie, worked to deny it its proper scope. Latin American countries often have growth rates comparable to those in East Asia, but have generally not been able to sustain those rates, and high growth has often been accompanied by increasing disparities of income. A suggested explanation is that the elites in those countries are threatened by the structural changes required for a real social and economic transformation, and use their power to prevent that change.

We don't have to be Marxists to appreciate that there may be at least a half-truth in this kind of interpretation or to recognize the advantages of a strong state in dealing with problems of social change. If the state is really autonomous from society (and if the state is itself strong—these concepts should probably be kept distinct from each other), social elites will not be able to block the state from implementing polices designed to foster successful modernization. We don't have to assume the military, bureaucratic, and party bosses that dominate the state have a public spirited, altruistic commitment to the common good. Their commitment, no doubt, is often to their own comfort, prestige, and convenience. But their own interests may best be secured by seeking the classical Legalist goal of a strong state and a wealthy people.

This "model," of course, requires some adjustment. China has not modernized as successfully as Japan or Taiwan (taking that island as an entity distinct from China as a whole). State autonomy obviously doesn't guarantee development; rather, it leaves state elites relatively free to choose it—but they may have reasons for not doing so. There are also different kinds of state autonomy. In the 1800s the Chinese state was weak and the political-social elite was a product of a particular kind of state structure incompatible with modernization. This pattern probably contributes to paralysis or stagnation: the state has no motive to modernize, and society has no force to push it to do so.

The KMT and CPC were both modernizing elites. The KMT never had full control over the system on the mainland. The CPC did have that control and also more autonomy than any previous elite. Their autonomy, combined with China's position in the international system, gave them the freedom to choose policies detrimental to development. They were able to indulge ideological visions and to quarrel with each other about those visions, with the quarrels themselves partly related to maneuvering for personal or political advantage within the elite. The Japanese rulers had the advantages of a politics less normatively tied to a particular system and strong incentives, both in the 1870s and after 1945, to make sure the country could adapt to a threatening international system. Somewhat similarly, the KMT on Taiwan after 1949 had incentives to make the best of an inherently weak position by consolidating its control and forestalling potential obstacles to control, whether these be political opposition or social unrest.

The personalism of the East Asian systems sometimes encourages corruption. On a more mundane level it helps humanize institutions that, in modern times, often verge on the dehumanizing. According to much modernization theory, modernizing social change is marked by the spread of impersonal rules. State or private bureaucracies take over functions once performed by the family or smaller groups. Ties of sentiment are replaced by the cold calculation of instrumental reason, what Marx called the cash nexus. The person can be reduced to the abstract individual. If lucky, he will be protected in his rights, but he will not have the right to demand anything of any other individual.

In East Asia human relationships remain important: relationships based on custom and institutionalized practice, not dependent on whether those you come into contact with happen to like you or find you appealing. Despite demographic pressures, the family system has remained strong. These relationships can be directly relevant to modernization or development: they may become the context for networks of mutual trust, obligation, and help in business dealings, for example. They also give the person psychological and material support. People may be thoroughly alienated from the political system or other institutions in the society, but can avail themselves, if they choose, of claims on other persons. This group orientation can often be oppressive. In Maoist China and militarist Japan it was even directed toward totalitarian goals. But it can also give the individual support and direction in a changing and often unfriendly world.

The relative weakness of society above the level of personal groups means there is no force spontaneously pushing the East Asian states in a democratic direction. At the same time, democracy has a widespread and long-standing appeal among the politically conscious in East Asia. In fact, democracy may be a natural part of the modernized Confucian mind-set. The appeal of democracy, combined with the difficulty and even unlikelihood of attaining it, creates problems of legitimacy in East Asia despite good economic performance.

The weakness of social institutions reinforces the moralism of post-Confucian culture. Neither regime nor opposition represents distinct social bases. They do not argue with each other in terms of interest but in moral categories: the regime are tyrants, the opposition traitors. The lack of social base makes the opposition vulnerable to co-optation by the regime, which can offer rewards to those willing to play by the regime's rules. This vulnerability induces a certain extremism among the opposition, as elements of the opposition strive to convince each other they are not about to sell out. This extremism does not show itself in the advocacy of bizarre or impractical ideas, but, rather, in a flat refusal to cooperate constructively with the regime. A good example is the Chinese democratic movement of 1989, but a milder form is evident in the relationship of the Japanese opposition to the LDP. The lack of social base, combined with personalism, also encourages factionalism in both regime and opposition. Factions of the opposition may strive for advantage against each other as well as the regime. The fact of holding power gives regime factions some incentive to cohere.

Japan and now probably Taiwan are democracies. Although post-Confucian society has nothing propelling it toward democracy, neither is there anything, apart from the desire of those with power to hold onto it, to prevent democracy. This may go far toward explaining how democracy could be imposed on Japan from the outside. The process on Taiwan was more complex, the adaptation by an outside elite to the changes it itself had instituted and to changes in the international environment. The Taiwan case is still a little unclear, but there is no reason to fear that Japan will somehow abandon democracy. There are questions, however, about how democracy will actually function in either society.

Japan and Taiwan still do not have great experience as *competitive* democracies. In a way, lack of competition has had advantages: it gave the state the good name of democracy and the freedom of action of autocracy. In Japan particularly, however, the lack of competition reached a point that it detracted from the reality of democracy, especially in allowing blatantly irresponsible behavior by the political leadership. The future will be more competitive than the past. We still don't know whether competition will undermine the political and economic advantages of the East Asian societies or enhance the legitimacy of their political systems, or both. If the cohesion of the regimes does in fact depend on the hold on power, a challenge to that hold could crack that cohesion, leading to a fragmented political system and unpredictable political style.

I hope this work will help people understand how the political systems of China and Japan operate and how they came to work the way they do. Like much of the world, both countries may be on the verge of major changes, and it would be both pretentious and mendacious to try to predict in detail how they will change. I think, however, that an appreciation of the culture and current conditions of these countries is necessary to understanding the change as it occurs. East Asian civilization is one of the major glories of human achievement, and it will play an ever-increasing role in shaping the human future.

Index

♦

Abe Shintaro, 301

Abe faction, 328

Abortion, 211

Administrative guidance, 287

Agriculture, 17–18, 29, 54, 224
  in Great Leap Forward, 183, 226–228
  political role in Japan, 292–293, 313,
    332
  reform in China, 187, 210, 214,
    219–220, 248–249, 250–251
  in Tokugawa Japan, 97

Agriculture, Ministry of (Japan), 313

Aïnu, 27, 29

Altaic languages, 28

Altars of the spirits of land and grain,
  36–37

Amur River, 161

Analects, 41–42

Anarchism, 137

Ancestor veneration, 38

Antipolitics, 221

April 5 (1976) incident, 189, 243, 245

Arendt, Hannah, 204–205

Aristotle, 34, 108, 339–340

Arlington National Cemetery, 73

Article 9 (of Japanese constitution),
  284–285

Asiatic society, 25

Assassination, 162

Atomic bomb, 167

Back door, 205

Bandit extermination campaigns, 145

Banners, 86, 114

Baseball, 10, 28

Beijing. *See* Peking

Bill of Rights, 284

Birdcage economy, 219, 246

Black Dragon Society, 161

Blue Shirts, 143, 148, 158

Bodhisatvas, 61

Bolshevik faction, 144, 145–146

Bolshevik Revolution, 138

Book of Poetry (*Book of Songs*), 41, 90

Bourgeoisie, 103, 221
  bourgeois liberalism, 252

Boxer Rebellion, Boxers, 118, 159, 262

Brainwashing, 163, 216–217

Buddha, 61

Buddhism, 10, 16, 32, 60–63, 65, 68
  Mahayana Buddhism, 61
  political role in China, 63, 90
  Soka Gakkai, 307
  Zen Buddhism, 49, 62

Bull Mountain, 47

Burakumin, 29

Bureaucracy, 83, 84–85
  and policy making in Japan, 312–314
  position of bureaucrats in LDP, 300
  role in Japanese politics, 286–288, 324
  role in Taiwan government, 264, 279

Burke, Edmund, 89

Bush, George, 252

Business, 104
  and KMT, 26
  Japanese business dealings with China,
    318
  Japanese management style, 289
  political role in China, 152
  political role in Japan, 286–288
  private enterprise in China, 213,
    220–221